THE COURT OF APPEAL FOR ONTARIO

Defining the Right of Appeal, 1792–2013

To Drew with thanks!

THE COURT OF APPEAL FOR ONTARIO

Defining the Right of Appeal, 1792–2013

CHRISTOPHER MOORE

Published for The Osgoode Society for Canadian Legal History by

University of Toronto Press

Toronto Buffalo London

ISBN 978-1-4426-5014-5

Publication cataloguing information is available from
Library and Archives Canada.

University of Toronto Press acknowledges the financial assistance to its
publishing program of the Canada Council for the Arts and the
Ontario Arts Council, an agency of the Government of Ontario.

Canada Council   Conseil des Arts
for the Arts   du Canada

ONTARIO ARTS COUNCIL
CONSEIL DES ARTS DE L'ONTARIO
an Ontario government agency
un organisme du gouvernement de l'Ontario

University of Toronto Press acknowledges the financial support of the
Government of Canada through the Canada Book Fund for its
publishing activities.

With research by

Caitlin Beresford, Niko Block, Todd Brayer, Helen Ruth Button, Matthew Capotosto, Brent Craswell, Tyler D'Angelo, Stephanie Rae Doucet, Julie Goldstein, Lydia Guo, Andrew Heard, Andrew Karavos, Christopher Los, Natalia Makuch, Jeffrey Minucci, Kate Moore, Simone Ostrowski, Danilo Popadic, Donald Pyper, Steve Taylor, Ziad Yehia, and Hartlee Zucker

Contents

viii   Contents

Illustrations follow page 146

List of Tables

Foreword

THE OSGOODE SOCIETY
FOR CANADIAN LEGAL HISTORY

In 1850 the Court of Error and Appeal for Canada West met for the first time. It was the first appeal court for what is now Ontario that was both independent of the Executive Council and staffed only by professional judges. It is therefore appropriate that Christopher Moore's study of the court's history sees this as a landmark event, the final departure from vesting appeal in a political body. Moore's account of the court over more than two hundred years is part institutional history, charting the various and at times complex reorganizations since 1850 and identifying the most significant changes in jurisdiction, such as the opening up of criminal appeals in the late nineteenth century. This is also partly a biographical history, highlighting dominant figures, especially chief justices, in the court's development. Along the way the book looks at the court's workload, its internal administration, relations with the bar, and connections to the politics of the province.

The purpose of the Osgoode Society for Canadian Legal History is to encourage research and writing in the history of Canadian law. The Society, which was incorporated in 1979 and is registered as a charity, was founded at the initiative of the Honourable R. Roy McMurtry and officials of the Law Society of Upper Canada. The Society seeks to stimulate the study of legal history in Canada by supporting researchers, collecting oral histories, and publishing volumes that contribute to legal-historical scholarship in Canada. It has published ninety-six books on the courts, the judiciary, and the legal profession, as well as on the history of crime and punishment, women and law, law and economy, the legal treatment of ethnic minorities, and famous cases and significant trials in all areas of the law.

Current directors of the Osgoode Society for Canadian Legal History are Robert Armstrong, Kenneth Binks, Susan Binnie, David Chernos, J. Douglas Ewart, Violet French, Martin Friedland, Philip Girard, William Kaplan, C. Ian Kyer, Virginia MacLean, Patricia McMahon, Roy McMurtry, Madeleine Meilleur, Jane Minor, Dana Peebles, Paul Perell, Jim Phillips, Paul Reinhardt, William Ross, Paul Schabas, Robert Sharpe, Alex Smith, Lorne Sossin, Mary Stokes, and Michael Tulloch.

The annual report and information about membership may be obtained by writing to the Osgoode Society for Canadian Legal History, Osgoode Hall, 130 Queen Street West, Toronto, Ontario, M5H 2N6. Telephone: 416-947-3321. E-mail: mmacfarl@lsuc.on.ca. Website: www .osgoodesociety.ca.

R. Roy McMurtry
President

Jim Phillips
Editor-in-Chief

Foreword

THE HONOURABLE
WARREN K. WINKLER

Tradition and history have always played an important part in defining our legal landscape. The Court of Appeal for Ontario, one of Canada's most important institutions, is no exception to this general rule. Tracing the evolution of the court from its inception more than 200 years ago to the present involves an intricate chronology of structural changes to the court interwoven with a mosaic of personalities that would challenge the creativity of any novelist. A final component requires an analysis of a myriad of jurisprudentially groundbreaking cases that were decided by some of the foremost legal scholars our country has ever produced.

Over two centuries, history, tradition, structural change, judicial personalities, and jurisprudential growth have evolved and melded to shape and define the Court of Appeal for Ontario as we currently know it. To incorporate all of this material into one work is a daunting task. It is a matter of great pride and profound satisfaction for me, and all of the members of the court past and present, that Christopher Moore has completed this project and done so with immense panache. He has written a work that captures not just the facts and chronology, but also the character and personality of this marvellous, beloved institution.

How did this book come into being? As a student, lawyer, and judge, I had an abiding love of history and, in particular, history of the law and of the courts. When I was appointed Chief Justice of Ontario in 2007, I set out almost immediately in search of a court history. There was no such thing to be found. Given the stature of the court over such an extended period, the dearth of material was surprising. It was then that I decided to make the publication of the history of the Court of Appeal a priority for my tenure as Chief Justice. How to begin the task of creating a historical record of our court? I had a "vision" in mind, but a vision is only a beginning. My first move in carrying this notion forward was to seek the sage advice of my friend and colleague Justice Robert Sharpe. Justice Sharpe, in addition to being a pre-eminent legal scholar and a member of the Royal Society of Canada, is a talented historical legal writer in his own right. I knew that as an adviser and strategist relating to the delivery of a high-quality historical legal book he would have no equal. Once I declared my intention to create a historical record of the court, Justice Sharpe was fully supportive.

We began by meeting with John Honsberger, QC. A long-time friend and an icon in the legal profession, Mr Honsberger is the historian emeritus of the Law Society. He has produced numerous books and articles relating to the Law Society and Osgoode Hall. Mr Honsberger's reaction to the project was predictable. He was excited beyond measure and in no time came up with a useful set of notes sketching the history of the court. The three of us – Bob, John, and I – quickly concluded that producing a book of the type we had in mind would be a gargantuan task, calling for the commissioning of a professional writer supported by a full cast of researchers.

Meanwhile, I attended the book launch in Vancouver for the history of the British Columbia Court of Appeal. On that joyous and happy occasion, I was fortunate to meet Christopher Moore, the renowned historical writer who had produced the British Columbia book. I broached the possibility of a book on the Ontario appellate court with Mr Moore. His response was positive and enthusiastic. I mentioned this conversation to Bob Sharpe upon my return and he was enthusiastically in favour of asking Chris to do the book. Bob knew Chris and respected his work. Soon afterwards, we met with Chris and mapped out a plan for the book, much along the lines of my opening couple of paragraphs to this foreword. A consensus emerged for the scheme for the book. All that remained to be worked out were "minor details": obtaining funding and securing a publisher.

The Law Foundation of Ontario came to the rescue in respect of funding for the project. Chair Mark Sandler and Chief Executive Officer Elizabeth Goldberg put together a funding scheme for the book. So far, so good.

Bob and I then met with Professor Jim Phillips, Editor-in-Chief of the Osgoode Society, and, after a brief but fruitful discussion, we had a publisher.

All that remained was for Christopher Moore to produce the book. That he has done. The book is a spectacular tribute to the court, its members and staff past and present, and to the body of the court's work. It justifies the stellar reputation and leadership role that the court so rightfully enjoys among the judiciary and the public throughout Canada. The court's reputation is built on the quality of its jurisprudential work. Ever mindful of this, the members of the court have always been and will continue to be committed to excellence. This history fills a vacuum created by the absence of a historical record of the court since its inception. In addition, it has a second, equally significant purpose. The court is currently experiencing a period of unprecedented change to its complement. Many of our esteemed colleagues have in the recent past either retired or elected supernumerary status. A cadre of new appointments to the court has been added to replace them. This is a natural process of rejuvenation, but when the extent of the transitional change to complement is large, there is always a risk that continuity of custom and tradition will suffer. The book serves as an invaluable resource to help protect these important values during a process of renewal.

In concluding these remarks, I would like to express my sincere appreciation to everyone who played a role in producing this much-needed and enjoyable historical work. I begin with author Christopher Moore, whose assiduous effort has surpassed our expectations. The book is a true tribute to his genius as a historical writer. I thank Justice Robert Sharpe and Mr John Honsberger, QC, for their inspired thought and effort in getting the project off the ground. It would not have happened without their ideas, encouragement, and support. Both shared the vision and dream to the fullest.

My expression of gratitude would not be complete if I did not mention Dr Jim Phillips, Mark Sandler, and Elizabeth Goldberg. All three of them trusted us to deliver a comprehensive history on time. Without their significant roles in bringing the project to fruition, the book would still be a mere dream.

Any project that becomes a reality begins with the creative ideas and suggestions of visionaries. We also need those who act and deliver on our dreams and thoughts if we are to succeed in making those dreams come true. As Thomas Edison observed, "a vision without execution is hallucination."

Now that the book is completed, this day should be one of great celebration and joy and … relief. My sincerest thanks to all who helped to make this dream a reality – from the bottom of my heart.

The Honourable Warren K. Winkler, QC
Former Chief Justice of Ontario and President of the Court of Appeal

Introduction and Acknowledgments

Introduction

Three judges of the Court of Appeal for Ontario share the raised bench at the front of the court. The courtroom may be one of the antique rooms, all dark wood and elaborated carved mouldings, near the central rotunda of Osgoode Hall, or it may be one of the sleek, paneled, modern rooms farther back in the additions to the hall. Either way, the room is usually quiet. A typical appeal will have no jury, no witnesses, no direct and cross-examination, no need for the careful placing on the record of the facts of the case, indeed little of the drama we associate with televised or dramatized trials. There are rarely many spectators in the courtroom. In a criminal appeal, there may be the prisoner, sometimes manacled and attended by custodial officers, bringing a hint of a grim world outside, but most appeals engage only the three judges, a few court personnel, and two legal teams: the lawyers for the appellant seeking to have the decision of a trial court overturned, and the lawyers for the respondent seeking to have it sustained.

At the heart of the appeal lies the record of the case "below": that is, the record of the trial whose verdict is being appealed. The judges have already immersed themselves in the record. They have received memoranda summarizing the issues on appeal, studied the transcript of the trial, read factums in which the opposing lawyers have set out their argument about the case. In 2013, the judges and the lawyers have computer screens beside them on which they can pull up all this material, but paper is also much in evidence. What is at stake is rarely ascertaining the facts of the case. What is at stake is the search of error.

An appeal is not a chance to do the trial over, for justice is not best two out of three. To succeed, an appeal needs to establish that "the learned trial judge erred": allowed a procedural error that invalidated the trial, or made some error in law. That is a high threshold to reach, but if the appellant can establish it, the appeal judges have broad powers to require a new trial, to substitute their own decision and remedy, or to dismiss the matter entirely. Many appeals turn on some error the trial court has made – an improper procedure allowed, a sentence outside the parameters, a decision contradicted by higher judicial authority – and on applying the appropriate remedy. In some cases, however, the law itself may be in dispute. There may be a new law with aspects not yet tested, or an older body of law being challenged by new developments. Here the duty of the appeal judges is to determine and proclaim what the state of the law actually is.

Most times, the decision of the Court of Appeal for Ontario will be the end of the matter. Of the many thousands of matters litigated in Ontario each year, of the thousand or so heard annually in the Court of Appeal, fewer than twenty will go for a final review at the Supreme Court of Canada in Ottawa – and in many of those, the Ontario court's decision will be sustained.

The Court of Appeal for Ontario has been about this business for a long time. Appeal is an ancient part of the justice system. The oldest constitutional document for Ontario, the *Constitutional Act* of 1791, provides for a tribunal to hear appeals, and the meaning of appeal then would be familiar enough to today's lawyers and judges. Ontario's appeal tribunals have given judgment in Osgoode Hall for more than 150 years.

Still, much has changed. For a time in Ontario, some of those qualified to hear appeals were not judges or even lawyers. Once, the concept of separating the political executive from the judiciary barely existed. How many judges should hear appeals, and whether they should be specialist appellate judges or simply trial judges taking on another duty, has long remained in dispute. Appeals in criminal matters are surprisingly new: into the twentieth century, two farmers litigating over a horse had an absolute right to appeal a trial verdict, but a citizen could be convicted of a crime and sentenced to death or a long prison term with no possibility of appeal beyond a plea for mercy addressed to the Queen.

It is the aim of this book to follow changing ideas of what appeal has meant and how the Court of Appeal for Ontario has evolved and changed since the late eighteenth century, and how these changes reflected ideas about the law and changes in Canadian society as well. As a result, institutional history looms large in these chapters. The governments of Ontario have experimented for more than 200 years with the form and structure of the province's final appeal tribunal: the Executive Council, the Court of Error and Appeal, the Appellate Division of the Supreme Court of Ontario, the Court of Appeal for Ontario. "Ontario's court system is very complex," wrote Margaret Banks, a historian of Ontario who became a scholar of its courts, and "its history is filled with conflicts and confusion." But the details are important, and I have taken a good deal of space here in an effort to sort them out.

I have tried also to present the people who have made the court. Politicians from William Hume Blake through Oliver Mowat to Ian Scott who have reformed and restructured. Judges from John Beverley Robinson, upholding a loyalist vision of society into a province of railroad charters and married women's property rights, through William Mulock, spritely and alert on the appeal bench into his nineties, to Bora Laskin, bringing a jurisprudential revolution to an ossified court. Advocates, many now forgotten, from James Bethune in the nineteenth century, through Newton Rowell in the early twentieth, to the peerless John Robinette and Charles Dubin later in the century.

Courts are ultimately about judging, about cases, decisions, precedents, and jurisprudence. Ontario's appeal tradition has too many cases, too many subtleties, too many issues and precedents to be captured within the covers of a single survey history, and much remains to be done, but I have tried to at least suggest some of the leading cases, some of the evolution of legal thought Ontario has seen in the last 200 years, and some of the avenues worth pursuing for future research.

The Court of Appeal for Ontario has always been the highest and final court in the province's hierarchy of justice. The experience of most Ontarians with the courts has been with "low" or "local" justice, far from the rarefied haunts of the Court of Appeal in Toronto, in Osgoode Hall. In the legal hierarchy of Ontario, indeed, most cases could be heard, appealed, and reviewed without ever reaching the Court of Appeal at the top of the pinnacle. This is a history near the top of the hierarchy. Fortunately, the importance of the histories of other courts is understood and they are not being neglected. But the top court, the final court, the place where most binding determinations are made about what the law is in Ontario, is a key piece in the mosaic of justice, and important in its own right.

Acknowledgments

When Warren Winkler determined that a history of the Court of Appeal would be one of the legacy projects of his time as chief justice of Ontario, he turned to one of the world's great legal history societies, the Osgoode Society for Canadian Legal History, and to the institution that underpins most innovative projects related to Ontario law, the Law Foundation of Ontario. This book would not have come into being without the vision of Chief Justice Winkler, the organizing initiative of the Osgoode Society, and the funding support of the Law Foundation. I am grateful to all three for inviting me to be part of this ambitious project.

At the court, I had enthusiastic cooperation from Chief Justice Winkler and many of the judges of the court, who were unfailingly welcoming, interested in, and perceptive about the history of their court. I benefited constantly from the help of Court of Appeal staff, including legal counsel Jacob Bakan, chief justice's secretary Michelle Robinson, senior legal officer John Kromkamp, research lawyer Alison Warner, judges' librarian Louise Brown and others. The staff and resources of Osgoode Hall's Great Library were an indispensable support throughout, as were Paul Leatherdale and his staff at the Law Society Archives. Court Registrar Huguette Thomson found space in her busy registry so that I could have the great pleasure and convenience of having an office inside Osgoode Hall for two years. The registry staff proved unfailingly welcoming to a historian somehow dropped into the midst of their busy workspace. Thanks particularly to Sandra Theroulde, Charlene Attardo, Christopher Lue, and Maria Broccoli.

Jim Phillips, Editor-in-Chief at the Osgoode Society, has been involved with this history from the beginning, as organizer, as adviser, as colleague, and as editor, and I am immensely grateful to him and to Marilyn MacFarlane. Jim assembled and coordinated an advisory network that included Chief Justice Winkler; former Chief Justice Roy McMurtry; Justices of the Court Robert Armstrong, Kathryn Feldman, Stephen Goudge, and Robert Sharpe; and lawyers and law professors Blaine Baker, Jamie Benedickson, Marty Friedland, Philip Girard, Ian Kyer, and Mary Stokes. Jim also organized and led a legal history seminar at University of Toronto Law School in the fall of 2012 focused on the jurisprudential history of the Court of Appeal. It proved innovative and stimulating for me and a very keen team of students. I have drawn extensively on research papers they prepared.

At the Law Foundation of Ontario, the support of Chair Mark Sandler and Chief Executive Officer Elizabeth Goldberg and their teams was appreciated immensely. One great benefit of Law Foundation support was our opportunity to hire a score of law students, representing all the law schools of Ontario, to do case law research on 150 years of Court of Appeal cases. We worked mostly by email, but I greatly appreciated the skill, diligence, and enthusiasm of these future leaders of the Ontario bar for their work during the academic year 2011–12 and the summer of 2012. I also benefited greatly from the research support of recent history graduate Niko Block during much of 2013, particularly in the compilation of the biographical dictionary.

THE COURT OF APPEAL FOR ONTARIO

Defining the Right of Appeal, 1792–2013

1

Give Us the Court of Appeal, 1792–1874

Canada West's new Court of Error and Appeal held its first sitting at Osgoode Hall in Toronto on Friday, 8 March 1850. The west wing of Osgoode Hall, constructed between 1844 and 1846 as the seat of the superior courts of Canada West, was then still the property of the Law Society of Upper Canada, which had agreed "to provide fit and proper accommodations for the superior courts of law and equity for all time to come."[1] At the request of the Crown, therefore, the Law Society had made hasty renovations to the building to provide chambers and courtrooms for two newly established courts, Common Pleas and Error and Appeal, which now joined Queen's Bench and the enlarged Chancery court as the resident courts of Osgoode Hall. At its foundation, the Court of Error and Appeal had nine judges: three each from the three superior trial courts, Queen's Bench, Common Pleas, and Chancery, and they would sit *en banc* as the final court of appeal for the province. So on March 8, the long-serving chief justice of Canada West, John Beverley Robinson, took the central chair as president of the appeal court. Eight of the nine founding members of the Court of Error and Appeal took seats on either side of him for a brief, ceremonial first sitting of Canada West's new court of appeal.

The creation in 1849 of the Court of Error and Appeal by the legislature of the Province of Canada, and particularly Solicitor General Hume Blake, brought into being the first independent and professional court of appeal for the future Ontario. It was a judicial landmark that had grown out of a significant political transformation. Though Error and Appeal would last only twenty-five years, until reforms in 1874 and 1876 created the Court of Appeal for Ontario that has existed (with various changes in name) ever since, the opening of that court in 1850 marked the real foundation of the province's highest court in its recognizable modern form.

The Governor's Council as Appeal Court, 1792–1849

The jurisdiction that became Canada West in 1841 and Ontario in 1867 had been established in 1792 when the predecessor colony called Quebec was divided into two: Lower Canada and Upper Canada. For the new jurisdiction of Upper Canada, the *Constitutional Act, 1791*, provided a lieutenant governor and a Parliament, and it did not neglect the question of judicial appeals. For the time being, Upper Canada would continue with the court system it had inherited from Quebec but, in its only statement on the courts of the new colony, the *Constitutional Act* declared that, in Upper Canada, as in Quebec before it, the lieutenant governor, "together with such executive council as shall be appointed by his Majesty for the affairs of such province, shall be a court of civil jurisdiction ... for hearing and determining appeals within the same." The appeal court for the new colony, in other words, would be the governor's political council, his cabinet.[2]

Three years later, Upper Canada's new legislature replaced the court system inherited from Quebec. Upon passage of "An Act to establish a Superior Court of Civil and Criminal Jurisdiction and to regulate the Court of Appeal" – the *Judicature Act, 1794* – the Court of King's Bench was founded as Upper Canada's superior trial court, "a court of record of original jurisdiction" with "all such powers and authorities as by the law of England are incident to a superior court of civil and criminal jurisdiction." At the same time, small modifications were made to the appellate authority of the governor's council:

The governor, lieutenant governor, or person administering the province, or the chief justice of the province, together with any two or more members of the executive council of the province shall compose a court of appeal for hearing and determining all appeals from such judgments or sentences as may lawfully be brought before them.[3]

It was no longer the executive council in toto that would be the appeal court. Henceforth only selected councillors would constitute the court, and the chief justice could sit on the court whether he was a councillor or not. Judges of King's Bench who were executive councillors (there was no restriction on dual appointments to the judiciary and the executive) could speak about cases that they had themselves heard and decided, but the act specified that they could not give an opinion about the disposition of those appeals. A further avenue of appeal was also confirmed: for matters of a certain value, generally over £500, decisions of the council's appeal tribunal could be appealed all the way to His Majesty's Privy Council in London.[4]

So, from the beginnings of the colony, there was a hierarchy of courts – not only a superior trial court, but also two levels of potential appeals from it: first, to a court composed of the chief justice and members of the lieutenant governor's executive council (some of whom might be judges), and second (at least in theory), to the Privy Council in Britain. The governor's political cabinet and the court of appeal remained enmeshed, and judges and non-judges could sit together on the appeal tribunal, without the separation of judicial and executive functions that would later be seen as fundamental to the rule of law.

In this fusion of executive and judicial functions, the colony of Upper Canada was not backward or out of step with British legal institutions of the late eighteenth and early nineteenth centuries. At that time, separation of executive and judicial functions was not a firm principle of the English legal system. From its origins, English justice had always been the king's justice; it was the king, assisted by the councils and judges he appointed, who offered law and justice to his subjects. In that system, it was not thought incongruous for cases that had been decided by the king's judges to be reviewed by the king's councillors. In England, principles of judicial independence and security of tenure began to develop after Parliament's overthrow of the Stuart dynasty in 1688, but there remained much overlap between judicial and governmental functions. The Lord Chancellor was simultaneously a member of the cabinet, the speaker of the House of Lords, and the head of the judiciary (and, indeed, remained so throughout the twentieth century), and, until 1824, the full House of Lords was the final court of appeal for cases from within Britain. In 1794 and after, the ultimate appeal from British colonial courts was to His Majesty's Privy Council, not to a court. Only in 1833 was the specialized "judicial committee," consisting of judicially trained members of the House of Lords, formed within the Privy Council for hearing colonial appeals.

In all British colonies, well into the nineteenth century, a governor's political council normally served as the highest court. As late as 1846, for example, when the judicial system of the new colony of New Zealand needed an appeals process, that function was entrusted to the colonial governor in council.[5]

In the United States as well, legislative and judicial roles were still not fully separated in the mid-nineteenth century. After the foundation of the state of New York during the American Revolution, its highest court was a body in which the chancellor of equity and all the judges of the state supreme court sat alongside all the elected members of the state senate to comprise the Court for Trial of Impeachments and Correction of Errors. After 1821, this became the State of New York Court of Error, consisting of the chancellor, three judges of the state supreme court, and thirty-two elected senators. In 1848, when the New York State Court of Appeal was established with eight members, four were judges appointed from the state supreme court, but the other four were directly elected and could be non-lawyers. In this mix, New York's situation resembled that of several other American state appeal courts at mid-century.[6]

It was not only the separation of executive and judicial authority that was incompletely developed when Upper Canada was founded. In the twenty-first century, the right of appeal is deeply rooted in the Canadian system of government and of law. Not only courts of law but tribunals and administrative agencies of every kind have procedures for appeal built into them. Opportunities to redress miscarriages of justice or errors in law or procedure are now fundamental to the rule of law, and it is easy to assume the origins of the right of appeal must go right back to the medieval beginnings of the English legal tradition. But in the 1790s, the right of appeal was far from being a fundamental part of the English legal system. British legal historian David Bentley has identified eleven requirements for a fair trial, and he estimates that perhaps three were in place in English courts in 1800, with the rest only gradually emerging in the following century.[7] Among those missing requirements was "the right if convicted to appeal against conviction and sentence."

In early-nineteenth-century England, civil proceedings did offer avenues of appeal, however limited, but appeal as a fundamental aspect of criminal law procedures, something now taken for granted, is a particularly recent development. Sir James Stephen, the nineteenth-century authority on English criminal law, wrote as late as 1883, "It is a characteristic feature in English criminal procedure that it admits of no appeal properly so called, either upon matters of fact or upon matters of law," although he acknowledged some exceptions and extenuations (notably when there was a technical error in the record, and through an extensive system of royal pardons that could substitute for appeals).[8] The right of criminal appeal was developed during the late nineteenth and twentieth centuries in England and in societies that had inherited the English legal system. The courts of Canada, and of Ontario, participated in this development of the appeal principle, often at a different pace than in England itself.

For the appeals that could be pursued in Upper Canada and Canada West, the appeal tribunal within the executive council continued to be the colony's final court until 1849. Almost no record survives of the cases and the jurisprudence of the executive council as an appeal court from the 1790s to the 1840s, but some small changes in the structure of the council-as-court were made. In the 1790s, no conflict had been seen in having members of the judiciary holding positions in government, but by the 1820s, such mixed roles had become controversial in Upper Canadian politics. Reformers and radicals were calling into question the tightly interlocked networks of legislative, executive, and judicial power that sustained the ruling clique they called the "Family Compact," and they regularly petitioned the British government to make reforms. The involvement of judges in the executive council became one of the reform movement's key grievances. In 1826, an assembly resolution deplored as highly inexpedient "the connection of the Chief Justice ... with the Executive Council, wherein he has to advise his Excellency upon executive measures, many of which bear an intimate relation to the judicial duties he may have thereupon to discharge."[9] In 1831, in a first step towards separating judicial and executive authority, the British government ordered the chief justice of Upper Canada, John Beverley Robinson, to withdraw from the executive council. His membership on its appeals tribunal, however, was independent of his position as councillor, so it was not affected by the reduction in his formal political role. In 1834, Upper Canadian judges secured judicial independence equivalent to that of British judges. They continued to be appointed by the British government until responsible government was achieved, but they served on good behaviour, and could be removed only by means of a joint address of the assembly and the legislative council to the Crown. (None actually were.) By an 1831 act of the Upper Canadian legislature, their salaries had become payable from a new Upper Canadian civil list, so they would not be dependent on the favour of either the legislature or the executive. Their pensions, however, continued to depend on decisions of the colonial executive.[10]

In 1837, further small changes were made to the appeal tribunal when the Upper Canada Court of Chancery was established. The vice chancellor of Upper Canada, judicial head of the new court and its sole judge (until 1849, the title of chancellor was honorific and belonged to the lieutenant governor), became a member of the executive council's appeal tribunal, much as the chief justice was. The statute that established the chancery court also declared that in order to provide a panel for appeals from the one chancery judge, all the judges of Queen's Bench would join the chief justice on the appeal tribunal, but only for cases coming from Chancery – much to the disapproval of equity lawyers, given the high wall that generally existed between law and equity. The Queen's Bench judges were not authorized to rule on appeals from their own court, but no specification was made as to who would hear common law appeals coming from Queen's Bench.

In the 1840s, two former judges of Queen's Bench, Henry John Boulton and Levius Peters Sherwood, were made executive councillors, and case reports show them sitting on appeal cases.* In a published volume of case reports on appeals for the years 1846–7, appeal panel members included Chief Justice Robinson, Vice Chancellor Jameson, Queen's Bench judges Jonas Jones, J.B. Macaulay, and Archibald McLean, plus executive councillors Boulton and Sherwood, and also "Attorney General Smith" (presumably James Smith of Canada East, a temporary and mostly apolitical member of the cabinet of the Province of Canada). Since Sherwood and Boulton were lawyers and former judges, their participation may testify to a practice of relying mostly on legally trained members of the executive council, rather than its more political cabinet members, on the appeal tribunals. Executive councillors such as Attorney General William Henry Draper, then the government leader in the legislature and political adviser to the Governor General, seems not to have participated in the appeal tribunal despite his legal credentials.†

---

* Upper Canada and Lower Canada having merged in 1841, the councillors now sat as members of the Executive Council of the United Province of Canada.

† It is not clear why such panels could rule on chancery cases and not on common law cases (with the Queen's Bench judges simply recusing themselves), but the law reformers were adamant that this was so, and no Queen's Bench cases appear in the case reports from the 1840s published by Alexander Grant as *Cases ... in the Court of Error and Appeal* in 1885.

In Upper Canada, there was never a formal "judicial committee of the executive council" equivalent to the Judicial Committee of the Privy Council, the final appeal tribunal for colonial matters, which was established in 1833, but it appears that by the 1840s appeals were mostly being heard by professional judges rather than by the governor's political councillors.[11] Hume Blake, who would abolish the judicial function of the executive council in 1849, knew this appeal tribunal well. In the 1840s, the court of appeal "in the Executive Council" frequently heard appeals of chancery decisions, and Blake, in his private legal practice as an equity lawyer, was among the most frequent and most successful advocates in appeals before the court.[12]

Despite this partial professionalization of the appeal tribunal, the formal link between the political cabinet and the appeal court remained, and it continued to be a matter of controversy. In his report of 1839, Lord Durham, who as governor of Lower Canada sought to reform the appeal courts of Quebec City and Montreal, had referred to appeal procedures in Lower and Upper Canada as "anomalous" and looked forward to something better in a future federation of British North America. By the 1840s, both the fusion of executive and judicial functions and the propriety of non-judges sitting as appellate judges had become contested issues in Canadian politics. By that time, Canadian reformers were campaigning vigorously to remove the appointed governor from active politics, and they had no wish to have him continue to preside as a judge, even theoretically.

In any case, the lawyers of Canada West, after fifty years of building up the dignity, independence, and standing of their profession, were determined that all judges should be legal professionals from their own community, no longer politicians or royal appointees.[13] They were determined that Canada West's superior trial judges and appeal judges should be qualified members of the bar of Canada West, selected not by the Crown's appointed governor on his own authority, but by a Canadian cabinet empowered by the new rules of responsible government, with judicial independence and life tenure guaranteed during good behaviour.

1849: Hume Blake's Idea of Appeal

In Montreal on 16 May 1849, William Hume Blake rose in the legislature of the Province of Canada to speak about the *Administration of Justice (Canada West) Bill* he had introduced two months earlier.[14] Blake was solicitor general in the new Reform government, elected a year previously with majority support from both Canada East and Canada West. This was the first new government elected in the province under the constitutional principle of responsible government, under which the Governor General would no longer wield power independently. Policy-making responsibility had shifted to a cabinet accountable ("responsible," in the terminology of the time) to the elected representatives of the people of the province. On all matters within the purview of the Province of Canada, the governor henceforth would act on the advice of that cabinet. After years of campaigning and organizing, the reformers had achieved the constitutional principle on which they insisted – and formed a government empowered to act upon it. The court of appeal would swiftly draw their attention.

The new government was reformist in more than the constitutional realm. It had plans for financing railroads and canals, for municipal and county government, for new public works. It also had, as an alliance between LaFontaine's francophone reformers from Canada East and Robert Baldwin's anglophone reformers from Canada West, an ambitious program for bicultural accommodation between the two communities, despite the fact that Britain had united the two colonies in 1841 with the expectation that the French minority would be submerged and assimilated. A key part of the new government's plan was its recently introduced Rebellion Losses Bill, intended to exorcise memories of the 1837–8 rebellions through payment of compensation for anyone in Canada East who had suffered losses in the violence. For the judiciary, there was Hume Blake's *Administration of Justice Bill*, a plan to remodel the courts of Canada West that fitted both the reform program of the government and his own powerful faith in law.

In his speech introducing the justice bill to the Canadian legislature, Blake "powerfully advocated the necessity of the utmost care and attention in the construction of courts of justice." Indeed, he identified "as the cause of all misgovernment in any country the maladministration of the laws in the courts of justice."[15] Even before he entered politics, Blake and other lawyers had been campaigning for a fundamental restructuring of the superior courts of Canada West, but they had lacked the political power to implement it. Now that Blake was Solicitor General for Canada West, he was ready to act. Some of what he introduced in 1849 was simply expansion that the rapidly growing province required: more trial courts, rationalization of court costs, and the streamlining of litigation procedures. But some of Blake's changes were more ambitious. Blake's bill promised for the first time a full separation of the executive and the judiciary in what would become Ontario, taking the governor out of the courtroom as well as out of the cabinet room. It also promised to entrench in the province's courts the fundamental principle of appeal.

Four years earlier, in a public letter to Robert Baldwin, Blake had condemned as an affront to liberty this particular failing of Canada West's judicial system, the lack of the right of appeal:

We by a strange oversight have neglected to provide any appellate tribunal within the province, before which the validity of the judgments of our Court of Queen's Bench could be tested. And this state of things, for the continuance of which during so long a period I am unable, considering the love of liberty so generally prevalent amongst us, satisfactorily to account, has led to the startling result that the whole body of law, civil as well as criminal, is at present administered by that court without control.[16]

Blake called this lack of an appeal tribunal "evil ... a grievance of the most pressing kind." Later he called it "monstrous." In a private letter to Baldwin, he denounced the Court of Queen's Bench as "despotic" and an "Inquisition."[17] Again and again, Blake described a well-designed system of courts, one that included the right of appeal, as a keystone of liberty and a reform comparable to responsible government itself. "Give us the Court of Appeal," he declared, "and you do more to liberalize the people and the bar than can well be conceived."[18]

Now, in the spring of 1849, Blake presented his court reform bill in fulfilment of those large ambitions. At the trial level, he reduced the Court of Queen's Bench from five judges to three and created alongside it a second superior trial court, the Court of Common Pleas, also with three judges. Since Common Pleas would have precisely the same jurisdiction and authority as Queen's Bench, there would always be two three-judge superior courts available for common law litigation and criminal trials in Canada West. (The term "Common Pleas" came from English usage; at Westminster there were three superior courts of common law: Queen's Bench, Common Pleas, and Exchequer.) Blake, a chancery lawyer himself, also restructured the Court of Chancery, forming a panel of three chancery judges instead of one and revising its procedures.[19] He also did away with the system by which court officials lived on the fees they collected. Henceforth court clerks, registrars, and others would be salaried employees, and all court fees would go into Crown revenues.

Blake's bill addressed the appeal situation as well. To ensure that the superior trial courts of Canada West would no longer be "without control," his bill provided that the nine judges of Chancery, Queen's Bench, and Common Pleas would be members ex officio of a new court. This was the Court of Error and Appeal, which would put an end to the old expedient of having the province's appeal tribunal drawn from the governor's executive council. The bill gave the Court of Error and Appeal full civil and criminal appellate jurisdiction to hear appeals from all judgments of the Courts of Queen's Bench and Common Pleas and from all judgments, orders, and decrees of the Court of Chancery.[20]

With the backing of the reform majority, Blake's bill was assured of passage, but it came at a stormy moment in the history of the Canadian legislature. On 25 April 1849, while the courts bill was before the house, Governor General Lord Elgin gave royal assent to the Rebellion Losses Bill, passed in February. This act, to provide compensation for civilians' property losses suffered during the 1837–8 rebellion in Lower Canada, did not distinguish between opponents and sympathizers of the rebellion as claimants, and the conservative anglophone elite of Canada East denounced it as the radical new government rewarding its traitorous supporters. When it passed, they demanded that the Governor General reassert his former authority and either disallow the bill or reserve it for the decision of the British government. Elgin, however, accepted the new rules of responsible government. The bill had been recommended by his ministers and approved by the legislature, and so he signed it into law. Conservative Montreal responded with rioting. The rioters invaded the Montreal legislative building in mid-debate and burned it to the ground, sending legislators and spectators fleeing for their lives. In subsequent rioting, the governor and the premier narrowly escaped death.[21]

For the rest of the parliamentary session, including the consideration of Blake's court bill, the legislators had to move to a temporary chamber hurriedly set up in Bonsecours Market. There, in mid-May, Blake defended his bill. After some debate, it was passed and given assent on 30 May 1849, the final day of the session. Blake had his court reforms and his appeal court.[22]

Blake's Vision of Appeal

Since it was Hume Blake's vision of an independent, professional, local court of appeal that was passed into law in 1849 and remained the template for Ontario's appeal courts thereafter, it is worth examining in some detail what that vision was. During the 1840s, there had been much discussion of court reform among the leading lawyers and judges in Canada West. In 1843, a government-mandated committee had explored reforms to chancery. Little came of this work, but in 1845 Robert Easton Burns, a prominent young lawyer from the committee, organized a petition of lawyers for judicial reform.[23] John Godfrey Spragge, the master in chancery for Canada West, published his own pamphlet proposing "a good court of appeal" in 1847, and after becoming Solicitor General, Blake canvassed the judges of Queen's Bench and Chancery, who all had ideas to contribute about restructuring the courts.

Of the lawyers seeking a new court system, Blake was the most determined and ultimately the most successful. He was thirty-six in 1845, a wealthy, well-educated immigrant from the Protestant gentry of rural Ireland, who had turned to the law after discovering how difficult it was for even wealthy individuals to prosper as agricultural landlords on the Upper Canadian frontier. After being called to the Upper Canadian bar in 1838, he prospered in equity practice. In 1843, while continuing to practise, he was named the first professor of law at Toronto's King's College. He became a political supporter of Canada West's reform leader Robert Baldwin and was elected with him in the great reform sweep of 1848. Baldwin, Spragge, Burns, and Blake came from broadly similar backgrounds: at once socially conservative and committed to political reform, they shared a deep faith in the law and the legal profession as fundamental guarantors of rights and liberties.

Blake knew well that avenues of appeal had existed in Canada West before his 1845 pleas to "give us the court of appeal"; indeed, he had a large appeal practice in Toronto. Despite his declaration that the province was without "any appellate tribunal," leaving Queen's Bench "without control," Blake had hedged his attack with careful qualifications that did acknowledge – but dismissed as inadequate – the forms of appeal that did exist.

There were three elements to Blake's critique of the forms of appeal that prevailed in Canada West before 1849. First, he acknowledged the existence of the executive council as an appeal court, but he dismissed and derided it as virtually no court at all:

It is true that an appeal is permitted to the Governor in Council; but that proceeding is so palpably an idle unmeaning form, that it is not referred to, even by the most unthinking, without a smile of contempt.[24]

This was clearly a political critique. In practice, the judges who actually acted as the appeal tribunal of the executive council were mostly present or former members of the bench and bar, and Blake himself had often appeared before them. What allowed Blake to dismiss them as illegitimate was their association with the governor's political council. They were still the governor's chosen men rather than an independent judiciary chosen by a government accountable to the people's representatives.

The second part of Blake's critique was his dismissal of the right of appeal from Upper Canada to the Privy Council in England. Courts in the colonies were still understood to exist by royal prerogative, and so were accountable to the royal Privy Council, not to the superior courts of Britain, which had achieved a degree of independence from the Crown. In 1833, the colonial appeal functions of the royal Privy Council had been reconstituted with the founding of the Judicial Committee of the Privy Council (JCPC). This was still formally part of the Privy Council, rather than a court of law, but it was now composed entirely of senior judges, separate from the political functions of the larger body.[25] In 1845, however, the JCPC did not loom as large in Canadian law as it would a few decades later, when its reputation had grown and when fast steamships and telegraphic communications made Canadian appeals to it feasible, indeed, routine. In Blake's view:

The appeal to His Majesty in Council is, for all practical purposes, equally unavailing ... [It] is so ruinously expensive, and requires for its completion so great a portion of time, that it amounts in effect to a total denial of justice.[26]

It was unacceptable, Blake continued, that the appeal court should be "a court situated in another country at a distance of some thousand miles." An authoritative court, he declared, had to be "situated within the province ... in the presence of the people affected by such decisions." The principle of judicial independence was insufficient, Blake argued, if the conduct of judges and the working out of their decisions could not be subjected to public scrutiny in the jurisdiction where their rulings were binding. Blake's view on the irrelevance of the Privy Council in 1845 was not unique. Spragge, the master in chancery, wrote that the appeal to London was "scarcely looked on as an appeal to a legal tribunal" and that its procedures were unknown to Canada West's lawyers.[27]

The final and crucial element of Blake's critique of appeal as it existed pre-1849 focused on a specific failing: the lack of a proper appeal tribunal for the Court of Queen's Bench. The *Judicature Act* of 1794 had provided a forum for such appeals and, in 1837, the court of appeal "in the executive council" had been modified to put more reliance on trained judges, rather than political councillors, to perform its appellate functions. As in the Privy Council in England, the executive council's judicial function was being delegated from the whole council to judges who were appointed to the council specifically to perform its judicial functions. In Upper Canada, however, this had an unforeseen consequence for Queen's Bench appeals: none could be heard. The three judges of Queen's Bench could sit on the executive council for judicial purposes, but they could hardly decide appeals from their own Queen's Bench decisions, and since there was only one chancery judge, he could not alone provide a quorum of judges without them.

From 1837 on, therefore, Blake and his colleagues argued, Upper Canada/Canada West had had no equity judges, only common law judges, authorized to hear appeals from Chancery, and only a single equity judge able to hear appeals from the court of Queen's Bench. As a lawyer supportive of Blake's reforms put it, there was "an appeal in effect from the court of chancery to the court of Queen's Bench and from the court of Queen's Bench practically to the Court of Queen's Bench itself, a glaring anomaly in both cases."[28] These facts provided the basis of Blake's passionate complaint about the effective absence of appeal in Canada West. The only appeal tribunal for Canada West's superior courts was one he found illegitimate, indeed contemptible, not only because it was ultimately a political forum, but also – for Blake the chancery lawyer – because it empowered common law judges to review the decisions of an equity court, while providing no proper appeal at all from the only superior trial court of common law in the province. Clearly it was time to rebuild and reform, as a matter of both constitutional and judicial reform.

The lawyers' proposals and pamphlets about court reform during the 1840s reflected agendas that went beyond simply improving the courts. Chancery lawyers like Blake, Spragge, and Burns were concerned to rebut claims that chancery should be abolished, merged, or simplified as part of court reform, but many of them were dissatisfied with the lone judge of chancery, Robert Sympson Jameson. Vice Chancellor Jameson had been an English patronage appointment, the last senior legal officer sent out from Britain to the province, where he served first as Attorney General and then as judge of chancery. Many of the Toronto equity lawyers found him ponderous and slow, even by chancery standards.[29] Indeed, Blake's ally Robert Baldwin once suggested that getting rid of

Jameson was one of Blake's principal motives for advocating court reform.

As well, Blake and many of his supporters at the bar looked at court reform as an element of political reform. They found the Queen's Bench judges who had been appointed by the governor before responsible government too politically conservative and too ready to impose old ideas in both politics and law and, as Blake told Robert Baldwin, their conservatism encouraged the bar to be just as conservative:

It is the thought of offending judges, whose decrees are absolute, and who thus hold the fate of transgressors in their own hand, which has driven the bar into the ranks of our opponents. It requires more firmness than falls to the lot of most youths to offend a court so constituted.[30]

Blake wanted to enlarge the courts at least partly to permit a Reform government to expand the range of judges sitting in them. (The Kingston bar, meanwhile, urged that if the superior courts were to be enlarged, at least some of them should sit in Kingston to serve the eastern part of the province.)[31]

Blake was no slavish imitator of English models in considering how best to provide courts for Canada West. "We have indeed followed the letter of English practice," he complained when describing the structure existing in 1845, "… but in so doing, we have been altogether unmindful of our social condition, and thus our literal adoption of the English institution has, I very humbly think, betrayed us into serious error."[32] In Canada's courts, Blake argued, English principles had to be adapted to Canadian circumstances. He argued that in Canada West's particular circumstances, its chancery court required three-judge panels, even though single judges heard all chancery cases in England. British judges, even sitting alone, had many colleagues to compare themselves against and to consult, he observed, but in Toronto, a lone chancery judge would become isolated, overworked, and probably arbitrary.

In their reforms to the courts of Canada West, Blake and his allies in the profession were also concerned to defend what they saw as fundamental principles of English justice against a popular outcry for fewer judges, fewer lawyers, the outright abolition of chancery, and a general reduction in legal costs and legal complexities. The success of responsible government had produced a taste for radical changes among some Upper Canadians. Indeed, Robert Baldwin, co-leader of the Reform government, had initially hesitated to endorse Blake's court reforms precisely for fear of opening the floodgates to more sweeping changes. "The country has long groaned under the law system," said the Toronto *Globe*, even though it defended Blake's proposals,[33] and reformers more radical than Blake and Baldwin saw Blake's reforms as motivated by the self-interest of lawyers and judges.[34] Looking for simple, inexpensive courts where all citizens would advocate for themselves and justice would be cheap, available, and populist, they proposed replacing even the superior courts with simple conciliation councils that would allow farmers and mechanics "to settle matters of dispute among themselves."*[35]

Some politically astute lawyers had bowed to the popularity of such proposals, but Blake, Baldwin, and Spragge dismissed them absolutely. Blake's remedy, in fact, was more courts with broader jurisdictions, more judges, and more work for lawyers. He admitted the expense, but pointed to the efficiencies his system would provide and the incalculable value of "the able and impartial administration of the law." A single misjudged case in Queen's Bench, he declared in his 1845 open letter, could cost a litigant more than the entire cost of the additional courts he proposed. Where the radicals emphasized access, Blake emphasized justice, which in his view could come only from formal law in professionally staffed courts following time-honoured legal procedure. Blake shared Baldwin's view that the radicals' plans would "reduce us to a state of barbarism." Indeed he frequently implied that of the two reforms he favoured, responsible government and court reform, the second was the more important. [36]

With lawyers who shared Blake's point of view well represented in the Reform government (and the conservative opposition) in 1849, this opinion was sure to prevail. Blake's reforms did add new costs and new layers of courts, but he could also claim that his court bill promised an antidote to injustice and maladministration. After 1849, all appeals in Canada West would be heard by independent legal professionals appointed by governments responsible to an elected legislature. Officials would no longer profit from the fees they charged. Procedures for pursuing debtors and others would be simplified and reduced in cost.

---

* Since the foundation of the colony, there had been lower courts headed by lay magistrates and justices of the peace. The populist campaign was partly against the superior courts, particularly chancery, but also against moves to professionalize the lower courts.

Chancery would be enlarged and modernized, with oral argument replacing exclusively written pleadings, and its judges going on circuit around the province as Queen's Bench judges always had. Above all, at least for Blake, the immunity to appeal of trial judgments would cease; all the superior courts of Canada West would come under the authority of the new Court of Error and Appeal, which would have sufficient judges of both law and equity to handle every kind of appeal, at least in civil matters. Despite the anti-court, anti-lawyer sentiment roiling the province around mid-century, Blake had good reason to boast that his *Administration of Justice Act* of 1849 really was a significant reform to the courts, and, given his belief in the courts as vital protectors of rights, even to the climate of liberty in Canada West.

As we shall see, however, there remained a significant limit on appeals, one that Blake neither mentioned in his 1845 pamphlet nor remedied in his 1849 reforms: criminal law appeals.

The Court of Error and Appeal as Founded

The statute establishing the Court of Error and Appeal and other new courts came into force on 1 January 1850, and it required many judicial appointments. Under the new rules of responsible government, the appointment of judges was no longer a prerogative of the governor or the British government to which the governor reported. The governor in council – that is, the cabinet of the Province of Canada, specifically Robert Baldwin as the Attorney General for Canada West, with Solicitor General William Blake at his hand – held the authority to choose the judges whom the governor would appoint in the name of the Crown.

Many of the first judges of the court, however, were already in place. The *Administration of Justice Act* made all the incumbent superior trial court judges into members of the Error and Appeal bench ex officio, while retaining them in their trial court roles. As a result, there was much reshuffling among the judges, but only a few new appointments, most of which were made public in the fall of 1849, though some were not officially gazetted until early 1850.[37]

The presiding judge at the centre of the new bench of Error and Appeal was John Beverley Robinson. Robinson had been chief justice of Upper Canada and Canada West since 1829, and he retained that role and title, taking on the leadership of the new appeal court in addition. With him on the Errors and Appeal bench sat one other continuing judge of Queen's Bench, William Henry Draper, and one new ap-

pointment to that court, Robert Easton Burns. Before being appointed
to Queen's Bench in 1847, Draper had been the conservative political
leader in Canada West (until the Reformers' election triumph in 1848),
and he was the last judge appointed in Upper Canada by the British
government under the old regime.[38] Robert Burns, the new appointment to Queen's Bench, was not a particularly partisan choice. [39] He
had held no elected offices, had practised with both conservative and
reform lawyers, and had previously been a judge of the district courts
of Niagara and the Home District. To the extent that his appointment
was a reward from Blake and Baldwin, it mostly reflected their professional ties to him and his prominent role in the judicial reform campaign. Burns was controversial only because he had been chosen over
Henry John Boulton, a prominent lawyer, politician, and former judge
from a distinguished legal family, whose nomination had been widely
expected. [40] Though Burns's practice had been principally in chancery,
his appointment was to the court of law, not the chancery court.

Also joining the Errors and Appeal bench ex officio were the three
judges newly appointed to the Court of Common Pleas. This court was
a new creation in 1849, providing Canada West with a second superior
court panel with jurisdiction identical to that of Queen's Bench. Blake's
legislation had reduced the complement of Queen's Bench judges from
five to three, and three of its judges had moved to the new court. James
Buchanan Macaulay, who had sat in Queen's Bench with Robinson
since 1829, became the first chief justice of Common Pleas.[41] He was
joined on that court by Archibald McLean, a judge of Queen's Bench
since 1837, and Robert Baldwin Sullivan.[42] Macaulay and McLean had
been school friends, War of 1812 comrades, and political allies of Robinson even before they sat together on Queen's Bench. Though all three
were only in their late fifties in 1849, they personified the old conservative elite of Upper Canada's Family Compact, now being marginalized by the reform politics espoused by Baldwin and Blake, but still, in
Blake's view, too powerful in the judiciary and the bar.

It is unlikely that in moving away from Queen's Bench, where Robinson presided as chief justice of Upper Canada, either man meant any
disrespect to him, for they were friends and ideological allies. Macaulay, after twenty years on the bench, was getting a promotion to chief
justice. The two men may also have calculated with Robinson that by
moving to Common Pleas, they could ensure that the new court began
in harmony with Queen's Bench, heading off any chance that Blake and
Baldwin might pack Common Pleas with their own favoured candi-

dates. The third judge moving from Queen's Bench to Common Pleas had been Baldwin and Blake's first judicial appointment in 1848: Robert Baldwin Sullivan, who was Baldwin's cousin, former law partner, and frequent (though inconsistent) political ally. He sat briefly on Queen's Bench until Common Pleas was established.[43] With these three shifting from Queen's Bench to Common Pleas, there was no room for new appointments there.

The Court of Chancery had had only a single judge until 1849. Now it acquired a complement of three, all of whom also became ex officio judges of Error and Appeal. Robert Sympson Jameson, vice chancellor since 1837, remained only briefly on the reconstituted chancery court. He did attend the first sitting of Error and Appeal in January 1850, but even before it began hearing cases, he agreed to retire from both chancery and the new appeal court, creating a sensation because he was able to negotiate a pension of £750 for life (his salary had been £1,000), and he was only fifty-four.[44] After his departure, all three chancery judges (who became judges of Error and Appeal as well) were new appointments. James Christie Palmer Esten was unusual among Canada West's lawyers in that he had been raised in Bermuda and trained at the Inns of Court in London before immigrating to Canada, where he became an early specialist in equity.[45] The other vice chancellor, who succeeded Jameson in 1850, was John Godfrey Spragge, an equity lawyer who had served the chancery court as master and then registrar since the court's foundation in 1837.[46] Spragge and Esten were both uncontroversial appointments, appointed more for their standing in the equity bar than for any political connection. Besides them, only one seat remained to be filled in the reformed chancery court: that of the chief judge, who now held the title of chancellor, Blake's legislation having abolished the governor's titular chancellorship. This appointment was neither apolitical nor uncontroversial. Vaulting over Jameson, the incumbent vice chancellor, to become the first judicial chancellor of Canada West was William Hume Blake.

Blake had not adapted well to a political career. He had strong principles, formidable oratory, and a brilliant mind, but he showed little taste for compromise and no great skill in getting along with his colleagues, let alone his opponents. In 1848, he had nearly resigned from the new Reform government over the question of whether he would have a cabinet seat – Solicitors General were not automatically cabinet members in the mid-nineteenth century – and while in office he thoroughly alienated the political opposition. Though he was privately

dubious about the Rebellion Losses Bill of 1849, he had defended it
vociferously in the legislature, accusing the conservatives of being the
real traitors, the true saboteurs of British constitutional principles.[47] His
speech was acclaimed as one of the most powerful ever given in the
Canadian legislature, but the unrestrained vehemence of his personal
attacks provoked fury among his opponents – and a duelling challenge
from John A. Macdonald, a fast-rising conservative. Blake accepted
the challenge but failed to show up for the duel, possibly a sensible
choice in a society in which duelling was on the verge of extinction,
but not one that enhanced his reputation among his peers. By the summer of 1849, the leaders of the government seem to have agreed that
Blake would do better on the judicial bench than in the House. Despite
opposition accusations that he had created the new judicial positions
simply to provide himself with one, Blake's hypersensitive conscience
did not prevent him from accepting the post – unlike Robert Baldwin,
who would later refuse all judicial appointments by saying that he
had been too closely involved in designing the courts to benefit from
them.[48]

In his brief foray into politics, however, Blake had managed to fulfil
his ambitions for court reform. His changes, while respectful of legal
and judicial forms and the prerogatives of the legal profession, had
successfully headed off a radical campaign against courts and lawyers
from the more advanced reformers, and he had wrought two fundamental changes in the superior courts of Canada West and Ontario.
Henceforth it was confirmed that the judiciary would be independent
of and separate from the executive. And the principle of appeal, at least
in civil cases, was firmly entrenched in all the courts.

These first ten judges appointed to Error and Appeal in 1849–50 (including both Jameson and his nearly immediate successor Spragge)
were a relatively youthful group for senior judges. Their average age
was forty-nine, and the two oldest, Robinson and Macaulay, were only
fifty-eight, each having already spent twenty years on Queen's Bench.
Blake, at forty, was the youngest. Six had been born outside Canada
(all in England or Ireland except Esten, born in Bermuda, where his
father was chief justice), but all except Esten and Jameson had received
their legal education in Upper Canada. They were all either Anglican or
Presbyterian, and they had nearly all practised in Toronto (McLean had
practised in Cornwall, and Burns in Niagara and St Catharines). On
average, they had practised law for almost eighteen years before their
first judicial appointment. Five of the ten – the four chancery judges

plus Burns of Queen's Bench – had been primarily equity lawyers, so chancery expertise was well represented on the appeal court.

Politically, the four most senior judges (Robinson, Macaulay, McLean, and Draper) were identifiably conservative and had become judges before the reformers came to power in 1848. Two judges (Blake and Sullivan) had been reform politicians, and four had not been very actively politically. Jameson and Sullivan were reputed to have drinking problems (Jameson retired in 1850 at only fifty-four, and Sullivan died in 1853, just fifty-one). Blake was prone to nervous complaints, and his health was uncertain throughout his judicial career.

Structure and Administration of the Court of Error and Appeal

Eight of the nine judges attended the first session of the Court of Error and Appeal on 8 March 1850 (McLean was absent), but this was a largely ceremonial sitting and was almost immediately adjourned pending the completion of new rules of practice for the court. Blake's statute, noting that "practice heretofore adopted in appeal is in many respects unsettled and inconvenient and the costs in some matters of appeal excessive," had directed the new court to submit to the legislature within two years a draft of new rules to replace those of the old executive council's appeal tribunal. The new judges drafted the new rules promptly, for the legislature approved them in August 1850, but the changes to the existing procedures they made were modest and showed no ambition to greatly simplify court procedures or reduce costs.[49]

No terms or sitting schedule for Error and Appeal had been specified in Blake's bill. The court's first sitting was held after Queen's Bench, Common Pleas, and Chancery had completed their two-week Hilary terms in early 1850, but before the individual judges left on circuit to hold assizes all over Canada West. It rapidly became habitual that the appeal bench would convene between the end of the superior trial court terms in Toronto and the start of the judges' solo trial circuits around the province.

The court was called "Error and Appeal." In 1850, error and appeal were rather different legal concepts, to be handled separately by the new court. Appeal came from civil litigation; it was standard practice in Britain and (mostly) in British North America that civil litigation in both law and equity courts included a broadly defined right of appeal to a higher court. In criminal law, however, the concept of appeal was barely recognized. Traditionally, the only avenue for judicial review of decisions in criminal law was the "writ of error," which pointed out some technical error made in drafting the official documentation of the case. If criminal trial documents could be shown to have been errone-ously drafted, then the trial verdict could be nullified by a reviewing court. In eighteenth-century Britain, writs of error had led to verdicts being overturned with some frequency. By the nineteenth century, im-proved record-keeping and statutory changes had reduced the likeli-hood of successful writ-of-error applications, and they were gradually becoming almost obsolete. Writs of error were the Court of Error and Appeal's only means of reviewing criminal verdicts of the trial courts of Canada West when the court was founded in 1849, and calling the court "Error and Appeal" acknowledged its dual civil and criminal ju-risdiction. In reality, given the rarity of writs of error, the court's man-date to review criminal cases was extremely limited. Those convicted of criminal offences might petition the government for clemency, but there was virtually no opportunity to appeal a criminal verdict or sen-tence to Error and Appeal. Queen's Bench and Common Pleas panels could and did review verdicts of single judges on assize, and there was a theoretical right of appeal from these to the Privy Council, but they were extremely rare.[50]

Hume Blake's passionate arguments that effective avenues of ap-peal were fundamental to liberty did not extend to criminal law. Blake did not practise criminal law, and none of the reforms he proposed or implemented in the late 1840s proposed any expansion of appeals in criminal cases. The near complete absence of avenues for criminal appeals was part of the design of English law at that time, not some in-advertent mistake simply needing legislative attention. Criminal trials, even more than civil litigation, were jury trials, and trials by jury had long held nearly sacred status in English criminal law. Unlike continen-tal Europe, where the legal codes empowered judges to investigate and decide most criminal matters according to "objective criteria of proof," English criminal law depended on juries, on "the collective judgment of an ad hoc panel of the folk." The legal historian John Langbein ar-gues that in England, "[t]he trial jury required for condemnation not certainty but only persuasion ... There were no firm rules establishing minimum standards for conviction, *and consequently no appellate review of verdicts for insufficiency of the evidence.*"[51] By the mid-nineteenth cen-tury, the English criminal trial had been greatly formalized, and the scope of a jury's powers significantly curtailed, but "the jury standard of proof" remained powerful: no appeals.

In the 1840s, as Blake and other Toronto lawyers were agitating for reforms to the appeals system in Canada West, some English lawyers began a campaign for appeals in criminal law, arguing the illogic of unfettered appeals in civil suits when there were almost none in criminal cases, in which lives and liberties were at stake. A commission then considering a criminal code for England supported the idea of criminal appeals, and private members' bills were introduced. The codification proposal died, however, and parliamentary consideration showed the depth of opposition to appeals in criminal law. The sacredness of juries and their verdicts was only one of the reasons offered. The superior trial judges, consulted on the proposal, told the select committee that wrongful convictions were rare and were satisfactorily dealt with. They argued that criminal appeals were unnecessary because, compared with civil litigation, the cases were relatively simple in both law and fact, and because the criminal law provided safeguards for the accused unknown in civil law. In addition, they reported, criminal appeals would create "inconveniences": courts would be overwhelmed by the volume of appeals, fraud and perjury would be encouraged, costs would rise, poor convicts would have to be provided with lawyers, juries would be encouraged to make reckless convictions, and the deterrent effects of swift punishment would be lost. Furthermore, if prisoners could appeal, prosecutors must have the same right, and the principle that an acquittal was final would be lost.

Such arguments, at least some of which drew on deeply held beliefs about English criminal law, successfully stopped the movement for criminal appeals in England. Only one small change was made. In 1848, legislation provided English jurisprudence with the Court of Crown Cases Reserved, in which a panel of five superior trial court judges could review and either affirm or quash a criminal conviction – but only if the trial judge "reserved" his own decision for examination by Crown Cases Reserved. This did provide a window for trial judges to challenge jury verdicts they thought unwise, but mostly it required judges to put into question their own determinations of law, and such selflessness proved rare. The Court of Crown Cases Reserved had a light caseload for the rest of the century.[52]

Nevertheless, the example of the Court of Crown Cases Reserved inspired a temporary but striking expansion of criminal appeals in the Province of Canada. In 1857, when England was again considering an expansion of criminal appeals, trial judges in Canada West were empowered by statute to reserve their decisions for review "of point of fact or question of law" by a higher court, including Error and Appeal. The appeal court hearing such cases had the authority to not merely affirm or quash a verdict but also order a new trial – something hitherto unknown in English criminal jurisprudence. And even if the trial judge chose not to reserve his decision for review, "any person convicted ... of any treason, felony or misdemeanour" was entitled to apply to a higher court for a new trial "in as full and ample a manner as any person may now apply to such Superior Court for a new trial in a civil action." Upon such application, the trial judge was required to "state in a case to be prepared by such person so convicted and approved by such court ... the question or questions of law or fact upon which such new trial was applied for." In most cases, the appeal by reserved or stated case was from a lower trial court to the Court of Queen's Bench or Common Pleas, but when the superior court bench affirmed a conviction, that decision could be appealed to Error and Appeal, "provided always that no such appeal shall be made to such Court of Error and Appeal unless allowed by such Superior Court," or unless otherwise ordered by the Court of Error and Appeal.[53] Otherwise "no other appeals from a decision of the Court of Queen's Bench or Common Pleas shall be allowed unless the judgement, decision, or other matter appealed against appears of record" – in other words, unless there was a technical error in the documentation. It was recognized at the time that appeals by reserved or stated case were effectively replacing the old writ of error as the only significant means for having a criminal verdict reviewed, and a separate Canadian statute that year declared writs of error abolished in favour of "memorandums of appeal."[54]

In 1859 Error and Appeal considered one criminal appeal, *R. v Gray*, which was based on the new appeal provisions of the 1857 statute. Gray had been convicted at trial of robbery, and Common Pleas had affirmed the conviction, but he appealed to Error and Appeal (with the consent of Common Pleas, presumably) on the ground that new witnesses with new evidence had since been discovered. The Error and Appeal judges noted their new authority to order retrials in criminal cases, but they dismissed this appeal, declaring that they could order a new trial upon "point of law or question of fact," but not because new evidence had come to light.[55] In 1863 in *Dickson v Ward*, Error and Appeal declared it had no jurisdiction to hear an appeal because the decision in question was not "of record."[56]

The limited right of criminal appeal established in Canada West in 1857 does not seem to have been much used, and it did not survive long. In 1869, as the Dominion of Canada began harmonizing criminal law across the new country, the convict's right to seek review and the appeal courts' power to order new trials in criminal matters were both abolished, perhaps because similar appellate reforms that had been expected in England had never been implemented.[57]

Another 1857 statute of the Province of Canada enacted a broad range of administrative and procedural matters concerning Error and Appeal.[58] The court for the first time acquired prescribed terms, being directed to open its three sittings, all in Toronto, on the second Thursday after the end of the Hilary, Easter, and Michaelmas terms (meaning it sat in late February, late June, and mid-December) and continuing as needed to transact its business. It also acquired a quorum: seven judges (reduced to six in 1869). The nine superior court trial judges remained the core of the court as members ex officio, but retired judges of those courts could also be appointed to the appeal court. Chief Justice James Buchanan Macaulay lost his seat on Error and Appeal when he retired from Common Pleas in 1856, but upon passage of this act he was reappointed, giving Error and Appeal ten members instead of nine until his death in 1859. In subsequent years, John Beverley Robinson (1862–3), Archibald McLean (1863–5), and William Henry Draper (1868–74) were also continued as justices of Error and Appeal after having retired from their trial court duties.

Confederation produced no sharp change in the Court of Error and Appeal. In criminal law, there had been efforts to harmonize laws and practices across Canada West and East before Confederation.[59] The new federal government was empowered to legislate in criminal law on a national basis in 1867, and it immediately began to do so. There was also an attempt at a more unified Canadian jurisprudence in common law matters. The *British North America Act, 1867*, looked forward to laws relating to property and civil rights gradually becoming uniform in all the common law provinces. Once such uniformity was achieved, there would be a unified common law bar, and judges could be appointed across provincial boundaries. These provisions, however, were to come into force only when the affected provinces agreed to their implementation. Despite some abortive efforts, no province ever did, and common law unification has remained unimplemented ever since. Just as Quebec retained its distinctive civil code system, the other provinces have each retained their own particular adaptations of English common law, and the unification of the common law provinces' benches and bars never came to pass.

Confederation made the administration of the courts a provincial responsibility, except that the federal government would appoint and pay the superior court judges of all the provinces. The constitution provides no clear explanation for this divided authority over the courts, which extended to the provinces of the new nation that which had been the case in Canada East and Canada West: largely separate provincial courts and bars combined with central control of judicial appointment. As Martin Friedland has observed, key players in the Confederation project who were moving to the federal stage were determined to keep control over these plum appointments in their own hands, but he also notes assertions at the time that appointments from Ottawa would be less narrowly partisan, because "external and local pressure will not be so great" on the national government.[60] Federal appointment enhanced the independence and prestige of the provincial superior courts; it would have eased the path to an eventual integration of Canada's provincial bars and courts, had that proceeded as foreseen in the original confederation plan. A federal statute of 1868 provided that provincial chief justices would be paid $5,000 and regular judges $4,000, with pensions (upon seniority) of two-thirds salary, all to be paid from the Canadian civil list, since it was "not expedient that the payment of ... salaries and pensions of the judges of the courts ... should depend on the annual vote of Parliament." (The Province of Canada had made a similar stipulation as early as 1859.)[61]

Appointments to Ontario's Court of Error and Appeal, as well as to Queen's Bench, Common Pleas, Chancery, and the county courts, became the responsibility of the federal cabinet.* Reforms to the administrative structures of the Ontario courts, however, would be the responsibility of the provincial government of Ontario. In the first years after Confederation, Error and Appeal remained virtually a final court of appeal, for the Supreme Court of Canada was not established until 1875 and appeals to the Judicial Committee in Britain remained rare. From the foundation of Error and Appeal in 1849 to the foundation of the Supreme Court of Canada in 1875, only seven Canada West and Ontario cases are recorded as having reached the Judicial Committee of the Privy Council.[62]

---

* The first few federally appointed judges were sworn in by the Governor General of Canada, but it was soon decided that the provincial lieutenant governor would perform that function in each province.

The Judges of Error and Appeal, 1849–74

From 1849 until 1874, the Court of Error and Appeal was constituted by the judges of the three superior trial courts of Canada West/Ontario, plus the handful of retired trial judges appointed to the appeal court after 1857. In 1874, this system would be changed. That year, four full-time judges of appeal were named, after which trial judges sat on appeals only in special circumstances.

For the first fourteen years of the twenty-five-year period 1849–74, John Beverley Robinson (Sir John after 1856) led the court, first as chief justice of Canada West (that is, the head of Queen's Bench) and then, after he retired from Queen's Bench in 1862, as presiding judge of Error and Appeal until his death a year later. Archibald McLean, who had retired from the trial court but remained on the appeal court, succeeded Robinson as president of Error and Appeal from 1863 to 1865. William Henry Draper succeeded McLean as president and received the title "Chief Justice of Appeal" in 1869.[63] He would continue as the first chief justice of the reorganized four-judge court in 1874. Draper too had retired from his trial court duties (in 1868), so the head of the appeal court had no trial court duties from 1862 to 1874. Hume Blake, who retired as chancellor in 1862, returned to Error and Appeal from 1864 to his death in 1870, but he never headed the court that he had established.

Between 1849 and 1874, twenty-two men sat as justices of Error and Appeal. William Henry Draper was the only member throughout its existence, though Spragge, appointed in 1850, missed only its first few months. Robert Jameson, who retired in 1850, and Skeffington Connor, who died the year he was appointed (1863), each lasted less than a year. The average tenure was less than twelve years (with tenure for seven of them shortened by the restructuring that removed them from the court in 1874). More than half the judges had held political office before their appointment (and, indeed, political service was very common among leading lawyers in mid-century Canada), but few seem to have been appointed strictly as political rewards. Most had had notable careers at the bar, and several were not of the same political party as the Attorney General who appointed them.

Though they came from both major political factions of their time, the judges were broadly similar in ethnicity, religion, and social origin, and they included a father and son, Hume Blake and his son Samuel Hume Blake. Several (Robinson, the Blakes, Esten, Connor) came from backgrounds of social eminence and education, but some (John Wilson,

Oliver Mowat) were sons of farmers or merchants. Most had been born and educated in the province, and even those few immigrants trained at the Inns of Court spent most of their legal careers in Canada West. By mid-century, in other words, the senior judges and leading lawyers of the province were local products. The judiciary of Canada West of the mid-nineteenth century looked to Britain for its jurisprudence, but not for its personnel.

The dominant figure on the court in its early years was John Beverley Robinson. Robinson held great sway for his long eminence, his powerful reputation, and his tremendous dedication and industry, and he led the Court of Error and Appeal from 1849 until 1863. His political ideas had been shaped by eighteenth-century ideas of landed property, aristocracy, and rule by appointed elites rather than elected officials. However, these views were tempered by his strong conviction as a judge that the law must be based on principles and precedent rather than by ideology. Robinson was an active chief justice. In the most complete surviving collection of Error and Appeal judgments prior to 1874, Robinson wrote opinions in twenty of the twenty-three cases he heard. He was not unchallenged, however. Most cases had opinions from several judges, and the chief justice was often enough in the minority.

Considering his reputation at the bar and his confidence in his own judgments, Chancellor Blake might have been a match for Robinson during his years on the court. There are hints in the few judgments that have survived that he was more prepared than Robinson to allow principles of equity to modify strict applications of procedural rules and precedents,[64] but Blake was plagued by ill health in the 1850s. He did not sit regularly.

Other prominent judges of Error and Appeal included William Henry Draper and Philip VanKoughnet. Draper, a sailor in his youth, immigrated to Upper Canada in 1820, studied law, and thrived as a common law barrister and protégé of Robinson. His eloquence, first at the bar and then in politics, earned him the nickname "Sweet William," and in the 1840s, he was the leader of the Upper Canadian conservatives, with John A. Macdonald among his protégés. Draper was named a judge at age forty-six in 1847, launching a thirty-year judicial career. His appointment as chief justice of Common Pleas in 1856 so deeply offended Archibald McLean, who was senior to him, that McLean transferred to Queen's Bench (and later became chief justice there). Still, Draper, who had been a successful coalition builder in politics, seems to have been an effective leader on the bench as well. He served as chief justice of both Common Pleas and Queen's Bench and led Error and Appeal and the Court of Appeal from 1865 until his death in 1877.

VanKoughnet, who came from a long-established family of eastern Ontario loyalists, had been successful both in common law and equity practice. After a brief political career – during the Province of Canada's experiment with an elected upper house in the 1850s, he became the first person elected to its legislative council, the forerunner of the Canadian Senate – VanKoughnet was named chancellor of Canada West in 1862, aged just forty. He was an active judge of Error and Appeal, writing opinions in almost 90 per cent of the cases he heard during the mid-1860s, but his very promising career was cut short in 1869 when he died suddenly, aged just forty-seven. Like VanKoughnet, several of the later appointments to Error and Appeal had little of the patrician antecedents of Robinson or the Blakes, or the English background of Jameson and Esten. Successful legal careers enabled John Wilson, a farmer's son; Adam Wilson, who worked in a country mill before articling in law; and Oliver Mowat, whose father came to Upper Canada as a soldier in the British army, to rise from these plain backgrounds to leading positions in Canadian law, politics, and society.

Relatively little is known of the workload of Error and Appeal judges. The annual number of appeals was small – two to five cases a year to start with, perhaps as many as twenty a year by the mid-1860s, and sometimes more than thirty in the 1870s – but hearing appeals was only one responsibility of the judges. The appeal judges also sat in the superior trial courts in Toronto, and twice a year (three times within York County) they undertook long assize circuits to bring the superior court to all the counties of the province. In 1874, when four full-time appeal judgeships were created, the *Canada Law Journal* doubted the wisdom of appointing lawyers directly from practice to the appeal bench, because the trial bench needed "younger men more fitted for the toils of circuit work."[65] These circuits presumably became somewhat less arduous during the 1850s and 1860s, as railroads replaced horses and stagecoaches, but train travel had its own dangers. The Grand Trunk, the main line between Toronto and Montreal, was notorious for the frequency of its delays and derailments, and other dangers lurked. In 1864, Mr Justice Joseph Curran Morrison of Error and Appeal boarded the train back to Toronto after holding an assize in Cobourg. He and John Hillyard Cameron, a leading barrister and treasurer of the Law Society, found no seats available in the passenger cars and many passengers standing in the aisles. They moved to the sleeping car and occupied seats that had not been made up into berths. When the conductor told them their tickets did not entitle them to sleeping-car accommodation, judge and lawyer declared that their tickets did entitle them to seats, and since there were none in the passenger cars, they would sit where they were. This equitable remedy did not persuade the conductor. He stopped the train, called in some burly brakemen, and had the legal gentlemen hauled bodily from the car. The *Globe* report read:

... a scene of a very unusual character indeed ... a Judge of one of her Majesty's Supreme Courts, [and] a Queen's Counsel and leading member of the bar, were struggling in the hands of three or four railway officials.

Mr. Morrison received three or four violent blows and kicks, by which he was considerably injured, besides which he was subjected to a hauling process to get him out of the car. Mr. Cameron was also roughly handled and, making a somewhat stouter resistance than His Lordship, sustained perhaps more injuries.[66]

At this point, just before the pair was left at trackside, other passengers persuaded the conductor they should not be "left on the road," and they continued on to Toronto among the other standees, vowing legal action.[67] The Grand Trunk was frequently litigating cases before Morrison and his fellow judges in both the trial and appeal courts, and it seems that the dispute was quickly resolved, for there is no further record of the matter.

In 1864, after the death of Justice James Esten at the age of fifty-nine, an anonymous correspondent in the *Canada Law Journal* alleged that Esten, Robinson, and Macaulay had all been "done to death" by their excessive workloads, and that Chancellor Blake, though still living, had been "driven from a life of eminent usefulness by the excessive sedentary work of a chancellorship." The letter argued for an increase in the number of judges of all the courts "so as to lighten their labours."[68] An editorial, perhaps by the journal's secret owner and editor, James Gowan, who was himself a county court judge, declared in response that "there is no doubt also of the fact that our judges of superior jurisdiction ... are overworked."[69]

In 1849, no provision had been made to pay justices of Error and Appeal. As judges of Queen's Bench, Common Pleas, or Chancery, the regular justices earned £1,000 (or $4,000; the provinces of British North America were decimalizing their currencies during the 1850s) and the chief justices £1,250 ($5,000), except for John Beverley Robinson, who received £1,666 ($6,664), presumably in recognition of his pre-eminence as chief justice of Canada West. Sitting *en banc* as the Court of Error and Appeal was part of the job, with no extra salary attached. Salary became an issue only when judges began to retire from the trial court but remain on the appeal bench. In 1862, a statutory amendment provided that a retired judge serving as presiding judge of Error and Appeal could have his retirement annuity topped up to full pay while he was serving on Error and Appeal.[70]

In 1867, the *British North America Act* passed the responsibility for paying judges of the provincial superior court from the Province of Canada to the new Dominion government. In 1868 an early Canadian statute affirmed Canada's authority to pay judges, while continuing the pay and pension rates established earlier by the province.[71] In 1869, however, an Ontario statute declared that because "judges of the superior courts are inadequately paid," the province would pay them an additional $1,000 each annually. The province may have been informed of the unconstitutionality of this measure, for another statute passed later that year affirmed that the judges' extra pay would be for their work as members of Ontario's Heir, Divisee, and Assignee Commission, not as federally paid judges.[72] This began a long tradition of small provincial payments to federal judges for services they provided to the province.

To critics of the judicial system, these were generous salaries at a time when a skilled worker might earn less than $500 a year, but lawyers saw it differently. In 1864 the *Canada Law Journal* complained that "the pittance doled out to our judges ... is a disgrace ... The respectable poverty of those holding judicial offices serves little to encourage those who may be needed to succeed them." Indeed, successful lawyers could earn two or three times the judicial salaries; Oliver Mowat made much more in his equity practice during the 1850s than as a judge of chancery, a fact that may have influenced his resignation from the bench in 1872.

The Error and Appeal Bar

The establishment of an appeal court for Canada West in 1849 encouraged the development of a distinct appellate bar, mostly but not entirely based in Toronto, which was the only place where the appeal court sat. There had always been a corps of leading barristers who not only practised in the superior courts in Toronto but also travelled the assize circuits to argue cases around the province. These specialist advocates soon added the Court of Error and Appeal to their repertoire. In sixty-five cases (1849–66) reported in the three volumes of *Error and Appeal Reports* edited by court reporter Alexander Grant and published in the 1880s, five lawyers – Edward Blake, Adam Crooks, John Hillyard Cameron, Samuel Strong, and John T. Anderson – each made more than ten appearances, and several other lawyers were not far behind, but sixty-two different lawyers were involved in the sixty-five cases, many just once or twice, and not all were Toronto practitioners.[73] Thus was established a long-standing custom: relatively open access to appeal for lawyers wishing to argue there, coexisting with a distinct bar of appeal specialists to whom other lawyers were in the habit of referring appeal cases.

The Jurisprudence of Error and Appeal, 1849–74

Though it had nine (or more) judges, Error and Appeal did not subdivide into smaller panels. All judges who were available sat on all cases, and from the start there were rarely fewer than seven judges. After 1857, legislation established a quorum of seven, and trial court judges joined the panels when needed to make up the required number.

The court's large panel usually produced many opinions for each reported case. A few concluded with a single *per curiam* decision for the whole court, but for most cases there were several concurring opinions, and in 37 per cent of the fifty-four cases reported between 1862 and 1866 (the largest continuous run of Error and Appeal decisions reported), there was at least one dissent.[74]

Given the way the Canada West courts had been structured after 1849, with all the superior trial court judges on the appeal panel, it was inevitable that the Error and Appeal judges would frequently be confronted with appeals from decisions they had made in their capacity as trial court judges. Far from recusing themselves from the appeals, they regularly wrote opinions to defend the conclusions they had made in the lower courts. "When the case was before me at Nisi Prius [that is, when he tried the case on circuit] ... I considered that the plaintiffs were entitled to their verdict. The Court of Common Pleas taking a different view of the law has granted a new trial, but as I have not with the advantage of further consideration come to that conclusion, I must give the opinion which I entertained," wrote Chief Justice Robinson in an 1856 Error and Appeal case, *Coleman v McDermott*.[75] The other seven judges of appeal disagreed: they sustained the Common Pleas decision.

In 1864, Chancellor VanKoughnet grumbled, "I think the opinion I expressed in the court below is in accordance with the rule of decision in England," even as the appellate bench overturned it despite his dissent.[76] An 1869 statute required that no more than two judges who had tried the case now being appealed could sit on the appeal panel. After 1874, there was less overlap between the personnel of the trial courts and Error and Appeal, and judges were prohibited from taking part in appeals from their own trial decisions.[77]

Cases heard by the court were virtually all civil appeals. Common subjects included litigation over debts and mortgages and the nature of the security given for them, disputes over titles to land and the boundaries to property, contested interpretations of wills, and appeals against the actions of county sheriffs and tax collectors. Some appeals involved railroad companies, banks, and insurance companies suing each other or their debtors, but many involved contests between rural landowners from various parts of Ontario, few of whom seem notably wealthy or well connected. Some cases ranged more widely. In 1854, the court reviewed a Common Pleas decision on a parishioner's claim to hold an easement in a pew rental that the churchwardens intended to cancel.[78] In 1862, three lawyers (one a future appellate judge) appealed a Chancery decision taxing a legal bill they had submitted.[79] In 1863 the court ruled on how a Canada East marriage contract affected the dower rights of a widow now living in Canada West.[80] In 1865, a judgment in favour of a father whose unmarried daughter had become pregnant was appealed on the grounds that since the child had not yet been born, the father had not yet suffered any loss of services.[81] Had the rector of Woodstock acquired a right to free passage on the Great Western Railway in exchange for conveyancing rectory land needed for the railroad? No, said the court, though equity judges Mowat and Spragge cited British and American cases in dissent.[82] Could a Queen's professor of classical literature overturn his dismissal by asserting tenure during good behaviour? The trial judge had found he could, but Justice Hagarty, in a decision that strengthened the authority of universities over professors, found that the court had no jurisdiction; "neither a court of equity nor law should interfere."[83]

In determining all these cases, the judges wrote at length and in detail, with many case citations. They frequently declared the authority of English cases, but not in a mechanical fashion. In his court reform pamphlet of 1845, Hume Blake, a founding member of Error and Appeal, had insisted that English institutions had to be adapted to local conditions. The court sometimes followed his lead, acknowledging the authority of principles derived from English decisions but seeking to apply them in light of local circumstances. In a railroad liability case of 1866, William Buell Richards, a future chief justice of Canada, declared, "The principles laid down in ... England seem to me broad enough for general application and are adapted to the mode of travelling which obtains in this country" – suggesting the possibility that English principles might not always be so well adapted to local needs.[84] "We are, of course, bound by English decision," Vice Chancellor Spragge wrote for the court in 1864, "but there is so much force in the reasoning in favour of the law of the place of performance of the contract being the law to govern on the question of prescription, as well as of the interpretation of the contract, that I think the doctrine of the English courts upon that point should not be carried further than it had already gone."[85] Dissenting from the overturning of his own lower court decision, Chancellor VanKoughnet acknowledged the sound reasons for what he considered a rejection of English precedent by Error and Appeal:

The opinion I expressed in the court below is in accordance with the rule of decision in England, which the statute law of this province and my judicial oath compel me to observe, and I cannot conscientiously concur in any other view, *though the conclusion at which the court has arrived may probably be the more just one as between the parties.*[86]

In 1862 John Hawkins Hagarty declared that the weight of English authority compelled him to concur in a decision, but observed "the principle of equity which is here enforced must, in this country, be often attended with the harshest results."[87]

The judges frequently cited American case law, though more as a supplement than an alternative to English decisions. In an 1862 debts case, Robert Easton Burns cited case law from Pennsylvania, New York, Connecticut, Massachusetts, and the United States Supreme Court, noting that "many other cases before courts in other states of America might be added."[88] Often, like Oliver Mowat in 1866, the judges found that these "foreign courts take the same view ... as English courts do," rather than choosing to adopt American over British precedents.[89] Surviving case reports show that lawyers and judges arguing appeal cases made abundant citations from a wide range of Canadian, American, and English cases, suggesting that even a brief appeal session three

Table 1.1 Statistical Notes on 22 Judges of Error and Appeal 1849–74

Birthplace

Lower Canada   1
Upper Canada   7
England   5
Scotland   2
Ireland   6
Bermuda   1

Ethnic Origin

Great Britain and Ireland   22

Legal Education

Upper Canada   19
England   2
Ireland   1*

Years of Law Practice before Judicial Appointment

Average 20 years (low 7, high 31)

Location of Legal Practice (some in more than one place)

Toronto   19
Cornwall   1
Niagara   1
Brockville 1
London   1

Identified Political Commitment

Reform   8
Conservative 6
Mixed   2
None   6

Religious Affiliation

Church of England   18
Presbyterian   4

Judicial Appointment prior to E&A

Yes   7   (6 Queen's Bench pre-1849, 1 district court pre-1849)
No   15

Table 1.1 (*Concluded*)

Age at E&A appointment

48.1 years

Years on E&A bench

Average 11.3 years[†] (minimum less than 1, maximum 25)

Reason for Leaving E&A

Died	10
Retired	2
Term ended (1874)	8
Promoted	2

Age on Leaving

All 22 judges	59.6 years
Omitting those whose E&A terms ended in 1874	58.8

---

[*] At Trinity College, not called to bar.
[†] Four full-time E&A judges were appointed in 1874, and the other judges then on E&A
     ceased to sit there while continuing their trial court appointments.

times a year required substantial time for research, reading, and draft-ing by the judges and by the lawyers.

Error and Appeal had, by its nature, to deal flexibly with both law and equity, though at the time these were largely separate and had very distinct rules of procedure. In the 1840s, arguing for the reforms that produced Error and Appeal, Hume Blake had been adamant that chancery had to be preserved and reinvigorated, rather than abolished. Against a substantial popular campaign for abolition, he had expanded the court from one judge to three, simplified its procedures, and sent the Chancery judges on circuit to hear cases around the province. Blake's intention was to reinforce chancery but, by making it more familiar and more widely practised, he may also have helped set in motion its eventual merger with the common law courts. In the Error and Appeal court that Blake established, there were always at least three Chancery judges on the panels, but they were not given any special mandate to determine the Chancery appeals. All judges weighed in on equitable is-sues as much as on common law ones. "I think nothing in a court of eq-uity would turn upon [those words]," wrote Robinson, a common law judge throughout his career, in an 1858 appeal from Chancery. "There would be a clear equity of redemption without those words."[90]

The chancery judges, perhaps demonstrating the chancery practitioners' belief that theirs was the most sophisticated and intellectual branch of practice, were among the most prolific writers of opinions, including appeals from the common law courts. There are cases in which three chancery judges were united in dissent from a common law majority, but mostly the Error and Appeal cases show the judges taking on equity and common law questions and remedies with equal confidence, producing few strictly law/equity splits among them. That developing habit at the province's senior court must have helped break down the barriers that had previously been fiercely maintained between equity and common law.

Nevertheless, tensions evidently continued between law and equity. William Buell Richards, a common lawyer, seems to have been criticizing chancery when he observed how chancery judges inevitably had a "character of extending their jurisdiction" into cases "in which there was a remedy at law."[91] And, much later, upon the death of Chief Justice Hagarty in 1900, the *Law Times* recalled the difficulty he had sometimes had with equity issues, and vice versa. "It may be easily imagined, with a bench of common lawyers, that equity cases had a hard time and some practitioners came to think, no matter how sound a judgment might be delivered in Chancery, there was never any certainty that it would pass muster in the Court of Error and Appeal."[92] Though the editorialist was mistaken in implying that equity judges did not sit on equity appeals, something of the lore of the chancery bar may have been preserved here.

2

Oliver Mowat's Court, 1874–1912

Oliver Mowat had been Mr Justice Oliver Mowat of the Court of Error and Appeal from 1864 until the day in 1872 when he resigned his vice chancellorship, having just been sworn in as premier and Attorney General of Ontario. Mowat, a Kingston-born son of a shopkeeper, had first found success as an equity practitioner in Toronto and as a reform-minded politician. In October 1864, when he was a cabinet minister engaged in the constitutional negotiations at Quebec City that would lead to Canadian Confederation, Vice Chancellor James Esten died in Toronto. Attorney General John A. Macdonald, Mowat's political rival and former articling principal, offered Mowat Esten's seat on the chancery bench (and therefore on Error and Appeal). Mowat accepted, and spent eight years as a judge of chancery and ex officio member of the Error and Appeal bench.[1]

From the surviving Error and Appeal case reports, Mowat seems to have been an active, productive judge. His chief justice, the common law lawyer William Draper, once called him "an equity fanatic," ready to overturn common law rules and statutes for "equitable extremes."[2] This jurisprudence may have put him out of step with his colleagues, and he chafed at his reduced income (in the mid-1850s, he had calculated his earnings from private practice at more than three times what a judge earned), and perhaps also at not being offered the chancellorship when it became vacant in 1869. Nor had his political ambitions been extinguished.

In October 1872, Mowat left the judicial bench for politics even more suddenly than he had left politics for the bench. A new Liberal government in Ontario had passed a statute seeking to strengthen the Ontario legislature against control from Ottawa by prohibiting its members from simultaneously holding seats in the provincial and federal Parliaments. The architect of this rule, Premier Edward Blake, the son of Hume Blake, intended to devote himself to federal rather than provincial politics. Seeking a successor as party leader and Ontario premier, he and other reform leaders persuaded Mowat to leave the judicial bench. There was some criticism of Mowat's abrupt shift from the bench to politics, but Mowat, who prided himself on being a "Christian statesman," loftily denied there could be any wrongdoing in choosing one form of public service over another. When Mowat replaced Blake in the premier's office, Prime Minister Macdonald appointed Blake's younger brother and law partner, Samuel Hume Blake, to replace Mowat as vice chancellor and judge of Error and Appeal.

Mowat's return to politics proved spectacularly successful. He would be premier of Ontario until 1896, winning majorities in six consecutive provincial elections and helping to establish provinces and provincial premiers as powerful players in Canadian politics. He had the good fortune to be premier when Ontario was consolidating its position as the keystone province of the new confederation.[3] With a population approaching two million in 1871 and over 2.6 million by 1911, Ontario was already Canada's largest province by population and growing rapidly in size, as Mowat pushed its boundaries west towards Manitoba and north to Hudson Bay. Across the agricultural expanse of southern Ontario, the rural population was approaching its peak, and intensive wheat farming was giving way to beef and pork production, dairy and cheese making, and fruit cultivation. Mining had hardly begun in Ontario at this time, although the transcontinental railroad projects of the 1880s were opening up the Sudbury basin, and the Cobalt discoveries of 1902 would help make Toronto the centre of finance (and legal counsel) for Canadian mining. The forest industry, on the other hand, still thrived on the Lake Ontario and Georgian Bay shores and was beginning to move north. The important Aboriginal rights case *St Catharines Milling*, heard in the Court of Appeal in 1886, arose from a southern Ontario lumber enterprise moving into northwestern Ontario.

Railroad development from the 1850s had led to commercial and industrial development in many Ontario towns, which were growing faster than the province as a whole: Toronto grew from 56,000 people in 1871 to 380,000 in 1911, and the city was home to about a quarter of Ontario's roughly 1,000 lawyers. The rise of corporations and industries was producing the first long-lived corporate law firms, but even those had only a handful of lawyers; most lawyers were sole practitioners or had informal associations with friends or family members. Law in Ontario in this era was a solidly established, self-governing, and self-educating profession. Law students learned the profession by articling with other lawyers, and they learned litigation by observing the courts, particularly those at Osgoode Hall, including Error and Appeal.[4]

While directing the growth of the province, Mowat served as his own Attorney General and never lost interest in the law and the judiciary. Two projects of Mowat's were particularly relevant to the history of the Court of Appeal, upon which he exercised more influence as premier than he had as a member of the court. First, Premier Mowat reshaped Ontario's courts through a series of reforms that replaced Hume Blake's vision for the courts with his own. Second, Mowat fought a long constitutional battle in the courts to assert the province's autonomy against Ottawa, and many of the cases that determined which would be the victor made their way through Ontario's appeal court. As Mowat was reshaping the courts and vindicating the independent authority of the provinces, however, the relationship of Ontario's appeal court to courts beyond Ontario was also being redefined. In these years, Ontario's Court of Appeal ceased to be a *de facto* final court of appeal and became part of an emerging national and imperial judicial hierarchy.

A Specialized Court of Appeal, 1874

Oliver Mowat was a cautious politician, preferring to follow rather than lead public opinion and inclined to incremental steps rather than bold leaps towards his goals. Nevertheless, as an ex-judge of appeal, he had firm views on what he wanted the court to become, and he began implementing changes soon after he took office. In the spring of 1874, he introduced legislation that abolished Hume Blake's appeal court of trial judges sitting *en banc* to hear appeals. Blake's expansion of courts and judgeships had been controversial in 1849, but by the 1870s, there was little opposition to the contention that the fast-growing province once more required more courts and more judges.

Introducing his *Administration of Justice* bill in the Ontario legislature in March 1874, Mowat felt obliged to underline that the new federal

Constitution, still just seven years old, empowered Ontario to create new courts and judicial positions, although it was Ottawa's responsibility to name and pay the judges ("It would of course be highly improper to ask the appointment of a greater number than the actual necessities of the country required."). He outlined the growth of Ontario's population and commerce since the 1849 reforms, setting out how the expansion of the counties and the county courts required expansion in the superior courts as well. He highlighted instances of court congestion, such as a recent Toronto assize that had been "unable even to try all the cases left over from the previous assize."[5]

The Ontario legislature's debate on the new court structure was generally approving. Mowat ignored backbenchers who asked for more radical steps (Simpson McCall, Liberal MPP for Norfolk South: "He thought the house should regulate the fees of legal gentlemen who are now gnawing the vitals of the country" – Hear, hear, laughter – "and he hoped the strong desire of the people for the fusion of law and equity would increase in strength"). The bill, defined in the legislative preamble as intended "to secure the due dispatch of the increased business of the superior courts ... and the due hearing and early determination of cases in appeal," was quickly passed into law.[6]

Mowat's principal change in 1874 was to the appellate court. "Some change was necessary in the court of appeal," he told the legislature, "and after much consultation and conference ... he had thought it most advantageous to procure three judges and reconstitute the court." Error and Appeal (in 1874 the name remained unchanged, though Mowat generally referred to it as "the Court of Appeal") would be reduced in size to a chief justice and three full-time judges, who would always sit as a panel of four. This quorum was deliberately chosen to require a high threshold for overturning trial court verdicts, so a two-two split was to be a definite rejection, not an awkward tie. "There being four judges," Mowat told the House, "it would be necessary for three of them to concur before any reversal of judgment could be made."[7] Just four years later, new amendments specified that only appeals from the superior trial courts required four judges, while three would suffice for appeals from the lower courts,[8] but the four-judge panel would have a long life. A majority or near-majority of cases would be determined by four-judge panels until 1931, when odd-numbered panels became obligatory.[9] Mowat's 1874 amendments also confirmed that Error and Appeal could wield all the powers of the lower courts it reviewed, could review all parts of a lower court decision, not just the parts directly appealed, and could hear new evidence of fact in the course of an appeal. The court could also dispense with the traditional terms and sit when it chose during the year.[10]

The superior trial court judges, though they retained their ex officio appointments as justices of Error and Appeal, would no longer be routinely engaged in hearing appeals and would give undivided attention to trial court work. The four new full-time appellate judges, meanwhile, were intended to be a small panel, working together as Ontario's final court on all matters of substance. This change made Ontario the first Canadian province to establish what has been called a "specialized" court of appeal – one with a small, collegial body of permanently appointed judges hearing appeals more or less exclusively and therefore, at least in theory, developing and applying a consistent jurisprudential philosophy as the final judicial law-making body in the province.[11]

Mowat, however, was not committed to letting the appeal court be completely specialized. Anticipating that the volume of appeals would not occupy the whole time of the four appellate judges, Mowat "proposed to utilize them by requiring them to aid in the original work of the various courts. This would be a great advantage to themselves as it would give them fresh and enlarged experience" in the trial courts.[12] The new appeal judges of 1874 were authorized, and expected, to sit on the trial courts at least part of the time. In addition, trial court judges could still be invited to fill appeal court quorums when needed. (The bill specified for the first time, however, that no judge could hear an appeal of a case he had decided at trial.) The *Law Journal* disapproved of this mingling: "What the country really wants [is] a strong and effective Court of Appeal. The judges of that court should have only their appellate work to do."[13] Mowat's 1874 compromise did not end debate on the appropriate separation of trial and appeal roles for judges. For the next century and more, nearly every court reform proposal in Ontario would revisit this issue, usually to permit some interchange between the trial and appeal benches.

The year 1874 was a good time for an Ontario reformer to be creating new judicial positions. In Ottawa, the scandal over the Pacific railway contract had recently brought down John A. Macdonald's government, and Mowat's ally Alexander Mackenzie was now prime minister. Mackenzie's government would appoint not only the new Ontario appeal judges, but also five members (two from Ontario) of the new Supreme Court of Canada that it established in 1875. As a result, Mowat-approved judges would have a lengthy tenure on the country's senior courts in the following decades, despite Conservative control of the federal appointive power for most of the late nineteenth century.

When the *Administration of Justice Act* came into effect on 1 July 1874, William Henry Draper, then seventy-three, retained his position as head of the appeal court, a position he had held since 1865. Draper was already a full-time appeal judge, having retired from the trial court in 1869 and been given the title Chief Justice of Appeal; previously the head of Error and Appeal had merely been titled its "presiding judge." . Named to join him on the new Error and Appeal bench in 1874 were Samuel Henry Strong, previously vice chancellor of the Chancery court and therefore already a judge of Error and Appeal, and two lawyers appointed directly from the bar, George Burton and Christopher Salmon Patterson. Strong remained only briefly. Named to the new Supreme Court of Canada in Ottawa in 1875, he was replaced by Thomas Moss, another direct appointment from the Toronto bar. Eight justices of the old Error and Appeal bench – J.G. Spragge, William Buell Richards, John H. Hagarty, Joseph C. Morrison, Adam Wilson, John Wellington Gwynne, Thomas Galt, and Samuel H. Blake – effectively lost their appellate roles while continuing their superior trial court functions.

Moss's replacement of Strong meant that all three puisne justices of the new four-judge Error and Appeal panel had been appointed directly from practice, the 1874 amendments having done away with the requirement that they be judges or retired judges of the trial courts. Evidently Prime Minister Mackenzie's government (probably in consultation with Premier Mowat) was determined to have its own men, or at least new men, on the courts. Only Moss, an MP until his appointment, had been an active Liberal. Strong's previous judicial appointment had come from a Conservative government, and he had been a legal adviser to Macdonald on plans for the Supreme Court of Canada, while Draper, the chief justice, had been a Conservative premier of the Province of Canada back in the 1840s. Like Strong and Moss, Patterson and Burton were respected lawyers and legal educators, but they had no strong political identifications.

Even before Strong, a relatively young judge, was replaced by Moss, who was even younger, the *Canada Law Journal* questioned the wisdom of appointing "younger men more fitted for the toils of circuit work" to the appeal court instead of the trial courts. The *Law Journal* suggested that the appeal court seats should have gone to the chief justices of the three trial courts: John Godfrey Spragge, who was sixty-eight in 1874; William Buell Richards, fifty-eight; and John Hawkins Hagarty, also fifty-eight. None of them was promoted, however, and the new appeal judges were indeed younger: Burton, fifty-six; Patterson, fifty-one; Strong, forty-nine; and Moss, just thirty-eight. Chief Justice Draper was seventy-three. "We fear," wrote the *Law Journal*, "that for a time at least the new court will not, as a Court of Appeal, owing to the strength of the courts below, secure that confidence which such a court should command. Nor can we be surprised at this when we see that the new court is partly composed of men taken directly from the bar."[14]

Having restructured the court, Mowat soon renamed it as well. In 1875, the commission to consolidate the Ontario statutes (consisting of Mowat, the four appeal judges, and some junior members drawn from the bar) recommended that the Court of Error and Appeal be renamed.* They observed that "court of appeal" was the term used in England, that the head of Error and Appeal was already called the Chief Justice of Appeal, and that the term "error" was now "superfluous," presumably because the near extinction of the writ of error meant that all the matters it heard were now technically "appeals." An 1876 statute duly changed the court's name to the Court of Appeal for Ontario. It also authorized the appointment of the Court's first registrar; until then, the Chancery registrar had doubled as Error and Appeal registrar. The first registrar seems to have been Alexander Grant, who had been a court clerk and a court reporter and published three volumes of Executive Council and Error and Appeal case reports in 1885. He apparently served as registrar from the mid-1870s until 1899.[15] At this time and long after, registry appointments were order-in-council – that is, patronage – appointments. This act also directed that appeals from the county courts should henceforth go directly to the Court of Appeal, thus shifting more appeal responsibilities from the superior trial courts to the higher court alone.[16]

The *Judicature Act* of 1881 – Merging Law and Equity

Mowat returned to make more changes to the Ontario courts in 1881, establishing a new structure for the superior courts, substantial elements of which would endure more than a century. The *Judicature Act*,

---

* Commissions to revise and consolidate Ontario's statutes consisted principally of superior court judges until 1927. Subsequently the duty passed to the Office of the Legislative Counsel.

1881, created a new institution, the Supreme Court of Judicature for Ontario, not as a court with judges and a jurisdiction of its own, but simply as an umbrella for all the superior courts.[17] The Court of Appeal for Ontario, otherwise unchanged, became the appellate division of this Supreme Court. The Supreme Court's trial division, now given the name "the High Court of Justice for Ontario," consisted of the existing superior trial courts, Queen's Bench, Common Pleas, and Chancery, each of which retained its individual name and its own chief justices and judges until 1913. In 1903, a fourth three-judge superior trial court, called the Court of Exchequer, also with a chief justice, was added to the High Court.[18] This largely titular Supreme Court, comprised of the Court of Appeal based in Toronto and a larger superior trial court called the High Court, also based in Toronto but whose judges went on circuit around the province, would survive into the late twentieth century.

The *Judicature Act, 1881*, also took the step that had been intolerable to Hume Blake in 1849 but had remained in the air ever since: the fusion of law and equity. In 1849, a substantial gulf had existed between equity and common law. Blake, John Godfrey Spragge, and other equity lawyers found it unacceptable that chancery decisions would be reviewed by the common law judges of Queen's Bench. The campaign for fusion had begun as a populist complaint that equity was too expensive, too complicated, and too inaccessible for ordinary litigants, and dominated by the interests of landlords and moneylenders.[19] By the 1870s, however, even the equity lawyers' devotion to equity's separate existence had faded. As premier of Ontario in 1871–2, Hume Blake's son Edward, by then a leader in the equity bar, had favoured rapid progress towards the fusion of law and equity. In England, chancery and common law were merged by statute in 1873, and several American states and other Canadian provinces had also moved towards fusion. Mowat, also an equity specialist, had not rushed to implement Blake's proposals when he came to office. When he joined the movement in 1881, his program to merge law and equity closely followed the English precedent from 1873 – always a course likely to find favour with the nineteenth-century Ontario bar.

Prior to 1881, the courts of Queen's Bench and Common Pleas had held identical jurisdiction and followed identical common law procedures, while Chancery was the equity court. From 1881 to 1913, the three courts retained their individual names within the new High Court, but now all three shared identical jurisdictions and a new common set of rules of practice. All three courts of the High Court (four after Exchequer was added in 1904) could apply common law procedures and precedents, and all three could also grant a plaintiff or defendant the equitable claims and defences formerly available only from the chancery court. Judges could be transferred freely between the three, and Queen's Bench lost its precedence; whichever chief justice was senior would henceforth be "President of the High Court."

Despite Mowat's cautious approach, fusion in Ontario must have been facilitated by the province's appellate experience in the preceding decades. From 1850 to 1874, equity and common law judges sat together on Error and Appeal panels. Hearing both law and equity arguments, Error and Appeal routinely made decisions that drew on both traditions and that bound the lower courts and the lawyers practising in them. After the restructuring of Error and Appeal in 1874, it was no longer automatic that there would be a bloc of chancery judges on the appeal panel, but equity specialists (such as new justices Strong and Moss) remained prominent there, and the court dealt confidently with both law and equity.

By 1881, both the British example and local experience had long been pointing towards coexistence between the two traditions and the two groups of legal practitioners. Mowat evidently concluded that he could follow the trend towards fusion without alienating his legal brethren. The long evolution of chancery – from a special appeal to the king's counsellors in cases where common law precedents could not provide natural justice, to a parallel court system with its own elaborate rules and procedures, to a gradual integration of equity principles and common law precedents in appellate decisions – concluded in Ontario in 1881 with a fused judicial system in which lawyers and judges could draw on both in all the Ontario courts. The *Judicature Act* specified that where law and equity could not be reconciled, equity principles would prevail, and in many fields, such as trusts (where all trustee relationships were defined by equity rules, not common law), equity remained essential, to the point that fusion in Ontario was called "a triumph of equity" and "the final vindication of the court of chancery."[20] In the longer term, however, the gradual rise of black-letter formalism in the courts may have reflected the growing influence of common law's reliance on the specific wording of statutes and precedents, rather than the more subjective quest of the chancery court for substantive justice.[21]

Until 1881, an "attorney" and a "solicitor" in Ontario had similar roles, the former serving the common law courts, the latter in chancery, and it was the same for "barrister" (in common law courts) and "counsel" (in chancery). With fusion, the terms "counsel" (from chancery) and "attorney" (from common law) were dropped, and "barrister and solicitor" thereupon became the normal appellation for lawyers in Ontario. Nevertheless, the distinct loyalties of equity lawyers (and their clients) were not immediately extinguished. Though the three branches of the High Court were now identical, Chancery remained the busiest and the first to be provided with additional judges, indicating that there were still many litigants who wanted their equitable arguments adjudicated by equity-trained judges. Curiously, despite chancery's reputation as a slow, expensive court favoured by deep-pocketed banks, landlords, corporations, and mortgage holders, it was an axiom among Ontario lawyers long after fusion that "all the leading members of the equity bar were reformers and all the leading members of the common law bar were Conservatives."[22] The appeal court's need for expertise in equity may help explain why several prominent reformers received appointments to the nineteenth-century Court of Appeal, even during Conservative administrations in Ottawa.

Confederation remained new enough in 1881 that the *Judicature Act* raised a small problem of jurisdiction. The act had not appointed any new judges in Ontario, but it did make them judges of courts whose roles and relationships had been redefined. This raised the question whether the province was encroaching on the federal power to appoint judges. To avoid doubt, all the judges were given new federal appointments to their redefined positions.[23]

Mowat and his successors would go on tinkering with the structure of the Court of Appeal. In 1883 Mowat agreed to remedy congestion in the Chancery division in a roundabout way, by appointing to the Court of Appeal a fifth judge who would also assist in chancery trials. Two years later, the extra seat was transferred to Chancery, and the Court of Appeal returned to four. A more permanent change came in 1897, soon after Mowat resigned as premier: the Court of Appeal was again expanded to five judges, and it could now sit in panels of either three or five, although the four-judge panels were not definitively prohibited until 1931. Five-judge panels made up 78 per cent of all panels in our sampling of cases from the decade 1900–10, but four-judge panels held a slim majority in the next two decades.[24]

An Intermediate Court of Appeal? The Divisional Court, 1881–1913

The *Judicature Act, 1881*, established procedures by which the Court of Appeal, "from pressure of business," could form two panels (or "divisions of the Court of Appeal," as the statute calls them), with the additional judges to fill out the panels to be selected from among the judges of the High Court by a vote of all judges of the Supreme Court of Ontario (that is, all the superior court judges, trial or appeal).[25] The act proposed that at least two regular appeal judges should, "where practicable," sit on each appeal panel, but in subsequent years, as it became common for High Court judges to sit alongside regular appeal judges on these panels, some were formed entirely of High Court judges.[26]

The act also created a new forum for appellate review that would long be part of the Ontario judiciary: the Divisional Court. From 1881, any three (sometimes two) trial judges of the High Court could sit as a "Divisional Court of the High Court," in order to hear appeals from High Court chambers rulings and other single-judge matters.[27] Litigants were entitled to take some of these matters directly to the Court of Appeal instead, and some Divisional Court rulings could be appealed to the Court of Appeal (and the nomenclature used in the statutes did little to clarify their roles*), but the Divisional Court, an intermediate appeal court comprised of panels of superior trial court judges, would become an enduring – though frequently changing – part of Ontario court structure into the twenty-first century.

In 1895, the rather limited appellate authority of this Divisional Court was reaffirmed, and in 1897 the Court of Appeal was enlarged from four justices to five.[28] In 1904, however, the jurisdiction of the Divisional Court of the High Court was substantially increased.[29] It could now hear appeals "from any judgment, order, or decision of a judge of the High Court," as well as appeals from the County Court and the other lower courts of Ontario. Furthermore, section 75 of the *Judicature Act, 1904*, seemed almost to abolish the need for the Court of Appeal, declaring that "the judgment, order or decision of a Divisional Court shall be final and there shall be no further appeal therefrom." Clauses surrounding section 75, however, provided a substantial list of exceptions to this no-appeal rule: when the case involved the Crown, when

---

* Since the 1881 Act made the Court of Appeal and the High Court into "divisions" of the Supreme Court of Judicature, and panels of the Court of Appeal were "divisions" of that court, and the three trial courts were "divisions" of the High Court, and there were also "division courts" within the county court system, the name "Divisional Court of the High Court" created further opportunities for confusion, but the name would come and go in various forms into the twenty-first century.

the value of the matter exceeded $1,000, when it involved the validity of a statute, when the Divisional Court was divided on a question of law or practice, when there were "special reasons" for treating the case as "exceptional," or in any matter where "an appeal would lie from the judgment of the Court of Appeal to the Supreme Court of Canada."[30] Thus there was abundant scope for appeal decisions of the Divisional Court to be appealed again. All appeals from the Divisional Court to the Court of Appeal would be heard by five judges – the whole membership of the higher court.

The motives for all this tinkering with the overlapping appellate functions of the Court of Appeal and the Divisional Court are not explained in the statutes, the legislative debates, or the law journals of the day.* Evidently there was still debate in Ontario judicial and political circles about layers of appeal and the value of a small, specialized, collegial appeal court to determine the law. The appellate functions of the Divisional Court were being expanded substantially, as if the Court of Appeal was henceforth to exist principally to hear appeals from it and not from the trial courts directly. Still, the exceptions and qualifications included in the statute preserved the Court of Appeal with broad appellate jurisdiction in civil and criminal matters. The whole question of the division of responsibility between the Divisional Court and the Court of Appeal would be revisited in the *Judicature Act, 1913*.

The Criminal Code and the Rise of Criminal Appeals

In the meantime, another significant change to the work of the Court of Appeal for Ontario was developing in Ottawa. Since Confederation, criminal law throughout Canada had been a federal responsibility. From 1867, criminal law across the provinces was gradually harmonized, but everywhere the rule remained that there was no appeal in criminal cases except when an error was alleged in the record of proceedings, or when a trial judge sought a review of the law in a case he was deciding. In 1875, the new Supreme Court of Canada, intended to provide final determinations of law for Canadian courts, was empowered to hear appeals of criminal cases decided by the provincial appeal courts, but in practice almost no criminal appeals reached the

---

* Debate about intermediate appeal courts would revive in Ontario in the 1900s and again in the 1980s.

provincial appeal courts, and therefore none proceeded to Ottawa. In 1886, federal law established that in criminal matters a trial judge who wished to reserve a decision of his own for appellate review would direct it "for the consideration of the justices of the court having, within the province in which such trial takes place, jurisdiction to hear Crown cases reserved," that is, to the appropriate provincial appellate court.[31] No Canadian province had a court formally named "Crown Cases Reserved," but such a court existed in England from 1848 to 1907, and Canadian use of the term with regard to criminal appeals reflected the long-standing reliance of the federal justice department on English practices.

In 1892, the new Criminal Code of Canada came into force, a pioneering attempt to combine all the laws regarding crime into a single statute.[32] The Code, though it did not create any general right of appeal, cautiously expanded the circumstances under which a criminal verdict might be appealed. It once more authorized trial court judges, when they were uncertain of the law in a case, to reserve their judgments for review by a higher court. The trial judge could initiate such a review himself, or either the Crown or the accused could request the trial judge to "state the case," that is, to refer the trial court's interpretation of the law for appellate review. That much was familiar practice, but the 1892 Code breached the absolute control the trial judge had formerly held over reviews of his decisions. It provided for the first time that if a trial judge had refused to reserve a decision for review, the provincial Attorney General could authorize a referral to the appropriate appeal court of any question of law or procedure regarding the case, at the request of either the prosecution or the defence, even against the wishes of the trial judge. The Criminal Code also broadened the authority of appeal courts in such cases not simply to clarify the law for the trial court, but to also substitute its own verdict or to order a new trial as it judged appropriate.[33]

This provision for appeals "by stated case," even against the trial judge's wishes, made appeals of criminal verdicts more frequent. In 1896, counsel for a man named Brennan, convicted of murder in Barrie, persuaded the Attorney General of Ontario to refer his conviction for appellate review. In the event, the venue for this "Crown case reserved" was not the Court of Appeal for Ontario but the Divisional Court, as established in 1881. The Divisional Court panel threw out the trial court verdict and ordered a new trial with a classic appellate finding, ruling that the trial judge had erred by misdirecting the jury when he refused to put the option of manslaughter before it.[34] The overruled trial judge, as it happened, was John Douglas Armour, then chief justice of Queen's Bench and a future chief justice of Ontario and justice of the Supreme Court of Canada. Chancellor John Boyd, who presided over the new trial at the next Barrie assize, saw Brennan convicted again, though his death sentence was later commuted. Boyd's biographer wrote that the Brennan case might have been "the first Canadian case where there was a new trial of a capital charge" – a direct result of the Criminal Code amendment that had opened the possibility of appellate review at the instigation of the provincial Attorney General.[35]

In 1900, there was a further expansion of criminal appeals. During parliamentary debate that year on amendments to the Criminal Code, two backbench MPs, both lawyers, the Liberal Byron M. Britton of Kingston and the Conservative Henry Absalom Powell of Saint John, NB, urged the government to allow litigants to go to their provincial appeal court and seek leave to appeal on points of law, without the consent of either the trial judge or the Attorney General. Britton was not proposing appeal as a right. "The administration of justice is fully protected by the accused being required to get the leave of the court," he declared, but he told the Commons that leave to appeal in criminal law should not depend on the Attorney General.

I do not think that any Attorney General will act upon caprice, or will take so strong a view of it that in any ordinary case he would not be willing to grant that. But I submit the principle is not fair … The Attorney General ordinarily gets his information of the case from the local prosecuting attorney and might be led to think that leave to appeal should not be granted.[36]

Powell, a law professor at New Brunswick's King's College law school, said he was urging the change at the request of several members of the New Brunswick bar, and he was blunt about the continued denial of appeals in criminal cases, telling Parliament, "This is one of those traditions from the Dark Ages."[37] The government was persuaded. The backbenchers saw their suggestion incorporated verbatim into the government's package of Criminal Code amendments, which was passed that year, and henceforth provincial courts of appeal could grant leave to appeal (to either the defence or the prosecution) in criminal cases, even if neither the trial judge nor the Attorney General had requested a review.[38] In England in the 1890s, some sensational cases of apparent wrongful convictions had produced renewed debate about the need for appeals in criminal cases there. The English controversy was not cited in the Canadian parliamentary exchanges that apparently led to the amendment of 1900, though it may have influenced the lawyers who advocated for change.[39]

Together the Criminal Code of 1892 and the 1900 amendment to it produced a significant expansion of appellate review in Canadian criminal law, shortly before England, the usual source of Canadian legal innovations, set up its Court of Criminal Appeal in 1907. The nineteenth-century Court of Appeal for Ontario had usually disclaimed jurisdiction for all but the occasional criminal case referred to it by a trial judge. In a sample of 100 reported appeal cases from the decade 1891–1900, there was one criminal case, but for 1901–1910, a quarter of the reported cases were criminal matters, some stated by the trial judges, but many with leave granted by the appeal court. In that decade, the court overturned an attempted murder conviction on the grounds that the defence had been denied permission to re-examine a witness on a crucial matter.[40] It upheld a bigamy conviction by confirming that a foreign divorce was invalid, upheld a burglary conviction by ruling that the trial judge had been within his rights in ordering a divided jury to go back and seek unanimity, and overturned a vagrancy conviction by finding the trial judge had misinterpreted the definition of "gaming."[41] In one case, the court in refusing leave to appeal ruled that the matter put to it was a question of fact and not of law.[42] In another, *R. v James*, the Crown was given leave to appeal an acquittal at trial, but when the appeal was heard, the court let the verdict stand even though it determined that the judge had wrongly instructed the jury. The Criminal Code clearly permitted appeals by the prosecution, but in this case the court declared that it disliked on principle any appeal by the Crown from the verdict of a jury, and it refused to change the trial verdict.[43]

In hearing these appeals, the court was taking up in the criminal law field the classic appellate function of correcting errors and providing jurisprudential certainty – subject, of course, to an appeal to the Supreme Court or JCPC (Judicial Committee of the Privy Council). The cases and the court's decisions make clear that criminal trials in this era often showed the kinds of prosecutorial or judicial behaviour for which appellate relief was clearly needed, and the court was willing to say so. In a 1904 appeal, the court vigorously corrected a magistrate who in mid-trial had amended a charge against two men to a more serious one without their consent and without allowing them to reconsider their decision to forego trial by jury.[44] Before 1900, such procedural abuses could not have been reviewed, except with the consent of the judge or (from 1892) the Attorney General.

Judging by the number of criminal appeals it heard, the post-1900 court clearly granted leave more readily than the Crown or the trial judges had done, but it was far from ready to concede a full-fledged right of appeal. Indeed, at least one judge evidently felt the new avenues for criminal appeals were being abused. Writing a majority opinion upholding a trial court verdict in 1908, Justice Richard Meredith denounced lawyers and judges whom he found all too eager to bring criminal cases to the Court of Appeal:

The frequency with which arguments are addressed to this Court, and, indeed, with which cases are stated, as if there were a general right of appeal in criminal cases, as ample at least as in civil cases, indicates an extraordinary lack of understanding of the subject, without excuse, as the statute makes it very plain that, generally speaking, there is no right of appeal except on a question of law.[45]

Many of these early criminal appeals concerned relatively minor matters, such as vagrancy, minor assaults, and even a prosecution for fortune telling, and they involved defendants who must have been of limited means. Yet the defendants frequently had lawyers of some prominence: the future bencher and Crown attorney Eric Armour, the prominent civil litigator E.A. DuVernet, and the noted defence counsel Thomas C. Robinette, for instance. Such lawyers may have been working pro bono to build reputations and attract paying clients, or perhaps the criminal law trial bar appreciated its new opportunity to challenge prosecutorial or judicial abuses of authority to the appeal court. However, the vigorous application between 1900 and 1910 of the court's new authority to grant leave to appeal in criminal cases appears to have been short lived. In our sample of 112 cases from the decade 1911–1920, criminal appeals fell from 25 per cent to just 8 per cent, seemingly without comment or explanation in law journals or in Parliament, and without further changes to the Criminal Code. After 1923, the question of criminal appeals would be transformed by new amendments to the Criminal Code that provided the first unambiguous right to appeal in Canadian criminal law.

An Emerging Judicial Hierarchy

Oliver Mowat resigned as premier and Attorney General of Ontario in 1896, when he went to Ottawa to serve briefly as Wilfrid Laurier's minister of justice. He soon returned to Ontario as lieutenant governor, and he died in that office in 1903. The Liberal government of Ontario continued under his successors Arthur Hardy and George Ross, but the Mowat era ended conclusively when the victory of James Pliny Whitney's Conservatives in 1905 launched a long era of Conservative dominance in Ontario. Before the end of the Mowat era, however, significant changes had been made to the hierarchy of courts in which the Court of Appeal for Ontario sat.

Error and Appeal had always looked to the courts of England for guidance and precedent, but throughout its existence, it had been very nearly a final court of appeal. In Upper Canada or in early Ontario, there had always been a theoretical right of appeal to the JCPC, but until the early years of Confederation that right was almost never used. Although the Privy Council was the only avenue of appeal beyond Error and Appeal until 1875, published reports show only six Canada West/Ontario cases at the Privy Council between 1851 and 1870 (compared to twenty-eight from Canada East/Quebec), and only one from 1871 to 1876 (against thirty-one from Quebec).[46] Hume Blake's 1849 opinion that the remoteness of the JCPC made appeals to it both impractical and barely legitimate had in effect been sustained. The *Canada Law Journal* declared in 1875 that in Quebec the right of appeal to the JCPC had been "abused by powerful and wealthy men," but that in Ontario public opinion in the courts kept appeal to Britain rare. It expected, indeed, that as Canada's new Supreme Court grew in stature, Canadian appeals to England would decline.[47] Instead, the number of appeals from Ontario to the JCPC began to grow quite rapidly after 1875, despite the establishment of the Supreme Court.

Both the Conservative and Liberal parties supported the creation of a Supreme Court of Canada, as authorized by the *British North America Act, 1867.* John A. Macdonald twice introduced legislation for the court, but neither of his bills had been passed before his government fell in 1873.[48] The Mackenzie government picked up the initiative, and in 1875 the Supreme Court of Canada, "the supreme constitutional authority," as the *Canada Law Journal* called it, came into being.[49] The new Supreme Court was empowered to hear appeals of all final judgments from the court of last resort in each province. It could also give advisory opinions on federal or provincial legislation referred to it and could rule on the constitutionality of federal as well as provincial legislation. It was understood from the start that constitutional cases would be an important part of the caseload of the new court. Indeed, historians of the Court have argued that the provision made in the *British North America*

Act for a Supreme Court indicated a commitment to having federal-provincial disputes arbitrated in court, with the provinces and Ottawa on a mostly equal footing, even though other parts of the Constitution authorized the federal government to reserve or disallow provincial legislation.[50]

The *Supreme Court Act* required that two of the new court's six justices must come from Quebec, to reflect that province's civil code particularity, and this quickly led to informal quotas for other provinces. On the founding court, there were two Quebec judges, two Ontario judges, and two Maritimers. After Edward Blake declined the chief justiceship offered by his Liberal colleagues, William Buell Richards, chief justice of Ontario as head of the Queen's Bench trial court and a member of the Error and Appeal bench until its 1874 restructuring, became the first chief justice of Canada. Appointed to the new Supreme Court along with him was Samuel Henry Strong, who had been named to the new four-person Error and Appeal bench the previous year and now, at fifty, became the youngest member of the new Supreme Court.

The government's bill to create the Supreme Court initially made no reference to JCPC appeals, but a government backbencher successfully added an amendment putting an end to appeals as of right beyond the Supreme Court.[51] At the time it was understood that Britain was about to replace the JCPC with a new statutory court for imperial appeals. Canada could have limited the authority of a new imperial court established by statute, but the new court was not created, and overcoming the royal prerogative power under which the JCPC operated was much less certain. British legal and colonial officials were deeply hostile to any reduction of the authority of the JCPC. Despite Canada's *Supreme Court Act* and vigorous efforts by Prime Minister Mackenzie and Minister of Justice Edward Blake, the JCPC continued to assert its right to maintain what it called "the silken bond of empire" by granting leave to cases from the Supreme Court of Canada and the provincial appeal courts, and so the appeal to London survived. Even as the Supreme Court began to hear appeals from Ontario, the number of Ontario cases heard in London began to grow: there were five between 1876 and 1883, including the constitutionally significant *Mercer* and *Parsons* cases, and many more followed, some appealed from the Supreme Court, some going directly from Ontario's Court of Appeal. From the mid-1870s, therefore, the Court of Appeal found itself placed in a hierarchy of appellate courts.

Leading Canadian lawyers gradually came to enjoy travelling by steamship to London each summer to argue Canadian cases before the JCPC. Many of them became vigorous opponents of any move to end appeals to Britain or to make the Supreme Court truly supreme. Edward Blake, however, who in his private practice became a leading Privy Council lawyer, continued to argue what his father had asserted in 1849: locally rooted justice was better justice.

Cases are, by this appeal, removed beyond the influence of local knowledge, of local experience, of local habits of thought and feeling, of much of that learning and training, not strictly legal, which is yet essential to the formation of a sound judgment.[52]

In the 1880s, the question of appeals to the JCPC briefly became a matter of partisan debate in Canada. John A. Macdonald, in opposition from 1873 to 1878, had attacked the Liberals as disloyal and anti-empire for their efforts to end JCPC appeals. Back in power, however, Macdonald and many otherwise imperial-minded Canadians were dismayed when the JCPC asserted its right to consider appeals of Canadian criminal cases, including the treason conviction of Louis Riel in 1885 and, even more, an 1886 case, *Sproule*, involving an American convicted of murder in British Columbia. In that case, it was the British government, under pressure from the American government, that persuaded the JCPC to intervene. It had been widely held in Canada, where criminal appeals were very rare in any case, that the JCPC should not consider Canadian criminal appeals, on the grounds that in general neither Britain nor Canada permitted criminal appeals and that even when a technicality made one possible, swift sentencing and exemplary punishment should not be delayed by lengthy transatlantic reviews. In the end, the JCPC denied Riel's application for leave to appeal and did not hear Sproule's before his execution, but it did not disavow its authority to hear Canadian criminal appeals. In response particularly to the *Sproule* case, Macdonald's new justice minister, John Thompson, introduced bills in 1887 and 1888 to abolish criminal appeals from Canada to London. Both bills passed, though with the Liberal opposition loudly noting the prime minister's hypocrisy. These were, however, ordinary statutory declarations, not a constitutional statement of Canada's right to prohibit such appeals. Without confirming that that the Canadian legislation was valid, the JCPC ceased to grant leave to Canadian criminal appeals, and the issue was not raised again for forty years.[53]

From 1875, the Court of Appeal for Ontario, after a quarter century of final responsibility for almost all of Ontario's jurisprudence, had to begin to learn deference to review by two higher courts. Premier Mowat shared the nationalist and Liberal sentiment in favour of Canadians running their own affairs, but he was also an advocate for provincial autonomy against centralization by Ottawa, and he would find that many of his greatest successes in that campaign would come from victories at the JCPC in London that overturned his many defeats in the Supreme Court in Ottawa.

For the Court of Appeal, the more direct consequence of the new hierarchy of appeals (as discussed in more detail in the jurisprudence section below) may have been a gradual shift from a jurisprudence that, while respectful of English decisions, had also drawn on American law and local conditions to create a local line of judicial thinking, towards one increasingly directed by decisions from higher courts, and increasingly limited to finding and applying precedents and interpretations established elsewhere, particularly in English courts.

Judges of the Court of Appeal, 1874–1912

When Mowat restructured Error and Appeal in 1874, William Henry Draper retained his position and acquired the title "Chief Justice of Appeal." A trial judge since 1847 and a member of Error and Appeal since the court's foundation, he had retired from his trial court duties in 1869, so he was already a full-time head of the appeal court. He was the only member of Error and Appeal to continue on that court after the restructuring of 1874. Draper had been called "Sweet William" during his political career, and he was said to have aspired to a quiet and peaceable life as a judge but, despite participating in some notable trials, he left little personal record of himself. One London, Ontario, lawyer recalled in his old age a vivid and unpleasant memory of how Mr Justice Draper, sitting as a trial judge (hence before 1869) "non-suited me in a *qui tam* action because my proof was not technically in accordance with my pleading … Upon his declaring a non-suit, the judge smiled, a complete Draperian smile, peculiar to the man, who seemed to derive comfort from what was disappointment and pain to me, a young and ambitious lawyer."[54] Draper was seventy-three and already infirm when his court was restructured in 1874, and he died in 1877. His successor as head of the Court of Appeal, Thomas Moss, was just forty-one and seemed destined for a long and distinguished tenure.

Moss was the eldest member of a remarkable legal and judicial family. The son of an Irish-Catholic immigrant family that had prospered as brewers in Cobourg and Toronto, Thomas Moss proved such a brilliant student at Upper Canada College and the University of Toronto that he was presented to the Prince of Wales in 1860 as Ontario's pre-eminent student. He soon succeeded in equity practice in a firm that included such partners as future Chief Justice of Ontario Robert Harrison, future Court of Appeal Justice Featherston Osler, and his own brother Charles Moss, who would also be a chief justice. At the time, no Catholics had been appointed to the superior courts of Ontario, but the Moss brothers had converted to the Anglican Church and seem to have faced few obstacles; they and the next generation of Mosses went on to high positions in the courts, the Law Society, the university, and other prominent institutions. Thomas Moss, his brother Charles, and fellow judge Featherston Osler were all brothers-in-law, each having married a daughter of the patrician Anglo-Irish lawyer and judge Robert Baldwin Sullivan.[55]

After being been appointed to the restructured Court of Error and Appeal in 1875, Thomas Moss became its chief justice in 1877. The title "Chief Justice of Ontario" continued to be held by the head of Queen's Bench until the same 1876 statute that renamed Error and Appeal "the Court of Appeal" also provided that the head of Queen's Bench, Moss's old partner Robert Harrison, would retain the title until his death or retirement, after which it would pass to the head of the appeal court.[56] As a result, Moss was "Chief Justice of Appeal" until Harrison died, aged just forty-five, in 1878, and then became the first leader of the appeal court to hold the title "Chief Justice of Ontario," as all his successors have done since. Moss's contemporary, the lawyer and legal historian David B. Read, quoted a Moss opinion in a mortgage case at length to demonstrate his "lucidity and beauty of diction" and his absolute command of "actual notice, constructive notice, registration, payment, and negligence,"[57] but Chief Justice Moss had little time to establish a record of appellate jurisprudence, for he became ill in 1880 and died seeking treatment in Europe the next year, aged just forty-five. In the same year, the fusion of law and equity, and the introduction of new simplified rules of procedure that accompanied it, did away with many of the elaborate rules Moss had mastered.

By the time of Moss's death, the frequency with which relatively young men were named to the court directly from practice had waned. Seniority prevailed in the next several appointments to the chief justiceship. John Godfrey Spragge was seventy-five and had been on the chancery court since 1850 when he was named head of the appeal court and chief justice of Ontario in succession to Moss in 1881; he was chief justice of Ontario for just three years before his death.[58] His successor, John Hawkins Hagarty, had almost thirty years' experience on the superior courts and was sixty-eight when promoted from chief justice of Queen's Bench to chief justice of Ontario. He led the court for thirteen years and retired in 1897. Hagarty had had a busy commercial practice before going to the bench at the age of forty and was both a prolific writer of judgments and a frequent dissenter during his time on the Court of Appeal. Upon his retirement, the *Canada Law Journal* reported he had an unparalleled record for having his decisions upheld in higher courts and praised his concern for avoiding "usurping or encroaching on the functions of the legislature." A modern scholar argues that Hagarty "gave much more thought to statutory interpretation than did his fellow judges."[59]

Hagarty had one lasting non-jurisprudential influence upon his court. When Hagarty became chief justice, Prime Minister Macdonald was developing a proposal to have knighthoods conferred ex officio on the chief justices of all the federally appointed superior courts in Canada. Hagarty, however, declined the knighthood he was offered and, even though he accepted one at his retirement, his example deterred some other judges and helped ensure that knighthoods never became ex officio for senior Canadian judges. Hagarty had no strong political affiliations, but in this era the Liberal party was somewhat less enthusiastic about British-conferred knighthoods and other honours than the Conservatives.[60]

Hagarty's successor as chief justice was another long-serving member of the court, George W. Burton, aged seventy-nine. Burton, who was knighted while chief justice, retired in 1900, just three years after becoming chief justice, and his successor John Douglas Armour, seventy upon his appointment (from Queen's Bench), served just two years, though his departure was for the Supreme Court of Canada, where he served briefly before his death in 1903. Both these appointments came to Armour from Wilfrid Laurier's government, though Armour had been a Conservative activist. Armour was succeeded in 1902 by Thomas Moss's younger brother Charles, a justice of appeal since 1897. Chief Justice Charles Moss, appointed at age sixty-two, would serve ten years. He too received a knighthood – the last so honoured in Ontario for his services as chief justice.[61]

These chief justices and all the seventeen men appointed to the Court of Appeal between 1874 and 1912 came from a bar that by their day was largely locally born and locally trained. Though all the judges were British in ethnic origin, only six were British born, and all seventeen got their legal education in British North America, though Hagarty had briefly attended Trinity College, Dublin, before immigrating. The seventeen appeal judges had substantial practice experience before coming to the court, having practised law an average of about twenty-two years before their first judicial appointment, mostly in Toronto (ten) or London (four). Nine of the seventeen had no other judicial experience when they came to the appeal court. Eight had Liberal (or Reform) loyalties, against five Conservatives, four whose political ties were unidentified, and one who had been in both parties. A bare majority, nine, were Anglicans. There were still no Catholic judges, the Moss brothers being converts to the Anglican Church, and no francophones.[62] The judges of this period averaged about twelve years of service on the appeal bench. Seven died in office, six retired, and four moved on to the Supreme Court of Canada, and their average age at leaving the court was seventy-three.

Among the other judges of the court between 1874 and 1912, two who stand out are Featherston Osler and Christopher Salmon Patterson. Osler, from the remarkable family that also produced his three brothers – the financier Edmund Osler, the medical pioneer William Osler, and B.B Osler, founder of the long-lived Toronto law firm bearing his name – was named to the Court of Common Pleas at the age of forty-one and to the appeal court four years later, in 1883. He remained for almost thirty years, declining an appointment to the Supreme Court of Canada in 1888, and was one of the most productive justices of the court throughout his tenure, writing opinions in more than half the reported appeal cases he heard. Osler also led the committee for the revision of the Ontario statutes in 1906–14 and, unusually in the era of lifetime appointments, he had a long post-judicial career. He retired from the court in 1910 at age seventy-two but was elected treasurer of the Law Society in 1921, serving three years.[63]

Christopher Salmon Patterson, appointed directly from practice in 1874, served fourteen years on the Court of Appeal before moving to Ottawa ("with reluctance, as his relations with his fellow judges, the legal profession, and the citizens of Toronto had been very pleasing") to take the seat on the Supreme Court of Canada that he held until his death in 1893, at the age of seventy.[64] Patterson's judgments stand out for the clarity and logic of their presentation, for his care to ground his arguments in statutes and precedents, and for the breadth of his legal knowledge. In *R. v Eli*, where the limits on the right to appeal were at issue, he gave a judicial history of the question back to the foundation of Error and Appeal in 1849.[65] Patterson was a relatively frequent dissenter, but without much rancour. "As my opinion differs from my colleagues, it is very likely wrong," he wrote in one case.[66] (Indeed, it was fairly common for a judge of this era to declare that he did not agree with the majority view but would not bother to dissent. Osler once signed what he called "a grumbling assent"[67] to the majority view.) Patterson's promotion to the Supreme Court seems to have been testimony to his work on the Court of Appeal: he was never active in politics and, while his first appointment came from the Liberals, his second was from the Conservatives.

Another judge whose judgments have an air of confidence and authority like Patterson's was James Maclennan, Oliver Mowat's long-time law partner.[68] Appointed directly to the Court of Appeal to succeed Patterson in 1888, he followed Patterson to the Supreme Court in 1905. Richard Meredith, a member of the court from 1905 until he became chief justice of Common Pleas in 1912, was a notable and fiery dissenter, particularly in his first years on the court, when he seemed to have had a point of disagreement in almost every case.

The Court of Appeal Bar, 1874–1912

Hundreds of lawyers made individual appearances at the Court of Appeal during the first four decades of the restructured court, but the court always had a core group of leading practitioners. Over the period 1876–90, the ten lawyers who appeared most frequently participated in no less than 141 of a sample of 150 cases – 94 per cent. For 1891–1910, the proportion was 75 per cent. The lawyer who argued the greatest number of appeal cases over the whole period was James Bethune, even though he died in 1884. Bethune, from a loyalist family of eastern Ontario, began his practice in Cornwall but soon moved to Toronto and joined the Blake firm. After 1873, Bethune led his own firm, Bethune, Moss, Falconbridge, and Hoyles. He was widely acknowledged as one of the leading Ontario and Canadian barristers of his day, and the appeal statistics confirm his dominance of that forum until his death, at just forty-four. His partner Charles Moss was also among the leading appeal counsel until his appointment to the bench in 1902.[69]

Bethune's previous firm, Blakes, was also well represented in our sample of leading appellate lawyers, notably by Samuel Hume Blake,

James Kerr, and W.D.G. Cassels. Edward Blake, the leader of the firm and a respected counsel, appears to have reduced his Ontario appeal practice even before moving to Britain in 1892, although he remained active at the Supreme Court of Canada and the JCPC, as well as in national politics. Even Premier Mowat occasionally argued cases at the Court of Appeal, sometimes as Attorney General and sometimes in his private capacity, for it was then possible both for an Attorney General to argue the province's cases personally and for a premier to maintain a private litigation practice. In 1878 Mowat participated in the appeal of a woman whose corporate directorship had been found invalid at trial. A director of the Toronto Street Railway had died, but one of the surviving directors objected to the way Mrs Smyth had been elected to the board. The issue was not gender but a struggle between the two major shareholder/directors, as she held two shares and the two men held 999 each. The appeal turned on the validity of the corporate election process, and the appeal court found she was a valid director – a win for Mowat and Bethune, who represented the woman and the director who had supported her candidacy.[70] In 1882, they acted together again, this time for the province, in the appeal of *R. v Hodge*, the landmark federal-provincial rights case testing Ontario's authority over liquor licensing, which continued to the JCPC.[71]

Like the Blake and Bethune firms, the firm of McCarthy and Osler (founded 1882, and parent to both the McCarthy Tétrault and Osler Hoskin firms that would remain prominent more than a century later) had several prominent appeal lawyers in this period. D'Alton McCarthy (died 1898), B.B. Osler (died 1901), Christopher Robinson (died 1905), and Wallace Nesbitt (appointed to the Supreme Court of Canada in 1903) all appeared regularly in pre-1900 lists of leading appellate counsel. After the turn of the century, the lawyer most frequently appearing was Allen Aylesworth. Aylesworth, from eastern Ontario, had joined the Bethune Moss firm and eventually became its leader and name partner. Aylesworth remained among the busiest appellate counsel, despite also serving in the Laurier cabinet 1905–11, but the onset of deafness restricted his courtroom practice soon after (though he lived until 1952).[72] Wallace Nesbitt disappeared from the list of appellate counsel when he was appointed directly to the Supreme Court in 1903, but he returned upon resigning from the Court after just two and a half years. George Shepley of the firm that became WeirFoulds; Isadore Hellmuth, a Canadian trained in law at the Inner Temple in England; and William Renwick Riddell, a future justice of appeal, were also prominent among appeal lawyers after 1900, but the counsel most frequently appearing in appeal cases between 1901 and 1910 was John Robinson Cartwright (whose nephew, another J.R. Cartwright, was chief justice of Canada 1967–70). Cartwright was deputy Attorney General of Ontario from 1889, and his prominence among the appeal court lawyers may reflect the rapid emergence of criminal appeals in this decade as well as other litigation involving the Crown. Cartwright's fellow Crown attorney Edward Bayly also appears in the lists of appellate counsel for that decade, as does T.C. Robinette, a noted criminal defence counsel.

The Jurisprudence of the Court of Appeal, 1874–1912

The Court of Appeal changed greatly in the four decades that followed the restructurings of 1874, 1876, and 1881. It went from part-time panels of seven judges or more to full-time panels of first four, and eventually either three, four, or five judges. After 1881, the court was engaged with the fusion of law and equity and a revised procedural rule book to replace their separate procedures. The court had to deal with important new legislation, both federal and provincial: the Constitution itself, the Criminal Code, new acts on bankruptcy and insolvency and insurance, expanded municipal powers, and the first *Married Women's Property Acts*, as well as frequent structural changes to the Ontario courts. It also came under the authority of the Supreme Court of Canada and the JCPC, though there are suggestions that some judges may have learned deference gradually and reluctantly. As late as 1898, when Justices Moss and Maclennan pointedly observed that, like it or not, the court was bound by "the law as laid down for us by the Supreme Court," Justice Burton argued in dissent for sustaining the Court of Appeal's own precedents. Despite the Supreme Court, he wrote, the Court of Appeal should not "reverse a case which has stood as law for so many years, unless now convinced that it was clearly erroneous."[73]

All these changes to the courts and their procedures gave the judges opportunities to debate past versus present practice. Procedural reform had reduced the number of cases determined strictly on technical errors and missteps, but judges continued to complain of the procedural failings of lawyers before them. In 1879, Justice Burton, in ruling that failure to meet a strict filing deadline voided the appeal in question, described the high procedural standards that he believed had prevailed during his time in practice. Justice Patterson, however, argued for a more flexible standard and the authority of the court to read the relevant statute "generously." [74] In 1883, Chief Justice Spragge complained that "a great deal of litigation arises out of the want of care of solicitors."[75] Osler observed tartly in another case that "at a moderate estimate I think the appeal book is twenty pages too long,"[76] and earlier Burton had threatened to assign costs to the parties responsible for the "unnecessary length of the appeal books."[77] Another frequent complaint was the trivial nature of cases litigated. Travelling on a highway includes a degree of risk, the court felt obliged to declare in 1895, and a turkey frightening a horse was not grounds for legal action.[78] Justice Moss declared in another case, "It is impossible to suppress a feeling of regret and surprise that there should have been such protracted and expensive litigation in a case where the amount at stake was so insignificant."[79]

In general, the court was deferential to English precedents, perhaps more than the early and rather eclectic Error and Appeal days. It once dismissed as "bombastry" the argument that English law should be adapted to Canadian conditions.[80] It also conscientiously deferred to trial courts, ordering new trials rather than giving judgment itself as much as possible and frequently endorsing the discretion of juries and trial court judges. In the same vein, the court showed substantial respect to arbitrators, rarely overturning an arbitrator's decision and sometimes chastising litigants who had entered into arbitration and then sought judicial review of the consequences. In a series of cases reviewing expropriations made to create the provincial park around Niagara Falls, the court asserted its right to review interpretations of both fact and law as determined by the arbitrators appointed by the Crown, but upheld them in almost all aspects.[81]

Oliver Mowat's constitutional struggles with Ottawa also kept the court busy. From the late 1870s, the Court of Appeal was drawn into the conflicts between Ontario and John A. Macdonald's Canadian government over the boundaries of federal and provincial authority. Premier Mowat was the principal advocate of the view that sections 91 and 92 of the *British North America Act* guaranteed provincial sovereignty within the fields allocated to them. Macdonald consistently held that Ottawa had the right to supervise the provinces through reservation, disallowance, and a broad interpretation of the section 91 powers assigned to Ottawa. Between 1878 and 1891, Mowat and Macdonald's conflicting views regularly confronted each other in the courts. The Supreme Court of Canada often upheld Macdonald's centralist views, but the JCPC crafted an interpretation of the *BNA Act* that reinforced the provinces against federal intrusion. "What luck Mowat has had at the Judicial Committee," wrote Macdonald to D'Alton McCarthy, the prominent Toronto litigator who was often his counsel in constitutional cases and suffered several defeats at the JCPC.[82]

Most of the constitutional cases were ultimately determined either at the Supreme Court of Canada or the JCPC, and those decisions on the federation have been widely studied.[83] Most, however, were launched in the Ontario courts, and the Court of Appeal tended to support Premier Mowat's positions. From the start, the court took the separation of powers between Ottawa and the provinces very seriously. In *Leprohon v City of Ottawa* (1878), a four-judge panel, citing mostly American law on division of powers in a federation, found unanimously that Ontario could not levy municipal tax on a federal civil servant who lived in Ottawa.[84] *Leprohon* was soon overturned by a Supreme Court of Canada finding in a similar case from New Brunswick. Thereafter, the Court of Appeal consistently, and most often unanimously, supported provincial authority: in *Parsons v Citizens Insurance*, in *Grand Junction Railway v County of Peterborough*, in *McLaren v Caldwell*, in *Hodge*, in *St Catharines Milling*, and in *Attorney General (Canada) v Attorney General (Ontario)*. *St Catharines Milling* concerned Aboriginal title as well as federal-provincial rivalries. In that case, Justice Burton declared for the court that the province held absolute title to the land, subject only to an Indian right of occupancy which the Crown could extinguish at any time: "The recognition of any right in the Indians has been on the part of the government a matter of public policy determined by political considerations and motives of prudence and humanity." The acceptance of this view at the Supreme Court and the JCPC meant that for decades, questions about Aboriginal rights were seen as questions for government policy, not judicial determination.[85]

George W. Burton took the lead on many constitutional questions, writing the court's decisions in several of these decisions, but usually with strong support from the other judges. Burton discerned broad scope for provincial authority in the *British North America Act*. He declared in 1882 that provincial legislatures had "plenary powers of legislation within their respective spheres as large and ample as those of the imperial parliament." He argued in 1888 for a flexible interpretation of the *British North America Act*: "It would be found almost impossible to work out the scheme of federation if the words of the act were to be read literally without any restriction or qualification whatever."[86] On the other hand, the Supreme Court of Canada often supported a centralist interpretation of the *British North America Act*, in 1880 declaring the federal government "a quasi-imperial power" and the provinces "subordinate to the dominion government," though its judges were appointed by the same federal ministers.[87] It may be that the Ontario-trained judges of the Court of Appeal had, like Mowat, absorbed the Upper Canadian political tradition, flourishing in the 1850s and 1860s but going back to the responsible government movement launched in the 1820s, which held that within a parliamentary system, colonial or federal, any legislature must be sovereign within its assigned sphere of activity. Just as important, however, were the decisions of the JCPC, which frequently overturned the centralist decisions of the Supreme Court of Canada, which would otherwise have bound the Court of Appeal.[88]

The appropriate judicial response to new legislation frequently exercised the court. In *Trumpour v Saylor*, an 1877 case hinging on the right to appeal in a civil matter, Justice Moss regretted that because of a clause in the *Administration of Justice Act, 1874*, "which I am convinced was passed in its present shape *per incuriam* [i.e., mistakenly], the plaintiff is precluded from having his appeal disposed of upon the merits."[89] In other decisions, the court quite explicitly called for legislative review of new statutes that had unexpected consequences, always emphasizing that it was the duty of the legislature, not the judges, to clear up errors or confusions.

With the rise of towns across Ontario and the growing responsibilities of local governments, issues of municipal law became a notable part of the court's docket in these years. Insolvency and bankruptcy also kept the court busy in the 1870s, as a consequence of the economic depression of that decade, but also because new *Insolvency Acts* of 1869 and 1875 frequently required interpretation. The sequence of *Married Women's Property Acts* in 1859, 1872, 1873, and 1884 that gradually expanded married women's rights to own and manage their own property, frequently brought cases to the appeal court. Lack of coherence in the early acts obliged the court to interpret the will of the legislature, and its criticism of the statutes helped lead to the greater precision in the 1884 statute. In many of the reported cases, the issue had less to do with women's rights than with frauds, with creditors alleging that a couple was abusing the law to prevent creditors from seizing assets to which they felt entitled.

As commerce and industry expanded, liability claims provided frequent appeals to the court. The court's nineteenth-century jurisprudence in liability matters was shaped by the principle that organizations

Table 2.1 Statistical Notes on 17 Judges of Appeal Appointed 1874–1912

Birthplace

Upper Canada   11
England   4
Ireland   2

Ethnic Origin

Anglophone/British   17

Religious Affiliation

Church of England   10
Presbyterian   5
Methodist   2

The Moss brothers, originally Roman Catholic, were converts to Anglicanism.

Legal Education

Upper Canada   15
Lower Canada   1
Ireland   1

Hagarty studied briefly at Trinity College, Dublin.

Average Years of Law Practice before Judicial Appointment

22.1 years

Location of Legal Practice (some in more than one place)

Toronto   10
London   4
Hamilton   1
Sarnia   1
Montreal   1
Goderich   1

Identified Political Commitment

Reform or Liberal   9
Conservative   4
None   5

Morrison, who began as a Reformer and became a Conservative, is counted twice here.

Table 2.1 (*Concluded*)

Judicial Appointment prior to Court of Appeal Appointment

Yes   8*
No   9

Average Age at Court of Appeal Appointment

61 years

Average Years on Court of Appeal Bench

11.8 years

Reason for Leaving Court of Appeal

Died   7
Retired   6
To SCC   4

Average Age on Leaving

73.2 years

Note: includes the CA tenure of Morrison, Spragge, and Hagarty, all of whom served
       previously in E&A up to 1874 and returned to the Court of Appeal later.
* Queen's Bench, Common Pleas, Chancery, Error and Appeal.

could rarely be liable for the errors or wrongdoing of their employees. When a Toronto Street Railway motorman threw a passenger from a streetcar, the court found "this act of pushing the plaintiff off the car was not of a class of acts entrusted to his discretion to perform," and therefore the employer was not responsible for the motorman's behaviour or for the appellant's permanent injuries.[90] When a shipper appealed a trial verdict that found the Great Western Railway was not liable for freight that had vanished after being accepted for shipment, the court accepted that the railroad's employee had acted fraudulently, but found that because the railroad had not condoned his action, it was not responsible for the loss. "I think to hold these defendants liable would be a terrible inroad upon the principles which have long been established," Justice Burton declared. "The consequence to a railway of adopting a different rule would be disastrous to them."[91]

Railroads and street railways were frequent litigants, partly because of the seemingly limitless ways that trains and horse-drawn buggies seemed able to be drawn into collisions, but also because these corporations were notorious for appealing every case of liability or negligence, allegedly to deter lawsuits by the sheer cost of multiple appeals. As with horses and railroads, there seemed to be endless bizarre and horrible ways for workmen to suffer injuries or death in the rail yards, lumber mills, and warehouses of industrializing Ontario. Employees who were injured at work could secure compensation only by suing their employers, and liability law placed a high threshold on such cases. Workers (or their survivors) who had been successful with trial court juries or sympathetic magistrates frequently had to defend their compensation entitlements on appeal, and the appeal courts often upheld the principle that any negligence or lack of care by the employee absolved the workplace from responsibility.

While the Court of Appeal was upholding a stern standard in questions of workmen's compensation and liability claims against railroads and other corporations, the same questions gradually became a political issue in Ontario. The argument that corporations and wealthy institutions were using multiple appeals to put the cost of litigation beyond the means of ordinary Ontarians became an election issue in the post-Mowat years and eventually contributed to another substantial overhaul of Ontario's appeal regime.

3

The Meredith-Mulock-Rowell Courts, 1913–38: Experiments in Court Reform

By 1913 Ontario, having secured and greatly extended its boundaries and its political autonomy within Confederation, was established as the province that would be the economic giant of Confederation for most of the twentieth century. At Confederation, the province had still been principally a wheat-growing agricultural economy, very much dependent on Montreal, then the commercial and financial capital of Canada. As Western Canada grew, slowly at first and then explosively after 1896, Ontario provided many of the early leaders (and lawyers) for the new communities there, as well as supplying the region with goods and transporting its grain and other products by rail and lake transport.

Behind the protection of the high-tariff "National Policy," Ontario's fast-growing cities had begun to develop industries during the late nineteenth century, and by the early years of the twentieth century, cheap and reliable hydroelectric power, particularly from Niagara Falls, was encouraging further modernization and industrial growth. With the discoveries of silver and gold around Cobalt and other Northern Ontario towns in the first decade of the twentieth century, Ontario's mining industry grew rapidly, which did much to underpin the new financial-services industries and mining law firms of Toronto. The population of the province continued to grow rapidly, from 2.5 million in 1911 to 3.7 million in 1941, and by 1911 it had become the first Canadian province with more urban than rural residents. Ontario was going to be tested by the stresses of the First World War, the uncertainties of the 1920s, and the Depression of the 1930s, but it was securely established not only as the population centre of Canada but, increasingly, as its commercial and industrial heartland.

Both federally and provincially, the country was developing political habits of partisan alternation. After the long ascendency in federal politics of Macdonald's Conservatives and then of Laurier's Liberals, the Conservative government of Robert Borden took power in Ottawa in 1911. In Ontario, the Liberal years of Premier Oliver Mowat and his successors (1872–1905) had given way to the government of James Pliny Whitney (1905–14), the first of the Conservative premiers who would govern Ontario during much of the twentieth century and shape much of the judicial structure of the province, even though Liberal dominance in Ottawa meant that most of Ontario's senior judges of the twentieth century would be appointed by Liberal governments.

By the beginning of the twentieth century, several of the long-lived business law firms of Bay Street were already well-established and thriving partnerships of prominent litigators and commercial lawyers, serving the banking and investment industry, manufacturers, railroads, and commercial enterprises. The legal profession was well established across the province, boasted a heritage of more than a century, and had several established dynasties of legal and judicial families. It was becoming rare for English immigrants to move rapidly into leading positions at the bench and bar; Ontario had long since been providing its own lawyers and judges.

The Meredith Court, 1913–23

In January 1912, Charles Moss, suffering from cancer, took leave of his duties at the Court of Appeal after a decade of service as chief justice of Ontario. He died at his Toronto home on 11 October at the age of seventy-two. The next day, Ontario's premier Whitney cabled William Ralph Meredith, the chief justice of the Court of Common Pleas: "Chief Justice Moss died yesterday. My colleagues and I desire to recommend you as his successor. Please cable your consent at once." Whitney also wrote to Prime Minister Robert Borden, calling Meredith "the best all-round man on the bench" and asserting that during the "reign" of Wilfrid Laurier, "not one" Conservative had been named to the superior courts in Ontario. Borden delegated the matter to his Ontario minister Frank Cochrane, who had recently moved from Whitney's cabinet to the federal one. The appointment was quickly secured, and a small complication smoothly handled. Since William Meredith's brother Richard was already on the Court of Appeal and the two brothers had agreed "we should never sit in the same court at the same time," Richard was quickly appointed to replace William as head of Common Pleas. William Meredith was formally appointed chief justice of Ontario in February 1913. He was seventy-two, the same age as his late predecessor.[1]

Meredith's appointment marked a transition in the career paths of Ontario chief justices. His six predecessors back to Thomas Moss (1877–81) had all achieved eminence primarily within the courts, as lawyers and judges. Meredith was a respected lawyer and judge – he had had a successful practice in municipal law and had led the Court of Common Pleas since 1894 – but he also had a very substantial reputation from his years as leader of the Ontario Conservative party in opposition to Premier Mowat. He had been a leading figure in Ontario politics, and even as a judge remained in the public eye as an adviser to the Ontario governments on public policy issues. His appointment introduced as chief justices a series of former politicians who had public as well as legal reputations. Meredith's successor, William Mulock, had been postmaster general and minister of labour in Laurier's cabinet, and Mulock's successor, Newton Rowell, was also a prominent political leader and government adviser. As chief justices, all three were personable, hardworking, and generally admired by their fellow appeal justices, and from their political experience they would seem to have been well placed to influence political decisions about the court. Yet none of them seems to have wielded much influence upon the Ontario government's frequent and sometimes bewildering reorganizations of the courts during these years. In evaluating these three men's successive tenures as chief justice of Ontario, historians have also seen the consolidation in the jurisprudence of the Ontario courts of an attitude of uncreative deference to precedent, perhaps even complacency.

William Ralph Meredith, the first of the three chief justices, had begun his legal career in London, Ontario, where the "eight Merediths of London" rapidly achieved prominence; his siblings included not only his fellow judge Richard, but also a president of the Bank of Montreal, a president of the Montreal Stock Exchange, and a mayor of London, who also ran the family law firm there. Elected to the Ontario legislature in 1872, William Meredith soon became leader of the Conservative opposition there, while continuing to build his legal career in Toronto. Unable to defeat Oliver Mowat in successive elections, Meredith accepted appointment to the bench in 1894, but he continued to advise the Whitney government on university reform, on the new Hydro-Electric Power Commission, on municipal law, and on workmen's compensation, a program he had championed while in the legislature.

"One Appeal within the Province"

Premier James Pliny Whitney, a country lawyer from Morrisburg, defeated the Liberals and became premier of Ontario in 1905 and held office until his death in 1914. Whitney ran a generally progressive Conservative administration credited with achieving "electoral and educational reform, developmental programs for the north, the dextrous and courageous management of the dangerous liquor issue, and creation of a great publicly-owned Hydro system."[2] But Whitney was also an ambitious party builder, keen to ensure that his Conservative party, having formed its first Ontario government under his leadership, would permanently displace the Liberals. He did not flinch from manipulating populist fervour for political advantage. Perhaps the most famous example was Regulation 17, a 1912 administrative order that sharply curtailed French-language education in the province. As the large population of English-speaking Irish Catholics in Ontario began to emphasize language issues over religious identity, Whitney used the language-of-education issue to win English-speaking Catholics away from their Liberal allegiance – at the price of creating long-lasting distrust between French Canada and English Canada on the eve of the First World War.

Courts administration was a less likely subject than language politics upon which to seek partisan advantage, but in the first years of the twentieth century Ontario had experienced a populist campaign against "the dominant power of the long purse in legal matters."[3] A particular target of criticism was the Toronto Street Railway Company. People injured in streetcar accidents won jury awards at trial, the argument went, only to have the TSR appeal every case again and again, until the accident victims either lost their cases or abandoned them for lack of funds. Similar ire was directed at employers, notably the Grand Trunk Railway, that allegedly used the same tactic in workplace injury litigation. The Toronto *Globe*, one of the newspapers behind the campaign, insisted that these abuses could be remedied only by limitations on appeals. "It is a mistake to say that the appeals ... are due to unfairly sympathetic verdicts by juries. Corporation managers recognize the helplessness of the courts and improve the opportunity, appealing all judgments, keeping the people in wise terror of the law and thus securing immunity." The accusation was partly that appeal courts were favouring corporate interests, but mostly that the corporations and the wealthy were able to overwhelm litigation against them by endless appeals, from the trial courts to the Divisional Court, to the Court of Appeal, to the Supreme Court of Canada, and even to the JCPC.[4]

In his 1908 re-election campaign, Whitney seized on this issue, "the only unfulfilled item on the government's programme," with a drastic solution. In a draft bill put before the legislature before the election, Whitney's Attorney General, the Toronto lawyer James Joseph Foy, proposed to abolish the Court of Appeal altogether.[5] His proposal was to return appeals to superior court judges sitting in panels, roughly as in the Error and Appeal regime before 1874. He also proposed to put new limits on appeals to the Supreme Court of Canada and to abolish Privy Council appeals completely. "One appeal within the province" – and as few as possible beyond it – became the government's promise. Whitney made appellate reform into the leading item of his election platform, and he easily won re-election.[6]

The 1908 draft bill on court reform created a difficult situation for lawyers who saw in the hierarchy of appeals that had existed in the province since the 1870s a guarantee against unjust, ill-considered, or erroneous judicial decisions. The *Canada Law Journal* criticized the government's one-appeal project as "an echo of the popular sentiment much in evidence before the last provincial election [rather than] the sober thought of those most capable of forming an intelligent opinion on the subject." In Toronto, a meeting of the newly formed Ontario Bar Association presented statistics to show multiple appeals were actually rare. J.H. Moss, son of former Chief Justice Thomas Moss and nephew of the incumbent Chief Justice Charles Moss, summed up the data as demonstrating that over several recent years, "an average of 31 cases in each year have been before more than one appellate court in the province ... an average of slightly more than 3% of all the cases tried" – hardly grounds for abolishing the appeal court, Moss argued, particularly when abuses in employers' liability cases could be addressed by other measures.

Defending the existence of a specialized appeal court, J.H. Moss deplored the proposal that "the tribunal that would hear all appeals in the province would be of a transient character and constantly changing membership." An appeal court, he declared, needed members who could engage in "consideration and mutual discussion" to impart "continuity and consistency to the jurisprudence of the country."[7] Both the Law Society and the Ontario Bar Association defended a "permanent Court of Appeal" and the right to appeal beyond the province.

The government was not dismayed to be in a fight with the legal profession. In a meeting with leaders of the bar, Premier Whitney declared there was "consensus in favour of the one appeal." His mentor D.R. McLennan, a Cornwall lawyer and Law Society bencher, argued that lawyers who defended multiple appeals were merely asserting pocketbook interests. "If the Attorney General's reforms are carried out, the lawyers will suffer a temporary loss. The client will save."[8]

Nevertheless, the next courts bill, introduced early in 1909,[9] differed substantially from the one in the Conservatives' election platform. In the meantime, Whitney had moved to reduce another source of frequent complaint about the Court of Appeal. In 1910 he appointed William Meredith, then a trial court judge, to lead the royal commission that inspired the introduction of a comprehensive workmen's compensation program, taking most workplace injury matters out of the courts altogether.[10] Whitney still spoke of limiting appeals to the Supreme Court of Canada and doing away with Privy Council appeals, but those matters required action by higher levels of government. He had already backed away from abolishing the Court of Appeal. In the post-election bill, it was the Divisional Court of the High Court and not the Court of Appeal that was abolished.

The *Act for the Better Administration of Justice, to lessen the number of appeals and the cost of litigation*, introduced in the Ontario legislature in March 1909, received royal assent the following month, but it was not proclaimed into force until 1 January 1913, suggesting uncertainty about it within the government. It was a disorganized statute, according to an editorial in the *Canada Law Journal*, "defective in regard to details" and raising new problems for lawyers and judges.[11] In May 1913, just four months after the legislation finally came into force and three months after Meredith's appointment, the Whitney government, perhaps recognizing its flaws, replaced the 1909 version of the *Justice Act* with a third attempt, a new *Judicature Act* that restated most of the provisions in the second one in more cleanly drafted language.[12]

The result was a substantial reorganization of the superior courts, beginning with new names. The Supreme Court of Judicature, encompassing all the superior courts, became the Supreme Court of Ontario. The Court of Appeal became the Supreme Court's Appellate Division, "not a new court but only a continuation of the Court of Appeal." At the superior trial court level, the historic names of Queen's Bench, Common Pleas, Chancery, and Exchequer finally vanished. Already little more than four identical panels of what had been called the High Court since 1881, they were combined as the High Court of Justice, with one chief justice instead of four. The 1909 legislation had proposed ten High Court judges plus the chief justice, but by 1913 the number had already grown to the chief justice and thirteen.

The Divisional Court, the High Court's appellate section since 1881, the jurisdiction of which had been substantially expanded in 1904, was abolished entirely. ("Where an appeal lies to the Divisional Court of the High Court, it now lies to the Appellate Division of the Supreme Court of Ontario.") It was not to re-emerge until 1972. The "one appeal within the province" that Whitney aspired to provide would be to the Court of Appeal, now renamed the Appellate Division of the Supreme Court of Ontario.

This Appellate Division had more than a new name. It was substantially changed by Whitney's reforms, principally by being reorganized into two parts, called Division Courts of the Appellate Division. The First Division court of the Appellate Division was pretty much the old Court of Appeal: the chief justice of Ontario and the four permanent sitting justices of appeal. The new Second Division would consist of five judges to be elected annually from among the High Court judges by all the judges of the Supreme Court.[13] These two permanent appeal divisions (there could be additional temporary divisions as well, if needed, but none was ever formed) were identical in jurisdiction, and the act made no stipulation about how appeal cases would be allocated between the two divisions, except that the divisions were to sit in alternate weeks and at least once monthly (though they could also sit concurrently). The act made no provision for appealing the decisions of the temporarily appointed judges of the Second Division to the permanent justices of the first division, so the new structure did fulfil the government's promise: there would be "one appeal within the province," to one or the other of the Appellate Division's two divisions. The act also confirmed the long-standing rule that four judges could be a quorum for many kinds of appeal. In the following decade, a majority of the court's panels had four judges, and almost all the rest had a full divisional panel of five.[14]

In the eternal debate between having a large number of appeal panels to correct errors swiftly, on the one hand, and having a small, collegial team to provide consistent and authoritative jurisprudence, on the other, the 1913 changes represent a confused compromise, one that gave the court a mix of full-time appeal justices formally appointed by Ottawa and temporary justices elected to annual terms from the trial court. Clearly, however, the emphasis was on a swift, one-level appeal process. From 1913, the Appellate Division, with its two panels of five permanent and five temporary judges, was effectively larger than the High Court, which had only fourteen judges, five of whom were always on secondment to the Appellate Division, to hear all the superior court trials in Ontario. Since the Second Division judges remained members of the High Court, however, they also continued to serve as trial court judges as needed.

The *Judicature Act* of 1913 instructed the nineteen appeal and trial judges who constituted the Supreme Court of Ontario to meet each December to elect five trial judges to be the second appellate division for the following year. This annual election was evidently taken seriously. Little information has survived about the process, but it was no mere formality. In the ten years 1914–23, these annual joint meetings elected fifteen different High Court judges to one or more annual terms on the Second Division. Membership on the Second Division changed substantially every year, and even judges who were elected to it several times rarely held consecutive terms. William Renwick Riddell was elected nine times, but no other trial court judge was elected more than four times, including William Mulock, a future chief justice of Ontario.[15]

Chief Justice Meredith, Whitney's long-time confidant, probably played a part in implementing the two-panel Appellate Division that came into being just as he became head of the court. It seems unlikely that the name changes, the elective procedures that bypassed the federal power of appointment, and the unwieldy nature of the new structure in general could have been pleasing to the appellate bar and the judges of appeal. The changes were driven more by Whitney's need to address his electoral commitment of 1908 than the needs of the court or the judicial system. Nevertheless, William Meredith appears to have yielded to political necessity for, in reply to Whitney's offer of the chief justiceship late in 1912, he committed himself to ensure "fair treatment for the Law Reform Act" if appointed. By that time, Premier Whitney had already modified his campaign promise to abolish the appeal court entirely and had proposed the two-division appeal court instead. Meredith may have accepted that as sufficient compromise.[16]

The Mulock Court

In 1923, William Meredith, aged eighty-two, still active and widely admired after ten years as chief justice of Ontario, became ill while visiting the United States and died in Montreal on his way home. The recently elected Liberal government appointed William Mulock as his successor. Mulock, a Toronto lawyer wealthy from his marriage into the Cawthra family, was less known for his legal practice than as vice chancellor and chancellor of the University of Toronto for the remarkable span of sixty-seven years, 1881–1944, during which he had done much to establish the system of colleges that the university has had ever since. He had also been a long-serving Liberal MP for North York. In 1896, Mulock became postmaster general in Prime Minister Laurier's cabinet. In 1900, he established the Ministry of Labour and became its first minister, with his protégé William Lyon Mackenzie King as deputy minister. In both positions, Mulock was reputed to be a successful and effective administrator. Pleading ill health, he resigned from the House of Commons in 1905 and was appointed chief justice of the new Exchequer section of the High Court.

He held that position until 1923, and his fellow judges elected him to the Second Division of the Appellate Division four times between 1913 and 1923. In 1923, he was seventy-nine when Mackenzie King, now prime minister, appointed him to succeed Meredith as chief justice of Ontario and head of the appellate division of the Supreme Court. Mulock had the reputation for being supremely well connected, socially and politically; it was jokingly said that he managed not only the courts and the university but also, discreetly, both the federal and provincial governments.[17] As a judge, he had a pragmatic and even a sympathetic side. In 1915, he had presided over the trial of the young household servant Carrie Davies for shooting her employer, a member of the Massey family. His charge to the jury helped secure her acquittal.[18] In 1930, a Ku Klux Klan leader, convicted for leading a cross-burning mob at the Oakville home of a black man who was about to marry a white woman, appealed the token fine he had received at trial. Chief Justice Mulock upheld his conviction and increased his sentence to three months imprisonment, but based his reasons on the need to punish and deter mob violence without reference to the racial issue.[19]

Like Meredith, Mulock began his tenure as chief justice just as the government of Ontario was once more transforming the organization of the court.

Another Restructuring

In 1923, Ontario ended the process of having trial judges elected to annual terms on the Appellate Division's Second Division. Seats on the Second Division became permanent appointments, formally made by the federal government. These five judicial positions were in effect permanently transferred from the High Court to the Appellate Division's Second Division, creating the bizarre situation of a High Court with just nine trial judges while the Appellate Division now had ten judges in two divisions. The Second Division became a mirror of the first, with identical jurisdiction and its own chief justice, who was second in seniority only to the chief justice of Ontario. Mulock served very briefly in 1923 as the first chief of the permanent Second Division. After he succeeded Meredith as chief justice of Ontario (and head of the First Division), Francis Latchford led the Second Division through the rest of its existence, first with the title "Chief Justice of the Second Division" and later "Chief Justice of Appeal." During the 1920s, the court sat in almost equal numbers of four-judge and five-judge panels.

Curiously, the expansion of the province's highest court in 1923 was introduced by the government of the United Farmers of Ontario, an insurgent agrarian movement that had ended the long Conservative tenures of James Whitney (1905–14) and William Hearst (1914–19).[20] The United Farmers were antielitist and populist – so much so that they did not permit lawyers to be members of their party, let alone its candidates. When the UFO won the provincial election in 1919, Ernest Drury, the new premier, had to recruit a member from the opposition Liberals, William Edgar Raney, in order to have a lawyer as his Attorney General. Raney's strongest commitment during his four years as Attorney General was to the rigorous prohibition of alcohol, but he seems not to have shared the anti-lawyer, anti-court attitudes of his UFO colleagues. The 1923 strengthening of the Appellate Division seems to have reflected Raney's professional loyalties to the legal establishment more than any sentiment likely to be favoured by the United Farmers. Soon after the restructuring of 1923, the UFO lost power, but Raney was soon appointed a judge of the High Court by Prime Minister King's Liberal government.

The 1923 reorganization of the court was accompanied by changes to the Court of Appeal Registry, a separate registry office with its own registrar since 1881. In 1923 it was absorbed into a single Toronto office, the Supreme Court of Ontario Registry. N.F. Paterson, KC, who had

been Court of Appeal registrar since 1909, now became head of the Toronto registry, a position he retained until 1934. Registry positions were
still patronage appointments, said to be dominated by Freemasons and
members of the Orange Lodge, but Paterson's successor as registrar
was D'Arcy Hinds, a prominent figure in Toronto's Irish Catholic community and a vocal Canadian supporter of Irish independence, but also
a Conservative active in military and militia matters, which seems to
have reconciled Protestant officialdom to him. Born in 1868, Hinds had
begun working at Osgoode Hall in 1905, was called to the bar in 1920,
and was honoured with a King's Counsel appointment at his retirement in 1938.[21]

The new Conservative government of Premier G. Howard Ferguson
(1923–30), which replaced the United Farmers soon after Mulock's appointment as chief justice, also wanted to restructure the Appellate Division. It attempted the kind of levelling that might have been expected
from the UFO. Premier Ferguson once said that he and Chief Justice
Mulock never had a disagreement "because he always took the chief
justice's advice."[22] However, there is no indication that Mulock or any
other judge had much influence on the Conservatives' 1923–4 proposals. Ferguson and his Attorney General, the Kingston lawyer William
Folger Nickle, had legislation passed declaring that henceforth Ottawa
would merely appoint judges to the Supreme Court of Ontario, while
the Ontario provincial cabinet would direct, from time to time, which
of the Supreme Court judges would serve on the superior trial court
and on the appeal court, and who would be chief justice of each court.[23]

Ontario claimed this was only an extension of the long-standing
practice of delegating appeal court judges to sit ad hoc on the trial court
and vice versa, and also of the 1913–23 practice of permitting the judges
as a group to select which trial judges would serve annual terms on the
appeal court. Still, the legislation raised a constitutional point: If the
provincial cabinet designated chief justices and moved judges freely
between the trial and appeal courts, was it appropriating the federal
power of judicial appointment? Ontario referred this question to the
First Divisional Court of the Appellate Division, led by Mulock. By a
four-to-one majority, it declared Ontario's legislation ultra vires and
rejected Ontario's claim to be able to reassign judges as it pleased.[24]
Justice Robert Smith, newly appointed to the court and a future justice
of the Supreme Court of Canada, found that the plan was unacceptable because "the duties assigned to each judge may be made pleasing or otherwise according as his decisions are pleasing or otherwise

to those for the time being in power in the province" – an unacceptable interference in judicial independence. On the other hand, Justice
Frank Egerton Hodgins, a member of the court since 1912, found in
dissent that the law might be bad policy but was not beyond Ontario's
power, given the long history of judges moving between the trial and
appeal courts without federal involvement. The government appealed
the rejection of its plans to the JCPC, but it sustained the decision of
the Appellate Division.[25] The legislation never went into effect, and the
Ferguson government lost interest in restructuring the courts. The ten-
judge, two-division appeal court would endure until 1931.

Expanding the Right to Appeal in Criminal Cases, 1923

The possibility of appeal in criminal cases – opened slightly by the new
Criminal Code of Canada in 1892 and more by its amendment of 1900 –
took a significant leap forward in 1923.[26] During the first two decades of
the twentieth century, appeals of Canadian criminal verdicts to a provincial appeal court could go ahead with leave of the trial court judge,
or the Attorney General, or the court of appeal. Though such leave had
been granted with some regularity between 1900 and 1910 (criminal appeals declined sharply in the decade 1911–20), the 1923 amendment to
the Criminal Code amounted to a significant further expansion. Henceforth a convicted person could appeal a conviction on any question of
law *as of right*, though leave of the provincial appeal court was still required for appeals on matters of fact or mixed questions of fact and law,
and for sentencing appeals.

The House of Commons debate on the 1923 Criminal Code amendments did not discuss the principle of criminal appeal in any detail, and
there were no passionate interventions by backbench lawyer MPs as
there had been in 1900.[27] The 1923 amendment was influenced more by
the work of a special committee of the Senate, driven mostly by a Winnipeg lawyer and senator, Lendrum McMeans. Senator McMeans seems
to have been unaware of the criminal appeals possibilities opened up
in Canada in 1892 and 1900. He denounced Canada's backwardness in
failing to allow appellate review of criminal convictions and looked to
England for a remedy. McMeans called for provincial appeal courts to
be given powers analogous to those held by the English Court of Criminal Appeal, which had been established in 1907 after public agitation
prompted by some spectacular cases of allegedly wrongful convictions
followed by executions.[28]

Despite McMeans's advocacy for the British model, the Criminal Code amendment of 1923 did not follow British precedent very closely. In Britain after 1907, a criminal appeal required leave of the Court of Criminal Appeal, and that court could only confirm or dismiss trial court sentences.[29] The Canadian amendment provided for appeals as of right, and it empowered appeal courts to order new trials when appropriate. It gave convicts the right to appeal a conviction, but it also removed, almost inadvertently, the Crown's right to appeal an acquittal, with the minister, MPs, and Senator McMeans all agreeing, quite erroneously, that such a right had never existed in Canada. The Crown's right to appeal – on questions of law – was restored in 1930. After 1930, both the Crown and the accused in all criminal matters had a broad right of appeal of convictions and acquittals on questions of law, and a more limited one on questions of fact and on sentencing matters.[30] The 1930 amendment also removed many of the limitations that the 1923 Criminal Code amendment had placed on criminal appeals from the provincial courts of appeal to the Supreme Court of Canada. Thereafter, appeals of criminal cases, which had been almost impossible for most of the nineteenth century, became as routine as civil appeals – at least as a matter of law. It took time for legal expertise in criminal appeals to begin to match the new freedom to appeal, and for several decades, the very limited availability of legal aid meant that, as a practical matter, legal representation for criminal defendants' appeals often depended on charitable measures by courts or the bar.[31] Criminal appeals had surged after the 1900 changes, but then declined again (perhaps because the Court of Appeal became less willing to grant leave) but the numbers increased again in the 1930s, when 24 per cent of the cases in our sample of appeals were criminal matters.

Shortly after the 1923 expansion of criminal appeals in Canada, but unconnected to it, the JCPC suddenly re-asserted its interest in criminal appeals from Canada. In 1925, the British cabinet was eager to ensure that English judges sitting in London would continue to hear final appeals in all matters from the new Irish Free State, self-governing since 1921 but still part of the British Commonwealth. Since the Irish Free State had been given a constitutional status specifically modelled on Canada's, the British government needed to forestall Irish legislation modelled on Canada's independent action in 1887–8. The JCPC suddenly found it expedient to support the British government by finding in *Naden v The King*, decided in February 1926, that Canada's 1888 legislation abolishing criminal appeals to the JCPC had always been ultra vires. It ruled that Canada could not interfere with the JCPC's prerogative right to hear any Canadian appeal it chose to accept, civil or criminal.[32]

Fearing protest from Canadians who resented the renewed subjection of Canadian jurisprudence to a British court, the British government offered to make a constitutional amendment specifically for Canada on this point. But Canada took no action. In the 1920s, influential members of the Canadian bar maintained reservations about the quality of the Supreme Court of Canada, and leading Canadian lawyers appreciated the privilege of arguing cases in London. As well, some provinces did not support the vesting of final authority in constitutional matters in a court appointed by the Canadian cabinet, and they might have challenged a Canadian attempt to change the constitutional status of the Supreme Court of Canada. The Canadian government, aware of such concerns and assured that the JCPC's new assertiveness concerned Irish matters, not Canadian ones, chose not to react. Despite the growing potential for criminal appeals in Canada after 1923's Criminal Code amendments, the JCPC took little further interest in criminal law after making its point in *Naden*, and few such cases were taken to Britain. In 1931, the *Statute of Westminster* confirmed the independence and equality of all the nations of the British Commonwealth. Canada restated the prohibition of Canadian criminal (but not civil or constitutional) appeals to the JCPC in 1933, and the JCPC acknowledged Canada's authority to do so.

One More Restructuring

In 1931, the government of Premier George Henry, who succeeded his Conservative rival Howard Ferguson in 1930, was retrenching in the face of the Depression. It decided something had to be done to find economies at an appeal court that was larger (ten judges) than the trial court (nine judges). "There were not enough judges taking trial work ... and many have thought [the Appellate Division] was a little top heavy," declared Henry's Attorney General, W.H. Price, a prominent Toronto lawyer widely known as Colonel Price for his military service. Price's 1931 amendment to the *Judicature Act* provided for the abolition of the two separate divisions of appeal and for the gradual reduction (through deaths and retirement) of the court from ten (two chief justices and eight justices) to eight (one chief justice and seven justices). As the appeal court was reduced in size, the High Court would expand from nine to eleven: a chief justice and ten judges. The 1931 amendment also simplified the names given the courts in 1913. The Supreme Court survived, but its Appellate Division became once more the Court of Appeal for Ontario, and its High Court Division the High Court of Justice for Ontario. Both courts remained parts of the Supreme Court of Ontario and the judges of each could still serve ad hoc on the other as needed.[33]

Premier Henry's government (1930–4) is mostly remembered for its campaigns against strikers and "reds" during the Depression of the 1930s, and Henry, overwhelmed by the economic crisis, was defeated by Mitch Hepburn's resurgent Liberals when Henry finally faced the voters in 1934. Premier Henry's restructuring of the courts, however, proved notably successful, or at least long lasting. The 1931 design for the appeal court remained in effect longer than the changes of 1849, 1874, 1881, 1913, or 1923. The Court of Appeal for Ontario, as defined in 1931, remained essentially unchanged in name and structure into the twenty-first century, and the High Court of Justice endured until 1990. Although the appeal court was slightly reduced in size, the 1931 amendments authorized it to sit in panels of three, where four or five had been the norm since 1913. The 1931 amendment also declared that an appeal court quorum would be not less than three "and always an uneven number." Oliver Mowat's 1874 concept of a four-judge panel requiring a high threshold of agreement to allow an appeal had finally been repudiated in favour of a simple majority.

Chief Justice Mulock soon seized on this amendment. To improve productivity at the court, he made the three-judge appeal panel the norm. Between 1911 and 1930, more than 90 per cent of all cases had been heard by panels of four or five judges. In the 1930s, panels were either three or five, and fewer than 30 per cent had five judges. Mulock reported proudly in 1934 that due to the administrative changes the court had made since 1931, principally by having more panels sitting, its backlog of cases had been eliminated entirely. "Throughout the judicial year 1932–3," he declared, "every appeal was heard in the month in which it was entered for hearing." In the month of June 1933, "the Court heard and delivered judgment in every case – a unique circumstance in the history of the Court of Appeal in this province, and perhaps of any other appellate court within the empire."[34] The judges did not immediately develop the habit of producing a single written majority decision. It remained common that three judges would write three opinions, even if they all agreed.

Chief Justice William Mulock had been sixty-one when he left politics for the bench, ostensibly for health reasons, in 1905 and seventy-nine when he became chief justice in 1923. He would lead the appeal court for another thirteen years. For Bill Gale, a future chief justice who began practising in 1932, "he was a majestic figure of a man with his snowy white hair and beard and his black gown and white tabs."[35] In 1933, he and four other senior members of the court survived an attempt to push them into retirement. That spring the House of Commons passed a bill introduced by the government of R.B. Bennett providing for federally appointed judges who did not voluntarily retire at age seventy-five to be paid only what their retirement annuity would provide.[36] Between 1920 and 1947, a chief justice was paid $10,000 and a regular judge $9,000, and their superannuation benefits had since 1859 been set at two-thirds of salary, once a judge had sufficient seniority.[37] The pay cut was the only means available to the government to encourage retirement at seventy-five, because life tenure at the provincial superior courts was constitutionally entrenched, and the government was unwilling to seek either provincial or British support for an amendment. Life tenure at the Supreme Court of Canada, by contrast, had been established by a statutory measure in 1875 and it was changed to mandatory retirement at seventy-five by statute in 1927. Chief Justice Mulock and Justices Riddell, Latchford, Magee, and Masten, all seventy-five or older already, were vulnerable to the pay cut, but in the end they were saved by the Senate.[38] Its life-tenure members saw that a similar stratagem might easily be applied to them. They rose up to defeat the bill, and it was not re-introduced.*

Mulock abruptly retired three years later. In 1934, he had made an unusual public attack on the government's plan to coerce the elderly judges through their salaries, telling the Canadian Bar Association that Prime Minister Bennett's bill was "unconstitutional" and an attack on the independence of the judiciary.[39] Two years later, in June 1936, the introduction of an amendment to the federal *Judges Act* gave R.B. Bennett, by then the leader of the opposition, an opportunity to strike back.

---

* Four years later, facing elderly and hostile judges on the Supreme Court of the United States, American President Franklin D. Roosevelt sought authority to nominate one additional justice for every sitting justice over seventy. The "court-packing" threat was never passed by Congress but was widely credited with persuading the court to temper its opposition to the president's legislative program: "the switch in time that saved the nine."

Regretting the failure of his 1933 plan and citing a supposed "unwritten rule" that no one over sixty should be appointed to the bench, Bennett declared the amendment then being considered would not be necessary "if all the judges in Ontario were physically fit." Bennett went on:

It is almost an intolerable condition in a country such as this that there should be men willing to accept positions on the implied condition that they will be able to continue to discharge their duties, and who, despite the fact that they are not – even on their own admission – continue to hold office and draw the emoluments of their positions ... There would appear to be a seeming unwillingness on the part of these men to realize their obligations in the same way as they compel litigants appearing before them to recognize their obligations.[40]

Chief Justice Mulock understood these remarks as aimed at him personally, even though most observers agreed that to the end he was (in the words of the future appeal judge G. Arthur Martin, who observed him while a student) "very alert and quite pleasant to counsel."[41] He announced his retirement at once, citing Bennett's words in the reasons he gave Prime Minister Mackenzie King. King, his old protégé, professed sympathy, but his private views were much like Bennett's: "The position of the bench as it is in Ontario is really shocking; almost a scandal with men of the age of those there at present, and incompetent," he wrote two years later.[42] Mulock, ninety-three when he retired in 1936, lived on in retirement until 1944 and died at age 101. Mulock was the oldest judge in the history of the court,* the last to hold a knighthood (received for his political service before he became a judge), and the last in a substantial line of magnificently bearded chief justices.

Chief Justice Rowell, 1936–8

In choosing a successor for Mulock, King gave little heed to his own reflections about elderly judges or to R.B. Bennett's view that no one over sixty should be made a judge. He considered lawyers D. Lally McCarthy and R.S. Robertson, both sixty-eight, before appointing Newton Wesley Rowell, who was seventy.[43] Rowell was the first chief justice of Ontario appointed directly from the practice of law. He was an evangelical Methodist and a prohibitionist who held progressive views on

---

* William Renwick Riddell died in office, aged ninety-two, in 1945.

many social questions, and he was both politically prominent and a leading member of the bar. After serving as opposition leader in the Ontario legislature from 1911, Rowell had led the pro-conscription Liberals who in 1917 split the federal Liberal Party during the wartime conscription crisis and went into Prime Minister Robert Borden's coalition government. Elected to the federal House on the unionist platform in 1917, Rowell spent the next three years as a senior member of Borden's cabinet. He left politics in 1920, but his public profile and reputation remained so high that Prime Minister King, who saw the Liberal Party reunited at the end of the war, reconciled with him. King turned to Rowell for counsel, appointed him to represent Canada at the League of Nations, and offered him senior cabinet positions. Rowell, however, preferred to concentrate on his already impressive litigation career. In the 1920s and 1930s, he was considered one of the two or three leading Canadian lawyers, particularly on constitutional issues, though by the mid-1930s he was reducing his practice to the most substantial civil and constitutional cases, mostly at the JCPC. In 1935 he had been elected treasurer of the Law Society.

During his term as chief justice, Rowell discussed with King and Justice Minister Lapointe draft legislation on a mandatory retirement age for judges, but King did not pursue the constitutional amendment that would have been required.[44] As chief justice, Rowell presided over almost seventy appeals, including a constitutional reference on separate school taxation and the sensational Millar will case, in which an eccentric Toronto lawyer offered his fortune to the woman who could produce the most children in the decade following his death. The will provoked a bizarre competition and litigation among several possible "winners." In one of thirty-nine opinions he wrote, Rowell upheld the trial court decision that the Millar bequest was not contrary to public policy and could stand, but that "children" meant legitimate children. The decision was affirmed at the Supreme Court of Canada, and a substantial payment was duly shared among several claimants.[45] But Rowell's tenure as chief justice was brief. Within a year after appointing Rowell, King chose him to lead what became the Rowell-Sirois Royal Commission on Dominion-Provincial Relations, and Rowell never returned to the court. His health collapsed in May 1938, during the commission's work. He retired from the chief justiceship and all his public offices in November, and he died in 1941. His appointment as chief justice had been a tribute to a distinguished legal career, but his contribution to the court was slight.

Judges of the Court of Appeal, 1913–38

On 12 October 1938, Crown counsel Clifford Magone was having a bad day in court. Trying to argue an appeal, he found himself constantly interrupted by questions from William R. Riddell, who was acting chief justice of Ontario during Chief Justice Rowell's illness. Eventually Justice Robert Fisher came to the lawyer's aid, declaring that he would like to hear Mr Magone set out his case uninterrupted.

"I intend to ask counsel any questions I wish," said Riddell, "without any objections from my brother judges."

Fisher declared that Riddell's interruptions were quite improper.

"I don't care a tuppence for you," said Riddell, who was eighty-six and had been a judge since 1906.

"I don't care a tuppence for you," retorted Fisher, who was seventy-three and had been a judge since 1922.

In the end, the three-judge panel (the third was Cornelius Masten, who was eighty-one) dismissed the Crown's appeal, and Riddell and Fisher were reported to be smiling and chatting by the end. But "Don't Care Tuppence" became a Toronto *Star* headline the next day, with photos of the two judges.[46] The incident nicely captured the reputation the Court of Appeal developed in the 1930s: elderly, anglophile, crotchety, and self-indulgent. The *Star* story also noted that among official circles in Ottawa, the story provoked only "amusement and reminiscences." One justice department official joked that since neither justice cared tuppence, it was a unanimous verdict and could not be appealed.

The fourteen judges appointed to the Court of Appeal between 1913 and 1938 had been appointed at about the same average age as earlier groups – about sixty-one – but by the 1930s and 1940s the appeal bench included several octogenarians and a couple who would mark their ninetieth birthdays on the bench. The judges of this period were all Canadian-born and Canadian-educated (except Norman Macdonnell, who also studied in Britain as a Rhodes Scholar), and all had trained in law in Ontario. Most had practised in Toronto. About half had Liberal allegiances when appointed, and they were exclusively anglophone, though now more Presbyterian than Anglican, and with the first Catholic, Frank Latchford, among them. They had had long experience at the bar – twenty-nine years on average – and most had been superior trial court judges before coming to the Court of Appeal, with four appointed directly from practice. Few had come from notable wealth or privilege, though most had had families able to support their education and apprenticeship, but for most their arrival at the pinnacle of the provincial bench and bar was a personal and professional achievement.

The court included able judges and some amiable and courteous ones. William Middleton, appointed in 1923 (at sixty-three), was so "polite, considerate, efficient, productive" that future justice of appeal John Arnup called him "the beloved judge."[47] John Gillanders, a First World War flying ace before he took up the law, was described by the distinguished advocate John Robinette as courteous, a great gentleman, and a good judge. Chief Justice Mulock long retained the interpersonal and administrative skills that had served him well in politics. But increasingly the style and reputation of the court were set by judges who were neither congenial to fellow judges nor polite to the lawyers who appeared before them. Of Riddell, Robinette said, "He was the most opinionated man who ever sat on the court ... Everyone hated the old boy. I have never appeared before a more difficult judge."[48] Arnup remembered Riddell as "quite lacking in the social graces ... rude to counsel, contemptuous ... cruelly sarcastic even to his own colleagues ... fond of quoting very old cases ... and of stating propositions in dogmatic terms. His judgments have not stood the test of time." Arnup described Riddell and Frank Latchford sitting together as "murderers' row."[49] In 1928, the year he joined the Court of Appeal at age sixty-three, don't-care-tuppence Robert Fisher told a spring assize that most criminals were foreigners, 70 to 75 per cent of whom were bootleggers. "We Anglo-Saxons" needed to take action, Fisher said, and a newspaper headlined his solution: "Judge would flog all bootleggers."[50] By the end of his career, even Chief Justice Mulock had few illusions about his judges. He described Riddell in 1936 as "a terrible man" and "partially insane." Latchford, he said, was impulsive and narrow and, as an "R.C.," too much given to the idea that even criminals deserved justice.[51]

Even the most irascible judges of this period were often acknowledged to know, or at least once have known, a great deal of law. John Arnup acknowledged that Riddell had been a capable lawyer and judge in his earlier years, and Robinette described W.T. Henderson as "rough" and "outspoken," but also as "a good judge." Robinette and Arnup, however, could afford to be generous; they had built their reputations precisely on their abilities to thrive in any tribunal and deal with any judge.

Something larger than personal failings may have been at work here. The judges of the early twentieth century had mostly worked themselves up from unpretentious backgrounds, but the majestic authority of the bench was as great as ever. Upon appointment, judges were expected to become remote and Olympian figures, standing outside society and even the bar, and clothed with large and unconstrained power. From the bench they were entitled to voice what they judged to be public morality, and they were accountable to no one throughout their lifetime appointments. With the benefit of better public health and medical advances, they also lived longer than their nineteenth-century predecessors, few of whom had lived to a great age. Perhaps inevitably, some as they aged became subject to arrogance, disdain for others, and petty abuse of authority. It was not a problem unique to the Court of Appeal or to Ontario. In Alberta in the 1920s, the chief justices of the trial and appeal courts litigated all the way to the JCPC as to which of them was entitled to be styled "Chief Justice of Alberta."[52] In British Columbia, Justice Archer Martin was renowned for abusive courtroom behaviour during thirty years of service on the Court of Appeal, and for his feuds with other judges and lawyers, and particularly with Chief Justice Gordon Hunter of the trial court.[53] The American Supreme Court that confronted President Franklin Roosevelt in the 1930s was routinely described as "nine old men." One of them, James Clark McReynolds, who referred to the president of the United States as "that crippled son-of-a-bitch," and was deeply hostile to Louis Brandeis, Benjamin Cardozo, and Felix Frankfurter, the Jewish members of the court during his tenure, was described by his chief justice as "someone who seems to delight in making others uncomfortable ... a continual grouch."[54] The Supreme Court of Canada had been riven by petty feuds among its judges almost from its start. The rudeness of Chief Justice Strong, who came to the court from Ontario's Error and Appeal, once provoked a group of Supreme Court lawyers into seeking his removal from the bench.[55] The eccentricities and ill health, both mental and physical, of several Supreme Court of Canada judges became the impetus for mandatory retirement to be imposed there in 1927.[56]

Ontario may have been notable only because its judges of the 1930s were unusually aged even by the standards of the time: by 1938, six of the eight judges of appeal were over seventy-five. One reason for the aging of the court was the brief tenures of some of the court's most highly regarded younger judges. Robert Smith served just four years on the court before being appointed to the Supreme Court of Canada in 1927. The very highly regarded Henry Hague Davis served just two years at the Court of Appeal before his own Supreme Court appointment. Norman Macdonnell, another highly regarded practitioner, was appointed directly from practice to the court in 1933 at age forty-seven, but he died just five years later. Almost the only personal note that survives about Macdonnell on the court was an episode when Justice Riddell was telling a young lawyer how he, Riddell, had been worked very hard as a law student and was not paid a cent. *"Quantum meruit,"* Justice Macdonnell was heard to murmur, applying a contract law term meaning "reasonable value."[57]

The Court of Appeal Bar, 1913–38

The appeal bar, the community of lawyers who argued cases at the Court of Appeal, remained large between 1913 and 1938. Our sampling of 100 cases per decade in this period shows 142 to 172 different lawyers appearing in each decade. But most made only one appearance in the sampled cases, and there is clear evidence of a pool of dominating counsel, less dominant than in the smaller bar of earlier decades but still a distinct and influential clique. Across the three decades 1911–40, the ten lawyers who appeared most frequently in the Court of Appeal acted in forty per cent of our sample of cases – far less than the 94 per cent and 75 per cent for 1876–90 and 1891–1910, but still a significant concentration. Across the whole period, D. Lally McCarthy, Robert S. Robertson, and W. Norman Tilley, three Toronto litigators with long careers and immense reputations, were the ones seen most frequently in the appeal court. Also among the leaders were Arthur Slaght, Thomas N. Phelan, and Isadore Hellmuth. Reflecting the rise of criminal appeals, Crown attorney E.J. Bayly remained among the leaders, as did W.D. "Bill" Common, a protégé of Bayly who would become a leading figure in the Crown prosecution department in Ontario for decades. Nearly all the leading members of the appellate bar were Toronto lawyers; one non-Torontonian among them was Sir George Gibbons, a lawyer and businessman of London, Ontario. They were almost exclusively white, Ontario-raised Canadians of British origins, and Protestant. B.J. Spenser-Pitt, an early black lawyer, appears in the appeal lists, and Vera Parsons, one of the first women criminal defence counsel, argued appeals from the 1920s, but in general women, Jews, and other ethnic minorities had not yet broken into the elite circles of the Ontario bench and bar, and it would be decades before any were even considered for appointment to the Court of Appeal.

There were lawyers who preferred taking their cases to the more cerebral, more law-centred Court of Appeal over arguing cases before juries in the trial courts, but into the 1930s there were limits to such specialization. Even lawyers whose rhetorical style and skill with juries made them better suited to the trial courts turned up in the appeal lists. Joseph Sedgwick, an example, an eloquent talker more than a cerebral lawyer ("A little more law, a little less Shakespeare," a judge once admonished him), was among the leading appeal counsel in the 1930s, acting for both the Crown and the defence. Some successful lawyers almost never took cases to the court. As future superior court judge Donald Morand put it after observing the appeal bench as a law student in the late 1930s, "They were incredibly arrogant and incredibly impolite in those days ... I said I would never set foot in this court." The London, Ontario, lawyer and law firm builder Mayer Lerner, on the other hand, decided never to ask anyone to take his appeals. "I took them myself, and I got hammered," he said, and he gradually learned how to face a hostile court.[58]

The late 1930s saw the first Court of Appeal appearances by Arthur Martin, a future member of the court who did much to "create" criminal law as a serious branch of practice. He was not called to the bar until 1940 but appeared on criminal appeals as a student. Back to 1900, lawyers had been appealing criminal trial verdicts with some success. T.C. Robinette, described at his death in 1920 as "during many years the chief defender of men indicted by the Crown on criminal charges," had a criminal appeal practice as well.[59] But most criminal defendants lacked funds, and there was no legal aid beyond loosely organized pro bono representation, with the costs occasionally subsidized by the Crown prosecution office. As a result, even after the right of appeal became more general in 1923, most criminal defence counsel had a reputation for doing little more than simply arranging guilty pleas or seeking mercy by colourful courtroom performances before lay magistrates and juries. "The bulk of their work was done in what was known as the Police Court in those days," Martin recalled. "And many of those lawyers weren't particularly learned. Some of them were quite witty and facile, but they weren't particularly learned ..."

Once the right to appeal was established, however, opportunities gradually opened for new developments in criminal law jurisprudence. By the end of the 1930s, Martin, a dedicated student of the Criminal Code and the rules of procedure, began appealing trial-court convictions on what would become classic grounds – inadmissibility of evidence, police or prosecutorial misconduct, improper charges to the jury – with enough skill, confidence, and expertise to sway even the hard-bitten, black-letter appeal judges of the 1930s. In 1936, aged just twenty-five, Martin, as co-counsel to the convicted murder Mickey MacDonald, persuaded the Court of Appeal that procedural errors by the Crown and the trial judge amounted to a miscarriage of justice, and won him a new trial.[60] Piece by piece, Martin would do much to develop a body of precedents in criminal law that would influence criminal law practice for decades.

Cases and Procedures in the Court of Appeal, 1913–38

One remarkable appeal from the 1920s and 1930s demonstrates that the Ontario appeal bench, for all its irascibility and rudeness, was capable of great loyalty – indeed of being more loyal to its friends than to impartial justice. The case Elizabeth Bethune Campbell launched in 1922, after she grew to suspect she had never received her due from her mother's estate, rapidly became an awkward one for the Ontario bench and bar.[61] Campbell, the wife of a Boston clergyman with a modest income, was also the daughter of James Bethune, Ontario's leading appellate counsel until his death in 1884, and the stepdaughter of William Pearce Howland, Confederation-maker and past lieutenant governor of Ontario. Most of the trial and appeal court lawyers and judges remembered her parents well, and Campbell had encountered them in her parents' elegant home. But by the 1920s, the bench and bar leaders were much closer to the trustee of Lady Howland's estate, William Drummond Hogg, who was Campbell's uncle but also a prominent Ottawa lawyer, a trust company director, and long-time bencher of the Law Society. Though he appears to have treated Lady Howland's estate more as family money than as a professional trust, most of Elizabeth Campbell's siblings, who were much better off than she was, preferred to avoid an unseemly squabble over Hogg's handling of the estate.

Campbell launched legal action against Hogg, but she found the bench and bar reluctant to uphold her case against their distinguished colleague, whatever the facts. Campbell's self-published memoir recounts in detail how leading lawyers declared themselves unable to represent her and withdrew from the case, and how one judge after another refused to think ill of his good friend Mr Hogg, whatever the evidence of his maladministration, and urged her to settle rather than cause further awkwardness. When she appealed a trial court loss to the Court of Appeal in 1928, four (Mulock, Magee, Hodgins, Ferguson) of the five judges hearing the appeal were Bethune family friends who had known her as a child (Grant was the exception), but all except Magee refused to rule against their colleague Hogg. Bringing her into his chambers, Chief Justice Mulock personally urged Campbell to cease making trouble and accept a token payment in exchange for Hogg's exoneration, and he then took her to the other judges to add their urgings to his.

According to Mrs Campbell, D. Lally McCarthy, one of the counsel who had withdrawn from representing her, told her that "nowhere this side of the water" would she find justice. At the JCPC in London, she believed, she would escape the cliquish solidarity of the Ontario bench and bar. There, representing herself, she won an unequivocal judgment against Hogg. The memoir she wrote about her case is a passionate salute to the glories of the JCPC and a forceful argument that in the 1920s and 1930s the upper levels of the Ontario bench and bar were an inbred clique where complacent professional solidarity had become stronger than impartial justice. Mrs Campbell's success at the JCPC should have been a sharp rebuke to the jurisprudence of both the High Court and the Court of Appeal, though not much attention was paid at the time, and she later had a hard time getting her claim against Hogg and his trust company enforced in Ontario.

The court in the interwar years heard its fair share of odd or sensational cases. About the same time as the Campbell case, there was a case of another self-representing woman, when Florence Deeks, a hitherto unknown Toronto writer, attempted to prove that H.G. Wells had plagiarized her unpublished work to write his bestselling *Outline of History*. Deeks's claim was less implausible than it seemed, and expert witnesses found the similarities between her text and Wells's striking, but after she lost at trial a four-judge panel dismissed her appeal, with Riddell, proud of his own historical work, being particularly dismissive. Deeks took a further appeal to the JCPC, but she did not share Elizabeth Campbell's happy experience there and lost again.[62]

In 1930, a federal law for the first time gave Ontario judges authority in divorces and annulments that had previously required an act of Parliament. The Court of Appeal handled the cases that came to it for review cautiously. Sharing the societal conviction that divorce should not be encouraged, the judges focused most of their attention on reviewing jurisdictional questions and setting standards for the evidence required as grounds for divorce, and they tended to display a sternly protective paternalism towards the female parties.[63]

During this period, the court continued to revisit some classic issues of law. The English law of nuisance (the right of a property owner not

Table 3.1 Statistical Notes on 14 Judges of Appeal Appointed 1913–38

Birthplace

Ontario   12
Quebec   2

Ethnic Origin

Anglophone/British   14

Religious Affiliation

Presbyterian   7
Church of England   4
Methodist   2
Catholic   1

Francis Latchford, of Irish-Catholic ancestry and the first Roman Catholic on the court, was replaced upon his death in 1938 by the second Catholic, Charles McTague.

Education

non-law academic degrees   6*
legal education through articling and examinations   7
Osgoode Hall Law School   7

Average Years of Law Practice before Judicial Appointment

29 years

Minimum: 12   (Latchford)
Maximum: 45   (Rowell)

Location of Legal Practice (some in more than one place)

Toronto   9
Ottawa   2
London   1
Orillia   1
Brantford 1
Cobourg   1
Cornwall   1

Identified Political Commitment

Held elective office or politically active   10
Liberal   7

Table 3.1 (*Concluded*)

Conservative   3
None   4

Judicial Appointment prior to Court of Appeal Appointment

Yes   10   (High Court of Justice and its predecessors)
No   4

Average Age at Court of Appeal Appointment

61.6 years

Minimum: 47 (Ferguson and Macdonnell); 48 (Davis)
Maximum: 73 (Riddell); 79 (Mulock)

Average Years on Court of Appeal Bench

11.6 years

Rowell, appointed at 69, had barely two years before he retired due to ill health.
Davis and Smith were promoted to the Supreme Court after two and three years, respectively.
Fisher, Middleton, and Masten had 21-, 20-, and 19-year terms, respectively.

Reason for Leaving Court of Appeal

Died   8   (At ages 49, 52, 60, 62, 71, 79, 84, and 85)
Retired   4   (At ages 71, 83, 84, and 92)
To SCC   2   (At ages 50 and 69)

Average Age on Leaving

72.4 years

Early death kept the average down; those few who retired did so late in life.

---

* Including MacDonnell, who had postgraduate experience as a Rhodes Scholar at Oxford.

to be disturbed by new development), once markedly sympathetic to landowners, had long been challenged by the needs of industrial development and urban growth, and the court's rulings were sensitive to the new balance that had been struck. A Rosedale homeowner got some support from the court in claims against a disruptive bridge builder because it was found that the builder should be able to mitigate the nuisance, but an Oakville property owner objecting to noise and odours from a new oil refinery was told that he would have to get used to the change.[64]

Negligence law had been decisively reshaped by the 1932 British case *Donoghue v Stephenson*, which defined the broad scope of a manufacturer's liability towards consumers. The court showed itself aware of the precedent four years later in *Shandloff v City Dairy*. It specifically cited *Donoghue* in finding both the manufacturer and the retailer of a chocolate milk product liable for pieces of glass found in it by a consumer.[65] In broader liability law matters, the court had accepted a reversal of its nineteenth-century jurisprudence in which employers could rarely be found liable for the harmful actions of their employees. In 1938, when the Joy Oil Company appealed a trial court decision finding it liable for a libel by one of its employees, the court dismissed the appeal, noting that nineteenth-century case law may have supported the company, but "more recent cases" had established that corporations could be liable for the actions of their servants or agents in the course of their employment.[66] In motor vehicle accidents, however, the court seems to have been reluctant to lay blame on careless drivers, tending to find that collisions were accidents and the *mens rea* required for a criminal conviction was lacking.

The court of this era was very much oriented to the rapid handling of a great many cases. Panels made up their minds quickly, often hearing the appellant counsel for only a few minutes and frequently not bothering to hear opposing counsel before rendering a quick dismissal. As Frederick MacKay, later a member of the court, recalled, there was "a disposition to dispose of cases, not to decide them."[67] Inevitably, decisions were based on familiar precedents, rigid procedural requirements, and on the court's long experience with the leading cases on the questions at hand, whether from an English court, the Supreme Court of Canada, or the Court of Appeal itself.

The legal historian R.C.B. Risk, after studying hundreds of judgments by W.R. Meredith, the first of the chief justices in this period, concluded that what drove Meredith was "the search for authority."[68] Meredith, he argued, did not see judges as lawmakers; their task was to find a statute or legal precedent covering the facts before them and to apply it. If the precedents disagreed, Meredith was more inclined to count them than to reason among them. It was as if, in the generation after the fusion of law and equity, the equitable concepts that earlier judges like Mowat had employed enthusiastically had been swallowed up in the black-letter precedents of the common law.

Yet not every decision of the court labels the judges of this era as mere automatons. In 1929, W.R. Riddell, the irascible bully of later years, considered a trial court decision that spared a railroad company from liability for damage to neighbouring properties because the legislature's *Railway Act* had a limitation clause protecting the railroad from such claims.[69] For a unanimous court, Riddell found that despite the protection of the statutory language, "this is a breach of a common law duty, imposed upon the company in common with all others." Riddell may have been traditional in his view of nuisance and liability, or even prejudiced against the mighty railroad, but here the court does not seem merely to be counting out authorities, but wrestling with the statutory authority on one hand and the common law principle on the other.

4

The Robertson-Pickup-Porter Courts, 1938–67

Ontario transformed itself between the late 1930s and the late 1960s. With the post-war baby boom and massive immigration, its population grew from about three and a half million to seven and half. Its economy, already dominated by automotive and machine manufacturing, and iron and steel production, saw continued expansion, and the standard of living improved constantly throughout the period. Toronto consolidated its place as a financial capital, and the period saw rapid growth in urban development and in the infrastructure of intercity transportation, hydroelectric development, and higher education. Labour unions secured their place as legitimate representatives of workers and expanded their numbers steadily. The Conservative government that took power in 1943 and would govern Ontario throughout the period was progressive as well as conservative, and the social welfare state grew rapidly. It had been said that the twentieth century did not really come to Ontario until 1950, but by the end of this period, small-town Protestant, loyalist Ontario values were challenged by rapidly increasing material prosperity, cultural transformations, the growing self-assertion of minority communities in commerce, education, and the professions, and by the ethnocultural diversity being heralded by immigration from southern Italy and (to a lesser extent) Eastern Europe, the Caribbean, and Asia. There was much that was modern about the province.

The same could not be said about the Court of Appeal. The extraordinarily elderly judges of the 1930s had passed from the scene, but their successors remained strongly committed to traditional jurisprudence. They were resistant to the claims of labour unions, dubious about racial and cultural diversity, hostile to most human rights initiatives, and committed to legal skills acquired by traditional apprenticeships rather than scholarship. It was a period when the Court of Appeal, hostile to much of the modernity blossoming around it, came to seem most spectacularly out of touch with currents of thought that were producing new ideas about society and new forms of jurisprudence.

Three Chief Justices Direct from the Bar

Despite his scathing comments about elderly and ineffectual judges, Prime Minister Mackenzie King replaced Chief Justice Rowell in 1938 with a near contemporary, sixty-eight-year-old Robert Spelman Robertson. Robertson, a product of small-town Ontario who came directly to the chief justiceship from the bar, as Rowell had, did not have his predecessor's public prominence, but he was as eminent in the legal community. A Liberal and once a candidate under Rowell's leadership, but not a very notable one, he built his reputation almost entirely on courtroom prowess in civil litigation. He initially practised in Stratford but when he was recruited to the Fasken law firm in Toronto in 1917, he was already prominent enough to secure a generous income guarantee and second ranking in the firm name, which became Fasken Robertson. David Fasken, the head of the firm, had built a large clientele among mining and financial businesses, and Robertson became their vital adviser. The morning after the Wall Street crash of October 1929, the firm's office was crowded with stockbrokers eager to have Robertson represent them in the litigation that was sure to follow. He argued cases frequently at the Supreme Court of Canada and the Judicial Committee of the Privy Council (JCPC), where he succeeded Rowell as one of Mackenzie King's favoured litigators in constitutional matters, and he was one of the lawyers most frequently seen in the Court of Appeal in the 1920s and 1930s. A bencher of the Law Society of Upper Canada from 1930, he was its treasurer when he was appointed chief justice. King, who had previously offered him judicial appointments, finally prevailed with the argument that at sixty-eight, with his children grown and provided for, Robertson could now afford to give up his large income for the $10,000 salary of a chief justice.[1]

Robertson, a slim, angular man and slightly stooped in his later years, was of the school of litigators who emphasized focus. From his juniors he wanted very brief memoranda, not encyclopedic surveys, and in court he tended to hit the key points and the key precedents briefly and forcefully. It was a style of litigation well suited to the black-letter, quick-to-judgment style that prevailed at the Court of Appeal. On the bench, Robertson could be just as brisk, but to future Court of Appeal Justice Arthur Martin, he was "a truly great jurist," and one who, at least in his first years as chief justice, discouraged the abuse of counsel that had often prevailed in the court before his appointment. Another future chief justice, Bill Gale, looked on Robertson as the best of the chief justices he had known, and John Robinette recalled how very well pre-pared Robertson was in the Evelyn Dick criminal appeal (which helped make Robinette's reputation). "You could never fool, or try to fool Rob-ertson on what the facts were ... He was just an ideal chief justice."[2]

Robertson began his term as chief justice in times of grim depres-sion, when the court was actually shrinking in size, and saw the court through the Second World War. He and his successors then saw the blossoming of the great post-war prosperity and social, economic, and cultural changes that went with it in Canada and Ontario, but the court changed remarkably little in structure or in attitude. During these de-cades, there was a lull in the endless tinkering with divisions of the court, methods of appointment, and relations with the superior trial court that had prevailed between 1913 and 1931. After 1938, most changes affecting the Court of Appeal were relatively small or else ex-ternal to the court itself. In 1949, Ontario passed legislation to expand the court from eight to ten judges, returning it to the size it had been be-fore the amendments of 1931 combined and shrank its two divisions.[3] Also during Robertson's tenure, the Canadian government, by a simple statutory declaration, abolished all appeals to the JCPC, effective 1 Jan-uary 1950. Both the Supreme Court of Canada and the JCPC had ruled, against the opposition of some provinces, that the *Statute of Westminster, 1931*, had definitively established the Canadian Parliament's authority in this matter.* From then on, the final court of appeal in all Canadian matters was the Supreme Court of Canada. The SCC was enlarged to

---

* Lord Jowitt of the JCPC, in a 1947 decision that confirmed Canada's authority to end appeals, seemed to echo Hume Blake's and Edward Blake's nineteenth-century argu-ments: "It is, in fact, a prime element in the self-government of the Dominion that it should be able to secure through its own courts of justice that the law should be one and the same for all its citizens."

nine members in 1949, saw the completion of its handsome new building on Ottawa's Wellington Street, and secured pay increases for its judges. The Court of Appeal for Ontario would still look respectfully to English precedents, but its decisions were now directly controlled only by the Ottawa court, which became the sole avenue of appeal beyond Ontario. The Supreme Court did not yet have the authority to "control its docket" by determining which appeals it chose to hear, and so the right of appeal to it remained broad.

Chief Justice Robertson had simple tastes; he called his fellow justices plain "Mister," and wanted to refuse the chauffeured car that was available to him as chief justice to bring him daily from his Rosedale home to Osgoode Hall. But he had strong views about the court, and when his health began to fail in the early 1950s, he apparently made it known that he would carry on until a successor of whom he approved was named. Rumour had it that he particularly did not want to be succeeded by James C. McRuer, an old litigation rival who sat briefly with him on the Court of Appeal before becoming chief justice of the High Court in 1945. Robertson agreed to retire, at age eighty-three, only when the appointment was promised to the lawyer he had trusted most while in practice: John Wellington Pickup, who had been his protégé, junior, and partner at the Fasken firm, and had then succeeded him as that firm's principal litigation counsel. Robertson retired in the fall of 1952 and was succeeded by Pickup.

Pickup, then sixty, became a lawyer as Robertson had, by articling for five years and attending classes at the Osgoode Hall law school, where he was gold medallist in 1913, just before turning twenty-one. He now became the last chief justice of Ontario without a university education. Pickup had spent his whole career as a litigator in Toronto, but he was not entirely a downtown, Bay Street type. Comfortable with the firm's rough-hewn mining clients, he liked to get away to northern fishing camps when he could. Described as "brusque" and "energetic" as a courtroom advocate, he had modelled himself on Robertson. Clients appreciated his plain, straight answers to their legal problems, and as a litigator he kept his arguments short and to the point. As chief justice, Pickup was an efficient administrator and brisk but polite on the bench, but his health broke down a few years into his term, and his medical leaves created a "long interregnum" at the court before he resigned in September 1957, just sixty-five.[4]

Pickup's retirement closely followed John Diefenbaker's election victory, and Diefenbaker became the first Conservative prime minister to appoint an Ontario chief justice since Robert Borden had appointed Meredith in 1912. Diefenbaker's choice was Dana Harris Porter, then fifty-seven, a fifteen-year veteran of the Ontario legislature and Attorney General in the Conservative government of Leslie Frost. Porter's appointment met with some controversy, partly because he was the first chief justice of Ontario (since John Beverley Robinson, at least) to be appointed directly from a political career, but also because the members of the court had been eager to see the appointment of one of their own, senior justice Robert Laidlaw, then sixty-six, who had been a member of the court since 1944 and its leader during Pickup's health leaves. Another potential candidate for the appointment was C.A. "Caesar" Wright, dean of law at the University of Toronto. After being interviewed by some influential Conservative party representatives, Wright apparently expected the appointment, but he may have been either too academic or too closely associated with the Liberal party, and no judicial appointment was ever forthcoming.[5]

Much as Porter had to confront the belief among his judges that Laidlaw, the most senior judge of appeal, should have been given the 1957 appointment, in 1967 his successor Gale would face a similar feeling that the then senior judge on the court, John Aylesworth, deserved to be chief justice. While Laidlaw and Aylesworth were both recognized leaders of the court, there was and is no tradition of seniority in the appointment of the chief justice of Ontario. Seniority influenced appointments of chief justices at the Supreme Court of Canada, but the lone instance of the most senior judge of appeal being named chief justice of Ontario was the appointment of G.W. Burton in 1900, after he had been on the court for twenty-six years.[6]

Porter, given his political career, had not built the legal reputation of his recent predecessors, but he had a distinguished academic record, including an Oxford MA, and had been successful in both law and politics. He became an effective administrator of the court and its judges, and John Arnup later concluded that Chief Justice Porter had both smoothed over the Laidlaw issue and exceeded the bar's expectations as a judge as well.[7] (Not everyone agreed: "Porter was a nice man, with very little knowledge of the law because he had not been in practice for a long time," was the verdict of Gregory Evans, who sat with him briefly before becoming chief justice of the High Court.)[8] Porter served almost a decade as chief justice, dying of cancer early in 1967, at the age of sixty-six.

The principal institutional change to the court in Porter's tenure was the new requirement in 1961 that all federally appointed judges retire at seventy-five. Because superior court judges' life tenure was specified in the *British North America Act*, the change required a constitutional amendment. The federal justice minister, E. Davie Fulton, secured the consent of every Canadian province, and also the support of the Canadian Bar Association, before requesting the amendment from the British Parliament, which quickly passed it. To the fury of many superior court judges who had accepted lifetime appointments, the amendment and the new rule applied to sitting judges as well as future appointments. Though some suggested such retroactive cancellation of their life tenures was illegal, the new rule was not challenged in court. Any sitting federally appointed judge over seventy-five had to retire at once though, as it happened, there were none in that situation at the Court of Appeal when the amendment became law.[9]

Another change of lasting significance, particularly in criminal law, was the agreement reached in 1966 between the Ontario government and the Law Society that established the province's first paid legal aid program. This permitted would-be litigants to apply to the program for a certificate with which they could retain a member of the private practice bar for trials and, if necessary, for appeals. Paid legal aid greatly increased the potential for criminal defendants, in particular, to pursue cases to appeal with specialized and adequately paid legal counsel, thereby gradually expanding the appeal court's role in the development of criminal justice matters. Legal aid was soon complemented by legal clinics, initially launched by university law schools, later publicly funded, that sought to assist poor and marginal groups who might not consult a lawyer even if legal aid funding was available.[10]

Another notable legal initiative of this period was the Canadian Bill of Rights, passed into law by the government of John Diefenbaker in 1960. The government chose not to seek a constitutional amendment that would entrench the Bill of Rights and confirm its primacy over ordinary statutes and administrative rulings. Instead, it sought to give the Bill of Rights similar force by shaping it as an interpretive statute, one that required other laws to be interpreted in the light of the principles it set out. As will be seen below, the Court of Appeal for Ontario took a strongly and consistently negative approach to applying the Bill of Rights in that way.

Judges of the Court, 1938–67

The ancient judges whom Chief Justice Robertson joined on the court in 1938 gradually succumbed to age. Latchford died at eighty-four in

1938, Masten at eighty-five in 1942, and Riddell at ninety-two in 1945. Middleton retired at eighty-three in 1943 and Fisher at eighty-four in 1949. No one ever again matched their longevity at the court. Indeed, R.B. Bennett's 1936 declaration that judges were not appointed over the age of sixty proved to be more accurate as a prediction than it was as history. None of the three men Bennett himself appointed to the Ontario Court of Appeal was over sixty – two were in their forties. From 1938 to 1967, the average age of judges when appointed was fifty-six. Chief Justices Rowell and Robertson, seventy and sixty-eight when appointed, were markedly older than all the other new appointments after 1930. Robertson was significantly older than all his judges when he retired at eighty-three in 1952, and he would be the court's last-ever octogenarian. When retirement at seventy-five became mandatory in 1961, no member of the Ontario Court of Appeal was obliged to retire immediately.

The Second World War seemed to have little direct impact on the Ontario courts beyond taking away many younger lawyers who went into the forces and some judges who were seconded to war-related work. Justice John Gillanders undertook many wartime labour arbitrations and then became a board chair for the Department of National War Services. When he died at age fifty-one, just after the end of the war, Chief Justice Robertson attributed his death to the way he had overtaxed himself in the service of the country.[11] In 1943, Charles McTague, already busy with wartime labour conciliation boards, took leave from the court to serve as chair of the three-person National War Labour Board. McTague worked closely with Prime Minister King in shaping the wartime labour settlement, and he briefed cabinet meetings regularly. ("McTague's view and mine are very similar … McTague is a real find.")[12] McTague saw himself creating "a sort of labour jurisprudence" through the NWLB, and while King was preparing P.C. 1003, the 1944 order-in-council that guaranteed collective bargaining in key wartime industries, he even contemplated making McTague his minister of labour. But McTague's interests lay elsewhere. He told King in February 1944 that having done war work steadily for four years, he was "fed up" and wanted to return to the bench. In April, however, when he left the NWLB, he also resigned from the Court of Appeal and became president of the Progressive Conservative Party – much to King's disgust.[13] He never again pursued his wartime ambition to see his ideas about labour regulation embedded in the jurisprudence of Ontario. In 1945, McTague, who had practised business law in Windsor before his appointment to the bench, was appointed head of the Ontario Securities Commission, which he thoroughly reorganized before returning to private practice, where he often represented brokers and financial organizations before the commission.[14]

In 1947, the justices of the court (and federally appointed judges in all the provinces) got their first raise in salary since 1920, bringing their salaries up to $13,333 for the chief justice and $12,000 for the judges. In subsequent years, increases were more frequent: in 1951 (to $16,000 and $14,000), 1955 ($18,500 and $16,900), 1963 ($25,000 and $21,000), and 1967 ($30,000 and $28,000). These judicial salaries provided a secure and comfortable living for the judges in the 1930s, when many private practice lawyers faced economic uncertainty along with their clients, but for most the pay remained well below what they could have earned in private practice, particularly when elite lawyers' incomes began to soar amid post-war prosperity. In 1945, judges' pension entitlements were adjusted for length of service and the first pensions for judges' surviving spouses were provided.[15]

The twenty-eight judges appointed between Robertson's appointment in 1938 and Porter's death in 1967 were all men, and nearly all were Ontario-born, with just one born in each of Quebec, New Brunswick, and Nova Scotia. About half were from Toronto and half from smaller places in what was still a rural and small-town province. They were nearly all anglophones. In 1953, Eugène Chevrier became the court's first francophone appointment. In 1965, Bora Laskin became the first Jewish member of the court, and also the first law professor to be appointed.

Most members of the court were mainstream Protestants, and though there were more Catholics than before – six were appointed in this period – politicians were still keeping very careful count of their Catholic appointments. Frank Latchford, the first Catholic on the court, was replaced by Charles McTague, the second. When McTague resigned in 1944, he was replaced by Wilfrid Roach, a Catholic, and when Roach retired in 1965, he was replaced by Gregory Evans, a Catholic. Evans, New Brunswick born and with a successful litigation practice in northern Ontario, rarely appeared in the Court of Appeal and preferred the trial courts, to which he eventually returned as chief justice, and he suspected that being a prominent Catholic litigator was a key reason why he had been offered the Court of Appeal appointment.[16] A second "Catholic" seat was created by the appointment of Eugène Chevrier in 1953, soon after the court was enlarged, and when Chevrier retired in

1956 he was replaced by Arthur LeBel, who was both a Catholic and (at least by name) francophone. In 1960, LeBel was succeeded by Arthur Kelly, a Catholic. At the end of this period, there were still two Catholics, Evans and Kelly, but no longer any francophones.

Like Chief Justices Robertson and Pickup, most of the judges appointed in these years had learned law through apprenticeship and practice. Just nine of the twenty-eight judges appointed between 1938 and 1967 had attended university, and just two had degrees from academic law schools: Keiller MacKay an LLB from Dalhousie University in Halifax, and Bora Laskin an LLM from Harvard. Twenty-seven of the twenty-eight (Keiller MacKay being the exception) had qualified to practise law in Ontario, where articling and attending lectures and passing exams at the Osgoode Hall law school run by the Law Society remained the only route into legal practice until 1957. These judges had spent an average of twenty-six years in practice before their first judicial appointment. About half had practised in Toronto, half in other Ontario centres. Thirteen of the twenty-eight had been Ontario High Court judges before being appointed to the Court of Appeal, the other fifteen being appointed directly from practice. Though their average age on appointment was just fifty-six, their tenure on the appeal bench averaged just ten years, due to early deaths (eleven), early retirements (nine), appointments to the Supreme Court of Canada or as chief justices of the High Court (five), and resignations (three). Before mandatory retirement, only two (Robertson and Hogg) sat beyond the age of seventy-five, though seven of the later appointments in this period would stay on until mandatory retirement or very close to it.

One judge who was appointed in 1954 never sat on the Court of Appeal. That year Justice Minister Stuart Garson offered a Court of Appeal appointment to John J. Robinette, then rapidly establishing his long pre-eminence among Canadian courtroom lawyers. Robinette accepted, and then almost immediately regretted his decision. By the time he informed the minister that he wanted to decline the appointment, it had been formally gazetted: he was a member of the Court of Appeal. Robinette was obliged to submit a formal resignation from the bench without ever having sat, and then to seek readmission to practice and reappointment as a bencher as well. Thereafter, Robinette declined all offers of judicial appointments, and he continued to practise in the Court of Appeal and many other courts into the 1990s. Walter Schroeder of the High Court took the appointment vacated by Robinette.[17]

For a time, the replacement of the ancient pre-war judges by newer, younger men may have made the bench led by Robertson a less irascible court than the 1930s had seen. The chief justices, particularly Robertson and Porter, valued calm and reason and were habitually polite in court. But the court remained brusque, confident of its jurisprudence, sceptical about new ideas and approaches, and not known for its sensitivity to the feelings of counsel. W.J. Anderson, who began appearing at the court in 1945 as a young lawyer, did not find Robertson's Court of Appeal a calm or polite venue:

The court of appeal in that period was the abode of ogres, man-eating trolls, and their diet of choice was counsel, preferably young counsel. It was not that I had led a particularly sheltered life. Indeed I had just come from something upwards of four years in the army where peremptory conduct and direct and abrupt language were commonplace. But I had no inkling that lawyers were subjected to that sort of treatment.[18]

Anderson's particular bête noire was Justice William Thomas Henderson, a member of the court from 1935 to his death in 1953, whom other lawyers also identified as a difficult and confrontational judge. One particular target of judicial baiting from anti-Semitic judges was Charles Dubin, a fast-rising young Jewish lawyer whom some of the judges insisted on calling "Mr Doobin" or "Mr Duboon." Dubin's ability to persevere despite such taunts was another sign of the brilliant career he would have as an appellate counsel, appellate judge, and chief justice of Ontario. But the name calling was not restricted to anti-Semitic jibes. Prominent and combative appeal counsel Walter Williston, the son of an Anglican missionary, found himself being addressed as "Wilkinson" or "Wilberforce" by judges with whom he clashed. The culture of the court was brusque and aggressive with everyone, hostile to most kinds of innovation, and equally provoked by weak lawyers and confrontational ones.

Robertson seems to have dominated his court's jurisprudence in the 1940s and early 1950s. He wrote many of its important decisions and was the most prolific writer of judgments for most of his term. Pickup also delivered many judgments during his much shorter time on the court, but several observers felt that, after Robertson, intellectual leadership at the court was passing to Robert Laidlaw, who sat from 1943 to 1963. After Laidlaw, the dominating personalities of the court, and also its most intimidating members, were John Aylesworth (1944–72) and Walter F. Schroeder (1955–75). Both were highly productive judges who knew vast amounts of law and could assess arguments and reach conclusions very rapidly. They were quick to dismiss lawyers and submissions that did not interest them and, if another member of a panel insisted on hearing out the argument, either of them might turn his chair away or even begin reading a newspaper.[19] "Some defence counsel thought the judges like Aylesworth and Schroeder were pro-Crown. It was my view that they were equally rude to everybody," recalled Archie Campbell. "You would be interrupted, scorn would be heaped upon you ... it was rough. You would just have to stand there and take it and do your best to get your point across. But it was a great learning experience."[20]

John Brooke, who argued cases before these judges and later sat with them and their contemporaries, saw Aylesworth and Schroeder as judges who knew vast amount of case law and were simply bored by unpersuasive arguments that were not going to affect their decisions. Brooke was initially puzzled by the fact that Aylesworth always carried a thinner sheaf of papers into court than the other judges did, but he learned that Aylesworth simply threw away all the pages he found uninteresting. Brooke said,

John Aylesworth ... had one of the most incisive minds I have ever encountered. He could just go straight to the core of the case in minutes, seconds. If there was a point in the case, he would just zero right in on it: bang. And when the lawyer stood up and started to talk, he would say, "Mr. Smith, there is only one point in this case and it is this one, talk about that." If the fellow couldn't talk about it, he would say, "Thanks, case dismissed."[21]

Brooke, a very successful and adaptable advocate, felt "it was the fellow who would try to spook them, who would get in there and repeat himself half a dozen times" that would run into trouble with these judges. Others acknowledged the skills of both Aylesworth and Schroeder, but argued that they stayed too long and became affected with what W.T. Anderson called "judgitis: boredom, fatigue, impatience, indifference, laziness, arrogance, bad manners."[22]

Soon after his appointment to the Court of Appeal in 1957, Ken Morden is reported to have called the Court of Appeal "not really a full time job," one that left a good deal of spare time.[23] Morden died in 1961, but Brooke, who was appointed in 1969, agreed, recalling they were often "finished by noon" in his early years, though he acknowledged that the pace increased and soon came to involve a great deal of night work preparing for the cases to be argued the following day. In the 1940s, half of all the court's reported cases in our sample for that decade were decided within a month of being argued. That pace slowed in the following decades, but in any event, relatively few cases were reserved for written opinions. Brooke estimated, "That crowd didn't write a lot of judgments ... We disposed of ninety per cent of our work right from the bench."

The move to three-judge panels initiated by Chief Justice Mulock in 1931 took firm hold during Robertson's tenure. The chief justice always had the option to strike a panel of five judges, but in the 1940s no less than 97 per cent of panels in our sample of recorded decisions had three judges. In the 1950s, the number of five-judge panels – by then reserved for constitutional cases or others of particular significance, or when the court was considering a review of one of its own earlier decisions – rose to 16 per cent of our sample, but in the 1960s, it fell back to 6 per cent. The degree of unanimity in panels was always more than 80 per cent of sampled cases, reaching 94 per cent in the 1950s. Justice Henderson, not much more respectful of fellow judges than of counsel, was the most active dissenter in the 1940s, dissenting in 6 per cent of cases sampled from that decade. In the 1950s, he was succeeded by Robert Laidlaw at 5 per cent. In the 1960s, Bora Laskin, though he was not appointed to the court until 1965, would quickly became that decade's most active dissenter, being in the minority in 6 per cent of cases sampled from 1961 to 1970, and in 17 per cent of all his cases at the court.[24]

As there had been for decades, there continued to be annual meetings of the superior court judges – the appeal judges and the High Court trial judges together – with a mandate to consider and recommend possible changes in legislation concerning the administration of justice, but little seems to have been recorded or preserved about what they discussed. In 1960, Donald Morand of the trial court recalled a meeting that happened to be presided over by Chief Justice McRuer of the trial court, not by Chief Justice Porter. Morand, a new and youthful appointment with some regrets about having giving up a well-paying law practice for a judge's salary of $16,900, spoke up to suggest that "since everyone has been complaining about their lousy salary all year, why don't they demand a raise from the Minister of Justice?" Justice Laidlaw of the Court of Appeal instantly denounced the idea as "unheard of." Aylesworth and Schroeder declared it would be "beneath their dignity" to ask for a raise. "Of course they both had money in the family," Morand recalled many years later, by which time judges were actually litigating over salaries and benefits. Morand swiftly withdrew his proposal, but he credited McRuer for securing the substantial raise that the judges received not long afterwards, and by 1967 judges received $32,500.[25]

In this period, each adjustment to judges' salaries and benefits required an amendment to the federal *Judges Act*, and judicial salaries remained substantially below what successful lawyers could expected in private practice. It would not be until 1974 that salaries were indexed to inflation. In 1975, judges for the first time were obliged to contribute to their own pensions – provoking one of the first lawsuits by a judge over benefits.[26]

Jurisprudential Trends, 1938–67

Despite the few direct changes it wrought on the court, the Second World War years saw the consolidation of longer-term transformations in Canada that did not spare the court system. A new post-Holocaust understanding of human rights and equality, as expressed in the 1948 United Nations Universal Declaration of Human Rights, gradually began to challenge both the traditional common law understanding of rights that underpinned much jurisprudence, and the presumption that the judicial bench should always be white, male, and mostly Protestant. At the same time, wartime growth led to bigger corporations and industrial projects, to more complicated finance and securities regimes, a vastly more complex tax system, and substantial growth in state administration generally. Wartime and post-war labour settlements, which included collective bargaining, the right to strike, and the closed shop, produced a new set of legal rights to be contested and adjudicated. Regulation increased, and with it a blossoming of regulatory bodies with quasi-judicial powers.

In response to these changes, the upper echelons of the legal profession, once mostly composed of general practitioners, began to be typified by legal specialists: tax lawyers, corporate finance specialists, labour lawyers on both the corporate and the labour side. By mid-century, virtually all new Canadian lawyers were coming into the profession not through apprenticeship but through universities and academic law schools. In the post-war years, the law schools grew rapidly in number and size, and in the scope of their legal scholarship, and they began to produce arguments for a more expansive jurisprudence, less bound to black-letter precedents.

In the 1950s and 1960s, the Ontario Court of Appeal was generally sceptical about many of the social changes taking place in Ontario and

Canada. It was equally resistant to the changes in law and jurisprudence associated with them. Its judges had largely been drawn from
the pre-war generalist bar, and their education had mostly been within
the legal craft. Schooled in the older common law understanding of
property, labour, and civil rights, they had learned established procedures and precedents and how to apply them successfully in court,
relying on time-honoured understandings about the nature of the common law and the relationship between courts, legislatures, and administrative agencies.

The Court and Human Rights Law

Post-war ideas of universal human rights came to the Court of Appeal
almost before the war was over. Previously, the English common law
tradition had determined rights to be rooted, not in the European tradition of human or natural rights, but in the "rights of Englishmen,"
principally associated with parliamentary representation, on one hand,
and property rights on the other. From the 1930s to the 1950s, judges of
the Supreme Court of Canada had developed what has been called the
"implied bill of rights," finding that freedom of speech and belief, and
protection from arbitrary state action, were essential to parliamentary
government as guaranteed in the *British North America Act, 1867*, and
therefore had constitutional protection derived from the ancient common law traditions of England.[27] This was not, however, a theory much
taken up at the Ontario Court of Appeal.

·In 1945, J. Keiller MacKay, then a High Court judge (he joined the
Court of Appeal in 1950), engaged with a more expansive theory of
rights in *Re Drummond Wren*, when Wren, the Toronto-based secretary
general of the Workers' Educational Association, sought a declaration that a restrictive covenant prohibiting the association from selling
a property it owned to "Jews or persons of objectionable nationality"
was void. MacKay specifically invoked the human rights commitments
of the new United Nations Charter, to which Canada was a signatory,
in finding the covenant contrary to an emerging public policy against
racial and religious discrimination, and therefore void.[28]

There was no opposing party in the *Drummond Wren* application,
and there was no appeal. The result was praised in the legislature and
the media. In 1948, however, the Court of Appeal took up another restrictive covenant case, *Noble and Wolf v Alley*, in which a vendor and
a buyer who wished to nullify a restrictive covenant on a Lake Huron

cottage were opposed by the other cottagers.[29] The covenant forbade selling or renting to "any person wholly or partly of Negro, Asiatic, coloured or Semitic blood" or to anyone less than four generations removed from southern and eastern European ancestors. *Noble and Wolf v Alley* was vigorously argued in both the High Court and the Court of Appeal by leading counsel for both sides. A unanimous five-judge panel led by Chief Justice Robertson sustained the judgment of the trial court judge, Walter Schroeder (who would join the Court of Appeal in 1955), who had found that the paramount public policy issue was not discrimination but the traditional ones of freedom of contract and freedom of choice. Indeed, the judges of appeal seemed hard pressed even to imagine what Noble and Wolf's grievance was. Justice Henderson found the *Drummond Wren* decision "wrong in law" and could "think of no reason" why people who exercised "a choice with respect to their friends and neighbours" could be infringing on anyone's rights. Chief Justice Robertson declared that the determination of the residents to enjoy a pleasant holiday at the beach by ensuring "a class who will get along well together" was "an innocent and modest effort." To conclude that it "offends against some public policy requires a stronger imagination than I possess," he wrote.[30]

On appeal to the Supreme Court of Canada, the restrictive covenant was overturned, but on narrow technical grounds, without any affirmation of MacKay's ruling against discrimination.[31] The Ontario decisions, however, produced demands for legislation on human rights. The distance between the courts and public sentiment was suggested in 1950, when the Ontario legislature's *Conveyancing and Law of Property Act* was amended to make void any covenant for exclusions based on "race, creed, colour, nationality, ancestry, or place of origin." In 1953, the United Nations Universal Declaration of Human Rights was endorsed in Ontario legislation and racial discrimination declared "contrary to public policy in Ontario."[32]

A few years later, the court sustained its traditional view of rights even against the legislative directive provided by the Canadian Bill of Rights passed by the Diefenbaker government in 1961.[33] The Bill of Rights declared that

every law of Canada shall, unless it is expressly declared by an Act of the Parliament of Canada that it shall operate notwithstanding the Canadian Bill of Rights, be so construed and applied as not to abrogate, abridge or infringe or to authorize the abrogation, abridgment or infringement of any of the rights or freedoms herein recognized and declared ...

But Canadian courts, and particularly the Court of Appeal for Ontario, could not be persuaded to apply the Bill of Rights. Until its thinking began to change in the 1970s, the court "went to much greater lengths, and showed considerably more creativity [than the Supreme Court of Canada], in its efforts to avoid application" of the Bill of Rights. It consistently sought "to avoid, narrow, and undermine" any application of the Bill of Rights, dismissed its applicability, and rebuked trial judges who did apply it. In *Sharpe*, it found that the right to a fair hearing established in the Bill of Rights did not conflict with the reverse onus clause then existing in the *Narcotics Act*, but declared that even if there was a conflict, the Bill of Rights could not invalidate the *Narcotics Act*.[34] In *O'Connor*, the court found that despite the Bill of Rights, the only issue with regard to admissibility of evidence was whether the evidence was relevant to the issue being tried – no matter how it had been obtained.[35] Even after the Supreme Court had applied a relatively broad interpretation of the Bill of Rights in the *Drybones* case, the Court of Appeal found in *Nevin* that a denial of trial by jury did not offend against the Bill of Rights' guarantee of due process of law.[36] Directly confronting the Bill's claim to be an interpretative statute governing other statutes unless they were specifically exempted from its sway, the court found the Bill of Rights to be "simply another statute" that could not affect the "settled canon of statutory interpretation." While the Supreme Court of Canada generally accepted that the Bill of Rights empowered the courts to strike down statutes inconsistent with it (though in practice it rarely did), the Ontario court vigorously resisted that conclusion, seeking to "freeze" rights to what rights had existed when a particular statute had been passed.[37] The judicial marginalization of the Bill of Rights exemplified by the Ontario court's decisions of the 1960s and 1970s would help strengthen the conviction of rights campaigners that the common law and the courts could not defend civil rights adequately and that a constitutionally entrenched charter of rights would be required.

The Court and the Regulatory State

Canadian courts had long had an ambiguous relationship with the regulatory state and the rising power of state boards and tribunals. Lawyers and judges frequently expressed concern about the encroachment of state agencies on the territory of courts, and about the danger that commissions and tribunals were making quasi-judicial decisions without the procedural guarantees and concern for the rights of individuals that the courts were expected to provide. In 1934, Chief Justice Mulock had warned about

... the ever-increasing practice of the Parliament of Canada and of our Provincial Legislature depriving our people of the protection of the law and of the courts, by vesting in autocratic bodies the power to arbitrarily deal with matters affecting our liberties and other rights without the intervention of any court. Let this invasion of the people's rights continue and the ultimate result must be despotism.[38]

Such views of the dangers of state despotism were frequently expressed by judges and lawyers in response to the rise of the regulatory state and its agencies, even before the peak of anticommunist fervour in the 1950s gave them new images of state tyranny to invoke.[39]

Nevertheless, judges of appeal had been active participants in sustaining the powers of tribunals in Ontario, or even in expanding them, as when Chief Justice Meredith laid the blueprint for the *Workmen's Compensation Act* of 1913, explicitly designed to take disputes between workers and employees out of the courts to be handled by an expert, and presumably impartial, tribunal.[40] Furthermore, despite the judges' expressions of concern, the court's deference to the legislature frequently led it to sustain the authority of boards empowered by provincial statute, even ones that denied judicial safeguards. In the nineteenth century, the court of appeal had rarely interfered with assessors' judgments in expropriations for highways, railroads, or public works, even while asserting its authority to do so. Upon the inauguration of workmen's compensation boards, the court largely vacated the field of workplace liability, which had been a constant source of appeals before 1913. In 1934, the year of Mulock's speech, Justices Middleton, Masten, and Davis had rejected the argument that the provincially established Board of Examiners in Optometry was appropriating powers reserved to federally appointed superior courts when it disciplined optometrists for misconduct. The court found unanimously that the board was entirely within its powers, indeed was exercising powers the court did not possess.[41]

Similarly, the Ontario Securities Commission, established by the province in 1928 and given very broad powers over the activities of securities dealers and brokers in the 1930s, rarely found its decisions being overturned by the post-war Court of Appeal. The Securities Commission was authorized to "examine any person, company, property, or thing whatsoever at any time," without being bound by common law rules of evidence. It could summon witnesses and compel evidence, override all claims of privilege, and use the evidence it obtained by these means in any subsequent proceedings, even notwithstanding the *Evidence Act*, and the commission chair could sit on panels reviewing his own decisions.[42]

A vital factor for the court was that a right of appeal to the courts was provided. With that principle respected by the statute, the Court of Appeal found very few cases in which interference with the commission's work was required. In an important trilogy of cases in 1946–7, Chief Justice Robertson acknowledged that the commission's powers were very broad and its rules of procedure very fluid, but he found such authority essential to the commission's task of protecting the public interest.[43] The court consistently upheld the authority of the commission, declaring that its activities were administrative rather than judicial and therefore within provincial powers and largely exempt from judicial review. All three cases in 1946–7 were appeals by brokers against the arbitrary powers applied by the commission in investigating them and cancelling their brokers' licences. "No doubt there are principles of natural justice that should be observed in proceedings under the *Securities Act*," Robertson found in *Re The Securities Act and Morton*, but he required no procedural safeguards other than the very limited ones given by the act, because "a registered broker has no vested interest that is to be weighed in the balance against the public interest."[44] Because of the vital importance of the smooth functioning of securities markets, Robertson found, the courts "should not interfere with its exercise of the powers and discretion that the statute had vested in them." The finding that the commission was "administrative" and not "judicial," consistently upheld by the court, was key to the determination that the courts should defend and defer to the tribunal's authority, despite the often expressed concern that such agencies were threatening the rule of law and the traditional functions of courts.

In 1959 and 1961, the Court of Appeal again considered appellants' claims that the Securities Commission's powers "had the effect of limiting or indeed destroying certain fundamental freedoms" – and the court rejected the argument again, declaring that the *Securities Act* was in place to protect the public, that far-reaching investigatory powers were essential to secure that goal, and also that the new Canadian Bill of Rights did not cover provincial legislation and was therefore inapplicable.[45]

Even in labour law, where the court was strongly committed to private property rights as a fundamental aspect of the common law, the court's resistance to administrative tribunals was muted. Many judges served as arbitrators (until their right to do so was removed in 1963), and the Court of Appeal in this period generally upheld the authority of conciliation boards and arbitration boards mandated by 1944's P.C. 1003 and its post-war adoption in provincial labour law. In 1958 in *Polymer*, the court sustained a trial court decision that an arbitrator could impose penalties upon parties to a collective agreement, even if such powers were not specified in the agreement itself.[46] In 1962, in *CPR v Zambri*, the court confirmed that the right to strike did exist, and employers could not circumvent it by dismissing workers when they went on strike,[47] but almost simultaneously, in *Hersees of Woodstock v Goldstein*, it closely circumscribed the right to strike by finding secondary picketing to be a common law tort, a decision that was not appealed.[48] The *Hersees* decision became widely followed across Canada.

The Court and Criminal Law

One area where the Court of Appeal of this era displayed some creativity was in criminal law, and that was perhaps due to lawyers more than judges. A broad right of appeal in criminal law had been established only in the 1920s, but no substantial criminal defence bar sprang rapidly into being, because without legal aid, there were few clients who could afford legal counsel. W.B. "Bill" Common, who prosecuted thousands of cases as a counsel in Ontario's department of the Attorney General from the 1920s into the 1960s, recalled routinely facing "so-called criminal counsel" who knew little about the tactics of defence and even less about the criminal code, and relied mostly on pleas for sympathy from juries and leniency from judges. Sometimes Common had cases in which "there would be nobody on the other side, and I would have to carry the Crown side and the defence side."[49] Occasionally, even the Crown felt an appeal was required – and the Attorney General would fund both sides. Coming into practice in that environment, Arthur Martin described criminal defence in his youth as "a very uncertain type of practice. And generally speaking, only a very few people engaged in it. Of course, only a very few people made their living in it."[50]

Martin brought to criminal defence a genuine passion for criminal law and for redressing its unfairness, as well as a monkish indifference to making a good living. He avoided representing anyone on criminal charges more than once, to avoid seeming dependent on, or too closely allied to, career criminals. A brilliant and largely self-taught scholar of the Criminal Code, he began bringing to the Court of Appeal criminal cases that raised arguments about due process, procedural fairness, the rights of the accused, and errors by prosecutors or by judges in their charges to juries, all matters that were rarely explored by most criminal defence lawyers of his time.

It took no great conceptual leap – or any softness on crime – for the Court of Appeal judges to see merit in the kinds of arguments Martin was making. They were arguments that resonated with the justices: focused, specific, rooted in common law principles and procedures, and hewing closely to the specifics of the Criminal Code – of which Martin had an encyclopedic knowledge. Criminal appeals based on judicial or prosecutorial error also reinforced the authority of the Court of Appeal over the trial courts and particularly over the magistrates' courts, where criminal cases were heard and adjudicated by lay magistrates whose legal knowledge and standing were not much respected by appellate lawyers and appellate judges.

Martin was the most prominent, but hardly the only, lawyer engaged in improving criminal law practice in the 1940s and 1950s. John Robinette did a good deal of criminal defence work early in his career, and Charles Dubin continued to do so, as did Roy McMurtry Sr. Indeed, given the extent to which the campaign of Martin and others to raise the standard of criminal defence practice concurred with the self-image of the Court of Appeal as an institution that treated criminal law and other matters of law in the same way, what may be most surprising is that it took from the opening of criminal appeals in 1923 until the 1930s for a G. Arthur Martin to appear.

In retrospect, the post-war years looked like a golden era for litigation in Ontario. The cost and complexity of litigation had not yet become prohibitive, and many skilled and colourful litigators came to prominence. During the 1940s, the busiest appeal counsel (at least in our sample of recorded cases) was John R. Cartwright, a future chief justice of Canada, but D. Lally McCarthy and Shirley Denison (both Law Society treasurers in the 1940s) were frequently in the Court of Appeal as well. Bill Common, the senior Crown prosecutor, was among the leading appeal counsel, and Arthur Martin's criminal defence practice also put him in the top ten of our sample, though he was only called to the bar in 1940. By the 1950s, John Robinette was dominant, though such future judges as Charles Dubin and John Arnup were also among leading appeal counsel, as were well-known Toronto counsel Walter Williston, Barry Pepper, and Andrew Brewin, and Crown prosecutor

Table 4.1 Statistical Notes on 28 Judges of Appeal Appointed 1938–67

Birthplace

Toronto	3
Ottawa	4
Other Ontario centres	18
Nova Scotia	1
New Brunswick	1
Quebec	1

Ethnic Origin

Anglophone/British	26
Francophone	1
Jewish	1

Religious Affiliation

Presbyterian	6
Roman Catholic	6
United Church	5
Church of England	4
Protestant, unspecified	4
Baptist	1
Jewish	1
Lutheran	1

Education

Non-law academic degrees	9
University law degrees	2*
Osgoode Hall Law School	27†

Average Years of Law Practice before Judicial Appointment

26 years

Location of Legal Practice (some in more than one place)

Toronto	14‡
Hamilton	3
Ottawa	4
London	2
Windsor	3
Owen Sound	1
Perth	1
Sarnia	1

Table 4.1 (*Continued*)

Stratford   1
Timmins   1

Identified Political Commitment

Liberal   8
Conservative   5
None/no data   15

Judicial Appointment prior to Court of Appeal Appointment

Yes   13   (Ontario High Court of Justice)
No   15

Age at Court of Appeal Appointment

Average 56 years

In their 40s   5
In their 50s   14
In their 60s   9

Minimum: 43   (Gillanders)
Maximum: 68   (Robertson)

Average Years on Court of Appeal Bench

10 years

Median 8.5 years.
Aylesworth at 26 years served the longest.
Greene (died) and McRuer (moved courts) at one year had the shortest terms.

Reason for Leaving Court of Appeal

A judge who left before age 65 or to take a non-judicial position is counted as resigned, not retired.

Died   11
Resigned   3[§]
Retired (65 or older)   9
Moved to another court   5[¶]

Age on Leaving

Average   66.2 years

Table 4.1 (*Concluded*)

Median   66.5 years

Minimum: 51   (Gillanders, died; Kellock, moved to SCC)
Maximum: 82   (Robertson, retired)

Two (Robertson and Hogg) sat beyond the age of 75 in the pre-mandatory retirement era.
Seven retired at or near age 75 after mandatory retirement was established in 1961: Roach and Gibson in 1965, followed by Aylesworth, F.G. MacKay, McGillivray, Schroeder, and Kelly.

---

* Keiller MacKay, LLB from Dalhousie Law; Laskin, LLM from Harvard Law.
† All but Keiller MacKay.
‡ Including Laskin, who taught at Osgoode Hall and U of T law schools.
§ LeBel, McTague, J.K. MacKay.
¶ Kellock and Laskin to SCC; McRuer, Kelly, and Wells to CJ HCJ.

Bill Common. In the 1960s, Bert MacKinnon and Douglas Laidlaw, son of Court of Appeal judge Robert Laidlaw, joined their ranks. But as the size of the bar grew, the proportion of all appeal cases handled by the top ten appeal lawyers continued to fall, holding in the 60-per-cent range in the 1940s and 1950s but falling to a still substantial 40 per cent in the 1960s.

Despite the strengths of the bar and the bench, the Ontario Court of Appeal reached the nadir of its reputation during the post-war period. The dismissive complacency experienced by Elizabeth Bethune Campbell in the 1920s had hardened into a positive resistance to change. The court seemed determined to rein in wherever possible new openings in law, whether it was a large legislative initiative such as the Bill of Rights or simply a creative legal argument by a young lawyer with a foreign name. It was more tolerant of familiar matters, even small ones. John Arnup recalled a typical scene in court in the 1950s: two lawyers and friends, R.M.W. Chitty and A.A. MacDonald – "and every month, practically, you would see [them] in the Court of Appeal" – arguing amicably over some very minor matter, "some county court case as a rule, sometimes even a Division Court case, which went to the full court of three judges if it was appealable at all, and it was appealable if there was more than $100 involved."

5

Renewal: the Gale-Estey-Howland Courts, 1967–90

For John Arnup, it was "the strongest appellate court in Canada."[1] Bertha Wilson declared it was "at that time the finest court in the country." Bud Estey, with his flair for vivid expression, said it was "the best single court in the western world."[2] The speakers were hardly dispassionate, certainly, for they had all been members of the court they praised so highly. But more than team spirit was at work here. These much-admired jurists were speaking not of the Court of Appeal for Ontario throughout its history, but making a claim about that court at a specific moment. Beginning about 1970, they argued, the court became something it had not been before. Instead of being generally perceived as "uncreative, precedent-bound, even reactionary,"[3] the Court of Appeal for Ontario had become a respected judicial institution whose judges and judgments commanded national attention and were steering Canadian jurisprudence in new directions. This transformation of the court may be epitomized by the roles played in the history of the appeal court during the late 1960s and the 1970s by three individuals: Bora Laskin, Roy McMurtry, and George "Bill" Gale.

Bill Gale: The Chief Justice as Leader and Recruiter, 1967–76

The new chief justice – christened George, but always known as Bill – had not initially been an insider in the Ontario judicial establishment. He was born in Quebec City in 1906, the son of a businessman who moved the family to British Columbia and eventually became mayor of Vancouver. Gale, a precocious student, formed an early ambition to be a lawyer and chose the University of Toronto and Osgoode Hall law school. He remained in Toronto after his call to the bar in 1932, practising initially in business law but rapidly shifting to civil litigation. Successful almost from the start, Gale became a trusted protégé of prominent and influential lawyers and judges. He appeared regularly before the Court of Appeal. In 1941 he represented the "junior bar" on a blue-ribbon committee to revise the Ontario rules of practice, and he would remain a member of the rules committee and chief editor of its rules compilation, *Holmestead and Gale*, until his retirement as chief justice of Ontario in 1976.

In 1946, aged just forty, Gale was appointed to the High Court, principally at the urging of future Chief Justice of Canada J.R. Cartwright, a confidant of Justice Minister Louis St-Laurent. After nearly twenty years there, and a brief six-month stint on the Court of Appeal, he succeeded James McRuer as chief justice of the High Court in 1964. There he presided over the *Texas Gulf* case, which pitted John Robinette against John Arnup in what was then the longest civil trial in Canadian legal history, described by Bertha Wilson as "Ontario's two most outstanding counsel facing off against each other under the keen and critical eye of its most outstanding judge."[4]

In 1967, the new Liberal government named Gale chief justice of Ontario, the first since William Mulock to come into the job with extensive experience on the bench. Despite the resentment of John Aylesworth, who believed that Gale had been part of a plot to keep him from the position,[5] he established himself as a strong leader – though he and Aylesworth never sat on a panel together during the five years they were both on the court. John Brooke, one of the first appointed to the court during his tenure, spoke of "the Gale force" and described how Gale was always in touch with his judges – and always aware when a judge was unprepared.[6] William Howland remembered Gale administering in "a very tight manner" and his sitting schedules as "stringent"; on one occasion, Howland found himself assigned to sit seven weeks in a row rather than the usual two. For Willard Estey, who succeeded him, Gale's ability to mix judicial and administrative skill was remarkable. "He could sit and preside and write brilliant judgments, and before he walked into the courtroom and as soon as he got out, he would be running the administration."[7]

Despite Estey's praise, Gale's leadership may have been more administrative than jurisprudential. He never ranked among the appeal court's most prolific writers of decisions. Indeed, an interview he gave after his retirement suggests a rather unreflective personality, focused more on results and outcomes than on any profound jurisprudential philosophy. He recalled, for instance, how as a trial judge he had sentenced the last two men executed in Canada, but he offered no reflection on capital punishment, merely noting that "the press got very wound up about it." Nor was he particularly progressive in other aspects of judicial proceedings. He had no time for supernumerary status, for bilingual courts, or for sabbatical leaves, and he had strong views about courtroom decorum. In 1974, discovering a television crew filming in "the dignified upper rotunda" of Osgoode Hall, Gale "asked the film crew to leave the building because [he] was satisfied that their operations constituted an interference with the administration of justice." Others recalled his intervention as being much stronger than a mere request; Gale believed, it was said, that "anyone who brought a camera to a courtroom should be put in jail."[8]

Gale's long judicial experience and insider role had familiarized him with the workings of court administration and judicial appointments, and he knew from the first what levers to pull. He had clear, strong views on what the courts needed and the personal, political, and administrative skills to get what, and particularly who, he wanted for his court. In 1974, Gale saw the court expanded in numbers for the first time since 1949. Against the inclinations of some of his judges, who were comfortable with the ten-judge court, the court expanded in a single step from ten judges (including the chief justice) to fourteen. William Howland, Lloyd Houlden, Bert MacKinnon, and Maurice Lacourcière were appointed simultaneously.[9]

Soon thereafter, Gale secured a fifteenth position. In 1976 the Attorney General's department proposed a substantial reform in courts administration, one that promised the judges great autonomy in running their courts. Gale declared that the added administrative burden would require an associate chief justice in each of the Ontario courts. The reform proposals were eventually abandoned, but Ontario did establish the associate chief justice positions in 1977, just after Gale retired, and Ottawa appointed Justice Bert MacKinnon as the court's first associate chief justice in May 1978. Chief Justice Howland told a meeting of the judges that the ACJO's role was "still to be defined," but would probably include management of the lists (that is, assignment of judges to the appeal panels) and leading the rules committee, as well as relieving other judges from administrative responsibilities. Still, he expected MacKinnon to maintain a full schedule of court sittings. There was some discussion at the time whether an ACJO could expect to succeed the chief justice, and whether the position should be term limited. In the event, neither proposal became an established rule. MacKinnon died in 1987, before Howland retired.[10]

In 1972 a federal-provincial agreement allowed superior court judges to elect supernumerary status, which permits a judge with sufficient seniority to vacate his or her position and be replaced by a newly appointed judge, but to continue to sit part time until opting to retire fully or reaching mandatory retirement. Gale initially thought his judges should either sit full time or retire, but in 1973 George McGillivray, then seventy-three and a member of the court since 1957, became the court's first supernumerary justice. In the early 1970s, mandatory retirement removed several older judges (John Aylesworth and Frederick MacKay in 1972, Walter Schroeder and Arthur Kelly in 1975). Others went supernumerary, and Bora Laskin left for the Supreme Court of Canada in 1970. These departures, combined with the five new positions, gave Gale substantial room to reconstitute his court, and he took eagerly to recruiting.

With the court's workload growing in the 1970s, Gale applied his intimate knowledge of the Ontario bar and his solid reputation among its leading practitioners to recruit the best potential judges to his court. As its size expanded he also wanted balance: the best commercial lawyer, the best advocate, the best civil and criminal specialists. John Arnup, then at the peak of his litigation career, recalled Gale's efforts to recruit him to the court with the argument, "If I can get you, I can get anybody." Within a few years, Gale "got" not only Arnup, but also Charles Dubin, the other leading advocate (Robinette being unpersuadable); Arthur Martin, the best criminal lawyer; Lloyd Houlden, a leading commercial lawyer; and the lawyer's lawyer Bertha Wilson, as well as Willard "Bud" Estey, Bert MacKinnon, William Howland, Maurice Lacourcière and others. This was a group that included three Law Society treasurers and three Osgoode gold medallists. Some came from the High Court but several, including Arnup, Dubin, Estey, MacKinnon, and Wilson, came directly from practice. "Gale really chose leaders of the bar, and it improved the reputation of the court. The judges were not all like that before that time," recalled Sydney Robins, another litigation leader soon appointed to the court. "Those direct appoints transformed the court," said Justice John Laskin, then a young litigator. Within a few years, the court gained a reputation for recruiting from among the best, not merely the best-connected, lawyers in Ontario. In

Robins's view, Gale could be "a tough judge," but as a group the new judges, having been so roughly treated by the court when practising before it, resolved to bring more decorum to court proceedings – and largely did.[11]

Both at the High Court and the Court of Appeal, Gale used the chief justice's prerogative of vetting and suggesting potential judicial appointments; he would "do a bit of sleuthing," consulting lawyers and judges about potential appointees, and then urge his suggestions on the politicians.[12] But a chief justice can only suggest appointments. Gale had the good fortune to be supported by changes to the federal judicial appointment process. The federal Ministry of Justice, led by Pierre Trudeau and then John Turner, had developed a new activism about judicial appointments, and the Landreville scandal that led to the forming of the Canadian Judicial Council had strengthened demands for politics and patronage to be removed from judicial appointments. From 1967, the minister of justice began consulting on appointments with a committee of the Canadian Bar Association. In 1973, the department retained a special adviser on judicial appointments who was an independent contractor, not part of the department, to consult and gather information on potential judges. In 1988, Ramon Hnatyshyn, justice minister in the Mulroney government, established the Commission of Federal Judicial Appointments and a network of provincial advisory committees. Thereafter, lawyers interested in judicial appointment (though not for transfers from, say, the trial to the appeal court) had to apply to the commission and be evaluated by the committees, though the cabinet still made the final selection.[13]

The new procedures did not remove political considerations from judicial appointment. Still, in developing formal criteria for appointments, consulting the Canadian Bar Association, and eventually requiring would-be judges to formally apply for appointments, the department of justice was pursuing a goal similar to Gale's, that is, to link senior judicial appointments more closely to ability and legal reputation than to political connections. In 1976, Ed Ratushny, the first special adviser on judicial appointments, pointed to the almost simultaneous appointments of Bud Estey, Arthur Martin, and Charles Dubin to the Ontario Court of Appeal in 1973 as evidence of the success of this new process. For Ottawa, if not for Gale, increasing diversity on the bench also became a policy goal. The 1975 decision to appoint Bertha Wilson, the first woman to sit on a Canadian appellate court, came from Ottawa.[14]

Gale had succeeded in getting Ottawa to ratify the selection of judges whom he had sought out and encouraged, and these new judges would thrive in the rapidly changing judicial environment over which he presided. Chief Justice Gale was transformative less for his jurisprudence than for his leadership. Already a veteran of the politics of judicial administration when he became chief justice, Gale was widely credited with securing most of the judges who, during and after his tenure, would revive the reputation of the court, as well as facilitating the beginnings of continuing education and other forms of judicial professional development. Mandatory retirement and the five judgeships added to the court during his term gave him unusual scope to act, but Gale stood out as a judicial leader who left the court staffed with strong judges attuned to the new currents of jurisprudence beginning to sweep through the courts of Canada.

During Gale's tenure as chief justice, Osgoode Hall received extensive renovations. In the 1960s, Gale had been one of the few judges to oppose a plan to build an eleven-storey tower on the west lawns of Osgoode Hall. That plan was cancelled, after some heritage-minded lawyers made an intervention directly to Premier Robarts, and between 1970 and 1973 a much more sensitive renovation of the old building was undertaken. The old courtrooms were restored to their original elegance. Six new courtrooms were added to the north of the nineteenth-century rotunda, making ten courts in all, and the expansion created twenty new judges' offices for a total of fifty-five. During the renovations, the Court of Appeal, for the first time in its history, moved out of Osgoode Hall into temporary space across the street in a court building at 145 Queen Street that was later demolished to make room for the Four Seasons Centre for the Performing Arts. In 1973, Chief Justice Gale and Law Society treasurer Sydney Robins, who was soon to join the court, welcomed Queen Elizabeth II to Osgoode Hall for the ceremonial reopening of the building.[15] In 1967, meanwhile, the Metropolitan Toronto Courthouse had opened at 361 University Avenue, directly north of Osgoode Hall. It became the principal home of the superior trial courts in Toronto and York County, and Osgoode Hall became more and more – though not exclusively – associated with the Court of Appeal.

For John Arnup, Gale was the best chief justice of his era, a strong judge who built a strong bench, administered the court effectively, strengthened relations with the bar, and enhanced the public image of the judiciary. In 1976, however, after eleven years as chief justice (and thirty as a judge), Gale rather abruptly chose to retire at the age of seventy, though he soon agreed to serve as vice-chair of the Ontario Law Reform Commission and lived another twenty years. His successor was Willard "Bud" Estey, Saskatchewan born, Harvard educated, and the son of Supreme Court of Canada justice James Estey.

Bud Estey, then fifty-seven, was highly regarded by Pierre Trudeau's government, which between 1973 and 1977 gave him four consecutive judicial appointments as well as appointing him to lead a royal commission inquiry. Estey was a member of the Court of Appeal from 1973 to 1975 and then served briefly as chief justice of the High Court in 1975–6 until he was named chief justice of Ontario. During his commercial law practice, Estey had administered some large corporations, and both at the High Court and as chief justice of Ontario, he looked forward to bringing new efficiencies to the Ontario courts. He "sparkled" with ideas, according to a contemporary, but never served long enough in either position to see many of them implemented in the Ontario courts. His term as chief justice of Ontario was particularly brief, though he enjoyed the job and the camaraderie of the judges there. He had been chief justice of Ontario for only nine months when Justice Minister Ron Basford telephoned him late in 1977 about "coming to Ottawa." At first Estey thought he meant for some meeting. When he realized Basford intended to appoint him to the Supreme Court of Canada, he complained that his own recommendations for the appointment were being ignored (who they might have been is unknown), but he felt unable to refuse the call of duty – and the chance to join the court on which his father had previously sat.[16] His appointment – one of only two chief justices of Ontario to go to the Supreme Court – demonstrated that politics had not been extinguished from appointments. Chief Justice Laskin had wanted Dubin, whom Prime Minister Trudeau vetoed as a Conservative, and Trudeau wanted the Toronto lawyer Pierre Genest, whom Laskin vetoed. Estey was their compromise.*

Estey was succeeded as chief justice of Ontario by another member of the court, William Howland, a doctor's son from an old Toronto family that included the lieutenant governor of Ontario who had been Eliza-

---

* Personal communication from John Laskin, 4 March 2013. Dubin had been a Conservative Party supporter, but he also was a common law lawyer who remained dubious about the need or value of entrenched charters of rights. How he might have shaped charter jurisprudence had he been a member of the Supreme Court of Canada after 1982 is impossible to know.

beth Bethune Campbell's stepfather. Like several of his fellow judges, Howland started on the path to a career in law through the undergraduate law program that flourished at the University of Toronto before university law schools began in Ontario in 1957. He was treasurer of the Law Society at the time of his appointment to the Court of Appeal in 1975. He recalled the offer of appointment as chief justice two years later as coming "out of the blue," but was told that his strength as both a judge and an administrative leader had been a factor. Unlike Gale and Porter, Howland sensed no resentment from rival seekers of the appointment among the judges. He suspected that John Arnup, Arthur Martin, and possibly others had been disinclined to accept the position.[17]

Howland was socially and perhaps politically conservative, but he was not adverse to innovations in the court, and he believed that a chief justice should advocate for the courts. Howland expanded the Opening of the Courts ceremony, previously a social event combined with a religious blessing. Picking up an initiative started by Estey, he used the annual opening ceremony as the occasion for a "state of the courts" address that he also published in the Law Society publication *The Gazette*. His declarations during the opening about underfunding and other judicial issues were intended, he said, "to defend openly the interests of the courts," and sometimes provoked official response from the government. He organized a Bench and Bar Council to bring together the province's courts and legal organizations, worked to develop a Courts Advisory Council, and expanded the scope of the annual meeting of Ontario judges, called the Council of Judges. Appointments of strong, respected judges to the court also continued during his term: Donald Thorson, a former federal deputy minister of justice and constitutional expert; John Morden; Peter Cory (later appointed to the Supreme Court of Canada); the legal scholar and rights expert Walter Tarnopolsky; Horace Krever; Marvin Catzman; and others, including the second woman on the court, Hilda McKinlay.

Howland was unusual in coming to the court as a commercial solicitor without experience as a litigator, let alone a judge; some colleagues felt that he remained insecure about being a jurisprudential leader. But as chief justice of a very strong court, he established himself as "chairman of the board," consulting and delegating, and organizing committees of judges. He also dedicated himself to the public role of chief justice, attending public events, giving speeches, and familiarizing the public with the judiciary in a way that would have been unthinkable behaviour from a chief justice not long before. Howland would serve thirteen years as chief justice of Ontario, longer than any except John Beverley Robinson and R.S. Robertson, in a period of rapid change for the courts. Throughout his term he would deal with the administrative and jurisprudential transformations that had begun during Gale's tenure.

The Court Administration Transformation

Roy McMurtry won election to the Ontario legislature in 1975 and was appointed Attorney General by Premier William G. Davis. McMurtry would hold the office for his entire ten-year career in politics, an unusually long tenure for an Attorney General. Throughout the decade 1975–85, Premier Davis gave McMurtry a notable degree of autonomy, and McMurtry used it to implement a wide range of reform measures in Ontario public policy, specifically in the administration of the justice system in the province. The transformation of court administration in the province had begun before McMurtry and continued after him, but McMurtry's years as Attorney General were central to the changes made to the Court of Appeal in particular and the Ontario courts generally.

Throughout the Western world in the post-war era, governments and bureaucracies had begun to examine court administration with an eye to rationalizing, professionalizing, and economizing. By the 1970s, provincial governments across Canada had newly expanded powers and tax bases, and newly professionalized civil services. They were growing concerned that courts had become too large and expensive to be administered in the spare time of a busy chief justice and a small staff with limited expertise and resources. Ontario was no exception to the trend. The civil services of Ontario and other jurisdictions began exploring new administrative processes that promised efficiencies and cost savings in the courts, and they became part of what has been called a revolution in court administration.[18] Court reform was a national and global trend, and would have come to Ontario no matter who was Attorney General. But the activist, reform-oriented ministry that McMurtry led between 1975 and 1985 initiated many projects that would have profound effects on how the Ontario Court of Appeal operated. After a long period with relatively few changes to the structure of the courts, McMurtry's department was building on changes that had started earlier, provoked by the province's Inquiry into Civil Rights, appointed in 1964 and headed by Chief Justice McRuer of the High Court.

New Courts

James Chalmers McRuer's inquiry into civil rights was focused on the threats to individuals posed by the power of expanding bureaucracies, whether they were government departments, police, public agencies, tribunals, or even licensed professions, including the law.[19] His analysis did not spare the courts themselves. In the 1960s, the magistrates' courts of Ontario, described in a 1969 study as "the forgotten child in our system of criminal justice," were still run by municipalities and largely staffed by lay magistrates with limited legal training, even though these were the principal courts for most kinds of criminal trials, including many serious offences.[20] They were often called "police courts," not least because of the strong police influence upon them. McRuer's first report called for the magistrates' courts to be staffed with legal professionals to be known as "judges," not "magistrates," upgraded in status and responsibility, and placed under central provincial authority. Many of these recommendations were incorporated in the legislation that created the Ontario Provincial Court in 1968.[21] Complementing McRuer's recommendations was the 1969 report of the federally established Ouimet Commission on Corrections, appointed in 1965, which argued forcefully for improving the criminal law justice system in the provincial courts. Such studies also helped launch a long debate about whether to integrate the federally appointed superior trial courts and the provincially appointed magistrates' courts – and if so, how.[22]

Another important section of McRuer's inquiry deplored the way in which the rapid development of administrative law in the twentieth century had placed many citizens' rights and interests under the purview of administrative tribunals which, in his view, failed to provide the safeguards and review procedures essential for the prevention of abuses of due process and of individual rights. McRuer's views on administrative law were controversial. Many experts in the rapidly growing field argued that his reliance on courts to defend citizens' rights amounted to turning back the clock, empowering courts in ways that undermined the autonomy of quasi-judicial administrative tribunals. The expansion of administrative tribunals dated back at least to the Workmen's Compensation Board recommended by Chief Justice Meredith in 1912. They had developed their own precedents and expertise in the specialized fields they supervised, and although judges had been worrying about potential abuses for just as long, the Court of Appeal had often tolerated the authority of tribunals (the fields of labour and human rights being exceptions where the court often disagreed with the tribunals).[23]

To his critics, McRuer seemed to be demanding a return to a court-centred version of administrative law in which the specialized knowledge and procedures of the tribunals would once more be eroded by subjection to the common law traditions of the judges. Nevertheless, Ontario passed an elaborate and widely imitated statute on the review of administrative agencies by courts, and in 1971, as one result of McRuer's advice, the Divisional Court was brought back into existence.[24] This new court, like the old Divisional Court abolished in 1913, was part of the High Court, staffed by panels of High Court judges assigned to it by their chief justice. The principal role recommended for the Divisional Court by McRuer would be hearing appeals from administrative tribunals of all kinds, municipal and provincial, though it acquired other appeal functions as well. (After 1984, most appeals involving less than $25,000 in value went to it rather than the Court of Appeal, and the dollar limit would rise over time.) The new Divisional Court was specially mandated to review how boards and agencies were applying principles of justice and individual rights. Its judges were expected to become specialists in administrative law and to relieve the Court of Appeal of some of its responsibility in that area. Decisions of the Divisional Court could be appealed to the Court of Appeal, with leave from that court, but in practice the re-emergence of the Divisional Court meant a transfer of certain appellate responsibilities from the Court of Appeal to the new court.

At almost the same time, and for some of the same reasons, the federal government substantially reorganized the Exchequer Court of Canada, which had been in existence since 1875 as a forum in which disputes with the federal government could be adjudicated. In 1971, the Exchequer Court became the Federal Court of Canada and Federal Appeal Court of Canada. As with the Divisional Court in Ontario, a key role for the Federal Court was judicial review of administrative tribunals, though it also inherited the Exchequer Court's jurisdiction in disputes involving admiralty, intellectual property, tax, and other claims against the federal government. Justice Minister John Turner saluted the Federal Court as "a national court exercising a national jurisdiction," but several aspects of it were controversial.[25] The new administrative law responsibilities being given to courts marked the waning of the old constitutional tradition that control of administrative bodies was principally the duty of governments and legislatures, not courts; it confirmed the substantial (and then controversial) judicialization of administrative law encouraged by McRuer. Furthermore, the Federal Court also suggested to some critics that Ottawa was moving towards "a dual system of courts: one for provincial matters and one for federal matters," instead of the unitary system that had prevailed in Canada since Confederation.[26]

Among those sceptical about the new Federal Court were Chief Justice Gale and other members of Ontario's Court of Appeal. Traditionally, appeals of decisions of federal administrative tribunals had been heard mostly in provincial courts of appeal. Because of Ontario's size and the fact that most federal tribunals were headquartered in Ontario, it was the Ontario appeal court that heard most of these cases. The emergence of the Federal Court challenged the court's pre-eminence in the field, and Gale and other members of the Ontario court suggested that the Federal Court was infringing on the inherent common law jurisdiction of the provincial superior courts. They had to accept the federal fait accompli, however, and their concerns were somewhat assuaged by the steady growth of the Court of Appeal's own workload, and also by statutory confirmation that the provincial superior courts would have concurrent jurisdiction with the Federal Court and not be frozen out of such matters.[27]

New Initiatives in Court Reform

A larger challenge to the traditional ways of the Court of Appeal came not from these relatively minor erosions of its jurisdiction but from the steady expansion of court administration within the provincial Attorney General's department. The provincial government, and specifically the provincial Attorney General, had always had constitutional responsibility for building, maintaining, staffing, and administering all the courts of Ontario, as well as for appointing the judges or magistrates of the provincial courts. Ottawa's role was limited to appointing and paying the superior court judges. Traditionally, the relationship between Ontario's court administrators and the judges, federal as well as provincial, had been informal and personal. The precise boundaries between civil service administration and judicial independence had hardly been tested.

A new Ontario Law Reform Commission established at the same time as McRuer's civil rights inquiry, with Chief Justice McRuer as concurrent head of both, took up an analysis of court administration as one of its early projects. In 1971, the judges of the Supreme Court of Ontario (that is, of the Court of Appeal and the High Court together) presented a report to the commission. Their presentation, named the Aylesworth Report for the head of the judges' committee that drafted it, noted that courts had traditionally been driven by litigants' needs more than their own agendas, but that growth had made enhanced planning and even centralization necessary. The judges called on Ontario to provide more support staff in the appeal court, under the direction of a new administrative officer reporting to the chief justice, and for the initiation of projects to control paper flow and to extend the courts' sittings. They also urged that the growing volume of appeal cases should be addressed by making the brand new Divisional Court a full intermediate-level appellate court independent of the trial court, with the Court of Appeal henceforth to be limited to nine judges, hearing only those cases in which vital law-making or law-defining issues were at stake. The Aylesworth proposals helped launch two decades of discussions about an intermediate appeal court for Ontario, but it was not taken up at the time.[28]

The Ontario Law Reform Commission's own report, submitted in 1973, also considered an expanded jurisdiction for the Divisional Court. Its more contentious recommendation, however, was to seek efficiency through centralization of court administration in the Attorney General's department.[29] This proposal marked the formal beginning of debate in Ontario about how to improve administrative efficiency without compromising judicial independence. There was a more than theoretical danger that a newly professionalized court administration run by the Attorney General's own department could give the Attorney General, who was always the principal litigant in the courts, undue influence on such matters as who heard cases and when they were heard. Seemingly routine administrative procedures, it was argued, could influence the way cases were heard and decided, raising concerns about the independence and impartiality of the court's decisions. In 1977, for instance, court schedules were still being drawn up by registry staff who reported to the Attorney General's department, and that year the Criminal Lawyers Association urged the Court of Appeal to see that it was "unwise and unnecessary to give even the appearance that one party to litigation has control over what case shall be heard by a given panel of judges."[30]

The judges' Aylesworth Report had proposed formalizing the division between external matters, which could be left to the Attorney General's department, and internal matters, which should be controlled by the judiciary. In 1976, the Attorney General's department, newly led by Roy McMurtry, took a bold approach to this internal/external division in a White Paper on courts administration. It proposed creating a Directorate of Courts Administration, headed by a civil servant but reporting to a judicial council led by the chiefs of the appeal court, the High Court, the county and district courts, and the provincial court. This council of judges, and their director, would administer all court services, employ all the court staff, and develop the courts' annual administrative budget for submission to the legislature. In effect, Ontario was proposing to solve the jurisdictional problem of court administration by turning the whole matter over to the judges and courts.[31]

Chief Justice Gale responded to the Law Reform Commission's White Paper by securing the appointment of associate chief justices to assist each of the Ontario courts with the administrative burden that was foreseen, but the White Paper's plan to transfer responsibility to the judges never took place.[32] The White Paper's view of court administration would be supported in 1981 by "Masters in Their Own House," a study undertaken by Quebec Superior Court Chief Justice Jules Deschênes for the Canadian Judicial Council that recommended a three-step progression towards independent control of courts administration by the judges, much as the White Paper had proposed.[33] But Chief Justice Howland (who had succeeded Gale in 1977) and his judges were concerned that if they took on full responsibility for court administration, they would gradually become more administrators than judges. Among both judges and politicians, concern also grew about a system in which the court budget would have no elected representative responsible for it – and therefore no one advocating for it in the cabinet or legislature.[34] The White Paper proposal was abandoned, although the principle that the court itself had to have clear control of its "internal" matters, notably scheduling and empanelling of judges, was informally accepted. In 1984, a new *Courts of Justice Act* (replacing the old, much-amended *Judicature Act* that had first come into force in 1913) declared that "the Chief Justice of Ontario has general supervision and direction over the sittings of the Court of Appeal and the assignment of the judicial duties of the court." It specified that judges had authority over trial lists and courtroom assignments "to the extent necessary to control the determination of who is assigned to hear particular cases," and that in matters assigned to the judiciary, court staff must act at the direction of the judges, not their civil service masters.[35]

Expanding the Court's Own Administrative Capacity

During the terms of chief justices Gale, Estey, and Howland, the court responded to the administrative challenge by gradually increasing its organizational and administrative capacity. Until this time, the court's only staff had been the employees of the court registrar's office, civil servants who could be transferred or reduced in number, without warning, in any governmental austerity drive or administrative reorganization. In 1975 an executive assistant (later "executive officer") to the chief justice was appointed: first George Taggart, and then Boris Krivy, who began a long tenure in judicial administration. From 1979, there was also a full-time director of administration for the Supreme Court, Warren J. Dunlop, whose responsibilities included both the Court of Appeal and the High Court. The two executive officers' responsibilities were mostly administrative, particularly in coordinating the Court of Appeal with the superior trial court, the county and district courts, and the provincial court, and liaising on behalf of all the courts with the rapidly growing court administration branch of the Ministry of the Attorney General. It was established that the staff responsible for scheduling appeals and organizing the panels to hear them would, while remaining officially members of the Ontario civil service, report to and be directed by the chief justice and his staff, not the Attorney General.[36]

The number of student law clerks fulfilling their articling requirement by working at the court for a term also grew. The court had had one clerk per year since 1956, when Chester Misener first held the position. From 1973 there were two law clerks annually. The clerks of 1975 were Kathryn Feldman, who became a judge of the court in 1998, and Richard Peterson, later a superior court master. As judges began to overcome engrained doubts about what use a law student could be, the work of the student law clerks expanded. Chief Justice Howland recalled discovering their potential during a contract law case soon after his appointment to the court. The intensive research done for him on one particular legal issue by Peterson helped make Howland an advocate for law clerks. "The heavy part of the Court of Appeal [is that] you are working against time, you only have the papers for roughly a week before you are sitting,"[37] he said, and timely research support could be of vital assistance. He began regularly assigning research tasks to clerks. Howland liked to stress that clerks did not write judgments, but researched assigned points and helped to review, edit, and annotate the judges' drafts. Some judges liked to have clerks prepare a memorandum summarizing each appeal before it was heard, though Howland liked doing his own, to "hammer the facts into his head" before oral argument of an appeal. By 1981, the court was hiring six law clerks annually and working towards Howland's goal of one clerk between two judges.[38] In 1977, the court hired its first professional law officer, the former law clerk Richard Peterson, giving the judges for the first time a permanent professional legal research capacity within the court itself.

The *Courts of Justice Act* still required the appeal judges to meet annually and report their recommendations for court administration to the Attorney General, but that was the extent of their formal powers independent of their chief justice. Howland believed, however, that by consulting regularly at the court's monthly meetings, he could give directions as chief justice without threatening the collegiality of the court. As a backlog of cases began to develop in the later 1970s, and particularly with the rush of Charter of Rights cases in the 1980s, he reached agreement with his judges on appropriate length limitations for both written factums and oral arguments before ordering them implemented on his own authority.[39]

The development of the administrative apparatus answering to the chief justice, and of statutory language stating the administrative authority of the chief justice, challenged the older understanding that a chief justice was no more than "first among equals" in his court. Strong personalities had always held some ability to shape a court in their own image, but now critics began to observe that the development of a bureaucracy answering to the chief justice might itself threaten judicial independence. As a 1995 study commissioned by the Canadian Judicial Council would observe, it was becoming possible "because of the unique nature of the chief judge's administrative authority and investigative, disciplinary and supervisory powers" that a chief justice might himself influence or coerce judges' decisions by giving or withholding favoured committee appointments, cases, working conditions, or accommodations. Some authorities began to speculate that chief justices should be chosen by their peers for fixed terms, as was becoming common for deans and department heads in universities, rather than being appointed for the rest of their career by outside selectors.[40] To date, however, chief justices in Canada continue to be appointed until retirement by the federal government and retain their broad formal authority, tempered by traditions of collegiality and consultation. At least since an order-in-council of 1935, it has been the prime minister's prerogative to propose nominations of chief justices to cabinet, while regular justices are proposed by the minister of justice, but some prime ministers have involved themselves either more or less in the process, and all the appointments are formally made by the governor in council.[41]

An 1985 amendment to the federal *Judges Act*, however, for the first time permitted chief justices to step down after at least five years in the office and hold instead the seat (and benefits) of a regular judge. Associate Chief Justice John Morden would avail himself of this provision in 1999.[42]

A very unwelcome need for the chief justice to defend his court in the most literal fashion arose in 1982 when a lawyer and his client were murdered in an Osgoode Hall court room. In general, appeal cases involve lawyers and judges almost exclusively, and Osgoode Hall may have seemed immune to violence, even after lawyer Frederick Gans was shot in an adjacent Toronto courthouse in 1978 by a party to a family law dispute. On 18 March 1982, however, a litigant brought a revolver into Osgoode Hall's Courtroom 4, where Mr Justice John Osler of the High Court was hearing a disputed injunction, and began shooting, killing lawyer Oscar Fonseca and a client. The tragedy led to increased security throughout Osgoode Hall. More security was added after a bomb threat in 1988, leading to a full-time police presence and the eventual installation of metal detectors and other security measures.[43]

Judicial Professional Development

During the 1970s, the judges of appeal began to venture into judicial professional development. As early as 1960, Arthur Kelly, on being appointed directly from practice to the Court of Appeal, found it odd that judges got no training at all; he followed Justice Fred MacKay (and Wilfred Judson of the Supreme Court of Canada) to an appellate judges' seminar at New York University, which he recommended to others.[44] John Arnup, who joined the court in 1970, had a strong interest in judicial writing and editing and was among the first members of the court to attend an innovative judgment-writing program sponsored by the American Bar Association in Boulder, Colorado. He came back an advocate for training in judgment writing, wrote a handbook on the subject, and began holding sessions for his fellow judges, some of whom began to follow him to Colorado.[45] Attention to the craft of writing well-organized, accessible, and clearly-argued opinions was in itself an acknowledgment that the day had passed when judgments needed little more than citations to decisive English precedents, and idiosyncratic opinion writing began to give way to judgments that followed standard models with recognizable structures.

In the meantime, there were new initiatives for Canadian judicial seminars and judicial education. In 1971, the federal government established the Canadian Judicial Council, a new body formed of the chief justices of all the Canadian superior courts and led by the chief justice of Canada. Its principal duty was to recommend on discipline for judges, and some of its members, particularly under Chief Justice Fauteux (until his retirement in 1973), were reluctant to see the council's disciplinary functions mingled with professional development matters.[46] Nevertheless, as the only venue for regular meetings of the leaders of the Canadian judiciary, the CJC meetings became a base from which they could act collaboratively, whether by commissioning reports like Deschênes's or by encouraging conferences and seminars. The Canadian Institute for the Administration of Justice, formed at Osgoode Hall law school in 1974 (and itself symptomatic of growing attention to issues of court administration) discussed with the CJC the need for a national forum for judicial continuing education.[47] Chief Justice Howland, asked by the CJC to study the question, was favourably disposed, and council began to apply its statutory authority to support judicial education programs, giving rise to the Canadian Judicial Institute, later the National Judicial Institute, in 1988.[48] Thereupon it became routine for judges from across Canada to meet regularly for their own continuing education. This kind of networking among superior court judges from across Canada also gave rise to the Canadian Judges Conference, which advocated for the judiciary on such matters as pensions and salaries – a project which would have been unthinkable to an earlier generation of judges. The judicial education programs subtly eroded the older image of judges as isolated, Olympian figures who came to their task fully formed and needing no further education or support.

Even more than Gale, Chief Justice Howland enjoyed and took seriously his public role as the judicial leader of Ontario and administrator of the province during the absences of the lieutenant governor. He attended ceremonies, gave speeches, and adorned the head tables at public events to a degree rarely imagined by his predecessors, many of whom had doubted whether judges should ever be seen, let alone heard, in public. Howland believed strongly that the court had to communicate with other courts, the bar, and the public. He formed the

Bench and Bar Council for liaison between the judges and the Ontario legal profession, encouraged the activities of the Council of Judges that brought together the appellate and High Court judges, promoted the creation of a Courts Advisory Council, and helped develop the Ontario Judicial Council, established in 1990 (just as his term ended) to discipline provincially appointed judges as the CJC did federally appointed ones.[49]

Bilingualism at the Court of Appeal

Bilingualism came to the Court of Appeal's attention in the late 1970s. The bilingual courts in Ontario were an initiative of Attorney General McMurtry. Premier Davis's government consistently resisted pressure from Ontario francophones and bilingualism advocates to make the province officially bilingual, but French-language services were expanded piecemeal within the province, and Attorney General McMurtry initiated a test of bilingual courts in 1976. A French-language common law program was launched at the University of Ottawa law school in 1977, and Ontario committed itself to translating its statutes into French in 1978. Within a few years, the Ontario courts were declared officially bilingual, and trials in either language became available across the province.[50]

At the Court of Appeal, Chief Justice Howland quickly and rather easily adjusted to the new requirements. The court had always been an almost entirely unilingual institution, but compared to the trial courts, where demand from unilingual francophone defendants, witnesses, and litigants was substantial, the demand for French-language hearings was less urgent at the Court of Appeal, because most of Ontario's francophone appeal counsel were bilingual and were prepared to be heard in English. Howland found that the court's sole francophone judge, Maurice Lacourcière, and its two bilingual anglophones, Peter Cory and Walter Tarnopolsky, could form a French-language panel when needed, and the court heard its first appeals in French in 1983.*

---

* Cory, a Windsor-born anglophone who practised law in Toronto, learned French out of a personal commitment to judicial bilingualism. He was one of the first to take the federally run language programs offered to superior court judges. Tarnopolsky, an academic lawyer of Saskatchewan Ukrainian heritage, also learned French as an adult.

Along with all the Ontario courts, however, the court faced challenges in developing consistent French equivalents for common law terminology that had been developed almost exclusively in English. The Court of Appeal continued to be a mostly English-language court that could hear appeals in French when needed, but it tended to translate court materials into French as required rather than operate equally in both languages.

Howland took French lessons regularly while chief justice but never felt able to hear cases in French himself. Early in the 1980s, however, he did give his first official speech in French at an Ottawa call to the bar ceremony and was gratified by applause and by the thanks of a francophone lawyer who said he had had "tears in his eyes" to hear a chief justice of Ontario speak French at an official function. Howland's judges joked that it might have been the chief justice's spoken French, not the significance of his gesture, that provoked the lawyer's tears, but Howland knew it had been a sincere compliment, and he continued to speak French as well as English at official functions. Demand for French-language appeals continued to be slight, however, and the court had just enough bilingual judges to be able to hear appeals in French, though Lacourcière remained the court's only native French speaker until 1990.[51]

All these structural and administrative changes meant that, between about 1970 and the early 1980s, the chief justice and his Court of Appeal had acquired a larger and more professional support staff, and the judges consulted more both among themselves and with the rest of the Canadian judiciary. The issue of control over courts administration was not settled, and perhaps never would be, but in response both the court and the government had professionalized their administrative teams and sought to clarify their separate roles.

A Flurry of Studies and Reports

One consequence of the judiciary's new organizations and the government's concerns about courts governance was a near-constant stream of studies and reports on the courts, unlike anything seen in the court's past. On the judges' side, the principal one was the 1981 report, "Masters in Their Own House," that the Canadian Judicial Council commissioned from Quebec superior court chief justice Jules Deschênes. "In Canada the current trend is for provincial departments which are heavily involved in litigation before the courts to assume increasing

and broad roles in court administration," Deschênes wrote, and he declared that it was the unanimous desire of the Canadian judiciary to see this ambiguity eliminated.[52] Deschênes made the case for a three-stage progress – consultation, decision sharing, and finally judicial independence – but in the end the CJC (and many judges) supported only the first two stages. The debate about the boundaries between government and courts in court administration continued, though Ontario's *Administration of Justice Act* was amended in an effort to clarify just which administrative tasks had to be controlled by the judges.[53]

The other topic that inspired reports and studies, particularly in the 1980s, was the potential for a new level of appeal court in Ontario. One possible solution to the court's growing workload that the judges regularly discussed was the splitting of criminal from civil appeals through the creation of a criminal appeals division or a separate Court of Criminal Appeal for Ontario.[54] A topic given more sustained consideration was a new intermediate-level appeal court below the Court of Appeal. By 1977, the Court of Appeal had grown to fifteen judges and had long since become accustomed to having several three-judge panels sitting simultaneously. Particularly after the Supreme Court of Canada decided in 1975 that it would "control its docket" and hear only the cases it judged vital, the provincial courts of appeal had become the final appeal venue for the overwhelming majority of cases. The demand for hearings obliged them to extend sittings and to continue adding more judges. Appeal judges in the larger provinces, particularly Ontario and British Columbia, began to question how a Court of Appeal could provide consistent, collegial, law-making certainty, if constant growth meant that judges of appeal rarely sat with each other and never sat together as a single court. One solution to which they gave extensive consideration was a new higher provincial court of final appeal, with a permanent panel of just seven or nine judges, as at the Supreme Court in Ottawa. Many American states, they observed, had long since adopted a top-level appeal court with a small bench, all of whose members sat together for the potentially law-changing cases, while a larger intermediate-level court disposed of the majority of more routine "error-correction" cases.[55]

In 1977, the Kelly Report, the work of a committee appointed by Attorney General McMurtry and led by the recently retired Court of Appeal judge Arthur Kelly, made the case for an intermediate Court of Appeal in Ontario.[56] Kelly proposed that the Divisional Court be divested of all appeal functions other than judicial review of administrative tribunals.

Henceforth the Court of Appeal would consist of two parts: a large and expandable "General Division," to hear appeals in which only error correction was foreseen, and a small "Juridical Division" (Kelly called it the "Special Division" in his draft reports) that would hear only those few appeals in which law-declaring and law-revising judgments were expected. Cases would go to one or other, though the juridical division would have the authority to give leave for appeal from decisions of the general division if a law-making issue arose. The judges of this new senior court would come from the existing Court of Appeal, with those not selected for it remaining in the general appeal division.[57]

Kelly had been a genial, sociable member of the appeal court, often inviting his fellow judges to hold their retreats at his country home, but his proposals proved contentious even among his former colleagues on the court, few of whom relished being relegated to a second-rank "general" appeal court.[58] Nevertheless, a growing backlog of appeals and the prospect of an endlessly growing appeal court kept the issue alive. In 1983, another Court of Appeal committee, led by Associate Chief Justice Bert MacKinnon, suggested an intermediate appeal process based on expanding and reforming the Divisional Court, so that the Court of Appeal could remain at its current size, then fifteen judges. In 1987, a report commissioned by the new Attorney General, Ian Scott, from Justice Thomas Zuber of the Court of Appeal revived the proposal for an intermediate Court of Appeal, as did the 1989 report of the Joint Committee on Court Reform struck by the Law Society and several legal organizations.[59]

Despite this interest in a small, collegial, specialized tribunal able to give final or near-final declarations of law, the new level of appeal court had two fatal disadvantages. The first was a matter of cost. A new level of appeal would increase the court administration budget, the cost of litigation, and the time required to move a case through all its potential appeals; it might even give rise to complaints like those that provoked the Whitney government's "one appeal" campaign in the early 1900s. Governments in Ontario and the other provinces never felt much enthusiasm for the proposal. Its second disadvantage was that it would have led to a selection among the appeal judges. Even among the judges of appeal convinced of the value of an intermediate court, few were willing to see themselves relegated to the second-rank, error-correcting court rather than appointed to the small, elite, law-making one. From his time as Attorney General, Roy McMurtry was sceptical of an intermediate appeal court, and he liked to say to judges who favoured it, including Chief Justice Charles Dubin, "I will take the idea seriously if you can tell me which nine judges will go to the superior level."[60] Even though such choices would have been different only in degree from the familiar selection of some appeal judges to move "up" to the Supreme Court of Canada – and it would have been the federal cabinet, not the judges themselves, who chose the seven or nine – McMurtry found this an effective conversation stopper. The intermediate-level court was never implemented in Ontario or elsewhere in Canada, although the same reports and studies that considered it produced substantial re-structurings in other parts of the judiciary. At the appeal level, the developing backlog was attacked in the short-term by efforts at pro-cedural efficiencies and – as reform advocates had feared – by regular increases in the number of judges.

The Jurisprudential Transformation of the Court, 1967–90

The truly fundamental change in the appeal court between the 1960s and the 1980s was not administrative but jurisprudential. Ian Scott, a successful appellate lawyer and later a controversial Attorney General of Ontario, later wrote that when he began to practise in the 1960s, "the courts were in the last throes of their adherence to the system of com-mon law built up through precedent." He recalled how in his first Court of Appeal case, the judges acknowledged that the legal principles he advanced in his argument were "persuasive" but refused to move from familiar English precedents and traditional canons of interpretation; they dismissed his appeal.[61] That was roughly where Ontario appel-late jurisprudence stood before the transformation that rather suddenly made the Court of Appeal hospitable to innovative legal thought. The representative figure in that jurisprudential transformation was Bora Laskin.

Laskin was a member of the court from 1965, shortly before Gale's term as chief justice began, until his appointment to the Supreme Court of Canada in 1970. His appointment was recognized at the time as transformative. As a non-partisan, as a Jew, and as an academic, he upended the norms of judicial appointments in the 1960s. His appoint-ment also demonstrated a growing backlash against political patronage in judicial appointments and helped render obsolete the careful tally-ing of "Catholic" and "Protestant" seats in Canadian courts. As those categories lost significance, Jews, women, and eventually Canadians of all ethnicities would henceforth be the new minorities that politicians would begin to consider for representation. In addition, the appointment of a law professor to a senior Canadian court heralded the arrival of jurisprudential scholarship that would move beyond established precedent and custom as the fundamental drivers of court decision-making.

The revolution in jurisprudence had many causes. More and broader education for lawyers was certainly one. Of the ten judges whose appointments to the Court of Appeal directly preceded Bora Laskin's, only half had attended university at all. They had trained in law mostly by apprenticing in legal offices, and they had learned how to win cases by observing in court which precedents and precepts the judges favoured and trying whenever possible to apply them to their own arguments.* Of the ten judges who followed Laskin to the court, by comparison, all were university graduates, and two had graduate training in law, as he did. The newer judges had more exposure to diverse legal scholarship, to debates about philosophies of law, and to efforts at determining principles of justice that should underpin the analysis of statutes and case law. One judge of the second group summarized the importance of education to the jurisprudential revolution by saying simply that "it all began in 1949" – that is, when Caesar Wright and the University of Toronto law school struck the decisive blow for academic control of legal education in Ontario. Many of the initiators of jurisprudential change at the Court of Appeal had actually been shaped just as much by the undergraduate law school run at Toronto by W.P.M. Kennedy before Wright arrived and abolished that program – but the point about broader educational horizons held. In Canada, the many constitutional judgments that had blocked government measures to relieve the Great Depression of the 1930s had galvanized legal scholars to pursue new ideas about the relations of law and society. The evolution of Canadian self-government between the wars stimulated their efforts to develop legal scholarship based on Canadian contexts rather than English case law. Laskin himself, as a Harvard Law graduate, a career academic, and the first law professor appointed to the Ontario court, had been shaped by all these trends in legal education and legal scholarship.

---

* In the midst of criticizing that tradition in his memoir, *To Make a Difference*, Ian Scott acknowledged that as a lawyer intent on winning his cases, he too cited the judges' favourite precedents whenever he thought he could win that way.

William Hume Blake. Solicitor General of the Province of Canada and founder of the Court of Error and Appeal in 1849, and then a justice of the court 1849–62 and 1864–70.

Oliver Mowat. Justice of Error and Appeal 1864–72, and then architect of the reorganized Court of Appeal as premier and as Attorney General of Ontario.

Osgoode Hall, Toronto. Home to the Court of Appeal for Ontario throughout its history.

William Henry Draper. Justice of Error and Appeal 1849–76 and Chief Justice of Appeal 1876–7.

John Hawkins Hagarty. Justice of Error and Appeal 1856–74 and Chief Justice of Ontario 1884–97.

George William Burton. Justice of Appeal 1874–97 and Chief Justice of Ontario 1897–1900.

Featherston Osler. Justice of Appeal 1883–1910, later treasurer of the Law Society of Upper Canada.

The Supreme Court of Judicature for Ontario, 1891. Chief Justice of Ontario J.H. Hagarty with judges from the Court of Appeal and the High Court. From left: Hon W.G. Falconbridge, Hon Thomas Robertson, Hon W.P.R. Street, Hon T. Ferguson, Hon F. Osler, Hon John A. Boyd (chancellor of Ontario), Hon J.H. Hagarty (chief justice of Ontario), Hon R.M. Meredith, Hon Sir Thomas Galt (chief justice of Common Pleas), Hon G.W. Burton, Hon H. MacMahon, Hon J. Maclennan, and Hon J.E. Rose.

William Ralph Meredith. Chief Justice of Ontario 1912–23.

The Court of Appeal for Ontario, 1923. From left: Justice Frank E. Hodgins, Justice John James MacLaren, Chief Justice William Ralph Meredith, Justice James Magee, and Justice W.N. Ferguson.

William Renwick Riddell. Legal scholar and famously peevish Justice of Appeal 1925–45.

Francis Latchford. Justice of Appeal 1923–38, the court's first Catholic judge. With Riddell, Latchford formed "murderers' row" of elderly and difficult judges in the 1930s.

The judges at cards, 1931. Chief Justice of Ontario William Mulock and some of his judges.

The Court of Appeal for Ontario, 1935. From left: Rt Hon Sir William Mulock, PC, KCMG (chief justice of Ontario), Hon Justice Riddell, Hon Justice Middleton, Hon Justice Masten, Hon Justice Davis, Hon Justice Fisher, Hon Justice Macdonnell, and Hon Justice F.R. Latchford.

The Court of Appeal for Ontario, 1951. Chief Justice Robert Spelman Robertson at centre, fifth from left.

John Wellington Pickup. Chief Justice of Ontario 1952–7.

The Court of Appeal for Ontario, 1956. Chief Justice Pickup, fifth from left.

Dana Porter. Chief Justice of Ontario 1957–67.

George "Bill" Gale. Chief Justice of Ontario and architect of the revitalization of the court 1967–76.

The Court of Appeal for Ontario, 1976. Chief Justice Gale front row centre, with Bertha Wilson, the first woman judge of the court, behind him.

Roy McMurtry. Chief Justice of Ontario 1996–2007.

Warren Winkler. Chief Justice of Ontario 2007–13.

Law clerks of the Court of Appeal. In Osgoode Hall's Convocation Hall during a reunion of former student law clerks in 2010.

The Court of Appeal for Ontario, 2013. Chief Justice Winkler at front row, left.

Causes of jurisprudential change went deeper than schooling. The post-war era carried a new awareness of human rights and the need to defend democratic principles against totalitarian challenge, and those views encouraged rule-of-law principles that went beyond the mere mechanistic invocation of the traditional, politically rooted "rights of Englishmen" that had once dominated Canadian politics and jurisprudence. Cases based on new human rights ideas and antidiscrimination statutes had little success at the Court of Appeal in the immediate post-war years, but more lawyers were beginning to at least hear the arguments. The grudging acceptance of labour unions in newly industrialized post-war Canada also led to new legal thinking about societal relations and rights, as the common law's presumptions in favour of property and contract were slowly remoulded by new statutory authority for collective bargaining, over not only wages but also working conditions. There were new campaigns demanding that the law consider interpretations of social and economic justice over blind allegiance to precedent. Again, Laskin, with his long record of involvement in the causes of academic freedom and civil rights and his long career as a labour-side labour arbitrator, personified the developing trend.

The growing diversity of Canadian society also produced demands for attention to the rights and claims of marginalized social and ethnic communities. In the Canadian legal system, much of this was led initially by Jewish lawyers who had gained entry to the legal profession in the 1930s and 1940s, and who remained viscerally aware of their outsider status even as they attained leadership positions in the legal community and eventually judicial appointments as well. Laskin was a successful Harvard Law School graduate, a tenured professor, and an establishment judge, always in a position to wield influence and shape public discourse, but at the same time he remained a Jew from a northern Ontario immigrant family, made vividly aware by his own life experiences about the prejudices and habits of the legal profession, the academic community, the public sector, and the judiciary. From all these economic, cultural, social and intellectual currents, there came new thinking about the law. Bora Laskin, a legal academic, a campaigner for workers' and human rights, a participant in social change, and a Jew, represented all of them.

Laskin's legal thinking was not particularly radical – there were certainly more radical thinkers when it came to the relationship of law to society – and his commitment to the common law tradition and the vital role of the judiciary was strong. He was a dissenter at the Court of Appeal of the 1970s, however, due to his belief that the law lost its legitimacy, and therefore its ability to serve, when it grew out of touch with the slowly but relentlessly shifting goals and needs of society. Like his teacher Kennedy, he believed that the law had to "serve social ends" and that it was a legitimate function of judges to mould the law to social ends. Like his mentor Wright, he believed that "the ends of law must always be found outside the law itself" and that law had to change as society's needs did. He held, therefore, that the common law could not be a prisoner of long-established precedents, but had to make room for constant jurisprudential review of how the deep principles of the law should be applied to the contemporary circumstances from which cases arose.

Such views, known as "sociological jurisprudence" or "legal modernism," were widely shared by Canadian legal academics by the 1960s, and they stood in stark contrast to the school of thought sometimes called "legal formalism" that still dominated the Court of Appeal. Legal formalists were committed to upholding legal principles already declared in court precedents and statutes. Far from expecting judges to adapt the law to social ends, they held that change should come from legislatures, and therefore they gradually found themselves defending visions of society laid down in the late-Victorian heyday of common law formalism and unrevised thereafter. Formalism had dominated Canadian jurisprudence through the first half of the twentieth century, and it was nowhere more strongly entrenched than at the Court of Appeal for Ontario that Laskin joined in 1965.

Laskin was appointed to the Court of Appeal less to launch a jurisprudential revolution than to serve the urgent political needs of a Liberal government struggling with corruption and patronage scandals involving lawyers and judges. It was the right moment to appoint a judge who was not a recently retired politician or a party crony, but would be seen as credible and forward-looking in ways the government itself wished to be seen when it was moving towards such legal innovations as decriminalizing abortion and homosexuality and reforming the Criminal Code and divorce law. On those grounds, Laskin's advocates among the government's advisers managed to outflank those who favoured a traditional patronage appointment – or who raised other objections. Laskin had been a tough professor in his early days, and two cabinet ministers who had suffered in his classes were not keen on his appointment.

Laskin joined a court that was sceptical of him on almost all counts. Judges, some of whom were seen as anti-Semitic, came from a generation that had dismissed Jewish lawyers as innately foreign and inadequately steeped in the great tradition of English law. As pragmatic, apprenticeship-trained lawyers, their resistance to an impractical academic thinker lacking practical skills would have been just as pronounced as their distance from his jurisprudential philosophy. Laskin had often been critical of the decisions of the Court of Appeal in his scholarly writing, and his arbitration rulings had drawn on legal principles antithetical to those that dominated at the court. As a result, Laskin quickly found himself a dissenter in the court's decisions: he was easily the court's most frequent dissenter during his time there.

Yet Laskin did not remain entirely isolated at the court. He soon proved well suited to its male-dominated, competitive milieu. His ferocious work ethic earned respect, and his productivity reassured colleagues who may have feared that an ivory-tower professor would be unable to keep up with their workload. No one on the court long imagined that the new judge was inferior to his colleagues in intellect or legal knowledge, and he quickly established that he was not the "alien" or "foreign" outsider they had feared, despite his background and legal formation. It may be that the legal modernist had a particular advantage that the formalists found difficult to resist. In the past, when a lawyer introduced a novel legal argument in court, or invoked some societal need as the basis for an appeal, it had been easy for formalist judges to dismiss him or her with a brief traditional judgment rooted in old precedents. But a fellow judge writing opinions laced with such arguments was more difficult to dismiss, and when the formalist judges engaged with modernist analysis, they allowed the ground of the dispute to shift, from precedents alone to jurisprudential principles.

Change in the court's jurisprudence, when it came, came rapidly and irreversibly. Laskin stayed only five years at the Court of Appeal before being appointed to the Supreme Court of Canada. Had he been a single, isolated example of a different style of legal thinking, he could easily have been marginalized and largely ignored as no more than a frequent dissenter. But within a few years, as Chief Justice Gale energetically recruited the province's best lawyers to his court, many of them proved to be Laskins rather than Aylesworths: lawyers shaped by new times, new kinds of legal education, and new climates of legal thought. As they came to prominence at the bar and then on the judicial bench, Ontario's Court of Appeal rapidly shifted from being a bastion of traditional legal thought to a wellspring of new legal ideas.

Robert Sharpe, like Laskin a legal scholar who became a judge of the Court of Appeal (a much less unusual thing at Sharpe's appointment in

1999 than it was in 1965), has examined how the JCPC's 1929 declaration in the Persons Case that the Canadian constitution was "a living tree capable of growth and expansion within its natural limits," had been ignored or redefined into irrelevance in Canadian jurisprudence for half a century and then suddenly became one of its central tenets.[62] At the Supreme Court, it was less Laskin than Brian Dickson (a traditionally trained establishment lawyer from Western Canada) who made the living tree principle into a standard reference in Canadian constitutional discourse. He began doing so in 1979, shortly but distinctly before the enactment of the Charter of Rights and Freedoms. The Canadian courts, and the Court of Appeal for Ontario among them, had been making the transition to legal modernism before the enactment of the Charter in 1982. As a result of the new jurisprudential thinking that Bora Laskin exemplified at the Court of Appeal and which soon came to prevail, the Charter got a completely different response at the Court of Appeal than had been given to the 1961 Bill of Rights.

The Judges of the Court, 1967–90

The twenty-eight judges appointed to the Court of Appeal between 1967 and 1990 were still mostly Anglo-Canadian in background, but they included five Jewish judges, a francophone, and two women. The five Jewish judges appointed had built their legal practices during a time when discrimination against Jews was still common at the Ontario bar – leading Toronto law firms had rarely hired Jewish lawyers before the 1980s, for instance – but they benefited both from Bora Laskin's path breaking and from the fading of overtly anti-Semitic public behaviour in Ontario and in the legal community. In the midst of this new social diversity, only two Catholics were named to the court in this period, evidently without comment or protest from the Catholic bar. Indeed, in this period, ever more judges ceased to make note of any religious affiliation in their standard biographical statements.

The appointment of the first woman to the court, however, met resistance reminiscent of that faced by Laskin a decade earlier. The decision to appoint a woman had been driven much more by Ottawa than by Chief Justice Gale, and Bertha Wilson, the first appointee, was hardly known to the court; she had made her career as a research lawyer and adviser, not a courtroom advocate. Many of the judges, having worked almost exclusively with other men throughout their careers, were alarmed about having a female colleague. "No woman can do my job," one of them was reported as saying. Even Chief Justice Gale, who supported the appointment, was taken aback by simple practical matters such as providing washroom facilities for Justice Wilson.

Wilson assuaged doubts about her appointment as Laskin had: courteous and sociable, she also demonstrated a prodigious work ethic, the ability to write well-written and persuasive judgments, and a vast knowledge of and love for the law – and she quickly proved herself. To address her limited background in criminal law matters, she sought Arthur Martin's guidance (as other judges had) and showed that she shared his concerns for the rights of the accused. She was an early attendee at the American judicial education seminars recommended by Arnup, who became a mentor. Wilson quickly became a strong, innovative contributor to the court's work, and after just six years she was named the first woman justice of the Supreme Court of Canada. On both courts, she was bold (even stubborn, some suggested) about advancing her interpretations of the law, sometimes in notable dissents. Her success at the Court of Appeal did not lead to a rush of other female appointments, however. She remained the only woman on the court from 1976 to 1982. The next woman justice, Hilda McKinlay, did not join the court until 1987.

The group of judges of the Howland years averaged twenty-four years at the bar, mostly in litigation practices, before their first judicial appointment. They were mostly graduates of Osgoode Hall Law School from the time when it was Ontario's only avenue to a legal career. Despite the importance of the "direct appoints," most (sixteen out of twenty-eight) came with prior judicial experience on the High Court. They had mostly received their first judicial appointments in their mid-fifties, with none older than sixty-two at first appointment. There were still few franco-Ontarian justices, and the court continued to have just enough bilingual judges to hear French-language appeals.

Only a handful of five-judge panels for significant cases interrupted the unbroken succession of three-judge panels (plus single-judge sittings in procedural matters and motions). Chief Justice Howland recalled among them the appeal of Rolling Stone Keith Richards on a drug conviction (appeal dismissed), the appeal of Holocaust denier Ernst Zündel (new trial, on one point), the Crown appeal against the acquittal of Dr. Henry Morgentaler on abortion charges (acquittal overturned), and a spousal assault appeal where the court anticipated making new law on the issue of spousal abuse.[63] By this era, the large number of panels, the caseload burden, and the growing unanimity of the panels made it impossible for any judge to write opinions in a large proportion of the court's cases. In a 200-case sample of reported appeals during the 1970s, 167 of the cases produced unanimous 3–0 decisions (against just fourteen 2–1 splits). Dissenters became statistically almost invisible; none had a rate greater than 2 per cent. Bora Laskin may have been not only a great dissenter but the last frequent one at the court.

The judges appointed between 1967 and 1990 differed from earlier cohorts of judges in having less elective political experience. Just two had held elective office at the federal or provincial level, although a third, Allan Goodman of Welland, was notable as the first identified New Democratic Party supporter ever appointed to the appeal bench (in 1979). Chief Justice Howland lobbied for Goodman's appointment on the basis of his demonstrated legal prowess, and was glad to cite his example as evidence that judicial appointment "wasn't basically a political situation."[64] The growing scarcity of ex-politicians on the appeal bench, partly due to the new appointments process, may have also reflected the fact that it was becoming difficult to build the kind of legal career that qualified one for an appellate court appointment while also maintaining an active political career, although "backroom" party work continued to be a factor in appointments.

The other distinguishing feature of these judges of the 1970s and 1980s was the new standard in legal education they began to exemplify. For the first time, all the judges appointed in this period had completed a university-based academic law degree (as was by then almost inevitable, given the changed requirements). In addition, six of the twenty-eight had at least one postgraduate degree in law, with Harvard, Columbia, Oxford, and London School of Economics among their credentials. The appeal bench, like the bar, was displaying more extensive and specialized legal training, and was being appointed and promoted by a process that gave education and other indicators of merit more emphasis. Some of the most admired members of the court – Arnup, Dubin, and Martin, for example – had had a traditional legal apprenticeship, but a profound reorientation in Canadian judicial thinking was taking place, and the Court of Appeal for Ontario was part of it.

Through the 1980s, Chief Justice Howland took a flexible approach to the selection of panels of judges. Martin, widely considered the greatest Canadian expert on criminal law matters, sat on all kinds of cases after he joined the court in 1973, but as Howland put it, "There were sort of joking references at times to the judgments he wrote on family law or various other things ... It was a terrible waste of that talent not to have him sitting on the criminal panels all the time. And that is what he wanted to do also, so that was done." Similarly, Lloyd Houlden was frequently assigned to the most complex commercial cases, as Howland, often with the assistance of the veteran Court of Appeal registrar Bill Shaughnessy, sought to match the judges' expertise to the cases coming forward.[65]

Cases and Procedures at the Court, 1967–90

One of the statutory duties of the Court of Appeal is to provide an advisory opinion to the government of Ontario when the government seeks an opinion on a question of law, usually constitutional in nature, without any specific case being argued. Although advisory in nature, the opinion the court gives in such a reference is a judgment in law and, like other judgments of the court, can be appealed to the Supreme Court of Canada.[66] In 1985, Ontario asked for such an opinion, when it referred to the court the government's plan to extend public funding to separate schools through to the end of high school, and asked whether the legislation was inconsistent with the Canadian constitution and the new Charter of Rights and Freedoms.

The five-judge panel, led by Chief Justice Howland, that considered this reference question on separate schools worked in the shadow of a 1929 case, *Tiny Township*. In *Tiny Township*, the court had ruled that the Confederation settlement required separate school education to be publicly funded only through elementary school; the Tiny township separate school system could not insist on funding beyond that as of right. The Court of Appeal had been sustained by the JCPC when the case was appealed there, and even though the JCPC had no authority in Canadian cases after 1949, the doctrine of precedent meant that decisions given when it was the final court continued to be binding on the Court of Appeal. In the reference question, the court of 1985 also had to consider the impact of the new Charter of Rights and the equality rights that it guaranteed.*

---

* No Catholic judges sat on the 1985 Tiny Township reference. Asked in his Osgoode Society oral history interview about his selections of judges for particular cases, Chief Justice Howland was unwilling to say that no Catholic could have sat on that case, but he observed that he would not have put judges with Holocaust victims or survivors in their families on the panel that heard the appeal of Holocaust denier Ernst Zündel.

Two judges, Sydney Robins and Chief Justice Howland, emphasized that *Tiny* remained the law: there was no right to separate school funding beyond elementary school. In any case, they found, the Charter might protect existing entitlements (such as funding for elementary schooling) but did not allow the legislature to expand a privilege that would be available only to one specific group of Ontarians. Their dissenting opinion – that Bill 30 was indeed unconstitutional – respected both sixty-year old precedent and the brand-new charter guarantees. Howland and Robins, however, were overruled by Justices Zuber, Cory, and Tarnopolsky. These three did not dismiss *Tiny* – they conceded it still meant the separate schools could not claim full funding as of right – but they found that the Confederation settlement had given the province discretion in choosing how broadly separate school funding should extend. Where the JCPC had – in classic formalist style – found the scope of separate school funding "frozen" at whatever existed in 1867, the majority found that Ontario, though not free to remove separate schools, was free to define the scope of what the province provided to accord with changing educational practice. They found that minority educational rights for Catholics in Ontario and Protestants in Quebec were an inextricable part of the Confederation bargain, embedded in the constitution, and not subject to being invalidated by the Charter. Since the ordinary definition of schooling had expanded since the mid-nineteenth century, it was within Ontario's powers to redefine the funding model to reflect that change. Bill 30 was constitutional.[67]

On appeal, the Supreme Court of Canada sustained the Court of Appeal majority on the Charter question and also overruled the *Tiny* precedent, finding that case wrongly decided.[68] At the Court of Appeal, the reference decision illustrated the state of jurisprudence, just as the Charter was beginning to be interpreted. In part, the reference was a Charter case, and both the majority and the minority assessed the legislation against Charter principles. But it was also a traditional constitutional case, and it was evident that even where the Charter did not reach, the court no longer followed the jurisprudential tradition of the 1920s, in which words set out in 1867 were fixed in their meaning, unless and until changed by legislation. A modernist jurisprudence, prepared to adapt principles of 1867 to circumstances of 1985, had become well entrenched at the Court of Appeal before 1982. As a result, it might be said that the Court of Appeal was prepared for the Charter era, in which courts, traditionally deferential to statutory language and legislative intent, had much more authority to assess legislative decisions against Charter principles and overturn them where they found inconsistency.

One of the most famous of early Charter decisions, *Oakes*, also shows this dual heritage operating at the Court of Appeal. *Oakes* is principally renowned as the case in which the Supreme Court of Canada, led by Chief Justice Dickson, set out the "Oakes test" to determine just how courts would interpret section 1 of the Charter, which authorizes the overriding of Charter-guaranteed rights when such an action could be justified in a free and democratic society. The Court of Appeal did not set out this procedural rule as the Supreme Court did when it heard *Oakes*, but its decision, sustained by the SCC, that Oakes's conviction (for drug trafficking) had to be overturned owed much to the criminal law jurisprudence, based on common law principles of the rights of the accused, that Arthur Martin had been championing over many years, and that had become increasingly influential at the court. Oakes had been convicted of trafficking because the pre-Charter law put the onus on anyone found with a substantial amount of illicit drugs to prove that he or she was not trafficking. Martin, on behalf of a unanimous Court of Appeal, found this reverse onus contrary to rights guaranteed by the Charter.

In 1983, Martin was among the first judges to apply the new Charter's section 11, the right to trial within a reasonable time, when he found in *R. v Beason* that a four-year delay in bringing a criminal charge to trial was unacceptable.[69] It would be the Supreme Court of Canada's 1990 ruling in *Askov*, however, that became the leading case on unreasonable delay, and in that case, the Supreme Court overturned the Ontario Court of Appeal's decision that those delays had been reasonable because the defendants had accepted them at the time.[70]

The court, however, was far from unrestrictedly committed to a right-based jurisprudence in the years before the Charter. In *R. v Shand* in 1976, it reviewed the decision of Stephen Borins, then a county court judge, later to join the Court of Appeal. Borins had found the mandatory minimum sentence of seven years for the importation of illegal drugs inappropriate to the specific circumstances of an individual who admitted to bringing cocaine into Canada. He applied the Canadian Bill of Rights' prohibition of cruel and unusual punishment and imposed a much shorter sentence and a fine. John Arnup, writing for Justices Brooke, Dubin, Martin, and Blair, found Borins's decision "particularly inappropriate," criticized Borins for substituting "his own discretion for that of Parliament," and restored the mandatory sentence. The

Table 5.1 Statistical Notes on 28 Judges of Appeal Appointed 1967–90

Birthplace

Toronto   8
Other Ontario centres   11
Prairies   6
Quebec   2
Non-Canadian   1   (United Kingdom)

Ethnic Origin

Anglophone/British   20
Francophone   1
European   2
Jewish   5

Gender

Male   26
Female   2   (Wilson and McKinlay)

Religious Affiliation

Protestant, various   12
Jewish   5
Roman Catholic   2
Orthodox Christian   1
Unspecified   8

Education

Non-law academic degrees   27*
University law degrees   7†
Osgoode Hall Law School   21
Post-graduate law degrees (one or more)   6‡

Average Years of Law Practice before Judicial Appointment

24 years

Minimum: 14   (Brooke and Galligan)
Maximum: 36   (Howland)

Location of Legal Practice (some in more than one place)

Toronto   20
Ottawa   2
Windsor   2
Hamilton   1

Table 5.1 (*Concluded*)

Sudbury	1
Welland	1
Out of province	2

Identified Political Commitment

Liberal	1
NDP	1

Judicial Appointment prior to Court of Appeal Appointment

Yes	16	(Ontario High Court of Justice)
No	12	

Average Age at Court of Appeal Appointment

55 years

Minimum:	44 years	(Morden)
Maximum:	62 years	(Grange and Griffiths)

Average Years on Court of Appeal Bench

14 years

Reason for Leaving Court of Appeal

A judge who left before age 65 or to take a non-judicial position is counted as resigned, not retired.

Died	3	
Resigned	1	(Thorson at 63)
Retired (65 to 75)	20	
Moved to another court	4	

Average Age on Leaving

69.5 years

Retired at or near the mandatory retirement age of 75	12
Moved to SCC	3[§]
Died in office	1[¶]

---

* All but Weatherston.
† U. of Saskatchewan (3); U. of Toronto (3); Dalhousie U. (1).
‡ Oxford (2); Harvard (2); Columbia (2); London School of Economics (1).
§ Estey at 58; Wilson at 59; Cory at 64.
¶ Tarnopolsky at 61.

Supreme Court of Canada denied leave to appeal.[71] While judges generally get used to seeing their decisions overturned, Borins resented Arnup's criticism for years, charging it had been motivated by earlier disagreements over opinions of the Law Society and of the courts expressed by Borins as a law professor. Borins characterized Arnup as "very black letter," and observed that the mandatory minimum sentence was overturned in later, Charter-based decisions.[72]

Before the implementation of the Charter, Bertha Wilson found a common law basis for recognizing the rights of individuals in her 1979 decision in *Seneca College v Bhadauria*.[73] When a would-be college teacher alleged that discrimination had kept her out of a job, the trial court found no cause of action in the courts because the Ontario Human Rights Commission had jurisdiction in such matters. Wilson, for a unanimous appeal panel, found that since the Ontario Human Rights Code, 1970, made it public policy that "every person is free and equal in dignity and rights," a tort of discrimination existed in common law, and the existence of the code did not remove the jurisdiction of the courts. Bhadauria was entitled to sue in the courts. In 1981, however, the decision was overturned at the Supreme Court, which sustained the jurisdiction of the commission: there had to be a tort that lay beyond the commission's jurisdiction for actions like Bhadauria's to proceed.[74] A few years later, when a teenaged female hockey player found herself prevented from playing in an elite amateur hockey league because it was reserved for boys, the Human Rights Commission found that the Code did not prohibit sexual discrimination in sports. In that case, Charles Dubin wrote the appeal judgment that upheld her right to play, finding that the Code itself was subject to the Charter and, indeed, violated the Charter by permitting this discrimination.[75]

Inevitably, most cases that generated new law based on the new Charter of Rights were appealed beyond Ontario to the Supreme Court of Canada, which made the definitive interpretations of what the Charter required. In criminal law matters such as *Oakes*, members of the Ontario court sometimes argued that they, and particularly Arthur Martin, were driving the evolution of Canadian jurisprudence, but that the Supreme Court inevitably got the final word and most of the credit. Another way in which the Charter affected the Court of Appeal was in the volume of work it produced. The court had become larger, more productive, and more hardworking over the years, and before 1982 the court was disposing of cases coming before it without much delay. "We didn't consider there was a backlog unless it was pending over six months, and we tried with most of the appeals to be able to dispose of them in one to three months and get the judgments out," said Chief Justice Howland of the pre-Charter years.[76] The volume of Charter litigation coming through the courts, the length and complexity that Charter decisions involved, and also the greater sophistication and argumentation implicit in modernist jurisprudence all led to a rapidly lengthening backlog, to the point that Howland even considered proposing that his court, like the Supreme Court of Canada after 1975, should be authorized to hear only those appeals for which it granted leave to appeal.[77] Civil appeals with a low dollar value were shifted to the Divisional Court in 1984, and Howland began imposing more stringent limits on the length of factums. He also revived a tradition that seems to have declined in earlier decades, making unprecedentedly frequent use of ad hoc judges seconded to the Court of Appeal from the High Court; at one point he had four sitting nearly constantly on appeal panels. Some of the appeal judges were concerned about both inefficiencies and the possible impropriety of having so many judges who were actually not members of the court but, as Howland recalled, the process was discussed at the Canadian Judicial Council in 1985 and found acceptable.[78]

The court's productivity was also affected by several royal commissions and inquiries headed by Court of Appeal judges, who therefore became unavailable to the court for long periods. Charles Dubin undertook a review of the Hospital for Sick Children in 1982 and led the very influential royal commission into drugs in sport that followed the Ben Johnson doping scandal at the 1988 Olympics. Samuel Grange investigated the Mississauga rail disaster of 1979 and was appointed in 1983 to report on deaths at the Hospital for Sick Children, after charges against nurse Susan Nelles were dismissed at preliminary hearing. Chief Justice Howland had only reluctantly approved Grange's appointment, not only because of the court's backlog, but also because of concerns that he would inevitably be drawn into matters that would end up before the courts.

6

The Dubin-McMurtry Courts,
1990–2007

Charles Dubin, who succeeded William Howland as chief justice of Ontario on 12 April 1990, had some reluctance about becoming a judge. From modest roots in Hamilton, Ontario, he had succeeded brilliantly in the law, confronting and overcoming the bar's endemic anti-Semitism and becoming one of the youngest lawyers in history to be named Queen's Counsel. By the 1960s, he was widely recognized as one of the two or three leading trial and appellate advocates in the country in both civil and criminal law. His love of legal practice was such that when offered an appointment to the Court of Appeal in 1973, aged just fifty-one, he was reluctant to leave the bar. But his sense that it was a leading barrister's duty to accept a judicial appointment when offered prevailed. Dubin spent seventeen years as a justice of the court, including three years as associate chief justice to William Howland, before becoming chief justice, the first and so far only associate chief justice to succeed to the office. When he was named, it was widely agreed that one of the country's finest jurists had been chosen to lead one of Canada's leading courts, and that the appointment of the first Jewish chief justice of Ontario was a landmark in the movement towards equal opportunity at the bench and bar.[1]

A lawyer's lawyer, Dubin quickly became a judge's judge, dedicated to judicial leadership in the courtroom, where he was an incisive, passionate, and engaged jurist, particularly in criminal law matters, though he was never among the most prolific writers of opinions. It was joked at his retirement in 1996 that Dubin had to retire, not because it was his seventy-fifth birthday but because he had asked his millionth question from the bench. However, he was not greatly engaged by administrative tasks. "Charlie was not a good administrator," said his admiring colleague Sydney Robins. "He left everything to his secretary."[2] Colleagues recalled that he preferred to discuss cases with them over sandwiches in his chambers rather than go out to bench and bar events or large meetings. Though charming and sociable, Dubin chose to make the court itself the focus of his activities as chief justice, and showed less interest in the public role of a chief justice than either his predecessor or his successor. He let slide many of the committees, councils, and consultations with the bar and the public that Howland had laboriously built up, including the Opening of the Courts ceremony, which Howland had made into a forum for the courts' needs and interests. Dubin intended to judge from the bench, not from the public podium.

Dubin's appointment coincided with a restructuring of the Ontario courts, though not one that he had particularly wanted. Dubin had supported the intermediate appeal court proposal that had been circulating for several years, that is, for a new final Ontario court that would always sit as a panel of seven or nine judges, to achieve consistency in the jurisprudence of the province on fundamental questions of law. This proposal had never had much traction among provincial governments, and Dubin was no more successful than the other judges and chief justices across Canada who advocated for it. The restructuring that did coincide with his term as chief justice was the most far-reaching revision of the Ontario trial courts in at least seventy-five years.

Ian Scott, the prominent appeal counsel, became Attorney General of Ontario in 1985, when the Liberal Party led by David Peterson replaced the long-serving Progressive Conservative government. New to politics but active and ambitious as Attorney General, Scott had influence in the Peterson government somewhat equivalent to that which McMurtry had had in the Davis government. Considering the court system "a kind of hodge-podge, dating back to colonial times,"[3] he intended to make changes in a hurry and showed little concern about upsetting lawyers or judges. In an interview after his retirement, Chief Justice Howland papered over his disagreements with Scott by noting the long friendship between the patrician Howland and Scott families, but he conceded that "life was more difficult with some of the things that Ian Scott was doing."[4] Their dealings left him ready to retire from the struggle when he turned seventy-five in 1990.

Restructurings

Ontario was one of the last two Canadian provinces to have a three-part trial court system: the provincially appointed provincial court, plus federally appointed county courts and district courts throughout the province, plus the federally appointed High Court, the judges of which were based in Toronto but went on circuit throughout the province. A unification of the county courts and the district courts had been undertaken in 1985, so Scott inherited two federally appointed trial courts and one provincially appointed trial court. Scott deplored the confusions in jurisdiction, the lack of coordination among the various courts, and the impossibility of rational use of courthouses and other resources caused by the proliferation of trial courts. He pursued root-and-branch reform, "a fundamental rethinking of all the assumptions on which our courts have operated since 1792."[5]

To start, Scott in 1986 had appointed an Inquiry into the Courts of Ontario, led by Justice Tom Zuber of the Court of Appeal.[6] In 1987, Zuber recommended the formation of a single superior trial court for Ontario, to be achieved by the gradual elimination of the District Court. He did not, however, support the long-standing proposal of the provincial court judges that their court should be merged with the federally appointed court. The jurisdiction and the standard of experience and expertise required of provincial court judges had increased steadily since the late 1960s, until there was increasing overlap between the federally and provincially appointed trial courts in family law and criminal law (where provincial judges handled almost all cases other than jury trials). The provincial court judges (almost 250 strong by 1990) argued for a single, unified trial court, with criminal, civil, and family divisions, and the end of all divisions between the federally appointed superior courts and the provincial trial court. Zuber, however, recommended keeping the provincial court separate from the superior trial court, even though he proposed giving the provincial court much of the jurisdiction previously exercised by the District Court, including responsibilities that would have required constitutional agreements to give the provincially appointed court powers until then reserved for federally appointed judges.

Zuber's recommendations were widely criticized,[7] and Attorney General Scott's eventual plan proved to be closer to the provincial court judges' ideas than to Justice Zuber's. Scott aimed at eventually combining the federal and provincial trial courts to form a single trial court, the

Ontario Court, which would serve the whole province, fully regionalized, with all its judges being assigned to one of seven new judicial regions in the province. Instead of letting the District Court gradually fade away through retirements, as Zuber had advised, Scott favoured its immediate merger with the High Court. All 150 District Court judges would become judges of what had been the High Court (which had 50 judges before the merger). The High Court circuits would be abolished, and the enlarged court would be dispersed across the new judicial regions of Ontario. Once legislation for that first step had been passed and implemented, Scott looked ahead to a second stage of court reform that would combine this enlarged High Court with the provincially appointed Provincial Court.[8]

Scott's 1989 legislation, effective 1 January 1990, merged the District Court and the High Court and replaced the High Court circuits with a new regional administrative structure. Zuber had recommended renaming the restructured and regionalized High Court "the Superior Court," leaving the provincial court unchanged in name. Scott, however, intended that the provincial court would soon join his trial courts merger. In anticipation of the second stage of the reform project, he established a new terminology in which all the trial courts became parts of a new entity called "the Ontario Court." He renamed the federally appointed part (the newly merged High Court/District Court) the "General Division" of the Ontario Court, and the other part, as yet unmerged, the "Provincial Division." In the process, the "Supreme Court of Ontario," since 1881 a term that encompassed the High Court and the Court of Appeal, ceased to exist. Since the Ontario Court was intended to encompass all the trial courts, the Court of Appeal for Ontario henceforth would stand alone (though General Division judges could still serve ad hoc on the appeal court, and vice versa).[9]

Both Scott's reorganization plan and the new names were resented by many judges. When Justice Zuber recommended a gradual extinction of the District Court as its judges retired, he had offended those judges by suggesting that some of them were not qualified to sit on the superior court. The provincial court judges were disappointed by his rejection of their proposals. Now Scott offended the High Court judges, many of whom shared Zuber's reservations about the District Court judges, not only by merging the two courts and dispersing the High Court's judges across the province, but also by ending the time-honoured name and tradition of the High Court, the heir to Queen's Bench, Common Pleas, and Chancery. Its judges, dispersed to the regions and combined in an entity four times its previous size, would henceforth merely be judges of "the Ontario Court (General Division)." Scott, who had already offended the senior bar by doing away with their cherished honorific "Queen's Counsel," was not much perturbed by the judges' disapproval. In a 1989 paper laying out his plans for restructuring the courts, he compared himself to Premier Oliver Mowat, recalling that Mowat's forward-thinking merger of common law and equity in 1881 had also antagonized hidebound traditionalists of the bench and bar.[10]

Shortly after establishing the Ontario Court and its General and Provincial Divisions, the Liberal government in which Scott served was defeated in the provincial election of 1990. The new NDP government of Bob Rae allowed Scott's reforms to stand but did not pursue his plan to consolidate the two divisions. As a result, Scott's second stage of court reform – a unified trial court that would have extinguished the differences between the federally appointed and provincially appointed trial courts of Ontario – never proceeded. Though discussions concerning greater unity in the family courts and other ventures have continued, and a pilot project has operated successfully in Hamilton since 1977, the constitutional problems of merging the federal and provincial appointment powers in a single trial court were never resolved. In 1999, when it was clear that the General and Provincial Divisions of Scott's Ontario Court would not be united, the General Division was renamed the Ontario Superior Court of Justice and the Provincial Division became the Ontario Court of Justice. Both trial courts continue to be divisions of the Court of Ontario, but they remain separate.

Within the new General Division formed in 1990, tensions had been running high. Frank Callaghan, chief justice of the High Court and therefore of the new General Division, took pride in running what he called the best trial court in Canada. Fearing dilution of the judicial quality and esprit de corps of the old High Court, he had opposed the merger of his court with the District Court, and some of the judges who came from the District Court felt themselves unwelcome there. As chief of the General Division, Callaghan controlled appointments to its Divisional Court for appeals in administrative law and lower-cost civil matters. Many of the judges considered these prestige assignments, but Callaghan refused to name any former District Court judges to them. For a time, relations within the court were so bad that some judges refused to share the judges' common dining room at Osgoode Hall, and the divisions between former High Court and former District Court judges remained stark. Stephen Borins, a future Court of Appeal justice who had been a law clerk to Chief Justice McRuer, a law school associate dean, and a Law Society bencher as well as an effective appellate counsel, was one of the District Court judges who joined the new General Division in 1990. In fifteen years on the county court and district courts, Borins had handled such significant cases as *R. v Shand*, in which he found mandatory sentences contrary to the Bill of Rights (and which was overturned by the pre-Charter Court of Appeal);[11] *R. v Rowbotham*, a complex drug conspiracy trial; and the tainted blood trial, in which he found the Canadian Red Cross liable for permitting HIV contamination of the blood supply.[12] When he joined the General Division, however, he found himself shut out of assignments to the Divisional Court. He felt that his record meant little, and that Chief Justice Callaghan "was never able to get over the fact that these people who weren't his equals got appointed."[13] Callaghan acknowledged the problems festering within the enlarged court by helping to recruit Roy McMurtry, under whom he had once served as deputy Attorney General, to become associate chief justice of the General Division in 1991. Callaghan, suffering from cancer, delegated much of the leadership of the court to McMurtry, hoping that his diplomatic skills could soothe some of the tensions roiling within the newly merged trial court. McMurtry succeeded Callaghan as chief of the General Division in 1994.[14]

The appeal court, meanwhile, had escaped Zuber's plans for it, and Scott's reorganization left it alone. Zuber had proposed abolishing the Divisional Court of the High Court, so that the superior trial court would do trials exclusively, and transferring its appeal functions to the Court of Appeal. With the support of Howland, Dubin, and many of the appeal judges, Zuber had also made what proved to be the final plea for a two-level appeal court. In Zuber's plan, there would be an enlarged Court of Appeal to handle most routine appeals, including the former Divisional Court matters. Above it, freed from having to "dispose of cases on a sort of assembly line basis," Zuber proposed a new seven-judge final appeal court to be called (and in fact to be) "the Supreme Court of Ontario."[15] This court would sit as a single panel to provide coherent, collegial decisions in the minority of appeals where it saw a need to determine and state the law, as well as to settle disputes from the new intermediate appeal court and give opinions on legal questions referred by the government of Ontario.

Attorney General Scott, however, decided not to change the Court of Appeal, except in facilitating its continual growth by providing that henceforth additional appellate judge positions would be established by regulation and would no longer need a statutory amendment for each expansion.[16] There would be no two-level appeal structure in Ontario. The trial court merger left the Court of Appeal more than ever a court apart. No longer included under the Supreme Court of Ontario umbrella, it became simply the Court of Appeal for Ontario. The Court of Appeal for Ontario endured, growing larger, but unchanged in structure and jurisdiction.

Chief Justice McMurtry

Charles Dubin retired at seventy-five in 1996, and Roy McMurtry, at the time chief justice of the General Division, was named to succeed him. McMurtry later wrote that he had not been particularly ambitious to be either a judge or a chief justice, but throughout his career he had chosen public service over private practice. After ceasing to be Attorney General, he had been Canadian high commissioner in Britain between 1985 and 1988 and then returned to law practice in Toronto. He joked that in going to the bench after just three years in private practice, he was confirming his friends' belief that he was determined "to avoid prosperity."[17] In an era when retired politicians were much less common on the judicial bench than they had once been, his transition from politics to the bench recalled that of previous chief justices Rowell, Mulock, and Meredith – though his first judicial appointment came from a Conservative prime minister (from whom he was estranged at the time) and his second from a Liberal.

McMurtry recalled one hesitation about becoming chief justice of Ontario. Dubin, his predecessor, had been associate chief justice before becoming chief justice, raising the possibility that the court might feel that John Morden, the incumbent ACJO (and a contemporary and friend of McMurtry), had some entitlement to the position. McMurtry began his relationship with his new judges by emphasizing his respect for them and for Morden, who remained associate chief justice until 1999 and a member of the court until 2003. The issue of "succession" was diffused, and McMurtry soon felt himself confident that he was leading a collegial bench of judges.[18]

Few doubted that as chief justice, McMurtry, a highly visible public figure throughout his career, would re-establish the high public profile that Dubin had preferred not to seek. Indeed, his appointment in 1996 had been partly a tribute to his judicial-political skills, as demonstrated by his success in deterring the Progressive Conservative government of Mike Harris from making deep cuts in the budget of the General Division.[19] In fact, McMurtry did continue in the spotlight, frequently using his new "bully pulpit" to speak publicly about social justice and other issues. As chief justice, he chaired a City of Toronto committee on a long-time concern of his, youth justice issues – a commitment honoured shortly after his retirement by the naming of Canada's largest correctional institution for youth, Brampton's Roy McMurtry Youth Centre (soon known as "the Roy"). He also remained active in outreach to black and other minority communities and continued his anti-apartheid and economic development activities through the Commonwealth.

McMurtry believed the office of chief justice should be a podium from which to advocate within the legal profession and to society in general on issues related to the law. During his term, he advocated that lawyers work for collegiality in the profession, expand their pro bono contributions, and contribute to educational outreach about the law. To those ends, he gave the court's support to programs on professionalism launched by the Law Society in response to incidents of incivility among lawyers thought to have taken their courtroom adversary roles beyond acceptable norms. He was also an active participant in the development of the legal-education organization called the Ontario Justice Education Network, and of Pro Bono Law Ontario, an organization for coordinating voluntary legal contributions by lawyers and to increasing the provision of such services by the profession. Organized in 2001, Pro Bono Law Ontario sought to organize the purely ad hoc provision of pro bono contributions and to "create a bridge between volunteer lawyers and people in need."[20] One beneficiary of Pro Bono Law Ontario's work was the court's long-standing program of prisoner appeals held in Kingston. For decades, panels of judges had held sittings in Kingston at which unrepresented prisoners could appeal their convictions or sentences. Soon after its foundation, Pro Bono Ontario developed a program through which even prisoners conducting their own appeals could count on guidance and counsel from leading members of the criminal defence bar when preparing their documents and arguments.

McMurtry took the Court of Appeal on visits to legal centres around the province, and revived the Opening of the Courts ceremony with its "state of the courts" addresses by the chief justices and the subsequent press conference, and he was notably open to media interviews and other activities that kept the chief justice in the public eye. By McMurtry's term, it was becoming accepted that while the chief justice handled the court's "outside" work – relations with other courts and with governments, judicial appointments, budgetary discussions, public outreach – the associate chief justice took on "inside" responsibilities, such as supervising case assignments and panels and ensuring efficient delivery of judgments, and also chaired the statutory committee of lawyers and judges that reviewed the rules of procedure. ACJOs also sat on the Canadian Judicial Council and played a significant role in interprovincial consultations on court practices. John Morden, ACJO throughout Dubin's term and the first years of McMurtry's, developed formal rules for case assignments and writing assignments. In 1999, he became the first associate chief justice to take up a new provision of the federal *Judges Act* that authorized chiefs and associates to retire from their administrative positions without leaving the court.[21] Morden remained a regular judge of the court until 2003. He was succeeded as associate chief by Coulter Osborne (1999–2001) and then by Dennis O'Connor, who came to the court directly from practice in 1998 and was associate chief justice from 2001 to 2012. Associate chief justices, like the chief justice, sat as judges half the time and devoted the rest of their time to administrative matters.

Like many judges, McMurtry found that judging in the appeal court lacked the drama of the trial court but he appreciated being able to spend about half of his time in court, unlike in the much larger trial court, where administrative responsibilities demanded much of a chief's time. There were, however, several administrative challenges for McMurtry.

The principal one was the backlog of cases, which had been growing throughout the 1980s due less to the number of appeals than to the growing complexity of the cases: more lawyers, more issues, more research, more need for lengthy and time-consuming written opinions. McMurtry estimated that in 1996 the backlog of cases was such that once an appeal had been "perfected" (that is, the documentary record on which the appeal hearing would be based had been completed and distributed to all parties), it took two to three years to get the case before a panel of judges. For years, the court had recommended the intermediate appeal court as the only solution to these delays. With that proposal dead, the court moved instead on organizational change.

Indeed, the key step in achieving progress on that front was already being implemented. In 1995, Chief Justice Dubin had appointed justices Coulter Osborne, George Finlayson, and John Laskin to a committee on judicial operations, and it recommended a step that would have a profound impact on appeal court practice.[22] It proposed placing stringent limits on oral arguments, with each case being examined by the court ahead of its hearing and assigned a given amount of time. Previously, counsel had a great deal of freedom with their oral arguments before the court. Subject only to the court's willingness to continue listening, lawyers could indulge in flights of oratory. But the new rules abruptly ended that era, and indeed the preceding decades, when leading counsel had been confident that they could win a case "on their feet," would be recalled as a golden age of oral advocacy. With the new strict time limits, a case that might have been argued over a couple of days might now be allocated an hour or two. Inevitably the rule was unpopular with many members of the appeal bar, and also with some of the judges, who declared that it denied procedural fairness and often refused to enforce the predetermined time limits. Counsel who had always been inclined to focus their arguments on one or two key points, however, thrived in the new environment, and quickly realized that limits on oral argument made the written factum critically important. Oral argument could still transform a case, but it was no longer simply that "the factum whets the judges' appetite" (a dictum of Chief Justice Dubin). The written factum was where the crucial arguments would be made and where the case would probably be lost and won. The shifting relationship of oral and written advocacy went far beyond merely improving productivity and ending the backlog of cases. It produced "a profound change in the culture in the court," according to ACJO Dennis O'Connor.[23]

Time limits on advocacy were not the only remedy applied to the backlog in the late 1990s. The court began exerting more control over scheduling, assigning hearing dates instead of waiting for the parties to bring the matter forward at their convenience. As they acknowledged the scale of the problem, the judges also agreed to a "blitz": starting in 1996–7, they sat more days, heard more appeals, and gave even more oral judgments from the bench than usual. They also began to attack their own backlog of reserved judgments that remained unwritten and undelivered. The *Courts of Justice Act* already empowered the chief justices of all the courts to take steps if a reserved judgment had not been delivered within six months, and the Canadian Judicial Council endorsed six months as the maximum allowable time for writing opinions, but in 2002 the court had about fifteen judgments that had been outstanding for more than a year and others that had exceeded the six-month limit. As a result, the new associate chief justice, Dennis O'Connor, was given responsibility for reviewing the progress of all judgments that had been in reserve for four months. If necessary, a judge could be relieved from other duties or given assistance to get a judgment written, but O'Connor recalled that peer pressure proved to be the most effective solution. Once monthly lists of the judgments about to become overdue were circulated, judges became determined not to find their own names there without very good reason.[24]

With all these efforts, the backlog began to melt away rapidly. In 1996, the court heard 50 per cent more civil appeals than in 1995 and double the total from 1990. The number of perfected cases ready to be heard dropped below 1,000 "for the first time in many years."[25] Litigants' lawyers who anticipated a three-year wait for an appeal hearing had developed the habit of appealing even hopeless cases, simply to have the trial verdict set aside for three years. With the delay shrinking fast, however, there was little point in "junk appeals," and so many were abandoned as their hearing dates loomed that for a time the court found it could schedule thirty hours of argument in a twenty-hour sitting week, confident that several of the scheduled cases would be abandoned.[26] The efficiency gains the court had made suggested that Ian Scott had had reason to prefer organizational changes over simply spending more, but Chief Justice McMurtry reached agreement with the government that three additional seats would be established on the court over a period of years, bringing the court to 21 judges (plus supernumeraries) in 2005.[27]

The Registry Office and Legal Research

Soon after his appointment as chief justice, McMurtry invited the courts administration branch of the Attorney General's department to assist in conducting "a review of the Court of Appeal's administrative operations and legal support," with a view to attacking the problem of backlogs and delays in areas beyond the responsibility of judges themselves. This study focused in particular on ways to improve the handling of court records in the Court of Appeal Registry. The registry, a separate institution within the Ontario registry system from 1874, then part of the Toronto court registry office after 1923, re-emerged as an independent registry in the 1990 restructurings. Senior registry officers often held a law degree, but in the nineteenth and much of the twentieth century, registry office positions were order-in-council appointments, a gift of governments. Sons of well-connected judges and court officials who had worked their way up in the Osgoode Hall court bureaucracy had often been well represented among the registry staff, along with retired military personnel, and some of that ethos had still lingered, though by the 1980s registry staff were all civil servants.[28]

The registry continued to play a dual function at the court, providing not only administrative functions that were properly the responsibility of the civil service but also judicial support functions that ought to have been independent of government. Registrars, for instance, continued into the 1980s to play a significant role in assigning judges and cases to panels. Chief Justice Howland described how in the 1980s, Registrar Bill Shaughnessy, with more than thirty years' experience in the registry and vast practical knowledge of how the court worked, often vetted cases "to determine who should sit."[29] Even later than that, Crown lawyers still sometimes treated the registry as an extension of the Attorney General's department to which they should have privileged access, and influential senior lawyers sometimes still expected that an informal understanding with the registrar would help them get their cases expedited.[30]

In 1991, Chief Justice Dubin, seeking to improve the legal research expertise available to the court, had secured the hiring, though a competitive process, of John Kromkamp, a former justice department prosecutor with appellate and legal management experience, as registrar, and for several years Kromkamp directed the court's legal research programs while also administering the registry. As registrar, Kromkamp oversaw the first steps in computerizing the registry process, beginning to create a system in which the registry's own records were stored in digital form and documents could be delivered electronically by appellants and respondents. Like many first-stage computerization projects in the 1980s, digitization at the registry began badly. It at first took twenty minutes for the computer merely to produce and assign an appeal number at the service desk, a task the paper-based process had handled in moments – forcing a quick "front counter" revision to ensure prompt service.[31] With improved programming, experienced staff, and some workspace reorganizations, the sophisticated database gradually began to deliver the promised efficiencies, and the Court of Appeal Registry continues to maintain its own customized records management systems separate from Ontario's main courts administration system. Renovations and additions conducted on the court side of Osgoode Hall between 1995 and 2000 included a substantial upgrading of the basement levels of the building – formerly "the dungeon" in registry staff parlance, now renamed "the concourse level" – to provide the staff of the Court of Appeal Registry with more and much improved work spaces.

The government's Court of Appeal Review team of 1996–9 recommended the separation of civil service tasks from jurisprudential functions entirely.[32] "At present the staff lawyers report administratively to the Registrar," the review report found, even though their task was to give the court independent legal advice and support, whereas the registrar was a civil servant accountable to the Attorney General.[33] The report also recommended that the court have more staff lawyers to handle scheduling and an enhanced program of case management for complex cases, as well as legal research; that such staffing increases should not substitute for increases in the number of student law clerks; and that both students and lawyers should become accountable to the chief justice, not to the registrar. As the result of these recommendations, Kromkamp became senior legal officer to the court in 1998. He took charge of legal research and direction of all judicial support functions that needed to be independent of government, and he was no longer tasked with administering the document management aspects of the registry. By 2013 the legal staff of the court had grown to nine lawyers and seventeen student law clerks.[34]

For the first time, the court acquired an Appeal Scheduling Unit whose members reported to Kromkamp, who in turn reported to the chief justice (though as court staff they remained members of the Ontario public service). The selection of judges for panels was removed entirely from the registrar's ambit to become the responsibility of the chief justice – usually delegated through the associate chief justice to Kromkamp and his staff. Selections of panels became even more randomized, so that over time all judges would sit with all, though discretion remained. Complex, potentially law-changing appeals in criminal law, family law, class actions law, and other such specializations often got a panel that included, not by accident, at least one of the court's experts in the field in question. "Let's say we have a big pension case," said Chief Justice Winkler about the process some years later. "If we see it coming, Eileen Gillese [a pension law scholar and former chair of the Pension Commission of Ontario] will be on it ... When scheduling is done, people are conscious of the subject matter. It is not a coincidence that with most of the class actions, I get on them."[35]

With the judicial functions removed from the registry to the chief justice's own staff, the registry could focus on the work that was properly the responsibility of the civil service, to be run by professional administrators from the courts administration branch. In September 1998, Huguette Malyon (later Thomson), who had risen through the courts administration service from the Provincial Court to the General Division, became Court of Appeal Registrar and Manager of Court Operations, charged with modernizing administrative aspects that had been outlined in the review of the registry, particularly with regard to paper flow. The court reform of 1990 had replaced "registrars" with court administrators in all the Ontario courts other than the Court of Appeal, though the name continued to be used. Thomson's dual title was a gesture to the independent tradition of the court.[36]

Paper flow, essential to efficiency at the court, had been the core responsibility of the Court of Appeal Registry since the foundation of the court. Appellants entered notices of appeal, respondents presented their replies, and eventually factums, trial transcripts, and other supporting documentation and sometimes physical evidence as well were filed at the court registry, until the complete case file was "perfected." Meanwhile, as cases were assigned to panels, allocated to courtrooms, and placed on the schedule of hearings, the registry delivered copies of the appeal materials to the judges who would hear the case an appropriate length of time before the appeal was to be heard. The registrar also held authority to rule on motions to dismiss for delay and other procedural matters related to the work of the registry. Once the appeal was heard, the paperwork began its reverse journey through the registry, with the records coming back from the judges and the decision papers going out to the public and to the parties involved.

These requirements of the registry had not changed, but Thomson concluded on her arrival that much of the process had hardly changed in a century. She and her staff implemented a fundamental reorganization to ensure efficient service both to the judges and to the lawyers, appellants, and respondents who were the registry's clients. Hiring, training, and human relations were modernized. Bilingual positions were established. The capacity of the registry to keep its own computerized records and to provide for electronic delivery of documents to and from the appellants and respondents and their lawyers was continually upgraded in subsequent years, as for instance in 2010, when the court announced that henceforth parties who did not need paper copies of decisions could receive their material by email on request.

The restructuring in the registry office, combined with the efficiencies made in court and chamber work (notably by the time limits on oral arguments), the judges' two-year-long blitz on overdue decisions, and the appointment of more judges all transformed "caseflow" at the court and served to reduce the backlog that had been developing through the 1980s. By 1999, the backlog had been extinguished, and the court could confidently promise that all appeals would get a hearing within six months of the filing of the perfected documentary record. By the mid-2000s, it was part of the culture of the court that even judgments that had been reserved for a lengthy written opinion would be delivered no later than six months after the hearing.

Judges of the Court, 1990–2007

The distinctive feature of the group of judges appointed to the Court of Appeal during the tenures of Charles Dubin and Roy McMurtry was their growing diversity. Where there had been only two women on the court before 1990, and not simultaneously, nine of the twenty-eight judges appointed between 1990 and 2007 were women: Louise Arbour, Karen Weiler, Rosalie Abella, Louise Charron, Kathryn Feldman, Janet Simmons, Eleanore Cronk, Eileen Gillese, and Susan Lang. Three of them (Arbour, Abella, and Charron) moved on to the Supreme Court of Canada during this period, and Arbour became the internationally acclaimed war crimes prosecutor for the United Nations. There were enough francophone appointments – Arbour and Charron, plus Jean-Marc Labrosse and Paul Rouleau – that the court no longer relied so heavily on its bilingual anglophone judges for its French-language panels. John Laskin, whose father, Bora Laskin, had been the first and only Jewish judge on the Court of Appeal in 1965, found when he himself joined the court in 1994 that fully a third of the judges were Jewish, and that anti-Semitism had ceased to be an issue. In another nod to merit over status, one of the first judges appointed to the court in the McMurtry years was Stephen Borins, who had felt treated as a second-class judge after the District Court–High Court merger in 1990, but was a valuable judge of the Court of Appeal from 1997 until his death in 2009. In one of his first Court of Appeal judgments, Borins dissented when the court dismissed the appeal of the murder conviction of William Mullins-Johnson. Years later, Mullins-Johnson would be exonerated by new forensic evidence.[37]

In 2004, the court set another milestone when two visible minority lawyers with non-European roots, Russell Juriansz, Indian-born of Sri Lankan ancestry, and Harry LaForme of the Mississauga First Nation,

joined the court. Juriansz had built a prominent practice in human
rights law and his appointment brought to two the number of ethnic
South Asians on Canadian appeal courts (the first being Wally Oppal of
British Columbia). LaForme, who had practised both corporate law and
Aboriginal law, had chaired the royal commission on Aboriginal land
claims before his judicial appointment and was Canada's first appellate
judge of First Nations ancestry.

Efforts to achieve gender balance in the judiciary helped bring down
the average age of first appointment among the twenty-eight judges
appointed between 1990 and 2007. They had served an average of
twenty-one years in practice before becoming judges (compared to
twenty-four for the 1967–90 cohort and twenty-six years for the 1937–
67 group). Rosalie Abella received her first judicial appointment just
six years after being called to the bar, and most of those who became
judges within fifteen years of their call were women. The new judges of
this era continued to be mostly Ontarians, with a few from other parts
of Canada, though Abella was born in Germany and Russell Juriansz
in India. Furthermore, the proliferation of law schools in Ontario after
1957 had finally broken Osgoode Hall's domination over legal education; nearly as many of the judges had earned their LLB at the University of Toronto as at Osgoode, and the other Ontario law schools were
also represented in smaller numbers. Seven of the twenty-eight had advanced degrees in law, and several had taught at Ontario law schools.
The trend to advanced education had become marked.

Of the twenty-eight appointed to the Court of Appeal during the Dubin and McMurtry years, only six (Armstrong, Cronk, Goudge, Laskin,
O'Connor, and Rosenberg, all veteran litigators) came directly from
practice, compared to as many as half in some earlier periods. Some
lawyers and judges argued that having judges appointed directly from
practice kept the appellate bench in touch with the concerns of the practising bar, and they noted that lawyers with the strongest appellate credentials sometimes chose to remain in practice rather than take a trial
court position, with its uncertain prospects of future advancement to
the appeal court. On the other hand, many judges argued the importance of trial court experience for judges who had to review trial court
decisions. And governments, it was sometimes suspected, thought that
when it came to assessing the jurisprudential inclinations of a potential
appointee, trial judges had more "track record" than lawyers. Whatever
the reason, relatively few judges came directly from practice in this period, and none after the appointment of Robert Armstrong in 2002.

Yet the court continued to boast judges of great talent: leaders of the bar, leading scholars, lawyers who had shaped the drafting of major laws, and admired trial court judges. David Doherty, Michael Moldaver, Marc Rosenberg, Louise Charron, and others provided expertise in criminal law that made them heirs of Arthur Martin. Robert Sharpe and James MacPherson had national reputations in constitutional, Elaine Gillese in pension law, Juriansz in human rights, Karen Weiler in family law, Robert Armstrong and Eleanore Cronk as leading advocates, and so on. Among the academic lawyers appointed to the court in this period – no longer the rare occurrence it had been in Bora Laskin's era – at least five (Arbour, Borins, Gillese, MacPherson, and Sharpe) had been deans or associate deans of law schools before taking judicial appointments. The later contributions of Louise Arbour, Louise Charron, and Michael Moldaver at the Supreme Court of Canada were further evidence in the talent on the Ontario court, and several others who were not appointed to Ottawa were frequently on shortlists as being both likely and deserving of appointment. Louise Arbour left the Court of Appeal in 1996 and won international renown as chief prosecutor for the International Criminal Tribunals prosecuting war crimes in Rwanda and the former Yugoslavia. She then joined the Supreme Court of Canada before becoming United Nations Commissioner for Human Rights from 2004 to 2008.

Panels of three judges had long since heard the vast majority of appeals – a five-judge panel was likely only if the court might be breaking with the *stare decisis* principle and overturning one of its own decisions. In the three-judge panels, unanimous 3–0 decisions had become very much the norm, to such an extent that there were no longer any judges on the court whose dissents were statistically notable. In a sampling of 200 cases per decade from the 1970s, 1980s, 1990s, and 2000s, the ratio of unanimous to split decisions began high and became steadily more skewed towards unanimity.[38]

The growing tilt towards unanimity was related to the growing emphasis on written argument and the way the court had refined its procedures during the blitz of the late 1990s. Operating under strict time limits, individual judges came to hearings well briefed and well prepared, although they did not discuss appeals in advance. From their preparation they often had a sense of whether an appeal should be allowed or rejected. Judges acknowledged, however, that in a quarter or more of cases, the nuances and interpretations they heard in oral argument would lead them to reconsider their original inclination. When a hearing was finished, the judges would confer briefly. The president of the panel (the chief justice or associate chief, if either was present, or the judge with the greatest seniority, even if supernumerary) would canvas opinions on the panel, starting with the most junior member. If they found agreement or settled on a 2–1 majority, they then had to decide: could this be an oral judgment or did it need to be reserved for a full written opinion?

The vast majority of appeals at the Court of Appeal for Ontario are error-correction matters that do not change or restate the established interpretation of the law. In most of these, the panel opts for an oral judgment. The president tells the parties to wait, sometimes for as little as twenty minutes, while the president (or sometimes another judge) quickly drafts a few paragraphs which are then read in court as an oral judgment (though with a written text). Such swiftly decided and delivered oral judgments had always been part of the court's repertoire, and they became very common during the backlog blitz. With the backlog reduced, however, and fewer open-and-shut cases coming to the court, many appeals, even of the error-correcting type, were decided by "endorsement." "Endorsements" had begun as brief decisions simply written on the back of the appeal book and entered into the record. By the twenty-first century, an endorsement was a longer written decision – it could be up to ten pages – to be delivered within a few days of the hearing. Endorsements did not have all the elements of a full written decision, but they constituted an official record of the judges' view. Oral judgments and endorsements constituted as much as 95 per cent of the court's decisions. Only a very small proportion of all appeals would be reserved for a long, detailed written opinion, with all the recognized elements of a formal judgment: introduction, the fact situation, the decision and reasons in the lower court, the appeal and its issues, the applicable law, the analysis, and the remedy, all fully supported by legal citations.[39]

When there was to be a full written judgment, the panel quickly decided who was going to write the majority opinion and the dissent, if any. But the culture of the court encouraged oral discussion and the circulation of draft reasons among the judges wherever there was dissent. Frequently a consensus could be found or a dissenter persuaded, or even the majority converted to the dissenter's point of view. When judges speak of the collegiality of the Court of Appeal, they usually point to this vigorous discussion that leads to a shared understanding of the law and a consensus on the decision required. Dissents remain possible, and vitally important, but in most case the judges find their way to a shared agreement on the case at issue and on the appropriate remedy.

The Jurisprudence of the Court

By the Dubin years, and even more during McMurtry's term, the profound reshaping of law and jurisprudence that resulted from the adoption of the Charter of Rights and Freedoms in 1982 had worked its way through the Canadian courts. During the 1980s, the Supreme Court of Canada, under the leadership of Chief Justice Brian Dickson, had made clear that the courts would not circumscribe and minimize the Charter of Rights as they had the Bill of Rights.[40] The Charter jurisprudence of the Supreme Court confirmed that courts would apply the Charter to review and overturn statutes that breached Charter values, and governments and their agents would be held to new standards of procedural fairness and respect for the rights of citizens in both criminal and administrative law. Some judges, including Charles Dubin, a committed supporter of the common law tradition, had not been admirers of the Charter, believing, as John Brooke said, that evolution in the common law would have delivered most of the goals of the Charter with less disruption in the law.[41] By the 2000s, however, the Charter had become accepted among judges and lawyers as the inevitable grounding of Canadian law.

Post-Charter, post-backlog, post–time limits, the court at the start of the twenty-first century emerged as a skilled, collegial, highly productive court, the final arbiter on most questions of law in Ontario, particularly in civil matters. Several prominent appeals during this period gave a sense of its jurisprudential style.

The 1999 case *English Catholic Teachers v Ontario*, once more confronted the vexed constitutional status of separate educational systems – a dispute that went back to Confederation.[42] The government of Ontario had centralized educational governance and funding and removed the right of local school boards, public and private, to support themselves by local property tax levies. The plan was challenged by both public and separate school supporters as an improper restriction on the autonomy of local schools, but the separate school teachers won at trial because of the constitutional protection for the independence of separate schools. The decision effectively overturned the cornerstone of the Ontario government's education policy, and it was appealed.

Aware of the possibility of revisiting the court's own judgments in *Tiny* from 1929 and the *Separate Schools Reference* of 1985, Chief Justice McMurtry appointed a five-judge panel (Brooke, Abella, Borins, and Goudge, with himself presiding) to assess once more the constitutional bargain of 1867. The respondents – the Catholic teachers – argued that removing the right to tax undermined the autonomy of the separate schools. The court however, found that the constitutional right was to separate schools, not to a particular funding mechanism. Since the new funding formula did not actually threaten the existence and autonomy of the separate schools, the court declared it constitutional. Stephen Goudge, a member of the panel, would later argue that the decision reflected the flexible, contextual jurisprudence of the court, focused on underlying principles rather than black-letter specifics:

The snapshot frozen in time as of 1867 could not be the sole determinant of the outcome of this debate. Rather, the court searched for the underlying essence of the compromise and found it to be a guarantee that there must be preserved a viable separate school system fairly and reasonably funded ... The choice made by the court might be described as that of a dynamic view of s.93 (1) as opposed to a static view.[43]

The Supreme Court of Canada agreed to hear an appeal of the case but sustained the Court of Appeal in 2001.

The most famous decision of the court in the McMurtry years was the same-sex marriage case, *Halpern*, an appeal from a decision by the Divisional Court that had overturned Ontario's prohibition on marriage between persons of the same sex.[44] When the court came to rule on the *Halpern* appeal on 10 June 2003, the constitutionality of the common law definition of marriage as the union of one man and one woman had already been reviewed in the British Columbia Court of Appeal and Quebec's superior trial court as well as Ontario's Divisional Court. All three courts had found in favour of gay marriage, but those three rulings had all been stayed pending the outcome of appeals and/or legislative action.[45] The Ontario Court of Appeal decision, by McMurtry, Gillese, and MacPherson, reached the same conclusion as the Divisional Court and the British Columbia and Quebec courts: the common law definition of marriage did breach the Charter rights of gay and lesbian couples who wished to marry, and therefore it could not stand. The court's unanimous decision declared that "to freeze the definition of marriage to whatever meaning it had in 1867 is

Table 6.1 Statistical Notes on 28 Judges of Appeal Appointed 1990–2007

Birthplace (some unreported)

Ontario	10
Other Canadian centres	5
Germany	1
India	1

Ethnic Origin

Anglophone/British	16
Francophone	5
Jewish	5
South Asian	1
Mississauga First Nation	1

Gender

Male	18
Female	10

Religious Affiliation

Few of the judges specify a religious affiliation in their biographical statements.

Education

Undergraduate degrees in Canada	28
Osgoode Hall Law School	10
University of Toronto Law School	10
Other law schools	8*
Degrees in law beyond the LLB	4

Average Years of Law Practice before Judicial Appointment

20 years

Minimum:	6	(Abella)
Maximum:	33	(McMurtry)

Location of Legal Practice (some in more than one place)

Toronto	21
Ottawa	4
Other Ontario centres	5
Out of province	3

Table 6.1 (*Concluded*)

Identified Political Commitment

Held elective office or politically active
Conservative   1   (McMurtry)

Judicial Appointment prior to Court of Appeal Appointment

Yes   22[†]
No   6

Average Age at Court of Appeal Appointment

50.8 years

Average Years on Court of Appeal Bench

In 2013, 16 were still sitting. Of 12 not still sitting, average service was just under 11 years.

Reason for Leaving Court of Appeal

A judge who left before 65 or to take a non-judicial position is counted as resigned, not retired.

Died	2	(Borins and Ducharme)
Retired (65 to 75)	8	
Moved to another court	3	(Abella, Arbour, and Charron to SCC)

Average Age on Leaving

68 years
Of retirees: 73.5
Of deceased: 71
Of those to SCC: 54

Note: 16 of the 28 Judges were still sitting at the end of 2013.
* Dalhousie, Western, Windsor, Oxford, Queen's, Ottawa, and Montreal.
† The court variously named the Ontario High Court of Justice, the Ontario Court (General Division), and the Ontario Superior Court; three of these also sat on the County/District Court before 1990, and two on the Ontario Provincial Court.

contrary to Canada's jurisprudence of progressive constitutional interpretation."

The court's innovation came less in the decision itself, since other courts had reached the same conclusion, than in the matter of when the ruling would be implemented. McMurtry, MacPherson, and Gillese concurred with the other Canadian courts on overturning the ban, but differed from them by declining to stay implementation of the decision to permit legislative revisions to the law of marriage. Their decision relied on previous Supreme Court of Canada decisions finding that common law definitions, such as the existing definition of marriage, were judge-made law, not statutory declarations, and therefore could be reviewed and changed by the courts without deference to the will of the legislature. As a result, the Ontario court did not stay its decision. Gay marriage became lawful in Ontario the moment the appeal was delivered. Some couples had their weddings declared valid at once and others married within hours of the decision. To provide nation-wide consistency in the application of the law, the courts in British Columbia and Quebec soon cancelled the stays they had previously imposed.

Here as in so much else, the decision of a provincial appeal court proved to be the final determination of the law. The federal government decided not to appeal the question, and soon enshrined the courts' new definition of marriage in the federal *Civil Marriage Act*. Gay marriage became established law throughout Canada and then rapidly in many other countries. The decision of the Court of Appeal for Ontario came to be seen as having played a notable role in the global shifting of both law and public opinion on this matter in the following decade.

Another significant decision of the court was its review of the conviction and sentence of Steven Truscott.[46] Since the 1980s, there had been a rising tide of calls for review of possible wrongful convictions. In 1995, the court directed a verdict of acquittal in the case of Guy Paul Morin, who had been convicted of murder some years earlier, and then convicted again on a new trial ordered by the Court of Appeal. But the Truscott case went much further back. Truscott, then fourteen, had been convicted of the murder of Lynne Harper in 1959 and given a death sentence (later commuted to life imprisonment), which both the Court of Appeal and Supreme Court of Canada had affirmed. Vigorous assertions of a wrongful conviction had let to a 1966 reference to the Supreme Court, which found the trial jury's verdict reasonable. In 2001, Truscott, by then paroled, sought a new review from the minister of justice, citing mishandling of trial evidence as well as new evidence about witness credibility and medical evidence. In 2004, the minister asked the Court of Appeal to "consider his case as if it were an appeal on fresh evidence." After extensive preparation by counsel – the appellant's factum was 3,000 pages long – the court heard the appeal over seven days in the spring of 2007.

Following the tradition that in the most serious matters, the chief justice takes the chair, McMurtry led the panel of five judges, which included David Doherty, Marc Rosenberg, and Michael Moldaver, perhaps the court's three leaders in criminal law matters at the time, and Karen Weiler. It was an unusual proceeding, for assessments of evidence and witness credibility are generally the responsibility of trial courts and juries – though indeed appeal courts can review matters of fact as well as law where warranted. In this case, furthermore, the testimony and evidence being reviewed was almost fifty years old. The review established that the medical evidence from 1959 of time of death was unreliable, suggesting that Truscott could not have been present when Lynne Harper died. In August 2007 (after McMurtry had retired, though he signed this decision), the court concluded that if a new trial were possible, "an acquittal would clearly be the likely result."[47] It quashed his murder conviction. Subsequently an inquiry by former Court of Appeal justice Sydney Robins recommended substantial compensation to Truscott for his wrongful conviction and his long imprisonment.

7

Into the Twenty-First Century: The Winkler Court, 2007–13

On 1 June 2007, Warren Winkler was named as Roy McMurtry's successor and became the twenty-ninth chief justice of Ontario. Winkler had been raised in Alberta (in the same small town, as it happened, as the slightly younger future chief justice of Canada, Beverley McLachlin). He came to Osgoode Hall to study law in the late 1950s, a very green country boy in his own telling, but gregarious and with a knack for joining organizations, making contacts, and finding mentors. He went on to earn a graduate degree in labour law with Harry Arthurs when labour law was still a new field of specialization, and he built a very successful practice in Toronto as a management-side labour lawyer with a gift for negotiations and arbitrations and a large and diverse network of friends and contacts in bar associations and the legal community in general. Urged on by friends, Winkler applied for a judgeship after twenty-eight years in practice, and he was appointed to the Ontario Court (General Division) in 1993. In 2004, he became that court's regional senior judge for Toronto, where he participated in reorganizing the court, taking steps to reduce backlogs and to ready the courts for large, complicated cases, including drug and gang cases for which extensive courtroom security was required. As a trial judge, he specialized in class actions and in judicial supervision of large, complex mediations, including the restructuring of Air Canada and the payments in the case of the Indian Residential Schools – some of which work he continued as chief justice.[1]

Given his jurisprudential and administrative record and his lack of political associations, his appointment as chief justice was controversial only because Chief Justice McMurtry had publicly declared that he and his entire court endorsed the associate chief justice, Dennis O'Connor, as the next chief justice. The Winkler appointment confirmed once more that decisions on judicial appointments always lie with the government, not with the chief justice, and also that the associate chief justiceship carried no right of succession. McMurtry remained of the opinion that O'Connor was vetoed because his work on the Walkerton Inquiry had made him unpopular with members of the federal cabinet who had been criticized in O'Connor's report,* but he emphasized that Winkler was indeed abundantly qualified for and successful in the role of chief justice.[2]

Like some of his predecessors, Winkler was initially surprised by the extent of a chief justice's public commitments, much of it effectively diplomatic and ceremonial: substituting for the lieutenant governor at official functions, attending dinners, receptions, and ceremonials. ("You could be out every night of the week.")[3] But he understood the importance of representing the judiciary and the courts to the public. Like his predecessors, he left much of the internal coordination of the judges' work to the associate chief justice and concentrated his attention (beyond judging, that is; the chief justice continued to sit on a half-time basis) on government relations and public functions, speaking frequently and in many public forums about the courts, the rule of law, and access to justice. Impressed by the lack of knowledge about the judiciary and the Court of Appeal among the public and even among insiders, Winkler initiated the project that led to this history of the court.

Winker attached the same importance to relations with the bar as with the wider public and the governing authorities. Winkler remembered when the Court of Appeal had been a "rough, rude place" and the judges at best formal and distant figures, even with practitioners who appeared regularly before them. Like his predecessor, he put great emphasis on outreach to the bench and bar. He launched a Court of Appeal annual report that summarized the activities of the court, reported

---

* O'Connor also conducted the inquiry into Canadian security services' role in the rendition of Maher Arar, a Canadian citizen, from the United States to Syria, and his report criticized actions of the Canadian government – which subsequently offered Arar an apology and awarded him compensation.

on the volume of cases heard, and noted changes among the judges and personnel of the court.[4] On his own or with the judges, Winkler continued to take the court out of Toronto to meet with the bench and bar, and he organized a series of visits to the law schools of the province. Concerned that the court be understood as a court for all Ontario, not merely a Toronto institution, Winkler secured a restructuring in Ontario's courts administration branch that formally separated the court from the local Toronto court administration with which it had been grouped. He considered having the Court of Appeal hold sittings in other Ontario centres, breaking nearly two centuries of the court sitting at Osgoode Hall in Toronto and practically nowhere else, although when he retired, no such sittings had yet occurred.

To give greater prominence to the Opening of the Courts ceremony, Winkler had the annual event moved from January to September and made it a more multi-faith and multicultural event, with an interfaith service in which much of the music was performed by members of the bench and bar, followed by the familiar courtroom event in which the heads of the appeal court, the superior trial court, and the provincial courts each reported on the state of their court. However, perhaps reflecting his career experience in conciliation rather than confrontation, Winkler discontinued the press conference, previously associated with the ceremony, at which issues (particularly funding decisions, where the judges and the government disagreed) had frequently been aired.

As chief justice, Winkler continued or extended the administrative improvements sought by McMurtry. He moved almost at once to increase the number of staff lawyers and of student law clerks (from twelve to seventeen). He secured an additional seat on the court as its workload continued to grow, so that after 2010 the court had twenty-two full time judges (including the chief and associate chief), plus two to four supernumerary judges in most years.[5]

The *Courts of Justice Act, 1990*, authorized the chief justice and the Attorney General to enter into an agreement that would formally define the vital boundary between court administration and judicial administration upon which the independence of the courts from governmental interference depended.[6] In 2012, Winkler and Attorney General John Gerritson signed the first such Memorandum of Understanding. In practice, the dividing line between court functions and civil service functions had become well understood, but the Memorandum of Understanding specified precisely how "the attorney general is accountable to the Legislative Assembly of Ontario for the proper use of public funds allocated to the administration of justice in the province," while also confirming "the constitutional principles of judicial independence and the maintenance of the judiciary as a separate branch of government" and the province's responsibility for "supporting the judiciary in providing fair and impartial adjudication."[7] The agreement confirmed how members of "the Office of the Chief Justice," including the registrar, senior legal officer, legal staff, articling students, appeals scheduling staff, and related administrative staff, would work under "the general supervision and direction of the chief justice." Even though the aforementioned remained part of the public service of Ontario, the Memorandum of Understanding put into writing the understandings about judicial independence and separation of powers that had prevailed since the reports of the McRuer commission, the Deschênes study, and other reports and studies dating back to the 1960s.

Judges of the Court

The court that Winkler joined upon his appointment in June 2007 remained remarkably stable in his first four years. Up to 2011, there were just four new appointments, including one to fill the new twenty-second seat that Winkler had requested and received. But in the twenty-four-month period that started with Alexandra Hoy's appointment to the court late in 2011, there were ten vacancies on the appeal court bench and ten new appointments, producing the most rapid transition on the bench in the court's history. Two of the court's sitting judges were named to the Supreme Court of Canada: Michael Moldaver, the criminal law specialist who had joined the court in 1995, and Andromache Karakatsanis, appointed to the appeal court in 2010 and to Ottawa just a year later. Several judges elected supernumerary status, so that by the end of 2013 there were six judges serving part time (Robert Blair, Russell Juriansz, Harry LaForme, Jean MacFarland, Robert Sharpe, and Karen Weiler), rather than the more usual two or three. Edward Ducharme, an English professor before he took up law, died of cancer in 2013, just a year after his appointment.

The appointments continued to reinforce the diversity of the court. The fourteen appointments from 2007 through 2013 included seven women and seven men, and when Dennis O'Connor retired after a decade as associate chief justice, one of the new female appointees, Alexandra Hoy, became the first woman in that post. Michael Tulloch, the first African-Canadian judge on the Court of Appeal, was appointed in 2012. There were no francophone appointments after that of Paul Rouleau in 2005. None of these judges came directly from practice. In fact, each one had prior trial court service at the Ontario Superior Court. Since the productivity reforms of the late 1990s, the court had made regular use of ad hoc judges from the Superior Court to fill out its panels when regular judges became ill, took leave, or were otherwise unavailable. As a result, new appointees from that court often had prior experience on the appellate bench. Still, they remained relatively youthful: the average length of legal practice before their first judicial appointment fell to nineteen and a half years. Long tenure on the Court of Appeal may have been a factor in the increase in the number of judges who requested supernumerary status before mandatory retirement, but early retirement remained an infrequent choice, and most judges professed enthusiasm for continuing their work. "I'm here for the duration," said one woman appointed relatively early in her career.

Though it has become relatively rare for elected politicians to move directly to the appeal bench, judicial appointments continued to be politically sensitive. The flurry of appointments from 2011 to 2013 provoked scrutiny of the appointment politics of the Conservative federal government led by Stephen Harper since 2006, particularly since the party had campaigned against activist judges and for tough-on-crime policies, and had shifted the composition of judicial selection panels to reflect those views. In 2011, the *Lawyers' Weekly* observed that across Canada the new government was appointing fewer women and a notably large number of former Crown prosecutors and government lawyers to the bench.[8] Neither observation applied to the Court of Appeal, however, where half the Harper government appointments were women and there was only one former Crown prosecutor, David Watt, and one government lawyer, Karakatsanis, among the new judges. (Tulloch had worked as both a Crown prosecutor and a criminal defence lawyer.)

Cases and Jurisprudence, 2007–13

There was a steady flow of appeals of criminal convictions or sentences, most of them of no great significance other than to the parties involved, but sometimes raising issues of national significance. In 2010, in *R. v Khawaja*, the court not only upheld the controversial antiterrorism law passed in the wake of the 9/11 attacks of 2001, but also increased the convicted terrorist's sentence substantially.[9] In *Attorney General (Canada) v Bedford*, a divided five-judge panel found aspects of federal prostitution law unconstitutional, setting up an appeal to the Supreme Court, which eventually threw out the entire law.[10] In November 2013, another five-judge panel gave its opinion on a matter that had been controversial since 2008, when the federal government, as part of its popular tough-on-crime agenda, imposed mandatory minimum sentences for gun crimes, implying, at least, that judges were too lenient in the setting of sentencing parameters. In a unanimous opinion written by David Doherty, the court struck down the three-year minimum sentence as cruel and unusual, noting that it obliged judges to give equivalent sentences for serious gun crimes and minor licensing violations. In *Smickle*, one of the group of cases the court reviewed, it rejected a mandatory three-year sentence imposed on an appellant whom police had found in an apartment wearing only underwear and sunglasses and photographing himself holding a handgun that belonged to his cousin, who was the actual object of their search.[11] The ruling produced media speculation about the government's response, but for some individuals there were rapid and direct consequences. At the court's regular Kingston sitting to hear prisoners' appeals barely a week after *Smickle*, none of the accused presented an error in law or procedure sufficient to overturn his or her conviction, but one who had been sentenced to a long term under the mandatory minimum rule was found to have already served a longer sentence than was reasonable, and he heard the court order his immediate release from custody.

In civil and commercial law, where there are fewer constitutional challenges or other issues that draw the attention of the Supreme Court, the provincial Court of Appeal is almost always the final court. One area where the court had influence during Winkler's tenure was class actions. Class actions have historically tended to reach settlement after being certified but before a final judicial determination; however, the Ontario court made new law in a number of cases, including one where it ruled that sanctions imposed by a securities regulator do not preclude a class action by investors, and another in which it loosened time limits within which actions can be launched. The court also authorized a controversial workplace class action by bank employees who claimed systemic underpayment for overtime work. In all these, the court declared the public interest in access to justice through class actions should not be hobbled by overly restrictive rules.

The court also took positions in Aboriginal rights law in *Keewatin*, when it upheld Ontario's right to implement the "taking-up" clause, without needing Canada's consent, in the part of northwestern Ontario covered by Treaty 3. Re-examining issues that went back to the court's *St Catharines Milling* decision of 1886, the court affirmed provincial authority, subject to the harvesting rights of the Treaty 3 First Nations.[12] In *Yaiguaje v Chevron*, a decision that broke new ground in international law, it authorized Ecuadorian plaintiffs to seek execution of an Ecuadorian court judgment against the energy giant in Ontario.[13] In *Rasouli v Sunnybrook Health Centre*, the sad case of a medical patient in a permanent vegetative state that raised complex issues of medical law and medical ethics, it ruled that doctors could not assert their professional authority to discontinue medical care without family consent, a decision later upheld by the Supreme Court of Canada.[14] In *Jones v Tsige*, the court declared that a common law "right of action for intrusion upon seclusion should be recognized in Ontario," in the case of a bank employee who used her position to spy on the financial situation of her partner's former spouse.[15] The Court of Appeal also broke new ground in bringing the "public interest responsible journalism defence" into Canadian law. In *Cusson v Quan*, the court observed that a long line of precedents in Canadian law gave journalists no qualified privilege against libel actions, but that the law needed to recognize newspapers' duty to serve the public by adequately covering matters of public interest. Justices Weiler, Sharpe, and Blair concluded that this tension should be resolved by judicial recognition of "public interest responsible journalism" as a defence against libel actions where the public's interest in the subject was clear and those who reported on it had followed responsible practices in their coverage. The court sustained the *Cusson v Quan* decision in a similar 2008 appeal, *Grant v Torstar Corp.* Both cases were appealed to the Supreme Court of Canada, and in *Grant v Torstar* the Supreme Court sustained the Court of Appeal and made the authoritative ruling that established the responsible journalism defence in Canadian law.*

---

* Some years later, when the mayor of Toronto was enmeshed in sensational reports of drug use and other improprieties, it was argued that without the responsible journalism defence, much of the journalism that broke the story would have remained unpublished and known only by rumour.

The Court in the Early Twenty-First Century: Achievements and Challenges

Looking back on his tenure in 2013, Chief Justice Winkler was moved to declare that he had "the best job in the world." He hesitated to boast about his court, but spoke of the skill, confidence, and collegiality of his judges and argued that through the way its jurisprudence and its procedures are studied and often followed by the other courts of the country, the Court of Appeal for Ontario played a leadership role among Canadian courts. These comments were said proudly, but they were not empty boasts. Several separate scales of measurement suggest Ontario's appeal court is both productive and influential.

In the years 2004 through 2012, the twenty or so judges of the court dealt with between 1,500 and 1,750 appeals each year.[16] Some of these inevitably were settled or abandoned as they worked their way from the initial notice of appeal, but the judges consistently heard and decided 830 to 1,085 appeals a year, as well as dealing with 800 to 1,000 single-judge motions and about 250 panel motions on procedural matters, plus 200 to 250 bail applications and 20 to 40 appeals from the Ontario Review Board.* These are substantial numbers for any court of equivalent size and jurisdiction, but it is difficult to measure or compare directly the productivity of courts. What constitutes optimal productivity for an appeal court is a subjective judgment. Appeal courts have different caseloads of appealable matters, different commitments to written versus oral opinions, and other distinguishing features. With that caveat noted, productivity calculations suggest that the judges of the Ontario Court of Appeal have consistently ranked high. The political scientists Michael Lubetsky and Joshua Krane conducted an analysis of cases dealt with by Canadian appellate courts for the years 2000 to 2007, and found that the Ontario court annually heard 159 cases per million people in the province, the highest rate among the large Canadian provinces, although some small provinces had notably higher rates.[17] On a simple cases-per-judge measure, the same analysis found that the Ontario court heard seventy-four cases per year per judge, the highest rate in the country, significantly higher than the average (forty-one cases) for all Canadian appeal courts.

---

* The ORB adjudicates in cases of individuals deemed unfit to stand trial or not criminally responsible for their actions.

Criminal matters (including inmate appeals) provided 50 to 55 per cent of the appeals heard each year in Ontario, civil matters about 40 per cent, and family law matters the remainder – less than 10 per cent.[18] Because Ontario is unique among the Canadian provinces in having a Divisional Court to hear many administrative and civil appeals (many of which therefore do not reach the Court of Appeal), the Ontario Court of Appeal has an unusually high ratio of criminal to civil appeals heard. Of all appeals heard, the court allowed the appeal– that is, revised the trial court decision to some degree – in some 30 to 40 per cent, distributed rather evenly among criminal, civil, and family matters. In 35 to 40 per cent of the appeals heard, the panels did not give judgment immediately but reserved judgment in order to deliver a written opinion later – though such opinions are often given soon afterwards in a brief endorsement. Throughout the period, appeals frequently took as much as ten months to move from initial notice to "perfection" of the record (less in civil matters, more in criminal), but once the matter was ready for a hearing, the court rarely took more than six months to deliver an opinion.

Productivity and timeliness are only two measures of a court's effectiveness. Another is how well its decisions hold up to appellate review. Here, too, the Court of Appeal has traditionally scored well. The Lubetsky-Krane study[19] found that of cases determined by the Ontario court between 2000 and 2007, the losing side sought to appeal to the Supreme Court of Canada about 8 per cent of the time. In only about 12 per cent of these appeals pursued did the Supreme Court agree to hear the appeal, and in the end only 4 per cent of cases decided by the Court of Appeal were overturned at the Supreme Court – a rate slightly "better" than the national average of 6.5 per cent of appeal court decisions overturned. Lubetsky and Krane concluded that the experience of the Ontario court's cases at the Supreme Court suggested it was a court that produced "uncontroversial decisions consistent with settled law which effectively end the dispute before it," though noting that appeal rates and rates of overturn have many complex causes not susceptible to simple explanations.[20] The general impression of a relatively productive and successful court, however, is confirmed by a book-length study by the political scientist Donald Songer covering the years 1970 to 2003. Songer's data showed that the Ontario court's low rate of overturn at the Supreme Court, both absolutely and compared to other provinces, has been long standing.[21]

Statistical analysis also tends to confirm the confidence expressed by

Chief Justice Winkler that the Ontario court's jurisprudence holds national influence. The appeal courts of the provinces and territories of Canada, while bound by the decisions of the Supreme Court of Canada, are coordinate in their authority, that is, there is no obligation on them to follow each other's decisions. Nevertheless, operating in the same country and applying a single Criminal Code and broadly similar statutory regimes and similar traditions of jurisprudence, they naturally look to each other, for guidance if not for direction. Provincial appeal courts have always taken note of each other's decisions. Throughout the twentieth century, as they gradually reduced their reliance on English jurisprudence, they began citing the decisions of the Supreme Court of Canada more frequently, and even more the other appeal courts of Canada.

Into the middle decades of the twentieth century, it was not surprising that the relatively new appeal courts of Western Canada and the small *en banc* tribunals that then heard appeals in Atlantic Canada would draw on Ontario's long record of appellate jurisprudence. A study by the political scientist Peter McCormick demonstrated that from the 1920s to the 1970s, the frequency with which Canadian appeal courts cited each other roughly doubled, so that "interprovincial citations constitute[d] a substantial element of the decision practices of Canadian provincial appeal judges."[22] In this period, the other provinces were clearly drawing on Ontario's appellate jurisprudence: the Ontario appeal court provided no less than 42 per cent of all citations by Canadian appeal courts to judgments of other Canadian appeal courts. Ontario, however, cited the other provinces' judgments much less frequently (half as often or less) than they did Ontario's. Even as the younger appeal courts matured and built up their own records of cases, the frequency with which they cited Ontario appellate judgments was hardly reduced. McCormick found that in the 1970s and 1980s Ontario still provided about 40 per cent of interprovincial citations, and continued to cite the other provincial appeal courts less than they cited it. Allowing for the volume of judgments each province produced, McCormick calculated that in the later part of the twentieth century, Ontario's contribution of citations actually grew from double what might have been its "share" (had all the courts been equally reliant on each other) to about four times its share. He concluded that this has constituted a "transmission of judicial doctrine from the Ontario Court of Appeal to its counterparts in other provinces, and this is as true in the 1980s as it was in the 1930s."[23] The Ontario court, he concluded, has been "a powerful provider of judicial precedent to other courts," influencing other Canadian appeal courts much more than any American state appeal court has done for other state courts.[24]

In 2013, judges of the Court of Appeal were quietly confident that their court retained that influence. While acknowledging the final authority of the Supreme Court, one of them argued that "we are the number one court in Canada for important everyday jurisprudence, because we do so many cases. It is a combination of the highly specialized skilled judges and the cases you just would not get anywhere else" – in criminal law, in class actions, in large commercial cases, and other fields.

Access to Justice: Challenges for Appeal Courts

For years, senior judges of the court had been observing what they called "the vanishing appellate bar." When they entered practice in the 1970s or perhaps earlier, a relatively small number of counsel were routinely retained by other lawyers to handle their appeals. This small clique of appeal giants were constantly arguing cases in the appeal court and demonstrated formidable expertise in formulating and arguing appeals. That tradition has survived, the judges say, in criminal law, but in civil law pure appellate specialists have become rare. This is partly an inevitable consequence of an ever-expanding bar and the much larger demands that preparing an appeal now put upon lawyers, but judges see it linked to deeper challenges to the way that the law and the courts serve the people of Ontario in the twentieth century. The number of appeals underwent a strange and barely explained decline, most sharply in the 1990s, and did not recover even after the court grew in numbers and in efficiency in the 2000s. It was a phenomenon seen across Canada and never authoritatively explained, but judges advanced two likely causes.

The first was the rise in private mediations. Since the 1990s, it had become common for retired judges and prominent lawyers to join private mediation chambers that offered ADR: alternative dispute resolution. Many corporations and their legal counsel found ADR attractive, both for major disputes with each other and for handling contract and service disputes with their customers. By going to ADR, the parties could in effect choose their own judges by the mediator they chose to retain. They could keep the whole matter absolutely confidential if they chose, and by mediating away their differences they could avoid the absolute win/lose of a binding court judgment on what the law required. ADR

was not automatically cheaper or even always faster, for the services of
the best ADR mediators were both expensive and in demand, but in the
twenty-first century there was no doubt that ADR was drawing a lot of
civil litigation away from the trial courts and the Court of Appeal. As
a result many leading civil litigators found themselves doing private
mediation cases, rather than trials and appeals. "The big stuff does not
come here," said John Laskin in 2013. "Courts cannot compete with the
arbitrators for the privacy, the speed, and the ability to choose one's
arbitrator."

This might be a good thing if it simply reduced the demand on the
public courts. But some judges expressed concern about a privatiza-
tion of justice. If all commercial cases went to private ADR chambers, a
body of binding public jurisprudence on many aspects of the civil law
would gradually cease to exist. Many members of the bench and bar
saw both the rise of private arbitration and the decline in the number
of appeals as aspects of the "access to justice" crisis in the Canadian
judicial system.

Courts are a subtle and complicated mechanism for settling disputes
and determining the law. Any service that demands large amounts of
time from highly trained professionals is expensive, and in the twenty-
first century more and more people and businesses were finding themselves unable to afford the costs of lawyers and litigation. Ontario had
introduced publicly funded legal aid (alongside traditional pro bono
contributions by lawyers) in the 1960s, on the principle that no one who
needed the service of a lawyer should be deprived of it simply because
of their inability to pay. Legal aid, however, was never quite like medi-
care and other aspects of the social safety net introduced in the 1960s.
By the 1990s, the large and difficult-to-predict burden of legal aid costs
upon provincial treasuries had led to budgetary restrictions and much
higher thresholds for access to legal aid, so that only very serious cases
or extremely indigent applicants were likely to be funded. Criminal defence, where an accused's right to a fair trial whatever his or her means
was a foundational principle, was better protected than civil litigation,
but across the court system, cost issues meant that growing numbers of
litigants either turned away from the courts or attempted to represent
themselves, because they either could not afford counsel or could not
accept professional advice and insisted on pursuing defences and appeals on their own.

In family law, many lawyers and judges vigorously urged that families avoid the adversarial procedures of the courts if they could possibly
deal with their issues through negotiation and mediation, but family

tensions inevitably prevented reasonable accommodations. Families ended up in court over divorces, child custody, property matters, and support payments, and it was estimated that 60 per cent of them ended up self-represented for at least part of their litigation.

Self-representation was most acute in the trial courts, but many appellants and respondents also represented themselves in the Court of Appeal, in both motions and the actual hearings of the appeals. In Chief Justice Winkler's view, this raised two different problems of access to justice. It was difficult, stressful, and time consuming for appellants to try to represent themselves effectively, and attempting to give appropriate guidance to non-professionals trying to negotiate the complex procedures of an appeal hearing cost the court much time. The second problem, however, was a deeper one which he summed up as follows: if a case cannot get to trial in the first place due to a potential litigant's lack of means, then it can never reach the Court of Appeal. Not only is the individual denied access to justice, but in addition, some definitive ruling on an important point of law may never be made, so that important social issues remain unresolved and new law goes unmade.

Winkler had made access to justice one of the hallmarks of his tenure, speaking frequently to the bar, to legislators, and to the public on the theme. Among the solutions regularly canvassed were more funding for legal aid, more pro bono contributions by the profession, more assistance for self-represented litigants, the streamlining of court procedures and of dispute resolution channels, and educational outreach to assist the public in resolving disputes as cost effectively as possible. Still, there was no quick fix and no simple solution. The chief justice, the courts, the bar, the government, and concerned members of the public continue to discuss and experiment with measures to preserve and expand access to justice, but the quest is permanent and without a single solution.

Meanwhile, in the courtrooms of Osgoode Hall, designated since 1846 as "fit and proper accommodation for the superior courts," the work of what Hume Blake called "an authoritative court ... in the presence of the people affected" goes on. Most days several appeal panels will be sitting in the original courtrooms from 1850, sensitively preserved in successive renovations, or in new courts built in renovations of the hall down to the end of the twentieth century. There is likely to be a single judge disposing of procedural motions regarding upcoming cases. In the other courts, panels of three judges, black robed, perhaps two men and a woman, perhaps two women and a man, are hearing

Table 7.1 Statistical Notes on 14 Judges of Appeal Appointed 2007–13

Gender

Male   7
Female   7

Education

Osgoode Hall Law School   5
University of Toronto Law School 4
McGill Law School   2
Queen's Law School   2
Windsor Law School   1
Degrees in law beyond the LLB   4

Average Years of Law Practice before Judicial Appointment

19.5 years

Minimum: 13   (Tulloch)
Maximum: 31   (Strathy)

Location of Legal Practice (some in more than one place)

Toronto   12
Other Ontario centres   2

Identified Political Commitment

None held elective office or was notably active politically.

Judicial Appointment prior to Court of Appeal Appointment

All 14 had previously sat on the Ontario Superior Court.

Reason for Leaving Court of Appeal

Died   1
Mandatory retirement 1
Moved to SCC   1

11 remain on the Court of Appeal.

appeals. On the bench, they have computer screens at their elbows but probably a good deal of paper before them as well. At the bar before them, there are one or two lawyers for each side, similarly arrayed with appeal books and factums, in paper and on their portable computer screens. In the appeal court, there are no witnesses, no "accused," no cross-examinations, and usually few spectators. Most of the sources of drama we expect from trial courts are absent in the appeal forum. An appeal is not a chance to do a trial over, and in general the facts have already been settled and determined. For an appeal to succeed, the appellant must convince the panel that there was an error in law or in procedure in the lower court. If the appellant can show it to have been of sufficient gravity, the appeal court will correct the error, state what the law is, and either cancel or amend the decision or send the matter back for a new trial.

The argument in the appeal courtroom is likely to be about technical interpretations of minute details of statute law or perhaps the precise phrasing of a trial judge's charge to the jury. The judges and the parties have read the record in advance and they have it before them, so the discussion, focusing on particular paragraphs or sections, is largely opaque to the few observers who may be there, and perhaps barely understood even by the appealing or responding parties. Most of the time, the decision will be of little importance to any but the parties involved. If a minor correction of error is the only result, the result is likely to be an unreported and swiftly forgotten case, just one of a thousand that will pass through the Court of Appeal for Ontario this year – but still vital to the parties who have pursued the matter so far, and who will almost certainly take it no further.

Once in a long while, an appeal is being argued that will produce headlines, overturn a statute, infuriate a government, make new law, or even free a wrongfully convicted person, notorious from media coverage of the alleged crime, from a long term of imprisonment. But even when the point of law is small and the outcome important only to the interested parties, the Court of Appeal is a mighty engine. The judges have benefited from the finest educations our society can provide. They have apprenticed through distinguished careers at the bar. They have spent years in courtrooms like these and the chambers nearby where they write judgment after judgment. They are supported by all the resources of the judiciary: research lawyers, law clerks, court clerks and bailiffs, the registry staff, and of course the lawyers who may have devoted weeks or months preparing for this brief hearing on this small point of law and who themselves may one day sit where the judges now preside.

In the end the mandate is always the same, barely changed since Hume Blake cried, "Give us the Court of Appeal": to correct error, to state what the law is, and to uphold as a guiding principle of the rule of law in Canada the right of appeal.

Note on Methods

In covering the cases and procedures of the Court of Appeal over the years, this book makes frequent reference to "our sample of recorded cases." This note sets out what we sampled and what our sample gave us.

With funding secured by the Osgoode Society for Canadian Legal History from the Law Foundation of Ontario, we retained nineteen law students, drawn from all the law schools in Ontario, and assigned to them to study the main series of published case reports in which Ontario Court of Appeal cases have been reported: the series *Ontario Appeal Reports* 1876–1900 and the series *Ontario Law Reports/Ontario Reports* (the name changed in 1931) 1901–2010.

With the reporting form provided below, the students examined cases for basic data: citation, name, dates of hearing and decision, panel of judges, opinions and dissents, names of the lawyers involved, and so on. They also provided a brief summary of the facts of the case and the opinions of the appeal judges. Finally, they were invited to note details of interest or significance about the case and to append further comment if they chose.

For the period 1876–1900, the students reported on all the published cases – because of the potential interest of such long-ago cases. For the period 1901–1970 the students sampled 10 cases per year (100 per decade) and, for the period 1971–2010, twenty cases per year (200 per decade).

Many cases heard in the appeal court were settled by oral judgment, of course, and were not reporting in the published case reports we used, and mostly we only sampled what was available. Nevertheless, the sample provided us with evidence on many questions related to the court not easily available elsewhere: the size of appeal panels and how they changed, the most prolific writers of opinions, the most frequent dissenters, the leading lawyers, the speed with which cases were completed, and so on.

Reporting Form
Ontario Court of Appeal Case Studies

Researcher Name: _____

Date Research Done: _____

Section 1. Data Collection

Case Reference [i.e., volume and page numbers] _____

Case Title: _____

Date of Hearing: _____

Date of Judgment: _____

Judges: _____

Majority judgment(s) written by:_____

Concurrences: _____

Dissent(s) written by:_____

Concurrences: _____

Appellant: _____
(name and summary description, if any)

Respondent: _____
(name and summary description, if any)

[If it is a "stated case," from which court?] _____

[If a reference, from where?] _____

Lawyers for the Appellant:_____

  Location and firm, if known: _____

Solicitors for the Appellant: _____
   Location and firm, if known: _____

Comment? [is this lawyer rare/frequent in CA cases, future judge, out-of-province, first woman you have found, anything of interest] _____
_____

Lawyers for the Respondent: _____
   Location and firm, if known: _____
   Comment? _____
_____
Solicitors for the Respondent: _____
   Location and firm, if known: _____

Section 2: Qualitative Analysis
Case Summary: Summarize Litigants/Fact Situation/Issues at Stake: _____
_____

Summarize Judgment and Dissents _____
_____

Case Analysis
Civil/Criminal

Substantive issue or mostly procedural? _____
Number of Cases Cited in the Court's Opinion(s): _____
   Supreme Court of Canada: _____
Other Canadian: _____
Other: _____

Worthy of Note?
[Make notes if the case seems of particular note or interest, whether for historical reasons, legal significance, personal glimpses, anecdotal value, or other. Quote vivid sentences, striking judgments, eccentric opinions.] _____
_____
_____

Other: _____
_____
_____

Appendices

Appendix 1: The Names of the Court

1792   Court of Appeal
1850   Court of Error and Appeal
1876   Court of Appeal
1881   Court of Appeal, division of the Supreme Court of Judicature
1913   Appellate Division of the Supreme Court of Ontario
1931   Court of Appeal for Ontario, division of Supreme Court of Ontario
1990   Court of Appeal for Ontario

Appendix 2: Size of the Court, by Statute

1849   9 justices (plus additional retired judges at times)
1874   CJ and 3 full-time justices
1883   CJ and 4
1885   CJ and 3
1897   CJO and 4
1913   CJO and 4 in 1st Division, CJA and 4 in 2nd Division = 10
1923   CJO, CJ 2nd Division, and 8 = 10
1931   to shrink by attrition to CJO and 8
1949   CJO and 9
1972   supernumerary judges permitted above the base number
1974   CJO and 13 (plus supernumeraries)

1977   CJO, ACJO, and 13 = 15
1989   CJO, ACJO, and 14 = 16 [numbers now change by regulation]
1998   CJO, ACJO, and 17 = 19, plus supernumeraries
2005   CJO, ACJO, and 18 = 20, plus supernumeraries
2006   CJO, ACJO, and 19 = 21, plus supernumeraries
2007   CJO, ACJO, and 20 = 22, plus supernumeraries
2010   CJO, ACJO, and 20 = 22, plus 2 supernumeraries
2012   CJO, ACJO, and 20 = 22, plus supernumeraries
2013   CJO, ACJO, and 20 = 22, plus 6 supernumeraries

Appendix 3: Terms of Justices of the Court of Error and Appeal and/or Court of Appeal, 1849–2013

Justices	Dates	Details
J.B. Robinson	1849–63	CJO 1849–62, president E&A 1862–3
Archibald McLean	1849–65	president E&A 1863–5
W.H. Draper	1849–77	president E&A 1865–76, CJAppeal 1876–7
Robert E. Burns	1849–63	EA en banc
J.B. Macaulay	1849–56	EA en banc
Robert B. Sullivan	1849–53	EA en banc
W.Hume Blake	1849–70	EA en banc
R.S. Jameson	1849–50	EA en banc
John G. Spragge	1849–74	and CA 1881–4 as CJO
J.C.P. Esten	1850–64	EA en banc
William B. Richards	1853–74	EA en banc
John Hawkins Hagarty	1856–74	EA, and CA 1884–97 as CJO
P.M.S. VanKoughnet	1862–9	EA en banc
J.C. Morrison	1862–74	EA, and CA 1877–85
G. Skeffington Connor	1863	EA en banc
Adam Wilson	1863–74	EA en banc
John Wilson	1863–9	EA en banc
Oliver Mowat	1864–72	EA en banc
J.W. Gwynne	1868–74	EA en banc
Thomas Galt	1869–74	EA en banc
S.H. Strong	1869–75	EA en banc, EA permanent 1874, to SCC 1875
Samuel H. Blake	1872–4	EA en banc

Appendix 3: (*Continued*)

Justices	Dates	Details
George W. Burton	1874–1900	EA and CA CJO 1897–1900
Christopher S. Patterson	1874–88	EA and CA; to SCC
Thomas Moss	1875–81	EA 1875–6, CA 1876–7, CJA 1877–8, CJO 1878–81
Fetherston Osler	1883–1910	
J. Maclennan	1888–1905	
J.F. Lister	1898–1902	
Charles Moss	1898–1912	CJO 1902–12
John D. Armour	1900–2	CJO 1900–2, then to SCC
J.J. Maclaren	1902–23	
J.T. Garrow	1902–16	
Richard M. Meredith	1905–12	
J. Magee	1910–33	
W.R. Meredith	1912–23	CJO 1913–23
F.E. Hodgins	1912–32	
William N. Ferguson	1916–28	
William Mulock	1923–36	CJ 2nd Div 1923, CJO 1923–36
Francis R. Latchford	1923–38	CJ 2nd Div 1923–31, CJA 1931–8
W.E. Middleton	1923–43	
J.F. Orde	1923–31	
Cornelius A. Masten	1923–42	
R. Smith	1924–7	to SCC
William R.R. Riddell	1925–45	
David A. Grant	1927–32	
Robert G. Fisher	1928–49	
H.H. Davis	1933–5	to SCC
N.S. MacDonnell	1933–8	
W.T. Henderson	1935–53	
Newton W. Rowell	1936–8	CJO 1936–8
Charles McTague	1938–44	
J.G. Gillanders	1938–46	
R.S. Robertson	1938–52	CJO 1938–52
R.L. Kellock	1942–4	to SCC
Robert E. Laidlaw	1943–63	
W. Roach	1944–65	

Appendix 3: (*Continued*)

Justices	Dates	Details
James C. McRuer	1944–5	to HCJ as CJ
J.A. Hope	1945–54	
F.D. Hogg	1945–57	
A.W. Greene	1945	
John B. Aylesworth	1946–72	
Charles W.R. Bowlby	1949–52	
J. Keiller MacKay	1950–7	
C.W.G. Gibson	1950–65	
Frederick G. MacKay	1952–72	
John W. Pickup	1952–7	CJO 1952–7
Eugène Chevrier	1953–6	
Walter F. Schroeder	1955–75	
Arthur M. LeBel	1956–60	
Kenneth G. Morden	1957–61	
George A. McGillivray	1957–73	
Dana Porter	1958–67	CJO 1958–67
Arthur Kelly	1960–75	
J.L. Maclennan	1961–8	
George A. Gale	1963–4	to HC as CJ, and then CJO 1967–76
Dalton C. Wells	1964–7	
Bora Laskin	1965–70	to SCC
Gregory Evans	1965–76	to HCJ as CJ
Arthur Jessup	1967–84	
John Brooke	1969–99	
John Arnup	1970–85	
Charles Dubin	1974–96	2nd ACJO 1987–90, CJO 1990–6
Willard Estey	1973–7	CJO 1976–7; to SCC
G.A. Martin	1973–88	
Lloyd Houlden	1974–97	
Maurice Lacourcière	1974–95	
Bert MacKinnon	1974–87	1st ACJO 1978–87; died 1987
William Howland	1974–90	CJO 1977–90
Tom Zuber	1975–90	
Bertha Wilson	1975–82	to SCC

Appendix 3: (*Continued*)

Justices	Dates	Details
F.S. Weatherston	1977–84	
Donald Thorson	1978–88	
John Morden	1978–2003	3rd ACJO 1990–9
Duncan G. Blair	1979–94	
Allan Goodman	1979–96	
Peter Cory	1981–9	to SCC
Sydney Robins	1981–98	
Samuel Grange	1982–95	
Walter Tarnopolsky	1983–93	died in office 1993
George Finlayson	1984–2002	
Horace Krever	1986–99	
Hilda McKinlay	1987–99	
W. David Griffiths	1987–95	
James Carty	1988–2004	
Marvin Catzman	1988–2007	died in office 2007
Pat Galligan	1989–95	
Louise Arbour	1990–9	to SCC
Osborne, Coulter	1990–2001	4th ACJO 1999–2001
Jean-Marc Labrosse	1990–	
David Doherty	1990–	
Karen Weiler	1992–	
Allan "Mac" Austin	1992–2003	
Rosalie Abella	1992–2004	
John Laskin	1994–	
Louise Charron	1995–2004	to SCC 2004
Marc Rosenberg	1995–	
Michael Moldaver	1995–2011	to SCC 2011
Roy McMurtry	1996–2007	CJO 1996–2007
Stephen Goudge	1996–	
Stephen Borins	1997–2009	died 2009
Dennis O'Connors	1998–2012	5th ACJO 2001–12
Kathryn Feldman	1998–	
James McPherson	1999–	
Robert Sharpe	1999–2013	supernumerary 2013
Jane Simmons	2000–	
Eleanore Cronk	2001–	

Appendix 3: (*Concluded*)

Justices	Dates	Details
Eileen Gillese	2002–	
Robert Armstrong	2002–13	ret'd 2013
Robert Blair	2003–	supernumerary 2013
Russell Juriansz	2004–13	supernumerary 2013
Susan Lang	2004–13	retired 2013
Jean Louise McFarland	2004–	supernumerary
Harry LaForme	2004	supernumerary
Paul Rouleau	2005–	
Warren Winkler	2007–	CJO 2007–13
Gloria Epstein	2007–	
David Watt	2007–	
A. Karakatsanis	2010–11	to SCC 2011
Alexandra Hoy	2011	6th ACJO Jun 2013–
Edward Ducharme	2012–13	died June 2013
Sarah Pepall	2012–	
Michael Tulloch	2012–	
Peter Lauwers	2012–	
George Strathy	2013–	CJO 2014–
K. Van Rensburg	2013–	
William Hourigan	2013–	
Gladys Pardu	2013–	
MaryLou Benotto	2013–	

Biographical Dictionary of the Judges of Appeal

Rosalie Silberman ABELLA (b. 1946), member of the court 1992–2004

Rosalie Abella was born in a displaced persons camp outside Stuttgart, Germany, in 1946, and came to Canada with her parents four years later. She graduated from the University of Toronto Law School in 1970, and after her call to the bar in 1972 set up a private practice. A well-known advocate for the rights of marginalized communities, Abella worked as a supervisor at Parkdale Community Legal Services, and served as an executive member of the National Action Committee on the Status of Women. She was appointed to the Ontario Family Court in 1976 and to the Court of Appeal in 1992. In 2004, Abella was appointed to the Supreme Court of Canada.

In 1982, she chaired the Study on Access to Legal Services by the Disabled, and in 1984 she conducted the Royal Commission on Equality in Employment – a report that introduced the concept of employment equity and influenced antidiscrimination legislation in Canada and around the world. She went on to chair the Ontario Labour Relations Board and the Ontario Law Reform Commission.

Abella is the recipient of over thirty honorary degrees and several other awards. She has authored over eighty articles, and written or co-edited four books.

* * *

Louise ARBOUR (b. 1947), member of the court 1990–9

Born and raised in Montreal, Louise Arbour studied law at the Université de Montréal, and after graduating with distinction in 1970 became a law clerk at the Supreme Court of Canada. She was called to the bar of Quebec in 1971 and to the bar of Ontario in 1977.

Arbour taught at Osgoode Hall Law School beginning in 1974, and for several years also sat as vice-president of the Canadian Civil Liberties Association. In 1987 she was appointed to the High Court of Justice for Ontario, and three years later to the Court of Appeal. She was appointed to the Supreme Court of Canada in 1999.

She has written extensively on issues of criminal procedure, domestic violence, and women's rights, and in 1995 led a federal investigation into human rights abuses at the Kingston Penitentiary for Women. The subsequent year, she emerged as a leading figure in international law when she was appointed by the Security Council of the United Nations as prosecutor for the International Criminal Tribunals for the former Yugoslavia and for Rwanda. She is the recipient of twenty-seven honorary degrees and several other awards. She left the Supreme Court in 2004 to accept an appointment as UN High Commissioner for Human Rights, and remained in that position until 2008.

* * *

John Douglas ARMOUR (1830–1903), member of the court as chief justice of Ontario 1900–2

Armour was born in Otanabee Township, Upper Canada, the son of an Anglican clergyman who emigrated from Ireland to the Peterborough area in the 1820s. He was an early graduate of the University of Toronto, earning his BA in 1850 before articling with his brother Robert, and later with the prominent equity lawyer and judge Phillip Van-Koughnet. Called to the bar in 1853, Armour practised in the Cobourg and area and was active in Conservative politics.

In 1877, the Liberal government of Alexander Mackenzie named Armour to the Court of Queen's Bench, and with the death of Adam Wilson ten years later, he was named chief justice of that court. In 1900, he succeeded George William Burton as chief justice of Ontario, but his tenure on the Court of Appeal was brief, for in 1902 he was named to the Supreme Court of Canada. After just seven months there, Armour resigned to serve on the Alaska Boundary Commission, and he died in London, England, while on commission business.

* * *

Robert Patrick ARMSTRONG, member of the court 2002–13

Robert Armstrong studied at Carleton, the University of Toronto, and the London School of Economics. He completed an LLB at the University of Toronto Law School in 1965 and was called to the bar two years later. From 1972 until his appointment to the Court of Appeal in 2002, Armstrong practised law at Torys LLP. He litigated several high-profile civil suits before the Court of Appeal and the Supreme Court of Canada, in addition to serving at various times as treasurer of the Law Society, president of the Canadian Institute of Advanced Legal Studies, and director of the Advocates' Society of Ontario. He is a distinguished lecturer and panellist at many legal education institutions, including the Law Society of Upper Canada, the Cambridge Lectures, the Canadian Bar Association, the American Bar Association, and others. He retired in March 2013.

* * *

John ARNUP (1911–2005), member of the court 1970–85

John Arnup was born and raised in Toronto, the son of a prominent Methodist minister and moderator of the United Church of Canada, and studied in the undergraduate law program at the University of Toronto before attending Osgoode Hall. Arnup articled with his father's friend Gershom Mason of Mason Foulds and went on to litigate in many high-profile cases before the Court of Appeal. During his three years as treasurer of the Law Society in the mid-1960s, Arnup was instrumental in the transfer of Osgoode Hall Law School to the York University campus, as well as the establishment of legal aid in Ontario – a program he defended well into the 1990s when it was faced with budgetary cuts.

He was appointed to the Court of Appeal in 1970, and would remain there until 1985. "He had wide legal knowledge and he was efficient in conducting his judgments," said his colleague John Morden. "It didn't matter what area of the law, he did whatever was required to get on top of it and to produce a very lucid, readable judgment." In his later years,

Arnup wrote several essays on legal history, as well as a biography of Justice William Edward Middleton.

* * *

Allan McNiece AUSTIN, member of the court 1992–2003

The son of a lumber merchant, Allan "Mac" Austin was born and raised in the small northern community of Chapleau, Ontario. He completed a BA at the University of Toronto in 1949, and then enrolled at the University of Toronto Law School. Following his call to the bar of Ontario in 1954, Austin practised for over thirty years at Mason Foulds (now WeirFoulds LLP), where he specialized in corporate law and civil litigation.

He was appointed to the High Court of Justice for Ontario in 1986 and to the Court of Appeal in 1992. After retiring from the Court of Appeal at age seventy-five, Austin returned to WeirFoulds as a consultant.

* * *

John Bell AYLESWORTH (1898–1990), member of the court 1946–72

Born in Newburgh, Ontario, John Aylesworth studied at Queen's University and read law with his uncle Allen Bristol Aylesworth – formerly a cabinet member in the Laurier government. Following his call to the bar of Ontario in 1923, Aylesworth practised with the Bartlet firm in Windsor, where he specialized in corporate labour law until his appointment to the Court of Appeal in 1946.

In his twenty-six years on the bench, he developed a reputation for prickliness and impatience, but was widely regarded as one of the top legal authorities in Ontario. "Aylesworth was a real man's man," said John Arnup. "When you got to know him really well, you were impressed with his … wisdom and his ability to express himself, particularly in oral judgements."

* * *

Mary Lou BENOTTO, appointed to the court 2013

Mary Lou Benotto earned a BA and an LLB from McGill University, and was called to the bar of Ontario in 1978. She practised in civil litigation and family law with Chapell Bushell Stewart in Toronto until her appointment to the Ontario Court of Justice (General Division) in

1996. From 2001 until 2005, she served as the senior justice of the Ontario Family Court, and throughout her career has authored several textbooks on family law. She was appointed to the Court of Appeal in November 2013.

* * *

Duncan Gordon BLAIR (1919–2006), member of the court 1976–94

Born in Regina, Saskatchewan, Duncan Blair earned his BA and LLB at the University of Saskatchewan. In 1941, he became a Rhodes Scholar and six years later graduated from Oxford University with a bachelor of civil law. During the war, he served as lieutenant in the Irish Regiment of Canada. Following his return to Canada in 1948, Blair set up a private practice in Ottawa, and in 1951 and 1952 worked as an executive assistant to the minister of justice. In 1968, he was elected to the House of Commons as a Liberal MP in the Trudeau government. He was defeated in the subsequent federal election, but in 1976 was appointed to the Court of Appeal, where he remained until 1994. Blair was instrumental in the establishment of the Canadian Judges Conference, and following his retirement from the bench spent four years as president of the Royal Canadian Legion. In 1998, he was inducted into the Order of Canada.

* * *

Robert Ashley BLAIR, appointed to the court 2003

Robert Blair completed his BA at Queen's University in 1965 and his LLB at the University of Toronto Law School three years later. He specialized in corporate litigation and administrative law during his time at the bar, and developed an interest in alternative dispute resolution. Following his appointment to the Ontario Court of Justice (General Division) in 1991, he served as co-chair of the Civil Justice Review, and as a member of the steering committee that established a judicially integrated Alternative Dispute Resolution centre in Toronto.

Blair has been closely involved with the Canadian Superior Court Judges Association throughout his time on the bench, and in 2005–6 served as its president. In recent years, he has represented the association at the International Association of Judges – a consortium that aims to protect the independence of the judiciary worldwide.

* * *

Samuel Hume BLAKE (1835–1914), member of Error and Appeal 1872–4 as justice of Chancery

The son of William Hume Blake, Samuel Blake was born in Toronto to a prominent legal family with close connections to the Liberal Party. He studied law at the University of Toronto, and worked at his family's law firm alongside his older brother Edward and his uncle George Skeffington Connor, both of whom went on to hold public office. Blake was called to the bar in 1858, and rapidly developed a reputation as a "successful and masterful advocate."

In 1872, Sir John A. Macdonald appointed him to the Court of Chancery of Ontario, making him a judge of Error and Appeal ex officio, but with the restructuring of Error and Appeal in 1874 he lost that role and sat only in Chancery.

Blake never achieved the same prominence or received the same respect as a judge that he had as a lawyer, however, and following his departure from the courts in 1881, returned to his old firm. For the remainder of his life, he remained in the public spotlight as an evangelical of the low Anglican Church, the treasurer of Wycliffe College, a public speaker, and author of approximately fifty pamphlets on politics and religious virtue. A skilled and well-connected corporate lawyer, he counted the Canadian Pacific Railway, the Canadian Bank of Commerce, and the city of Toronto among his clients, and donated much of his wealth to the church and other philanthropic causes. Never one to hold his tongue on issues of public or religious concern, Blake was a staunch proponent of temperance and foe of corruption. His writings were marked by strident proclamations on morality, a frivolous use of exclamation marks, and verbose titles such as "The Church of England in Canada should be Protestant until Rome dies," "A rebellious people, a God of Judgment. The end thereof? Who will have the last word? The Judge," and "Is the world's estimate of the position of Christ correct?"

* * *

William Hume BLAKE (1809–1870), member of Error and Appeal 1849–62 as justice of Chancery, and from 1864 as retired trial judge

William Hume Blake was born to a prominent Anglican family in the Irish county of Wicklow. He arrived in British North America at age twenty-three, along with his brother Dominick and brother-in-law George Skeffington Connor. After settling in York, Blake was called to the bar 1838 and rapidly established himself as a successful and dynamic lawyer, practising in both criminal and equity law.

He became increasingly enmeshed within the upper echelons of the Reform movement throughout these years, and in 1843 at the behest of Robert Baldwin began litigating on behalf of the Crown. That year he also accepted an appointment, alongside Robert Easton Burns and James C.P. Esten, to an inquiry into the structure of the chancery courts. With the executive committee holding final judicial authority in Upper Canada, and the superior courts consisting merely of a single unpopular judge of Chancery and three Family Compact Tories on the Queen's Bench, discontent with the courts had been fomenting at the bar for some time. In 1845, Blake petitioned Baldwin to put an end to the judicial power of the executive committee and form a court of appeal – a reform, he wrote, that would "do more to liberalise the bench and bar than can well be conceived." In 1848, he was elected to the legislative assembly, and following his appointment to Solicitor General, his recommendations soon made their way into legislation. In May of 1849, the Court of Error and Appeal was established, alongside the court of Common Pleas and an expanded Chancery. An anxious and fervent politician who sometimes alienated his allies, Blake was appointed chancellor in September of that year, where he remained until 1862.

He briefly returned to the Court of Error and Appeal in 1864, but was soon forced into retirement by failing eyesight and acute arthritis.

* * *

Stephen BORINS (1934–2009), member of the court 1997–2009

Stephen Borins was born and raised in Toronto, the son of a Jewish family with roots in the Ukraine. His introduction to law came through his father, who worked as assistant Crown attorney of Ontario throughout the 1930s and 1940s and was active in the Liberal Party. Borins worked at his father's firm, Croll, Borins, Orkin & Allen, while attending the University of Toronto Law School, and was called to the bar in 1961. He then worked for one year as a law clerk to the chief justice of the High Court, James Chalmers McRuer.

In 1969 Borins left the firm to accept a position at Osgoode Hall Law School, where he was instrumental in incorporating poverty law into the school's curricula. He was appointed a district court judge for Brampton in 1975, and in 1997 joined the Court of Appeal, where he sat until his death in 2009.

In his first case on the court, he dissented from the ruling of his fellow justices in dismissing the leave to appeal of William Mullins-Johnson, who had been convicted of first degree murder but was later exonerated by DNA evidence after spending twelve years in prison. As a judge, in the words of criminal lawyer Frank Addario, Borins "was principled and intellectually curious. He had an inspiring willingness to stand up for the underdog."

* * *

Charles William Reid BOWLBY (1892–1952), member of the court 1949–52

Born in Tapleytown, Ontario, Charles Bowlby served in the 26th Battery during the First World War and enrolled at Osgoode Hall upon his return to Canada. During his thirty years at the bar, Bowlby served briefly as assistant Crown attorney and then set up a private practice in Hamilton, where he later became president of the Hamilton Law Association. He was appointed to the Court of Appeal in 1949, and served until his death in 1952 at age sixty.

* * *

John Watson BROOKE (b. 1924), member of the court 1969–99

John Watson Brooke was born in Toronto, the son of a doctor and coroner, and studied at Trinity College and Osgoode Hall Law School. After his call to the bar in 1949 he worked alongside John Robinette at McCarthy & McCarthy of Toronto, where he specialized in litigation. He practised in several areas of law in the 1950s and 1960s and was especially known for representing the CBC and the Canadian College of Nurses in labour negotiations. Brooke joined the High Court of Justice in 1963, one of the youngest people ever to do so, and six years later was appointed to the Court of Appeal.

* * *

Robert Easton BURNS (1805–1863), member of the court 1850–63 as justice of Queen's Bench

Robert Easton Burns was the son of a Presbyterian minister who had arrived in the Niagara region from Pennsylvania in 1804. He was educated by his father until age sixteen, when he began studying law with the local lawyer John Breakenridge. He was called to the bar of Upper Canada by the time he was twenty-two, and set up a practice in St Catharines. He became a district judge for the Niagara region at the age of thirty, but after two years decided to return to the bar and move to Toronto, where he went into practice with Attorney General Christopher Alexander Hagerman and later became a bencher of the Law Society of Upper Canada. Focusing on equity law, in 1844 Burns entered a partnership with Oliver Mowat and Philip VanKoughnet, but shortly thereafter returned to the bench as judge of the Home District court. Burns was appointed to Queen's Bench in 1850, making him an ex officio judge of Error and Appeal. Known as a diligent and liberal judge, Burns was made chancellor of the University of Toronto in 1857.

* * *

George William BURTON (1818–1901), member of the court 1874–1900, as chief justice of Ontario 1897–1900

The son of an admiral, George Burton was born and raised in the English town of Sandwich. At age eighteen he moved to Ingersoll, Upper Canada, where he studied law with his uncle Edmund Burton. After his call to the bar in 1841 he practised in Hamilton, where he worked in commercial and railway law and served as solicitor to the municipality.

In 1874, he was appointed to the restructured Court of Error and Appeal, and in 1897 became chief justice of Ontario. Though known for his expertise in commercial law, he also made significant contributions to the interpretation of legal jurisdiction, writing several judgments of provincial and federal law, and chairing the 1885 commission charged with revising the provincial statutes. Throughout his career on the bench, Burton often demonstrated a sense of humour in addition to a fastidiously methodical approach to the law – qualities that according to the *Canadian Law Times* made him "a great favourite of the Bar, and we believe with the public also."

* * *

James Joseph CARTHY (1933–2006), member of the court 1988–2004

Born in Peterborough, James Carthy studied at St Catharines College, the University of Toronto, and Osgoode Hall, from which he graduated in 1958 with honours. He practised at Weir and Foulds for the following thirty years, specializing in civil litigation and administrative law. Carthy was involved in several legal organizations, including the Canadian Bar Association and the American College of Trial Lawyers, and sat for fifteen years as a bencher of the Law Society. He was appointed to the Court of Appeal in 1988, and remained there until his retirement in 2004.

* * *

Marvin Adrian CATZMAN (1938–2007), member of the court 1988–2007

The son of a Jewish litigator in Toronto, Marvin Catzman took an interest in law from a very young age. He completed his BA and LLB at the University of Toronto and was called to the bar in 1964. After working as a law clerk under James McRuer and George Gale at the High Court of Justice, Catzman joined his father's firm, Catzman and Wahl, where he specialized in civil litigation. He was appointed to the High Court of Justice in 1981, and in 1988 to the Court of Appeal, where he remained until his death in 2007. Throughout his time on the bench, Catzman developed a strong reputation for his congeniality and affability. "He had a very brilliant legal mind," said litigator Marie Henein following his death. "He was a forceful presence at the Court of Appeal, but he really had a wonderful manner about him."

* * *

Louise Viviane CHARRON (b. 1951), member of the court 1995–2004

Louise Charron was born in Sturgeon Falls, Ontario. She received her BA from Carleton University and her LLB from the University of Ottawa, and was called to the bar in 1977. Beginning in 1978, she served as assistant Crown attorney for Ottawa-Carleton, and additionally began lecturing at the University of Ottawa's faculty of law. She was appointed to the Ontario Court of Justice (General Division) in 1990 and to the Court of Appeal in 1995. In 2004, she was called to the Supreme Court of Canada, where she remained until her early retirement in 2011.

* * *

Edgar Rudolphe Eugène CHEVRIER (1887–1956), member of the court 1953–6

Eugène Chevrier was the first francophone judge appointed to Ontario's High Court and the Court of Appeal. Born in Ottawa, Chevrier studied at Osgoode Hall and was called to the bar of Ontario in 1912 and the bar of Quebec two years later. From 1926 until 1936, he sat as a Liberal in the House of Commons, representing Ottawa East.

Upon his appointment to the High Court of Justice in 1936, he became notorious for his stringent standards of courtroom decorum and was known to censure witnesses, lawyers, and court officers who slouched, rested their feet on the rungs of their chairs, failed to dress appropriately, or used the word "okay." His "unremitting sartorial campaign" did lead to improvements in the justices' gowns, although his bid to revive the judicial wig met with less success.

In June of 1940, the Communist Party was banned after Chevrier found three of its members guilty of sedition for their distribution of antiwar pamphlets – a ruling he later described as "the proudest judgment I ever rendered."

* * *

George Skeffington CONNOR (1810–1863), member of Error and Appeal in 1863 as justice of Queen's Bench

The son of a prominent lawyer, George Skeffington Connor was born in Dublin and enrolled at Trinity College at the age of fourteen. After settling permanently in Toronto in the late 1830s, he was called to the bar of Upper Canada in 1842 and established a legal practice with his brother-in-law William Hume Blake and Joseph Curran Morrison. A charismatic orator, he went on to lecture at King's College and the University of Toronto, and additionally worked as U of T's solicitor through the 1850s. In 1856 he was appointed to the commission to revise and consolidate the statutes of Upper Canada. Connor's first foray into politics came in 1844, when he ran as a Reformer for the legislative seat of the Simcoe area. He lost that election, but secured a seat thirteen years later (by a margin of a single vote) for the riding of Oxford South and during his time in the assembly served as Solicitor General under George Brown's short-lived administration. In 1863, he was appointed to the Court of the Queen's Bench, but soon died from a seizure.

* * *

Peter deCarteret CORY (b. 1925), member of the court 1981–9

Peter deCarteret Cory was born in Windsor. After serving in the Royal Canadian Air Force during the Second World War, he graduated from the University of Western Ontario in 1947 and from Osgoode Hall

Law School in 1950. He practised with Holden & Murdoch in Toronto throughout his twenty-four years at the bar, and served as president of the County of York Law Association, national director of the Canadian Bar Association, and president of the Advocates' Society.

In 1974, Cory was appointed to the High Court of Justice, and in 1981 to the Court of Appeal. From 1989 to 1999, he sat on the Supreme Court of Canada, and in the decade following his retirement he conducted arbitration and mediation at the Osler Alternative Dispute Resolution Centre.

* * *

Eleanore Ann CRONK, appointed to the court 2001

Eleanore Cronk graduated from the University of Windsor Law School in 1975. She worked for several years as a senior litigation partner at Lax O'Sullivan Cronk, where she specialized in environmental, commercial, insurance, and health law. She has been commission counsel and represented parties at many public inquiries, including investigations of infant mortality at the Hospital for Sick Children and the Walkerton E. coli disaster.

Cronk has served as the president of the Advocates Society, has gained fellowships at the American College of Trial Lawyers and the International Society of Barristers, and has been the recipient of multiple awards for her advocacy work.

* * *

Henry Hague DAVIS (1885–1944), member of the court 1933–5

Born and raised in Brockville, Henry Davis completed his BA, MA, and LLB, all at the University of Toronto. Following his call to the bar in 1911, he joined the Toronto firm Kilmer, McAndrew & Irving and remained until his appointment to the Court of Appeal in 1933. Two years later, he was appointed to the Supreme Court of Canada, where he chaired inquiries into the Canadian arms trade and labour practices at the Port of Vancouver.

He is known for having dissented against the ruling of his fellow Supreme Court justices in the 1939 case *Christie v York*, when the majority upheld the right of a tavern to deny service to a black man. Davis died in 1944 at the age of fifty-eight.

* * *

David Harold DOHERTY, appointed to the court 1990

David Doherty was appointed to the High Court of Justice in 1988 and
to the Court of Appeal in 1990. Formerly a Crown attorney, he is considered one of the foremost experts in criminal law. In recent years,
he has made news for his criticism of mandatory minimum sentencing
and the criminalization of the sex trade.

* * *

William Henry DRAPER (1801–1877), member of Error and Appeal
1849–74 as justice of Queen's Bench and Common Pleas 1849–68 and
head of Error and Appeal 1868–74; chief justice of the Court of Appeal
1874–7

The son of a minister, William Draper grew up in Oxford, England. He
began his career in his teens as a mariner with the British East India
Company, and for some time considered pursuing a life at sea. (During
his time as a cadet he is said to have once quelled a mutiny singlehand-
edly, "felling one of his assailants dead at his feet with a blow from a
handspike.")
    He came to Canada in the spring of 1820, and studied law with
George Boulton, and subsequently under Attorney General John Beverley Robinson, before being called to the bar in 1828. After eight years
in private practice, Draper, a moderate Tory, waded into politics. In the
subsequent years, he was a highly influential figure in Upper Canada,
sitting on the executive committees of the governments of Francis Bond
Head and Charles Metcalfe. As Solicitor General and later Attorney
General, Draper organized many of the prosecutions that followed the
Upper Canada rebellion of 1837.
    He went on to lead the government of the United Province of Canada
in the mid-1840s, during which time he passed important reforms in
taxation and educational policy but struggled to maintain a stable caucus. Frustrated with politics, he resigned in 1847 and was appointed to
the Court of the Queen's Bench, later moving to the Court of Common
Pleas. In 1868, he was appointed as the presiding judge of the Court of
Error and Appeal, where he would remain until his death in 1877.

* * *

Charles Leonard DUBIN (1921–2008), member of the court 1973–96, as
chief justice of Ontario 1990–6

Charles Dubin was born and raised in Hamilton, the son of New York

Jews who had moved to Canada in the 1910s. Mentored by Caesar Wright and Bora Laskin at the University of Toronto, Dubin graduated with the gold medal in 1941. Articling with Mason, Foulds, Davidson & Kellock while at Osgoode Hall, Dubin became the first Jew at a leading litigation firm in Toronto.

Throughout his career at the bar, he was known as one of Canada's most skilled and versatile litigators, taking myriad cases in both criminal and civil law. He defended clients on charges of drug possession, on charges of murder, in custodial battles, in labour disputes – and the list goes on. In 1966, he represented Prime Minister John Diefenbaker ("the most difficult client I ever had") at the judicial inquiry into the Munsinger affair. At another point, he successfully defended a Thunder Bay dog facing euthanization under the *Vicious Animals Act*.

Dubin was appointed to the Court of Appeal in 1973, later becoming chief justice of Ontario from 1990 until his retirement in 1996. He led several high-profile commissions, including the 1979 inquiry into aviation safety, and the 1990 inquiry into the use of athletic steroids.

* * *

Edward W. DUCHARME (1943–2013), member of the court 2012–13

Edward Ducharme grew up in Windsor. He studied English at the University of Windsor and earned his PhD at the University of Michigan, later returning to Windsor as a professor of English literature. He fostered an interest in hermeneutics throughout his academic career, studying questions of a text's intent and interpretation, and it was not until his mid-forties that he turned that interest towards the law and enrolled at the University of Windsor Law School. Working alongside his younger brother, himself a prominent criminal lawyer at Ducharme Fox LLP, Ducharme came to specialize in employment law and labour relations. In 2002, he was appointed to the Superior Court of Justice, where he later became regional senior judge for Southwestern Ontario. He was appointed to the Court of Appeal in April 2012.

* * *

Gloria Jean EPSTEIN, appointed to the court 2007

Gloria Epstein earned her LLB from the University of Toronto and was called to the bar in 1979. Specializing in administrative, commercial, and family law, Epstein began her legal career at Fasken & Calvin and later established her own specialized litigation. In 1993, she was appointed to the Superior Court of Justice of Ontario, and in 2007 to the Court of Appeal. She has held many positions in civil society organizations throughout her career – including director of the Ontario Superior Court Judges Association and director of the Canadian Women's Foundation – and has lectured at the University of Toronto, York University, the Advocates' Society Institute, Canadian Bar Association, and the American Bar Association.

* * *

James Christie Palmer ESTEN (1805–1864), member of Error and Appeal 1849– 64 as justice of Chancery

James Esten was born and raised in Bermuda, the son of the colony's chief justice. In his adolescence, he went to London, where he studied at Charterhouse School and Lincoln's Inn and went on to establish a successful legal practice specializing in land law.

He moved to Upper Canada in 1836, and following the establishment of the Court of Chancery the following year resumed his career as an equity lawyer. His practice in York became very successful, and in 1843 he was appointed to the commission on the Court of Chancery alongside William Hume Blake and Robert Easton Burns. He joined the courts as senior vice chancellor in 1849 and remained there until his death in 1864.

* * *

Willard Zebedee ESTEY (1919–2002), member of the court 1973–5 and chief justice of Ontario 1976–7

The son of a prominent litigator and Supreme Court judge, Willard "Bud" Estey earned his BA and LLB at the University of Saskatoon. He joined the army in 1942, and soon thereafter, the RCAF, flying missions over Japan. Following the war, Estey completed an LLM at Harvard, and was subsequently called to the bar of Ontario. He became a prominent and prosperous figure during his years practising law; specializing in tax and copyright legislation, he litigated on behalf of CTV, Famous Players, and other major corporations.

He was appointed to the Court of Appeal in 1973, and served briefly as chief justice of Ontario in 1976–7, before being named to the Supreme Court of Canada. Though known for an "air of crusty conservatism,"

Estey was also sympathetic to the rights of criminal defendants at a time when the court was beginning to interpret the Charter of Rights and Freedoms.

* * *

Gregory Thomas EVANS (1913–2010), member of the court 1965–76

Greg Evans was born and raised in McAdam, New Brunswick, the second of seven siblings in a Catholic family of modest means. After earning his BA at the University of Moncton, Evans moved to Ottawa to pursue a career in hockey. Finding no such opportunities (he was short and only 130 pounds), he moved to Timmins in 1934 to work in the beer parlour of his aunt's hotel. After two years, he had saved enough money to enrol at Osgoode Hall, though upon arrival he found the conservative pedagogy of the school rather tedious. ("I hated it," he later said.) Often he would often skip lectures to watch courtroom proceedings, but he nonetheless graduated near the top of his class.

Returning to Timmins after his call to the bar in 1939, Evans set up a private litigation practice, which by the 1950s had become the most prominent firm in Northern Ontario, with six other lawyers and offices in four cities.

In 1963, he was appointed to the High Court of Justice, and two years later to the Court of Appeal. In 1976, he took the position of chief justice of the High Court, and remained there until 1988. Perhaps his greatest legal legacy was to call attention to the issue of justice for the wrongfully convicted. Beginning in 1987, Evans chaired an inquiry into the wrongful conviction on charges of murder of a Mi'kmaq man named Donald Marshall Jr in Nova Scotia. His report found that racism had played a significant part in the fiasco and that the justice system had failed Marshall "at virtually every turn."

* * *

Kathryn N. FELDMAN, member of the court 1998

Kathryn Feldman completed a BA at University of Toronto in 1970, and went on to earn an LLB at the U of T Law School, where she co-edited the law review. Following her call to the bar, she worked as a law clerk at the Ontario Court of Appeal, and subsequently practised with Blake, Cassels & Graydon, where she focused on civil litigation and administrative law.

In 1990 she was appointed to the Ontario Court of Justice (General Division) and in 1998 to the Court of Appeal. Throughout her time on the bench she has been an active member of the Canadian Superior Court Judges Association and has participated in a number of continuing legal education programs. She currently sits as the director of the Canadian Chapter of the International Association of Women Judges.

* * *

William Nassau FERGUSON (1869–1928), member of the court 1916–28

William Ferguson was born in Cookstown, Ontario, to a prominent Anglican family with strong ties to the Conservative Party and the Orange Lodge. Of his five siblings, two of his brothers also went into law, and his sister Emily Murphy went on to make an indelible mark in the jurisprudence of gender equality through her involvement in the 1927 Persons Case.

Ferguson, who was known among friends as "Pat," articled with William Mulock while attending Osgoode Hall Law School and was called to the bar in 1894. His law firm, Millar, Ferguson & Hunter, was based in Toronto, and during his years there he specialized in railway law. He also took an active interest in outdoor sports, playing in and at times administrating local lacrosse, rugby, and baseball leagues. Throughout his time on the bench, writes historian and appellate judge Robert Sharpe, Ferguson developed "a solid reputation as a courteous, personable, and common-sense judge who took particular interest in encouraging the younger lawyers who appeared in his court."

* * *

George Duncan FINLAYSON (1927–2008), member of the court 1984–2002

George Finlayson was born in Winnipeg, and grew up partly in Ottawa after his father was hired as secretary to Prime Minister R.B. Bennett in 1930. He completed a BA at the University of Toronto in 1949, and enrolled that fall at Osgoode Hall. Beginning in 1951, he practised at McCarthy & McCarthy, and in his thirty-three years at that firm he litigated in several high-profile cases across the country, often winning them despite his habit of "brawling verbally with opposing counsel and even judges."

He was the treasurer of the Law Society of Upper Canada from 1978 until 1980, and in 1984 he was appointed to the Court of Appeal, where he sat until his retirement in 2002. In 2003, he published a biography of his colleague John Robinette entitled *Peerless Mentor: An Appreciation.*

* * *

Robert Grant FISHER (1865–1953), member of the court 1928–49

Robert Grant Fisher was born in London, Ontario. He was educated at Dufferin College and then studied at the Law Society of Upper Canada, during which time he articled with the prominent London lawyers Thomas Graves Meredith and William Meredith. Following his call to the bar in 1888, he practised in London and in 1913 ran unsuccessfully as a Liberal for a seat in the House of Commons. He was appointed to the High Court of Justice in 1922, and joined the Second Appellate Division of the Court of Appeal in 1928.

Fisher became a uniquely public figure during his time on the court, his comments frequently making headlines in the local press ("Jurist Urges Strappings" and "Judge Would Flog All Bootleggers," among others). Upon his retirement in 1949, he publicly lamented the social decay wrought by bars, dances, sports, and drive-in theatres. On the question of juvenile delinquency, he pronounced that "mothers must assume responsibility for the downfall and loss of good principles in their children," and encouraged corporal punishment, so that "they will know better how to behave in the future." Nonetheless, by the time of his retirement he denied that he had grown callous during his time on the bench: "I still believe in this moral and mercy stuff," he said.

* * *

George Alexander GALE (1906–1997), member of the court 1963–4 and chief justice of Ontario 1967–76

George Gale, known among friends as "Bill," was born in Quebec City to an Anglican family with deep roots in Quebec. When he was four, his family moved to Vancouver, where his father went on to become mayor from 1918 until 1921. At about the age of nine, Gale decided to become a lawyer, and upon graduating from high school moved to Toronto, where he enrolled in law at University College. Beginning in 1929, he articled with Donald, Mason, White & Foulds while attending Osgoode Hall, and was called to the bar in 1932.

Gale joined the bench of the High Court of Justice in 1946, at the time the youngest man ever to do so. In 1964, after a brief stint on the Court of Appeal, Gale was made chief justice of the High Court, and four years later was appointed chief justice of Ontario. Gale presided over several criminal cases in his early years as a judge, but his most high-profile case began in 1966 with the mining dispute *Leitch Gold Mines v Texas Gulf*, which became the longest and most expensive civil suit ever heard by the Ontario courts. As chief justice, Gale recruited several leading practitioners – including John Arnup, Bill Howland, Charles Dubin, and Arthur Martin – who revitalized the Court of Appeal from its previous rut of black-letter jurisprudence. He retired from the Court in 1976, aged seventy, and in subsequent years worked in various advisory roles to the Province of Ontario.

* * *

Patrick Thomas GALLIGAN (b. 1930), member of the court 1989–95

The son of a county court judge, Patrick Galligan was born and raised in Pembroke, Ontario. He attended Osgoode Hall Law School after completing a BA in English and economics at the University of Ottawa, and was called to the bar in 1956. He practised in criminal and civil law, first in Toronto, where he was a founding member of the ADR (Alternative Dispute Resolution) Chambers, and later in Ottawa, where he was a sessional lecturer at the University of Ottawa Law School.

In 1970, he was appointed to the High Court of Justice, and in 1989 to the Court of Appeal. Shortly after his retirement in November of 1995, he conducted a legal inquiry into the trial of Karla Homolka.

* * *

Thomas GALT (1825–1909), member of the court 1869–74

The son of the prominent Scottish novelist and colonist John Galt, Thomas Galt was born in London, England, and raised in Upper Canada from the age of three. He studied law under Attorney General William Henry Draper, serving as his clerk, and was called to the bar in 1845. Galt was a dynamic lawyer – making connections with big business by focusing on railway law, and simultaneously developing a reputation as one of the most skilled criminal lawyers in Toronto. He served as Crown prosecutor before his appointment to the bench of Common Pleas in 1869, and in 1887 he became the chief justice of that court. Following the court's incorporation of equity law in 1881, Galt's "almost exclusive devotion" to the common law became a slight handicap. But, noted the *Canadian Law Journal*, "his sound common sense very largely supplied the defect."

* * *

James Thompson GARROW (1843–1916), member of the court 1902–16

Born into a farming family, James Garrow was born in Chippewa, Ontario. He studied law by working in the courts of Huron County and was called to the bar in 1869. He practised in Goderich before entering politics, becoming reeve as well as warden of the county. In 1890, he was elected as a Liberal to the Ontario legislative assembly, where he sat on the standing committees on municipal law and railways.

Following his appointment to the Court of Appeal, Garrow served as a commissioner for the revision of the statutes of Ontario in 1906.

* * *

Colin William George GIBSON (1891–1974), member of the court 1950–65

Colin Gibson was born in Hamilton, the son of Major General John Gibson. He attended the Royal Military College before moving to Toronto, where he studied at Osgoode Hall and articled with Newton Rowell. Gibson became captain of an infantry regiment during the First World War, and was decorated by the governments of Belgium and Poland for his service.

Following the war he practised law with Gibson, Levy & Inch in Hamilton, where he would also become president of the local Liberal Club. In 1940, he was elected to the House of Commons and immediately appointed by Prime Minister King as minister of national revenue. In the later 1940s, Gibson went on to serve as minister of national defence for air, secretary of state, and minister of mines and resources. He was appointed to the Court of Appeal in 1950 and remained there until his retirement in 1965.

* * *

John Gordon GILLANDERS (1895–1946), member of the court 1938–46

John Gillanders was born and raised in Highgate, Ontario. After beginning his post-secondary education at the University of Toronto, he joined the Royal Flying Corps in 1917. After several victories in airborne combat, Gillanders was made commander of his squadron and awarded the Distinguished Flying Cross in 1918. He enrolled at Osgoode Hall after his return to Canada, and following his call to the bar in 1921 he established a firm in London.

He was appointed to the Court of Appeal in 1938, aged only forty-three, and during his eight years on the bench he also sat on the Ontario Cancer Commission, the Inquiry into Transport in Ontario, and the Department of National War Services. During the Second World War, Gillanders undertook several extra duties for the government, in particular by chairing the Department of National War Services and arbitrating in several labour disputes. Upon his death, Chief Justice Robertson stated that he "took on so many special duties at the request of the Government that he simply overtaxed himself."

* * *

Eileen Elizabeth GILLESE, appointed to the court 2002

Eileen Gillese was born in Edmonton. She earned a bachelor of business administration and Commerce from the University of Alberta in 1977, and subsequently studied law at Oxford as a Rhodes Scholar, graduating in 1980 with distinction.

After returning to Canada, Gillese was called to the bar of Alberta and worked with the firm Reynolds, Mirth and Coté in her hometown. In 1983, she moved to London, Ontario, where she became dean of the faculty of law at the University of Western Ontario, and taught trusts, pensions, property, and administrative law until her appointment as a Superior Court Justice in 1999. She was appointed to the Court of Appeal in 2002, and has been named a Leading Educator of the World, one of Canada's Top 100 Women, and a *Globe and Mail* Nation Builder for her part in the 2003 same-sex marriage decision.

* * *

Allan GOODMAN (1921–1997), member of the court 1979–96

The youngest of six siblings, Allan Goodman was born and raised 'in Hamilton to a family of Polish Jews. After graduating from McMaster University in 1940, he enrolled at Osgoode Hall, where he won the gold medal in 1943. Before he could collect his medal, however, Goodman enlisted in the RCAF and remained overseas until the end of the war.

In 1946, Goodman set up a one-man general practice in Welland, Ontario, where he became a well-known and respected member of the community and in the 1960s served as alderman and water commissioner. Although an ardent supporter of the NDP, he was appointed to the High Court in 1973 by the Trudeau government, and in 1979 to the Court of Appeal by Joe Clark's administration.

* * *

Stephen Thomas GOUDGE, appointed to the court 1996

Stephen Goudge was born in Toronto, and graduated with a BA from the University of Toronto in political science and economics in 1964. From there he went to the London School of Economics where he completed a Masters in economics, before returning to U of T for his LLB. He articled under Ian Scott (later Attorney General of Ontario) and was called to the bar in 1970. He became a managing partner at the Toronto firm Gowling, Starthy & Henderson, and from 1974 until 1985 lectured at U of T in labour law and aboriginal law. Throughout his time at the bar, he also was active in the Ontario Bar Association and the Canadian Civil Liberties Association. He was appointed to the Court of Appeal in 1996. In 2007, Goudge was appointed commissioner of the inquiry into pediatric forensic pathology in Ontario, and the following year released his extensive report on judicial investigation into child mortalities.

* * *

Samuel George McDougall GRANGE (1920–2005), member of the court 1982–95

Samuel Grange was born in London, and studied at the University of Toronto, graduating in 1939. The following year he enlisted in the Royal Regiment of Canadian Artillery; by the end of the war, he would be promoted to captain, and later awarded the Croix de Guerre by the government of France. As the son of two journalists, Grange had planned on pursuing his parents' trade, but during his time in the military he was selected several times to defend his fellow servicemen when they were brought before military courts. Having excelled as a counsel despite a lack of legal training, Grange enrolled at Osgoode in 1946 and was called to the bar in 1948.

He practised for thirteen years with Heighton, Symons & Grange, and in 1961 moved to McMillan Binch, where he remained until his appointment to the High Court of Justice in 1974. He was appointed to the Court of Appeal in 1982, and remained there until his retirement in 1995. During his time on the bench, Grange chaired several commissions, including the inquest into the spate of infant mortalities at the Hospital for Sick Children in 1980 and 1981.

* * *

David Inglis GRANT (1871–1933), member of the court 1927–33

The son of a Presbyterian minister, David Inglis Grant was born in Ingersoll and during his years in high school moved with his family to Orillia. Grant finished his studies at Osgoode Hall with the silver medal, and was called to the bar in 1894. After practising in Orillia for sixteen years, in 1911 he returned to Toronto to join the firm Johnston, McKay, Dods and Grant. In 1925 he was appointed to the High Court of Justice, and in 1927 to the Court of Appeal.

* * *

Ainslie Wilson GREENE (1880–1945), member of the court 1945

Ainslie Greene was born and raised in Ottawa. He graduated from the University of Toronto in 1901, and from Osgoode Hall in 1904. He then moved back to Ottawa to practise law, first with the firm MacCracken, Henderson, Greene & Herridge, and after 1919 with Greene & Johnston. Greene also became involved in municipal politics, first as an alderman and later as a controller. He was appointed to the High Court of Justice in 1936, and throughout the war undertook several extrajudicial duties for the federal government. "In national politics," wrote the *Globe and Mail*, "he was a zealous Liberal of distinct leftist tendencies, without being a narrow partisan." He died shortly after his appointment to the Court of Appeal in 1945.

* * *

Wilson David GRIFFITHS (1925–2004), member of the court 1987–95

David Griffiths was born and raised in Owen Sound. During the Second World War, he served in the RCAF as a leading aircraftsman, and later in the army as a corporal. Following the war, he completed a BA in law at the University of Toronto, and was admitted to Osgoode Hall in 1948. He practised law in Toronto following his call to the bar in 1951, and throughout his years in practice was an exceptionally active member of the legal community, serving as chairman of the Ontario Legal Aid Plan, the Medical-Legal Association, the Advocates' Society, and others. He sat on the High Court of Justice beginning in 1975 and on the Court of Appeal from 1987 until his retirement in 1995.

* * *

John Wellington GWYNNE (1814–1902), member of Error and Appeal 1868–74 as justice of Common Pleas

John Wellington Gwynne was born in the Irish town of Castleknock, outside Dublin. He studied at Trinity College Dublin beginning in 1828 and in 1832 left for Canada with his brother William Charles, where he articled under Christopher Hagerman and William Henry Draper in Toronto. Beginning in the mid-1840s, he took a keen interest in the railway business, and by the early 1850s he had successfully built a line to Guelph and secured a charter to extend it to Sarnia. (His company was ultimately merged with the Grand Trunk Railway Company.) Gwynne became one of the most prominent litigators in Toronto in these years; in addition to his extensive knowledge of railway law, he was one of few barristers to be well-versed in both common law and equity.

In 1868, Draper wrote to Prime Minister Macdonald recommending Gwynne's appointment to the bench ("notwithstanding he is at times crochetty"), and in November of that year he joined the Court of Common Pleas. During his time in the judiciary, Gwynne's politics drifted away from his previous Reform inclinations and further in the direction of Macdonald's Conservatives, whose centralist approach to Confederation complemented his own. But he also distinguished himself in the eyes of the federal government by chairing a commission on the fusion of law and equity in the early 1870s. In 1879, he was appointed to the Supreme Court of Canada, where he remained until his death in 1902.

* * *

John Hawkins HAGARTY (1816–1900), member of Error and Appeal 1856–74 as justice of Queen's Bench and Common Pleas, chief justice of Ontario 1884–97

The son of a judicial official in the courts of Dublin, John Hawkins Hagarty grew up in an Anglican household and in his adolescence studied at Trinity College Dublin. He moved to Toronto in 1835, and, after articling with the prominent Orangeman and politician George Duggan, he was called to the bar in 1840. Rapidly developing a reputation as an eloquent and effective counsel in the common law courts, Hagarty soon took several prominent positions in the political establishment, becoming an alderman in 1847, and president of the St Patrick's Society and the Canadian Institute.

He was appointed to the court of Common Pleas in 1856 and to Queen's Bench in 1862. He later became chief justice of both of those courts, and in 1884 became chief justice of Ontario – a position he held until his retirement in 1897.

Though admired by many at the bar for his "good natured sallies," Hagarty was also known as an austere and god-fearing traditionalist. "Strongly conservative in his views, he took no pleasure in change," wrote the *Canada Law Journal*, "and cared not for the fusion of law and equity, preferring to the last the ways of the common law."

* * *

William Thomas HENDERSON (1874–1953), member of the court 1935–53

William Henderson was born and raised in Stratford. After his call to the bar in 1894, Henderson moved to Brantford, where he practised law for the bulk of his career. His time there was interrupted only by his service in the First World War, during which he led an artillery battalion. A member of the Freemasons and multiple golfing clubs, he served as counsel and solicitor for the City of Brantford for thirty-six years, and occasionally as secretary of the Brantford Conservative Association.

In 1934 he was appointed to the High Court of Justice, and the subsequent year to the Court of Appeal, where he developed a reputation as one of the most belligerent judges on the bench. Litigator William Anderson described him as "a heavy set man, with a florid complexion, prominent jowls, and appalling judicial manners," adding that he was "without a doubt, the chief ogre in the Court of Appeal."

* * *

Frank Egerton HODGINS (1854–1932), member of the court 1912–32

Frank Hodgins was born and raised in Toronto, the son of prominent author and deputy minister of education John George Hodgins. He was

educated at Trinity College and called to the bar in 1879, thereafter joining the firm Heighington & Bastedo, which he went on to lead.

Throughout his time in practice, Hodgins worked as counsel to government bodies in various capacities: legal agent to the federal government in Toronto, counsel to the government of Ontario, and solicitor
for the Toronto Board of Education. He additionally served on multiple
commissions, including an inquiry into the municipal liquor licensing
system, and another into the "condition and care of the feeble-minded."

As warden of St Simon's Church and a lay delegate to the Synod
of Toronto, Hodgins's activities in the Anglican Church were, in the
words of the *Globe and Mail*, "almost as prominent as his professional
and judicial career."

He was appointed directly to the Court of Appeal in 1912, and remained there until his death.

* * *

Frederick Drummond HOGG (1879–1961), member of the court 1945–
57

The son of a barrister, Frederick Drummond Hogg was born and raised
in Ottawa. He studied at the University of Toronto and Osgoode Hall
before his call to the bar in 1904.

He practised in Ottawa, where he served for a time as an alderman,
and as chair of the Court of Revision.

He was appointed to the High Court of Justice in 1935 and to the
Court of Appeal in 1945, remaining there until his retirement in 1957.

* * *

John Andrew HOPE (1890–1954), member of the court 1945–54

John Andrew Hope was born and raised in Perth, and after studying
at Osgoode Hall was called to the bar in 1914. Having enlisted in the
military in 1910, Hope was sent to France during the First World War,
where he became company commander of a Canadian infantry battalion. He was later decorated by the military, and upon returning to
Canada remained active in local militias into the 1930s.

Hope set up a private practice upon his return to Perth, and became
chairman of the local board of education, and president of the Great
War Memorial Hospital.

He was appointed to the High Court of Justice in 1933 and to the
Court of Appeal in 1945, remaining there until his death in 1954. Begin-

ning in 1945, he also chaired the Royal Commission on Education and in 1950 released the "Hope Report," a 1,200-page document encompassing 300 recommendations. Calling for the elimination of Catholic secondary schools in Ontario, the abolition of Grade 13, and the expansion of programs for children with learning disabilities, the report stirred much debate but was ultimately ignored by the government.

* * *

Lloyd William HOULDEN (1922–2012), member of the court 1974–97

Lloyd Houlden was born and raised in Toronto, and earned a BA at the University of Toronto. He enlisted in the Canadian Naval Reserves during the Second World War and following the war enrolled at Osgoode Hall. Graduating in 1948 with several medals and awards, Houlden joined the Toronto firm Binkley & Harries and remained there for over two decades. Specializing in issues of creditors' rights, he co-authored the *Insolvency Act* and the textbook *Bankruptcy and Insolvency Law of Canada* alongside Carl Morawetz.

He was appointed to the High Court of Justice in 1969, and in 1974 to the Court of Appeal. Known as "an avid reader, vegetable gardener, and world traveller," Houlden also contributed his time to the ADR Chambers following his retirement from the bench in 1997.

* * *

C. William HOURIGAN, appointed to the court 2013

William Hourigan completed a BA at McGill University in 1987 before attending Osgoode Hall Law School. Following his call to the bar in 1992 he practised with Fasken Martineau, where he focused on commercial litigation. Formerly a member of the Advocates Society and the Ontario Bar Association, he was appointed to the Ontario Superior Court of Justice in 2009. He joined the Court of Appeal in October 2013.

* * *

William Goldwin Carrington HOWLAND (1915–1994), member of the court 1975–90, as chief justice of Ontario 1977–90

The son of an Anglican family with a long and prominent history of public service, Bill Howland was born in Toronto and attended Upper Canada College. He articled with Rowell, Reid, Wright & McMillan while studying at Osgoode Hall, where he graduated in 1939 with the silver medal. Following three years as a training officer in Western Canada during the Second World War, he returned to Toronto and became a partner at his previous firm in 1948. Howland worked primarily in corporate law until he was appointed to the Court of Appeal in 1975.

In his thirteen years as chief justice of Ontario, he implemented reforms aimed at rationalizing court procedure, and was instrumental in the establishment of such bodies as the Ontario Bench and Bar Council and the Ontario Courts Advisory Council.

He was closely associated with the UN Association of Canada throughout his adult life and travelled extensively throughout Russia, China, South America, Africa, the Middle East, and Australia.

* * *

Alexandra HOY, appointed to the court 2011, associate chief justice from 2013

Alexandra Hoy studied at the University of Alberta, l'Université Laval, and York University, from which she graduated with honours in 1975 with a bachelor of fine arts. From there, she went on to Osgoode Hall Law School, and was called to the bar in 1980. She became an associate and later a partner at Lang Michener, where she represented several high-level corporate clients. Hoy was appointed to the Superior Court of Justice of Ontario in 2002, where she went on to specialize in the adjudication of class action lawsuits and financial litigation. She was appointed to the Court of Appeal in 2011, and in 2013 was named associate chief justice of Ontario.

* * *

Robert Sympson JAMESON (1796–1854), member of Error and Appeal 1849–50 as justice of Chancery

Robert Sympson Jameson was born in England's Lake District, and as a friend of Hartley Coleridge, he grew up in the company of Samuel Coleridge and William Wordsworth. At twenty-four he moved to London, where he studied law at the Middle Temple and was called to the bar five years later. He worked in London for the subsequent six years, editing reports from the bankruptcy courts and editing a new edition of Samuel Johnson's *Dictionary of the English language*.

In 1829 Jameson was appointed chief justice of the colony of Dominica, where he spent the subsequent four years lamenting the local culture and struggling unsuccessfully to reform a court system dominated by slave owners. After declining the offer of chief justice of Trinidad and Tobago, Jameson was appointed Attorney General of Upper Canada, and commenced his position there in June 1833. He became a fixture of the Upper Canadian elite, serving in the legislative assembly through the late 1830s, becoming treasurer of the Law Society, and establishing the St George's Society and the Toronto Literary Club.

His reputation steadily declined, however, following his appointment in 1837 to the court of chancery, where his limited experience in litigation and painstaking devotion to precedent drew the ire of the legal community. With the reforms of 1849, William Hume Blake became chancellor; Jameson was unhappily pushed down to junior vice chancellor, and a year later he resigned from the judiciary altogether. He died in Toronto of tuberculosis in 1854.

* * *

Arthur Robert JESSUP (1914–1990), member of the court 1967–84

Arthur Jessup was born in Montreal and moved with his family to Toronto at age twelve. He studied at the University of Toronto, graduating in 1936, and enrolled at Osgoode Hall that fall. Shortly after his call to the bar, Jessup enlisted in the Canadian army, and by war's end had been promoted to the rank of major and decorated by the governments of France and Belgium.

Upon returning to Canada in 1946, he set up his practice in Windsor. Known for his air of "unpretentious dignity," Jessup was appointed to the High Court of Justice in 1964 and three years later to the Court of Appeal, where he sat until his retirement in 1984.

* * *

Russell Gordon JURIANSZ, appointed to the court 2004

Born in Kirkee, India, Russell Juriansz immigrated to Canada with his family in 1955. He studied at the University of Toronto, graduating in 1969 with a bachelor of science, and then at Osgoode Hall Law School, from which he graduated in 1972. He set up a general litigation practice in the mid-1970s, and soon became a consultant to the Metro Toronto Task Force on Human Relations, which examined problems of racial discrimination in the city. In 1987 he became an associate and later a partner at Blake, Cassels & Graydon, and in 1994 established an independent practice. Specializing in human rights law and the Charter of Rights and Freedoms, Juriansz argued several cases before the Supreme Court of Canada prior to his appointment to the Ontario Court (General Division) in 1998. In March of 2004 he became the first person of South Asian descent to be appointed to the Ontario Court of Appeal.

* * *

Andromache Rhea KARAKATSANIS (b. 1955), member of the court 2010–11

Andromache Karakatsanis studied at the University of Toronto and Osgoode Hall Law School, and was called to the bar in 1982. For several years, she litigated in criminal, civil and family law in Toronto. Beginning in the late 1980s, Karakatsanis took several jobs in the provincial civil service, first as CEO of the Liquor Licence Board of Ontario, and later as secretary for native affairs, deputy Attorney General, and secretary of the cabinet. She was appointed to the Superior Court of Justice in 2002, to the Court of Appeal in 2010, and to the Supreme Court of Canada in 2011.

* * *

Roy Lindsay KELLOCK (1893–1975), member of the court 1942–4

The son of a pharmacist, Roy Kellock was born in Perth, and in his adolescence moved with his family to Toronto. He earned a BA at McMaster University, and after studying at Osgoode was called to the bar in 1920. He practised law with Donald, Mason, White & Foulds for twenty-two years, and in 1942 was appointed to the Court of Appeal. Following his appointment to the Supreme Court of Canada only two years later, Kellock went on to chair several Royal Commissions, the most high profile of which was the inquiry into foreign espionage prompted by the revelations of the Gouzenko affair. He was called upon to mediate and adjudicate in labour disputes involving railway unions on three separate occasions in the 1950s, and additionally led investigations into safety protocols of the shipping and railway industries.

In 1955 he was made chancellor of McMaster University, and following his retirement from the bench in 1958 he returned to private practice, joining the firm Blake, Cassels & Graydon.

* * *

Arthur KELLY (1900–1986), member of the court 1960–75

Arthur Kelly was born to a prominent Irish Catholic family in Toronto. His father, Hugh Kelly, had been a prominent barrister and was appointed to the High Court of Justice in 1911. During his years at Osgoode Hall, Kelly articled with T.N. Phelan and Osler, Hoskin & Harcourt, and was called to the bar in 1923.

He went into practice with Day, Wilson, & Kelly in 1928, and stayed there until he was appointed to the Court of Appeal in 1960. He wrote the legislation that incorporated the Catholic school board of Toronto in the early 1950s, and became the first chairman of the Addiction Research Foundation, as well as the Ontario Mental Health Foundation. Towards the end of his career he conducted a number of important commissions – including one on stock market regulation and another on labour dispute arbitration. Following his departure from the court, Kelly was appointed to head a commission on the structure of the appellate process in Ontario. The Kelly Report, released in 1977, recommended that appeals be divided between error correction and law development, but was ultimately ignored by the Attorney General's office.

* * *

Horace KREVER (b. 1929), member of the court 1986–99

Horace Krever was born to a Jewish family in Montreal and raised in Toronto. He graduated from the University of Toronto with a BA in 1951 and proceeded to study law at University College and Osgoode Hall, articling with Goodman & Goodman. Following his call to the bar in 1956, Krever joined Kimber & Dubin, where he practised civil and criminal litigation for nearly a decade. Beginning in the mid-1960s, Krever taught law at the University of Toronto and the University of Western Ontario, and in 1975 he was appointed to the High Court of Justice. He joined the Court of Appeal in 1986, and sat there until his retirement in 1999.

In 1987, Krever chaired the Royal Society of Canada's study on the AIDS epidemic, which found that the struggle against the disease was being hindered by homophobia and the lack of human rights protections for gays and lesbians. He went on to write the decision in the landmark 1992 case *Haig v Canada*, the first appellate court ruling to determine that sexual orientation should be read into the Charter of

Rights and Freedoms as a proscribed basis of discrimination. The following year, he was appointed to lead the federal inquiry into the tainted blood fiasco of the 1980s that resulted in the spread of HIV and hepatitis C among clients of Canadian blood banks. In 2002, he received the Ally Award from the CBA's Sexual Orientation and Gender Identity Conference.

* * *

Jean-Marc LABROSSE (b. 1935), member of the court 1990–2007

Born in the town of Masson, Quebec, Jean-Marc Labrosse studied at the University of Ottawa, graduating with a BA in 1957 and with an LLB in 1960. He was called to the bar in 1962, and went on to become a senior partner in Lacroix, Forest & Labrosse in Sudbury, where he specialized in civil litigation.

A member of the Advocates Society and the Canadian Bar Association, Labrosse was additionally one of the founders of the Sudbury District Boys Home, a foster home for children in need.

He was appointed to the High Court of Justice in 1975 and to the Court of Appeal in 1990, where he sat until his retirement in 2007.

* * *

Maurice Norbert LACOURCIÈRE (1920–1999), member of the court 1974–95

The son of a prominent litigator, Maurice Lacourcière was born in Montmartre, Saskatchewan. He studied French literature at the University of Ottawa, graduating with a BA in 1940, and then enrolled at Osgoode Hall – although his studies were soon interrupted by the war. After four years in the RCAF, Lacourcière returned to Toronto and began articling with the firm O'Brian & Phelan. He was called to the bar in 1949, and joined his father's practice in Sudbury, where he went on to hold several positions in local civic institutions, including president of the Sudbury Law Association and governor of Laurentian University. He was appointed to the bench of the Nipissing county court in 1964, and to the High Court of Justice in 1967. Having developed a reputation as an "attentive, compassionate listener," and a staunch defender of the rights of Franco-Ontarians he was brought to the Court of Appeal in 1974, where he sat until his retirement in 1995.

* * *

Harry Smith LaFORME, appointed to the court 1994

A member of the Mississauga of the New Credit First Nation, Harry La-
Forme grew up on the New Credit reserve south of Brantford, Ontario.
After studying at Osgoode Hall Law School, LaForme articled with Osler, Hoskin & Harcourt, where, following his call to the bar in 1979, he
went on to practise in corporate law. He later opened an independent
practice, where he specialized in aboriginal law, constitutional law, and
the Charter of Rights and Freedoms.

In 1989 he was appointed to the Indian Commission of Ontario, and
that same year sat as co-chair of the National Chiefs Task Force on Native Land Claims. In 1991 he was appointed chair of the Royal Commission on Aboriginal Land Claims. LaForme has taught on the rights
of indigenous peoples at Osgoode Hall Law School and published extensively on aboriginal law and justice. In 1994 he was appointed to
the Ontario Court of Justice (General Division), and in 2004 became the
first aboriginal person appointed to an appellate court in Canadian history. In 2007 he was appointed to lead the Indian Residential Schools
Truth and Reconciliation Commission, but resigned the following year,
claiming that his fellow commissioners were insufficiently committed
to the objective of reconciliation. He has been presented with the Eagle
Feather by aboriginal elders on three occasions.

* * *

Robert Everett LAIDLAW (1891–1963), member of the court 1943–63

Robert Laidlaw was born in Durham, and attended high school in the
neighbouring town of Owen Sound. In 1911, he moved to Toronto,
where he studied civil engineering. Following his graduation, he took
a job in Detroit with the Federal Commission on Valuation of U.S. Railroads, but after one year returned to Toronto to study at Osgoode Hall.
Laidlaw graduated in 1919 with a silver medal in proficiency and a
gold medal in public speaking and began practising with McCarthy &
McCarthy, where he had previously articled.

In 1923 he joined the legal department of Canadian National Railways, and in 1937 co-authored an influential textbook on engineering
law. He was appointed to the Court of Appeal in 1943, and remained
on the bench until his death in 1963.

* * *

Susan Elizabeth LANG, member of the court 2004–13

Born in Sault Ste Marie, Susan Lang earned a BA at Queen's University in 1971, and from there went to Osgoode Hall Law School. After thirteen years in practice, in 1989 she was called to the High Court of Justice. The following year, she joined the Ontario Court of Justice (General Division), now the Superior Court of Justice. During her time there, she became president of both the Ontario Superior Court Judges' Association, and the Canadian Superior Court Judges' Association. She sat on the Court of Appeal from 2004 until 2013, and has co-chaired the Ontario Courts Accessibility Committee.

* * *

Bora LASKIN (1912–1984), member of the court 1965–70

Possibly the most influential jurist of post-war Canada, Bora Laskin was central to the transformation of Canadian jurisprudence from a strictly black-letter discipline to a more rigorously intellectual one.

He was born and raised in a family of Russian Jewish immigrants in Thunder Bay, and moved to Toronto after finishing high school, earning a BA at the University of Toronto in 1933. He then began his master's degree while simultaneously studying at Osgoode Hall and articling with the barrister W.C. Davidson. In 1936 he was admitted to Harvard, where he completed a masters of law within a year. After struggling to find work within the largely anti-Semitic legal establishment of Toronto, Laskin was hired as a professor by U of T in the fall of 1940. He remained in academia for twenty-five years, becoming one of the most prominent scholars of Canadian law and writing widely cited texts on constitutional and labour law.

He was appointed to the Ontario Court of Appeal in 1965, and after five years to the Supreme Court of Canada. He was the first Jew and the first academic to serve on either of the courts, and from 1973 until his death in 1984 sat as chief justice of Canada.

Often the most liberal jurist on the bench, Laskin's dissents on behalf of battered wives, native women, and iconoclastic artists won the admiration not only of burgeoning social movements, but also of Pierre Trudeau. "Known for his rigorous commitment to the highest ethical and intellectual standards on the part of the judiciary," writes biographer Philip Girard, "he symbolized a new spirit of openness and transformation in Canadian society and law."

* * *

John Ivan LASKIN, appointed to the court 1994

The son of Bora Laskin, John Laskin's introduction to law came early in life. He grew up in Toronto, and graduated from the University of Toronto Law School in 1969. Following his call to the bar, he spent twenty-three years in civil litigation and came to specialize in public policy law. During his years in practice he was made a fellow at the American College of Trial Lawyers, and served as counsel to several commissions of inquiry.

Since his appointment to the Court of Appeal in 1994, Laskin has been closely involved with several educational organizations for judges and barristers, including the Ontario Centre for Advocacy Training and the National Judicial Institute.

* * *

Francis Robert LATCHFORD (1854–1938), member of the court 1923–38

An inveterate polymath, Francis Latchford was among the most dynamic lawyers of his time, and in 1923 became the first Catholic ever appointed to the Court of Appeal. He was born to Irish immigrants who had settled in Aylmer, Quebec, and attended Ottawa University and graduated in 1882 with multiple awards for his writing. Following his call to the bar in 1886, Latchford became a leading barrister in the Ottawa region and a solicitor for several of the city's social clubs. He additionally became president of the St Patrick's Orphan Asylum, and the Ottawa Reform Club.

During these years he also fostered a hobby as an amateur conchologist, and beginning in the 1880s published several short reports on freshwater mollusks in *Nautilus*, *Ottawa Naturalist*, and other journals.

In 1899, he was elected as a Liberal to the legislative assembly of Ontario for the district of South Renfrew, and during his time in government was appointed commissioner of public works, and later Attorney General. After his exit from government in 1905, Latchford came to focus on industrial infrastructure, and became a director of the Cobalt Lake Mining Company and the Nipissing Central Railway. He was appointed to the High Court of Justice in 1908, and in 1923 to the Court of Appeal.

* * *

Peter LAUWERS, appointed to the court 2012

Peter Lauwers earned an LLB from the University of Toronto, graduating in 1978. He was called to the bar two years later, and in 1983 completed a Masters of Law at Osgoode Hall Law School.

As a partner at Miller Thompson LLP, Lauwers practised in human rights, constitutional law, labour law, civil litigation, and administrative law. He practised at every level of court, including the Supreme Court of Canada, and published and lectured widely throughout his years at the bar.

In 2008, he was appointed to the Superior Court of Justice of Ontario, and in 2012 joined the Court of Appeal.

* * *

Arthur Mahony LeBEL (1897–1988), member of the court 1956–60

Born to a Catholic family in Sarnia, Arthur LeBel was educated in the separate school system. He served with the Canadian artillery in the First World War, and after returning to Canada in 1919 remained closely involved in veterans' organizations such as the Veterans' Assistance Committee for several years. After completing his studies at Osgoode Hall, LeBel was called to the bar in 1921 and set up a private practice in Sarnia, which he later moved to London.

During the Second World War, he served as counsel to the Wartime Prices and Trade Board, and in 1944 was appointed to the High Court of Justice. LeBel joined the Court of Appeal in 1956, and following his retirement in 1960 returned to private practice.

* * *

James Frederick LISTER (1843–1902), member of the court 1898–1902

James Lister was born in Belleville and in his childhood moved to Sarnia, where he was later tutored by his uncle, a junior judge of Middlesex County. After a decade practising as a solicitor, he was called to the bar in 1875. Lister established strong ties in both the public and commercial sectors of Sarnia, serving at various times as county solicitor, as well as president of the Industrial Mortgage and Loan Company.

In 1882, he was elected as a Liberal to Parliament. After misappropriation of funds by a handful of Conservative parliamentarians was exposed 1891, he was given the nickname "Fighting Jim Lister" for his tenacious inquiry into the scandal, and in 1896 he became chairman of the committee of banking and commerce. He was appointed to the Court of Appeal in 1898, and remained there until his death in 1902.

* * *

James Buchanan MACAULAY (1793–1859), member of Error and Appeal 1849–59, as justice of Common Pleas 1849–56, as retired trial judge 1857–9

James Buchanan Macaulay was born in Niagara-on-the-Lake, then called Newark, to parents who had recently arrived from England. He was raised in York, where his parents had gained a sizable land concession, and at the age of thirteen left for Cornwall, where alongside the adolescent John Beverley Robinson and Archibald Maclean he studied under John Strachan.

In 1812 he was appointed a lieutenant in the Canadian Fencibles, and following the war, wounded but decorated, decided to pursue law. He began his studies with the Law Society of Upper Canada in 1816, and within three years was working in the office of Robinson, then Attorney General. In 1825, Macaulay was appointed a bencher of the Law Society and also to the Executive Council of Upper Canada. Working alongside Robinson and Strachan, Macaulay was a mainstay of the Family Compact under governor Peregrine Maitland. In 1829 he was appointed to King's Bench, and soon resigned from the cabinet in order to devote his energies exclusively to the judiciary.

Macaulay's judgments were consistently more liberal than his peers' and, writes historian Gordon Dodds, tended towards clemency in criminal cases. Taking a growing interest in questions of good governance, he wrote several influential reports towards the end of his career, examining the operations of the Indian Department and the Executive Council, and contributing in 1840 to the first revision of the statutes of Upper Canada. In 1849 he was made chief justice of Common Pleas, and in 1857, despite his failing health, was appointed to the court of Error and Appeal, where he remained until his death.

* * *

Norman Scarth MACDONNELL (1886–1938), member of the court 1933–8

The son of the minister of St Andrew's Presbyterian Church, Norman Macdonnell was born and raised in Toronto. After studying at Queen's

University, in 1907 he became a Rhodes scholar and pursued his studies at Oxford. He enrolled at Osgoode Hall upon his return to Canada, and was called to the bar in 1913. During the First World War, Macdonnell served with the British artillery in France and Palestine, and was promoted to the rank of major.

Following his return to Canada, Macdonnell became a senior partner in the firm Macdonnell, Mortimer & Kennedy, and in the mid-1920s represented the Presbyterian Church during the formation of the United Church of Canada. He was appointed to the appellate bench in 1933, but in 1937 fell ill and died a year later.

* * *

Jean Louise MacFARLAND, appointed to the court 2004

Jean Louise MacFarland received an LLB from Queen's University in 1971 and was called to the bar in 1973. She practised in litigation with the firm Smiley, Allingham, MacFarland & Stortini before her appointment to the High Court of Justice in 1987. From 1990 to 1996, she served as Regional Senior Justice for the central east region of Ontario, and in 2004 was appointed to the Court of Appeal.

* * *

Frederick George MacKAY (1900–1992), member of the court 1952–72

Frederick MacKay was born and raised on a farm in the Bruce peninsula. He enlisted in the Canadian artillery during the First World War, and upon returning to Canada in 1919 studied at Osgoode Hall. MacKay moved to Owen Sound following his call to the bar in 1923, and as one of the few lawyers in the area practising in both civil and criminal litigation, his practice flourished. He went on to sit on the Owen Sound Board of Education as well as the board of the local hospital. In 1952 he was appointed directly to the Court of Appeal, where he earned a reputation as a uniquely patient and instructive judge. "He spent a lot of his time talking to younger counsel after and pointing out what they had done and shouldn't have done, and how to help them along," said Arthur Kelly.

MacKay retired after twenty years on the bench, because, he said, "I've worked since I was knee-high to a grasshopper and I've never really had a holiday," adding that "I don't want to stick around until I lose my marbles."

* * *

John Keiller MacKAY (1888–1970), member of the court 1950–7

John Keiller MacKay was born in Pictou, Nova Scotia. He graduated from Ontario's Royal Military College in 1909, and then returned to Nova Scotia to earn a BA at St Francis Xavier in 1912. During the First World War, Mackay served as a lieutenant and later as a major, commanding three artillery brigades.

Following the war he enrolled at Dalhousie, graduating in 1922 with an LLD. He was called to the bar of Nova Scotia that year and to the bar of Ontario in 1923. He then went into practice with MacKay, Matheson & Martin in Toronto, where he specialized in criminal law. He was retained on occasion as a Crown prosecutor during his years in practice, and was appointed by the Dominion of Canada to serve on numerous inquiries, including one in 1932 into conditions within Canadian penitentiaries, and another during the Second World War to review the rulings of the courts martial.

A staunch defender of individual freedoms and the jury system, Mackay was brought on to the High Court of Justice in 1935 and to the Court of Appeal in 1950. The most significant case of his judicial career came in 1945, with *Re Drummond Wren*, in which he ruled against any restriction on the sale of land to Jews and people of colour. He retired from the bench in 1957 to become lieutenant governor of Ontario, a position he held for six years. In 1966 he chaired a royal commission on religious schooling, which recommended that religious curricula be inclusive and multicultural in their scope, and was instrumental in the subsequent establishment of the World Religions course in Ontario secondary schools.

* * *

Bert James MacKINNON (1921–1987), member of the court 1974–87

Bert MacKinnon grew up in the household of a Baptist farmer and beekeeper in St-Eugene, a small town on the Ottawa River just west of the Quebec border.

He studied history at McMaster, graduating with a BA in 1943, and immediately joined the Canadian Navy. After the war's end, he went to Oxford as a Rhodes scholar, and then to Osgoode Hall. He joined Wright & McTaggart following his call to the bar in 1949, and developed a reputation as a flamboyant and effective litigator whose style was best suited to the appellate courts. He was appointed to the Court of Appeal in 1974, and four years later became associate chief justice of Ontario – a position he held until his death in 1987.

* * *

John James MACLAREN (1842–1926), member of the court 1902–23

Born to Scottish parents in Lachute, Quebec, John James Maclaren was educated near Madoc, and then attended Victoria University in Cobourg, where he earned a BA, an MA, and an LLB. He then moved to Montreal, where he completed a bachelor of civil law at McGill in 1868 and set up a private practice.

He went on to litigate in several high-profile cases, some of which brought him before the Privy Council in England. His clients included politicians, the government of Canada, and on one occasion, the Mohawks of Oka.

He moved to Toronto in 1884, and soon after resumed studying, earning a DCL and an LLD in 1888. He became active in civic life in Toronto, becoming president of the Y.M.C.A., the Toronto Law and Order League, and the Dominion Prohibitory Alliance. He was appointed to the Court of Appeal in 1902 and remained there until his death in 1923.

* * *

James MACLENNAN (1833–1915), member of the court 1888–1905

James Maclennan was born in the town of Lancaster in eastern Ontario, and received a BA from Queen's University in 1849. He began studying law in 1851 and was called to the bar in 1857. After working in Hamilton for three years, in 1860 Maclennan returned to Toronto where he went into practice with Oliver Mowat.

He sat very briefly in the House of Commons, in 1874 winning the district of North Victoria for the Liberals, but the election was contested and declared void. He won a subsequent by-election, but in the fall of 1875 that too was annulled.

Maclennan returned to his law practice for the next several years. In 1888 he was appointed to the Court of Appeal, and in 1905 to the Supreme Court of Canada, where he sat until his retirement in 1909.

Throughout his time on the Court of Appeal, he was involved in the governance of both the University of Toronto and Queen's University, and additionally sat as the vice-president of the Toronto Conservatory of Music.

* * *

James Curry MacPHERSON, appointed to the court 1999

James Curry MacPherson was born in Yarmouth, Nova Scotia. He earned a BA at Acadia University in 1971, and proceeded on to an LLB at Dalhousie, and an LLM at Cambridge. He worked at several positions in government, education, and the judiciary throughout the 1980s, beginning as a professor of law at the University of Victoria, later becoming director of the constitutional branch of the Saskatchewan Department of Justice, then executive legal officer at the Supreme Court of Canada. In 1988 he was appointed dean of Osgoode Hall Law School, where he remained until his 1993 appointment to the Ontario Superior Court. He joined the Court of Appeal in 1999.

* * *

James MAGEE (1846–1938), member of the court 1910–33

Born in Liverpool, James Magee came to Canada with his parents as a child, and was educated at the Union School in London, Ontario. He was called to the bar in 1867, and became a leading barrister in the London area. After declining the offer of deputy minister of the interior in 1878, the following year he ran for Parliament as a Liberal candidate and lost.

Beginning in 1893, Magee was the Crown attorney for Middlesex County, and in 1904 he was appointed to the chancery division of the High Court. Known as a "careful and painstaking jurist," he was brought onto the Court of Appeal in 1910, where he remained until his retirement at age eighty-seven.

* * *

Goldwyn Arthur MARTIN (1913–2001), member of the court 1973–88

Arthur Martin is widely considered to be the most influential criminal lawyer in Ontario's history. The son of a lumber merchant in Huntsville, Martin moved to Toronto with his family in his teen years. He attended the Honours Course in Law at the University of Toronto, and enrolled at Osgoode Hall in 1935. Shortly after his call to the bar in 1940, Martin set up his own practice specializing in criminal law in downtown Toronto. "The penal system in Canada was very bad in those days," he said later. "I think I was interested in anything I could do to reform it."

At a time when Canada still lacked a single textbook on criminal law,

Martin rapidly became known as an authority in the field, and in 1942 was appointed to a faculty position at Osgoode. Throughout his career at the bar, he set several important precedents in criminal practice, pioneering the use of expert witnesses, the insanity defence, and other now-common conventions. He was instrumental in the establishment of the Legal Aid system, and was also a central figure in the Ouimet Committee, which in 1969 published an influential report on the reformation of Canada's penal system. "Criminal law wasn't a favourable part of law until Arthur Martin made it a respectable business," said lawyer Edward Greenspan following Martin's death. "He made people proud to be criminal lawyers."

* * *

Cornelius Arthur MASTEN (1857–1942), member of the court 1923–42

Cornelius Masten was born in Lacolle, Quebec, and earned a bachelor's degree at Cobourg's Victoria University, graduating with honours. He read law under John Bain and G.F. Shepley and was called to the bar in 1883, and later went into practice with Bain. In 1919 he chaired a royal commission on the insurance industry in Ontario, and the following year co-authored the book, *Company Law in Canada*. A firm believer in the common law, Masten was brought onto the Second Appellate Division court in 1923, and remained on the bench until his death in 1942. Following his death, friend and fellow lawyer G. Larrett Smith remembered him as "a man's man, and a lover of the out-of-doors, a sportsman, a man of culture, and a keen fisherman."

* * *

George Argo McGILLIVRAY (1900–1990), member of the court 1957–73

Born and raised in Whitby, George McGillivray enlisted in the Canadian military at the age of sixteen and during the First World War served in both the army and the air force. He studied at the University of Toronto and Osgoode Hall throughout his twenties, and was called to the bar in 1930. After working in private practice for two years, McGillivray was hired as assistant general counsel for the Toronto Transit Commission.

He enlisted in the military once again during the Second World War and was given the rank of major, though he remained in Toronto. In 1957 he was appointed to the Court of Appeal, and remained there until retiring in 1973. In 1966 he conducted a single-handed inquiry into the Workers' Compensation Act, and his recommendations for increased benefits for disabled workers and their beneficiaries were adopted two years later.

* * *

Hilda Margaret McKINLAY (b. 1927), member of the court 1987–99

In 1987, Hilda McKinlay became the second woman appointed to the Court of Appeal, following Bertha Wilson in 1976.

She graduated with a BA from the University of Toronto in 1950, then worked as Public Relations Director for the Canadian Bankers' Association, and later as the Executive Director of the Imperial Order Daughters of the Empire. She returned to school in the mid-1960s, graduating from Osgoode Hall with an LLB in 1965, and from Columbia University with an LLM in 1967. She taught law at the University of Toronto Law School from 1968 to 1973, and later went into private practice where she focused on commercial litigation. McKinlay was appointed to the High Court of Justice in 1983, four years later to the Court of Appeal, where she sat for twelve years before retiring.

* * *

Archibald McLEAN (1791–1865), member of Error and Appeal 1849–65, as judge of Common Pleas and Queen's Bench 1849–62, as retired trial judge 1862–5

Archibald McLean was born and raised in the Cornwall area of Upper Canada, where his father worked as a sheriff and public administrator. He was educated at the local school run by John Strachan, and at the age of eighteen moved to Toronto where he articled under Attorney General William Firth. Following his service in the war of 1812 (during which he spent seven months as a captive), McLean was called to the bar and returned to Cornwall, where he established his private practice.

He was elected to the legislative assembly in 1820 and became a prominent member of the Family Compact alongside Strachan and John Beverley Robinson. A staunch defender of British colonial administration, McLean served as colonel in the militia raised to suppress the rebellion of 1837. In March of that same year he was appointed to King's Bench, and throughout the subsequent three decades served in various judicial roles. In one of his most significant rulings, he dissented against his peers on behalf of John Anderson, an escaped American slave facing extradition.

* * *

James Laidlaw McLENNAN (1908–1968), member of the court 1961–8

James Laidlaw McLennan was the great-nephew of Justice James Maclennan, who had sat on the Court of Appeal and the Supreme Court of Canada in the early twentieth century. He was born in Lindsay, Ontario, and earned an MA from Queen's University in 1929. After studying at Osgoode Hall, McLennan was called to the bar in 1932. During his eleven years practising in Toronto with the firm Macdonald & Macintosh, McLennan worked as counsel to the *Globe and Mail*, and to the Law Society's committee on unauthorized practices. He was appointed to the High Court of Justice in 1951, and a decade later to the Court of Appeal, where he remained until his death.

* * *

Roy McMURTRY (b. 1932), member of the court as chief justice of Ontario 1996–2007

Beginning with his entrance into provincial politics in 1975, Roy McMurtry has been one of the most influential characters in the recent history of the Ontario judicial system.

The son of a barrister and a school teacher, McMurtry was raised in the Forest Hill area of Toronto. After completing a BA in history at the University of Toronto, he enrolled at Osgoode Hall and was called to the bar in 1958. He practised in general litigation in Toronto for several years.

In 1975 he was persuaded by Ontario premier Bill Davis – a close friend since their years together in university – to enter provincial politics with the Progressive Conservatives. He was elected in the district of Eglinton, and immediately appointed Attorney General of Ontario – a position he held for a decade. A far more public figure than his predecessors, McMurtry was an active reformer of the provincial legal system, and devoted to rationalizing and improving the fields of family law, disability law, misdemeanors, police-community relations, and others. In the words of Justice Archie Campbell, McMurtry was full of forward-thinking ideas, and "revived the idea of the Attorney General as the protector of civil liberties."

He resigned from politics following an unsuccessful bid for the P.C. leadership in 1985, and subsequently served for three years as the High Commissioner for Canada to Britain. He was appointed to the bench in 1991, first as associate chief justice of the Ontario Court of Justice, and in 1996 was made chief justice of Ontario, where he remained until retiring in 2007. Perhaps his most celebrated moment during those years came in 2003, for his role in the legalization of same-sex marriage.

He is the founder and president of the Osgoode Society for Canadian Legal History, and since 2008 has sat as chancellor of York University.

* * *

James Chalmers McRUER (1890–1985), member of the court 1944–5

James McRuer was born in Oxford County and attended the University of Toronto and Osgoode Hall. He enlisted shortly after his call to the bar in 1914, and throughout the First World War served as a lieutenant in the Canadian Field Artillery.

After returning to Toronto, McRuer was made assistant Crown attorney for the city of Toronto and the county of York, a position he held until 1925 when he established a private practice. He began lecturing at Osgoode Hall Law School in 1930, continuing there for five years.

He was appointed to the Court of Appeal in 1944, though he only remained there for a single year, before becoming the chief justice of the High Court of Justice.

Known as a diligent judge and a well-versed legal scholar, McRuer wrote extensively on legal history and participated in several inquiries during his years on the bench. Following his retirement in 1964, he simultaneously chaired the Ontario Law Reform Commission and the Royal Commission on Civil Rights in Ontario, the latter of which was highly influential in entrenching the right of appeal at all levels of Canadian public administration.

* * *

Charles Patrick McTAGUE (1890–1966), member of the court 1938–44

Charles McTague was born to a Catholic family in Guelph. He earned a BA at the University of Toronto in 1915, and went on to serve in the field artillery during the First World War.

During his years at Osgoode Hall, he articled with the Toronto firm Hughes & Agar, and following his call to the bar in 1920 he went into practice in Windsor.

McTague was appointed to the High Court of Justice in 1935, and three years later to the Court of Appeal. He was extraordinarily active during the war years, in particular as the chair of the National War Labour Board, which mediated in countless labour disputes. In 1944 he resigned from court in order to take the position of national chairman of the Progressive Conservative Party. "His departure," wrote the *Globe and Mail*, "will be felt most keenly in the ranks of labor, which, having complete confidence in his 'honesty of purpose and fair-mindedness,' has come to regard him as a friend in court ... None has studied the nation's labor problems more closely, and none has had greater experience in adjudicating them."

He later became chairman of the Ontario Securities Commission and chair of the royal commission on transportation. In December 1959, ill health forced McTague into retirement.

* * *

Richard Martin MEREDITH (1847–1934), member of the court 1905–12

Richard Martin Meredith was one of eight brothers, all of whom became distinguished in their fields. Following his primary education in London, he served in the Canadian militia during the 1866 Fenian raids. He began articling in the office of his older brother William and was called to the bar in 1869. Focusing on equity law, Meredith went into practice with another brother, Edmund, in London. In 1890 he was appointed to the chancery division of the High Court, and fifteen years later he joined the Court of Appeal, where he developed a reputation as an obstinate naysayer for his nearly constant dissents. He was nonetheless admired by his peers, as he consistently, in the words of the Ottawa Citizen, "distinguished himself in the vigor and originality of his judgments." He was also closely involved in the establishment of the University of Western Ontario, where he served as the first Chair of the Board of Governors from 1908 until 1914.

In 1912 he succeeded William as chief justice of Common Pleas, while William simultaneously moved to the Court of Appeal. He retired from the bench in 1930, returning to the home in London where he was raised.

* * *

William Ralph MEREDITH (1840–1923), member of the court as chief justice of Ontario 1912–23

William Ralph Meredith was the leader of the provincial Conservatives in the late 1800s, but upon his appointment to the bench he also became one of the most admired jurists of his time.

The eldest of fourteen children in the prominent London-based Meredith family, he articled with the barrister and politician Thomas Scatcherd in his late teens. He then studied law for two years at the University of Toronto, and joined Scatcherd's private practice following his call to the bar in 1861. Meredith took on cases in both criminal and civil law and rapidly became the most prominent barrister in London, eventually succeeding his mentor as the city solicitor.

He entered politics in 1872 with his election to the Ontario legislative assembly, and although he continued to practise law throughout the subsequent years, quickly rose within the ranks of the Conservative caucus. In 1879 he became the leader of the opposition, a position he held through four elections – all of which were lost to Oliver Mowat's Liberals. Identified by historian Peter Dembski as "the first clearly defined progressive Conservative in Ontario," Meredith supported the full suffrage of males over the age of twenty-one, suffrage for native men living off reserves, workers' compensation, and stringent regulation of industrial labour standards. But although he was often "more liberal than the Liberals," his strained relations with the Catholic Church as well as the federal Conservatives ultimately handicapped him in the face of Mowat's political acumen. (It is also true that he was vociferously conservative on some issues; he was among the vocal opponents of women's suffrage and their admission to the bar.)

After more than two decades in politics, in 1894 Meredith accepted an appointment as chief justice of Common Pleas, and in 1913 was elevated to chief justice of Ontario.

A devotee of common law jurisprudence, Meredith was known as a fastidious researcher of precedents during his time on the bench. He additionally led some of the most important commissions of his time, investigating issues of workers' compensation, university reform, and hydro-electric infrastructure.

* * *

William Edward MIDDLETON (1860–1948), member of the court 1923–43

Born in Toronto and raised partially in Montreal, William Middleton attended the University of Toronto, and read law with John Fosberry Orde. Called to the bar in 1885, Middleton practised for several years with the firm Macdonald, Shepley, Middleton & Donald, where he specialized in property and estate law. He was appointed to the Court of Chancery in 1910, and in 1923 joined the Court of Appeal, where he remained until his retirement in 1943. Throughout his time on the bench, Middleton earned a reputation as a fair and sympathetic jurist. "Murderers are not all bad," he said once. "I always tried to take the humanitarian view and I believe it is the solemn duty of juries to watch out for the element of reasonable doubt before passing judgments."

"He was a kindly man," commented Arthur Martin following his death, adding that in his later years, "if a lawyer was too long – he was quite deaf at this stage – he might tend to turn off his earphones if you were getting too boring."

* * *

Michael James MOLDAVER (b. 1947), member of the court 1995–2011

Michael Moldaver was raised in Peterborough, and by the age of twenty-four had earned a BA and an LLB from the University of Toronto. After articling with Thomson Rogers as well as Arthur Martin he was called to the bar in 1973, and began his practice in criminal law with Pomerant, Pomerant & Greenspan. An active member of the legal community, during his years in practice he served as director of the Criminal Lawyers' Association, and co-chaired the Advocacy Symposium in 1989 and 1990.

Moldaver additionally began teaching in criminal law at Osgoode Hall Law School and U of T in 1978, and following his appointment to the High Court of Justice in 1990 became active in judicial educational programs connected to the National Judicial Institute and the Canadian Institute for the Administration of Justice. He was appointed to the Court of Appeal in 1995, and in 2011 he was appointed to the Supreme Court of Canada.

* * *

John Wilson MORDEN (b. 1934), member of the court 1978–2003, as associate chief justice of Ontario 1990–9

The son of Kenneth Gibson Morden, John Morden was born and raised in Toronto. He earned a BA from Trinity College in 1956, and an LLB from the University of Toronto Law School in 1959. Throughout the 1960s and early 1970s he practised in Toronto with Day, Wilson, Campbell, and beginning in 1964 worked as counsel to the Royal Commission on Civil Rights. During his time at the bar, he additionally worked as assistant counsel to the House of Commons Special Committee on Statutory Instruments, and as editor of the Land Compensation Reports.

Morden was appointed to the High Court of Justice in 1973, and in 1978 to the Court of Appeal, where he sat for twenty-five years. Between 1968 and 1972, Morden sat as a senator at U of T, and during his time on the bench sporadically served as an adjunct professor in the Faculty of Law. Following his retirement, he became a counsel at the firm Heenan Blaikie.

* * *

Kenneth Gibson MORDEN (1907–1961), member of the court 1957–61

Kenneth Gibson Morden was born in Belleville and moved to Toronto in his adolescence to attend the University of Toronto Schools. He went on to win the gold medal from both the University of Toronto and Osgoode Hall. After articling with D.L. McCarthy, Morden was called to the bar in 1931 and went into practice with Armstrong & Sinclair. He soon became involved in education as well, lecturing at Osgoode Hall Law School, and sitting on the U of T senate.

Morden served as a Lieutenant-Colonel in the Queen's Own Rifles during the Second World War, serving in Britain, northwestern Europe, and the Mediterranean. Upon returning to Canada he became a partner at Day, Wilson, Kelly, Martin & Morden, and served as senior counsel to the Royal Commission on Workmen's Compensation and the registrar of the Canadian Bar Association. He was appointed to the Court of Appeal in 1957 and remained there until his death in 1961. His son John Wilson Morden later went on to sit on the Court of Appeal as well.

* * *

Joseph Curran MORRISON (1816–1885), member of Error and Appeal 1862–74 as justice of Queen's Bench and Common Pleas; member of the Court of Appeal 1877–85

Joseph Curran Morrison was born in Ireland and attended elementary school in Belfast. After moving to Toronto in his adolescence he attended Upper Canada College, and in 1834 enrolled as a law student. He became a partner in Blake, Morrison & Connor following his call to the bar, where he began to specialize in commercial law. In 1848, Morrison entered politics as a parliamentary representative of the York West riding. Initially a member of the Baldwin-LaFontaine government, Morrison was made Solicitor General. He moved towards the Conservative Party during his years in Parliament, however, and in 1856 he became receiver general under the government of John A. Macdonald. He also became closely associated with railway construction, sitting as president of the Northern Railway from 1852 until 1862, and additionally sat on the government's Board of Railway Commissioners.

After a series of electoral defeats in the late 1850s Morrison abandoned parliamentary politics and worked briefly as the registrar of the city of Toronto. In 1862 he accepted an appointment to the Court of Common Pleas, and the following year moved to Queen's Bench, in both positions sitting as an ex officio justice of Error and Appeal. He joined the Court of Appeal in 1877, and remained there until his death in 1885. Although, as the *Canadian Law Journal* pointed out upon his death, Morrison lacked the "depth of learning" of some of his peers, his business experience, his "strong common sense," and his amiability made him a valued member of the bench.

* * *

Charles MOSS (1840–1912), member of the court 1897–1912, as chief justice of Ontario 1902–12

The son of Irish immigrants and brother of appellate Chief Justice Thomas Moss, Charles Moss was born in Cobourg and moved to Toronto as a child when his father acquired a brewery there. He enrolled with the Law Society in 1864, and articled with his brother Thomas, quickly establishing a reputation as a capable and confident lawyer. By the time of his call to the bar in 1869, he had won four scholarships and published a book called *A Handy Book of Commercial Law*.

He went into practice alongside Featherston Osler and William Alexander Foster, and their firm, writes historian Alexander Reford, soon "became a source for Ontario's expanding bench," later taking on prominent lawyers such as William Glenholm Falconbridge and Allen Bristol Aylesworth.

Moss became involved in legal education early in his career at the bar. He was hired in 1872 as a lecturer at Osgoode Hall, specializing in equity law, and in 1889, following the school's eleven-year hiatus, he played an instrumental role in its re-establishment. That same year he was additionally taken on as a professor at the new law program at the University of Toronto.

Moss circulated comfortably among the political establishment, and, like his elder brother Thomas, transitioned out of the Catholic Church and into the Church of England. In 1897 the Laurier government – with Oliver Mowat sitting as Minister of Justice – appointed him to the Court of Appeal. Again following in his brother's footsteps, he was made chief justice of Ontario in 1902, and remained there until his death in 1912.

Among his lasting achievements was his contribution to the royal commission on university governance, which recommended that post-secondary institutions be protected from government influence and resulted in the 1906 University Act.

* * *

Thomas MOSS (1836–1881), member of the court 1875–81, as chief justice of Ontario 1878–81

The elder brother of Charles Moss, Thomas Moss was born in Cobourg and grew up in Toronto. Following his graduation from Upper Canada College he enrolled at the University of Toronto, where, upon his graduation in 1858, he won the gold medal in classics, mathematics, and modern languages. That same year, he began articling in the office of barristers Adam Crooks and Hector Cameron, and was called to the bar in 1861.

Moss would be closely involved with U of T for the rest of his life, first serving as the university registrar and later as a senator and vice chancellor. Upon his death the *Canadian Law Journal* noted that "he was always foremost in suggesting and promoting schemes for the advancement of the University, and the extension of its sphere of usefulness." He became directly involved in legal education in 1871, when he was hired as a lecturer in equity law at the Law Society of Upper Canada.

Two years later, he was instrumental in the establishment of a formal law school at Osgoode Hall.

In 1873, he ran as a Liberal for the riding of Toronto West and won, but only two years later he would be appointed to the Court of Appeal. In 1877 he was made chief justice of Appeal, and the following year, at age forty-one, became chief justice of Ontario. As a jurist he was known for his consistent defence of individual rights against the interests of the state, and became widely admired for the painstaking research and thought that went into his judgments. "Few beyond his intimate acquaintances were aware of the untiring energy with which he investigated those cases requiring more careful preparation," stated George William Burton after Moss's premature death, "or that the rising sun has occasionally found him still engaged in examining and verifying the authorities upon which he proposed to base his decisions."

* * *

Oliver MOWAT (1820–1903), member of Error and Appeal as justice of Chancery 1864–72

One of the pivotal figures in Ontario's early history, Oliver Mowat's judicial legacy stems more from his career in politics than law. Born into the Presbyterian establishment of Kingston, Mowat enlisted in the loyalist militias in 1837, and that same year began articling under John A. Macdonald. He later studied under the prominent equity lawyer Robert Easton Burns, whose Toronto practice he joined following his call to the bar in 1841. Mowat rose to prominence within the legal community in 1853, when he successfully prosecuted Toronto mayor John George Bowes and Premier Francis Hincks for a conflict of interest scandal involving several thousand pounds in railroad bonds.

Four years later, he was simultaneously elected an alderman for the city of Toronto and a representative in the legislative assembly, where he worked closely alongside George Brown. His most important contribution to the incipient project of Confederation came at the Quebec conference of 1864, where delegates sought to construct a legal framework for the division of powers between the federal and provincial governments.

In November of that year, he was appointed vice chancellor of Upper Canada – a position he held for eight years. On the bench, Mowat was a decisive liberal, although, writes historian Paul Romney, "His judgments were generally concise and unspectacular, consisting largely of quotations from the leading cases ... reinforced with brief statements of the principles they established."

In 1872, following Edward Blake's resignation from the premier's office, Mowat was nominated by the Liberal Party of Ontario to lead the province, an offer he happily accepted. A precedent-setting campaigner for provincial rights, Mowat undertook reforms that marked the emergence of a modern government in Ontario. He extended the franchise, expanded public education, modernized agriculture, and assiduously sought to strike a balance between business and labour. His most consequential reform of the judiciary came in 1874, with the *Administration of Justice* bill, which inaugurated an independent Court of Appeal, consisting of four full-time judges. In 1896, after twenty-four years as premier, Mowat entered federal politics as a senator and minister of justice in Wilfrid Laurier's new Liberal government, but the following year he was appointed lieutenant governor of Ontario and returned to his home in Toronto, where he died in 1903.

* * *

William MULOCK (1843–1944), member of the court as chief justice of Ontario 1923–36

From the 1880s until the time of his death, William Mulock was a fixture in Canadian public life, known as both an ardent patriot and a progressive Liberal. He was born and raised in the small farming community of Bond Head, and in 1859 enrolled at the University of Toronto, where he went on to win a gold medal in his graduating year. After four years of articling Mulock was called to the bar in 1867, and established the firm Ross, Lauder & Mulock. Around the same time, he became interested in some of the governance problems faced by U of T, and alongside his peers Thomas Moss and Edward Blake, Mulock petitioned successfully for stronger graduate representation on the University's governing body. Mulock would remain closely involved with the university for several decades to come, sitting on its board from 1874 until his death.

In 1882, he ran successfully for Parliament in the riding of York North, and rapidly became a leader in the Liberal caucus. He was appointed postmaster general under the government of Wilfrid Laurier in 1896 and went on to implement significant reforms in the imperial postal service. Perhaps his most lasting political achievement, however, came that same year when he passed legislation calling for the establishment of a branch of the federal government that would "aid in the prevention and settlement of trade disputes." Four years later, he became Canada's first minister of labour.

After his resignation from federal politics in 1905, Mulock was made chief justice of the Exchequer Division of the Ontario courts, and in 1923 became chief justice of Ontario. He retired at ninety-two in 1936, but even as he turned 100 years old still delivered speeches to his friends at the Canadian Club. Following his death, his friend and protégé William Lyon Mackenzie King remembered him as "a friend of the oppressed, a lover of liberty, a champion of freedom, one who held high and firm the standards of right and truth and justice."

* * *

Dennis O'CONNOR, member of the court 1998–2012, as associate chief justice of Ontario 2001–12

Dennis O'Connor was called to the bar of Ontario in 1966 and practised law in Toronto until 1973, when he became a magistrate in the Yukon Territory. He returned to Ontario three years later, teaching law at the University of Western Ontario, and returned to practice in 1980 as a litigator with Borden, Elliot in Toronto. During that time, he represented the Government of Canada in aboriginal land claims negotiations in the Yukon, and served as a bencher of the Law Society. He was appointed to the Court of Appeal in 1998 and became associate chief justice of Ontario in 2001. During his time on the bench he conducted inquiries into the Walkerton tragedy, and into the case of Maher Arar, a Canadian citizen illegally extradited to Syria.

* * *

John Fosberry ORDE (1870–1932), member of the court 1923–32

John Fosberry Orde was born in the town of Great Village, Nova Scotia. He attended secondary school in Ottawa, where, following his 1891 call to the bar, he went on to build his legal career with the firm Orde, Powell, Lyle & Snowdon. He worked with the municipal licensing commission for several years, and was closely involved with the Anglican Church, serving as chancellor of the Diocese of Ottawa. He was appointed to the High Court of Justice in 1920, and joined the Court of Appeal in 1923. At the time of his death, Orde was in the midst of an inquiry into a financial scandal involving the Hydro-Electric Power Commission of Ontario.

* * *

Coulter Arthur Anthony OSBORNE (b. 1934), member of the court 1990–2001, as associate chief justice 1999–2001

Coulter Osborne grew up in Hamilton and graduated with a BA from the University of Western Ontario in 1955. The following year he briefly put his studies at Osgoode Hall on hold in order to participate in the Olympics in Melbourne, Australia, as a member of the Canadian basketball team. Following his call to the bar in 1959, he practised law in Kitchener-Waterloo until his appointment to the High Court of Justice in 1978. He moved to the Court of Appeal in 1990 and in 1999 became associate chief justice of Ontario. In September 2000, after a year of struggling with a severe heart infection, Osborne ran in the torch relay inaugurating the Sydney Olympics. He retired from the bench the following year, accepting an appointment as the provincial integrity commissioner. In 2011, he was appointed to the Order of Ontario for his efforts at expanding access to justice in the civil court system.

* * *

Featherston OSLER (1838–1924), member of the court 1883–1910

Featherston Osler was born in Newmarket and educated in Barrie and Bond Head. The son of the prominent Anglican clergyman Featherstone Lake Osler, his siblings included the medical pioneer Sir William Osler, the lawyer Britton Bath Osler, and the banker and politician Sir Edmund Osler.

Following his call to the bar in 1860, Osler practised law in Toronto, working at various times alongside Thomas and Charles Moss. He went on to take leading positions at the Toronto General Trusts Corporation and the Working Boys Home. In 1879 he was appointed to the Court of Common Pleas, and in 1883 joined the Court of Appeal. He declined an appointment to the Supreme Court of Canada in 1888, and retired from the bench in 1910. Though he tended to shy away from the spotlight, he remained active in the legal community for several years, returning to the Law Society as a bencher. In 1921, at age eighty-three, he became treasurer of the Society and remained in that office until his death.

* * *

Gladys I. PARDU, appointed to the court 2013

Gladys Pardu completed a bachelor of science at Brock University in 1974, and went on to earn an LLB from the University of Toronto in 1975. Following her call to the bar, she practised with Pardu Macdonald in Sault Ste Marie. Since her appointment to the Ontario Court of Justice (General Division) in 1991, she has sat on the Rules Committee, directed the Canadian Superior Court Judges Association, and co-authored a report on the administration of criminal trials. She was appointed to the Court of Appeal in November 2013.

* * *

Christopher Salmon PATTERSON (1823–1893), member of the court 1874–88

Christopher Salmon Patterson was born in London, England, and studied in Belfast before coming to Canada in 1845. Settling in the small town of Picton, he articled in the office of Philip Low and was called to the bar in 1851. In 1856 Patterson moved to Toronto, where he practised for the next eighteen years, and became the chairman of the board of the Toronto General Hospital and a founder of the Building and Loan Association.

Among the most important moments in his career at the bar came in 1871, when he was appointed to the Law Reform Commission to assist in its assessment of fusing the common and equity law courts. He joined the Court of Appeal when it was restructured in 1874, and in 1888 – despite his strong ties among barristers and judges in Toronto – accepted an appointment to the Supreme Court of Canada.

* * *

Sarah E. PEPALL, appointed to the court 2012

Sarah Pepall graduated from McGill University's faculty of law in 1976. She was called to the bar of Ontario two years later, and in 1983 graduated from Osgoode Hall Law School with a Masters in Public Law.

Practising in Toronto, she became a partner at McMillan Binch, where she litigated in both civil and commercial cases. She has lectured extensively on mediation and firm management, and taught in the field of civil procedure and trial advocacy at Osgoode Hall Law School.

Pepall joined the Superior Court of Justice in 1999 and the Court of Appeal in 2012. She has sat as a director of the Advocates' Society and, from 2006 to 2008, served as president of the Ontario Superior Judges Association.

* * *

John Wellington PICKUP (1892–1973), member of the court as chief justice of Ontario 1952–7

John Wellington Pickup was born and raised in Millbrook, Ontario. He studied at Osgoode Hall Law School, graduating with the gold medal in 1913, and was called to the bar the same year.

He practised at the Faskens firm in Toronto for nearly four decades, taking on a wide variety of litigations. During his time at the bar, he became increasingly involved in government and judicial affairs, serving as counsel to multiple inquiries and to the Public Trustee of Ontario. He was also an active member of the Law Society, serving as a bencher and chair of the discipline committee.

He was appointed directly to the position of chief justice of Ontario in September of 1952, following the resignation of his former law partner Robert Spelman Robertson, and remained there until 1957, when illness forced his retirement.

* * *

Dana Harris PORTER (1901–1967), member of the court as chief justice of Ontario 1958–67

The son of a prominent medical researcher, Dana Porter was born and raised in Toronto. He earned a BA at the University of Toronto and an MA at Oxford before attending Osgoode Hall Law School. Following his call to the bar in 1926, he practised in litigation for eighteen years with Fennell, Porter & Davis, and in 1943 entered provincial politics as a Progressive Conservative. In his fifteen years at Queen's Park, he served as treasurer, Attorney General, minister of education, and minister of planning and development.

"Scholarly, given to quoting Shakespeare," wrote the *Globe and Mail*, "Mr. Porter was more at home, perhaps, in a social rather than a political setting. But he was also an aggressive speaker, trained in debate, and he soon learned to turn his wit to political advantage." Despite his antisocialist politics, Porter was a reformer in government, as Attorney General favouring probation over imprisonment and as minister of planning and development angling for the eradication of urban slums.

He accepted an appointment as chief justice of Ontario in 1958, and remained on the bench until his death in 1967. Among his most notable rulings was his lifting of the ban on the bawdy eighteenth-century novel *Fanny Hill*. He also fell into the spotlight in the mid-1960s as the author of a report on the liberalization of the banking system.

* * *

William Buell RICHARDS (1815–1889), member of Error and Appeal 1853–74, as justice of Queen's Bench and Common Pleas

William Buell Richards was born in Brockville. His early education took place there and in Potsdam, New York, and he went on to article in the office of his uncle, Andrew Norton Buell, whose practice he joined following his call to the bar in 1837. A member of the Belleville town council and several other organizations, Richards was elected as a Reformer to the legislative assembly of Canada in 1848, becoming Attorney General under the administration of Francis Hincks and Augustin-Norbert Morin.

He was appointed to the Court of Common Pleas in 1853 – a move that was at first challenged by some who pointed to his relatively brief career at the bar, but he went on to become respected as a sensible and sympathetic adjudicator. Richards later became chief justice of Queen's Bench after being consulted by the government of John A. Macdonald on the creation of the Supreme Court of Canada. In 1875 he was appointed the first chief justice of Canada by the government of Alexander Mackenzie.

Following his death in 1889, Richards was remembered by the *Canadian Law Journal* as "emphatically a man of the people," and one who was "remarkable for the simplicity of his manners and the entire absence of ostentation."

* * *

William Renwick RIDDELL (1852–1945), member of the court 1925–45

William Renwick Riddell was born in Hamilton and educated in Cobourg. After graduating from Victoria University with an LLB in 1878 he articled in law, and went on to win the Law Society's gold medal in 1883. He first established his practice in both civil and criminal litigation in Cobourg, and in 1893 moved to Toronto.

His connections in government grew over time, and in 1904 he was retained as counsel for an inquiry into municipal elections. Two years later, Riddell was appointed to King's Bench. He joined the Court of Appeal in 1925, and remained there until his death at age ninety-three.

Though known for a cantankerous disposition ("Everybody hated the old boy," said John Robinette), Riddell nonetheless commanded respect and admiration within the legal community. A compulsive polymath, he taught himself seven languages and wrote extensively on legal and social history, publishing over 1,200 articles and lectures, in addition to biographies of William Kirby and John Graves Simcoe. He was awarded twelve honorary degrees by the end of his career.

* * *

Wilfred Daniel ROACH (1891–1976), member of the court 1944–65

Wilfred Daniel Roach was born in Arthur, Ontario. A Catholic, he was raised in the separate school system until he enrolled at the University of Toronto, where he graduated in 1913. He then studied at Osgoode Hall and articled with Judge Moses McFadden of Sault Ste Marie before his call to the bar in 1917. Roach established his private practice in Windsor, where he became an alderman, a member of the Separate School Board, and president of the Essex County Bar Association.

After twenty years in practice, he was appointed to the High Court of Justice, and in 1944 to the Court of Appeal, where he remained until his retirement in 1965. Arthur Kelly later described him as very modest and hard working. "It was quite an experience to sit with him," he said, "because he had the ability to draw people out, and if counsel weren't getting along, he could kind of nudge them a little bit, to say the things that they should say."

* * *

Robert Spelman ROBERTSON (1870–1955), member of the court as chief justice of Ontario 1938–52

Robert Spelman Robertson was born and raised in Goderich, and studied law under James Thompson Garrow, later a member of the Court of Appeal. Following his call to the bar in 1894 he established a private practice in Stratford and worked alongside John Idlington, who later joined the Supreme Court of Canada.

He worked for a time as the Stratford city solicitor, and in 1914 ran unsuccessfully for Parliament as a Liberal. In 1917 he became a partner in the Fasken law firm in Toronto, and four years later additionally began work as a Crown prosecutor. An expert in constitutional law, Robertson litigated in several high-profile cases, and in 1935 represented the government of R.B. Bennett before the Privy Counsel in London. He served as counsel in several commissions, including inquiries into the Toronto Police, the Canadian penal system, and commuter railways. He was appointed directly to the office of chief justice of Ontario in 1938, and remained there until his retirement fourteen years later.

Following his death, Arthur Martin described Robertson as an outstanding jurist, and one of few on the Court of Appeal who would check the intimidating style of his fellow judges. John Robinette also praised him, saying, "You could never fool, or try to fool Robertson on what the facts were ... He was just an ideal Chief Justice."

* * *

Sydney Lewis ROBINS (1923–2013), member of the court 1981–98

Raised in Toronto's Jewish community, Sydney Robins graduated from the University of Toronto with a BA in Law in 1944 and enrolled at Osgoode Hall Law School the same year. Following his call to the bar in 1947, he studied at Harvard, where he earned an LLM.

Around the time of his return to Toronto, Caesar Wright – his former mentor and lecturer at Osgoode Hall – fell ill, and at the age of only twenty-four, Robins was called in to replace him. He lectured there for twelve years while also practising law, and went on to deliver several special lectures at the Law Society of Upper Canada. He became a bencher at the Law Society in 1961, and ten years later became the first Jew elected treasurer – a position in which he thrived.

Initially, Robins ran his practice on his own, but later took on his younger brother Hartley. Due in part to Wright's influence, Robins & Robins specialized in labour law and litigated on behalf of several unions before the Labour Relations Board. He was appointed to the High Court of Justice in 1976, and joined the Court of Appeal in 1981. Throughout his time on the bench, he arbitrated in labour disputes and served on several provincial commissions.

Following his retirement from the bench in 1998, he joined the corporate law firm Goodmans LLP.

* * *

John Beverley ROBINSON (1791–1863), member of Error and Appeal 1849–63, as justice of Queen's Bench 1849–62, as retired trial judge 1862–3

The son of a Virginian loyalist, John Beverley Robinson was born in the Lower Canadian town of Berthier. As a young boy he was mentored by the prominent young priest and politician John Strachan, who would become a lifelong friend and ally. At sixteen Robinson moved to the town of York where he articled under D'Arcy Boulton, then Solicitor General of Upper Canada. Robinson's public profile rose rapidly during the War of 1812, during which he served alongside Isaac Brock and later took command of a militia. Upon his return to York, he was made Attorney General of Upper Canada, and at the age of only twenty-one became responsible for the prosecution of settlers accused of committing acts of treason during the war, successfully demanding that eight of those convicted be executed.

He travelled to England to further his legal education in 1815, and upon returning to Canada two years later was reinstated to his former position in government. Working closely alongside Strachan, Robinson was a prominent fixture of the small clique of Family Compact legislators encouraging strong autocratic governance, British immigration, and anti-American policies. He became chief justice of Upper Canada as head of Queen's Bench in 1829, but remained highly influential in the political sphere as a legal adviser to governors John Colborne and Francis Bond Head. After 1862 he sat only as head of Error and Appeal, but by then his health was rapidly deteriorating and the following year he died.

* * *

Marc ROSENBERG, appointed to the court 1995

Marc Rosenberg earned a BA from the University of Western Ontario in 1971, and graduated from Osgoode Hall Law School in 1974. During his twenty years at the bar, he became a partner at Greenspan, Rosenberg & Buhr, where he specialized in criminal law. He became involved in several related educational initiatives, including the instruction of criminal procedure within the Law Society's bar admission course, and the Society's Legal Education Committee. He has taught in the fields of evidence and the administration of criminal justice at Osgoode.

As a representative of the Canadian Bar Association to the Law Reform Commission from 1982 to 1992, he served as a consultant on electronic surveillance, the jurisdiction of the Attorney General, and the role of the Crown prosecutor.

In 1995 he became assistant deputy Attorney General of Ontario, but only months later was appointed to the Court of Appeal. He has written extensively on criminal law, evidence, and the Charter of Rights and Freedoms, and currently sits as a Judicial Associate with the National Judicial Institute.

* * *

Paul-Sylvain ROULEAU, appointed to the court 2005

Paul Rouleau earned a bachelor degree in administration and an LLB from the University of Ottawa, as well as an LLM from Osgoode Hall Law School. Following his call to the bar in 1979, he became a partner at Cassels, Brock & Blackwell and later at Heenan Blaikie, and worked in the fields of education, constitutional, labour, and commercial law. From 1985 to 1987, he served as president of the Association des juristes d'expression française de l'Ontario. He was appointed to the Superior Court of Justice in 2002 and has sat on the Court of Appeal since 2005.

* * *

Newton Wesley ROWELL (1867–1941), member of the court as chief justice of Ontario 1936–8

Newton Rowell's career as a politician was far longer and more influential than his brief career on the bench. Born to a family of farmers in Middlesex County, he moved to London in 1883 where he took a brief course in commerce and worked for three years at a dry goods business run by his uncle. Lacking the funds to attend university, he articled with the local firm Fraser and Fraser and in 1891 successfully wrote the bar admission exam. After joining the firm of Isidore Frederick Hellmuth in Toronto, he rapidly established himself as a leader at the bar.

Rowell became influential in the Liberal Party and the Methodist Church at this time, and well known as a champion of temperance.

He lost a bid for Parliament in 1900, but in 1911 secured a seat in the provincial legislature and, within a Liberal caucus beset by scandal, the punctilious Rowell immediately became leader of the opposition. He moved into federal politics in 1917, as one of the leaders of the Liberal contingent that defected from the opposition and joined Robert Borden's pro-conscription Union government. Appointed to the cabinet, he sat as president of the Privy Council, chaired the war committee, and became the first federal minister of health.

A significant moment of his subsequent years in private practice came in 1928, when he represented the appellants in the Persons Case before the Supreme Court of Canada and the Judicial Committee of the Privy Council, which ruled for the recognition of female personhood in Canada. Appointed directly to chief justice of Ontario in 1936, Rowell sat on the bench for only two years before he was forced to resign due to ill health. During his term he also chaired the Royal Commission on Dominion–Provincial Relations, a task regarded as "one of the heaviest and most complex ever undertaken by a Canadian jurist."

As a public figure, Rowell attracted both admiration and ridicule. Seen by some as "a fanatic with a one-track mind," he in many ways epitomized the Victorian ideology of empire and order. Known, in the words of historian Margaret Prang, for his "excessive seriousness and an addiction to statistics," he fought doggedly for a ban on Sunday streetcars; he touted the "Providential design and purpose [of the Anglo-Saxon race] for the world's evangelization"; and it is little wonder that his "Abolish the Bar" campaign in 1914 won him little popular support. At the same time, many of his positions were progressive for his time, among them his support for women's rights, his support for international law under the League of Nations, and his staunch campaign for an eight-hour working day for miners. What everyone did agree on was that he was a tireless worker, seldom an opportunist, and always fought with the courage of his convictions.

* * *

Walter Frank SCHROEDER (1901–1983), member of the court 1955–75

Walter Schroeder was raised in Ottawa, and in his adolescence attended the Concordia Lutheran College in Indiana. After studying at Osgoode Hall, he was called to the bar in 1924 and returned to his hometown, where he became a partner at MacCraken & Fleming and went on to argue several cases before the Supreme Court. He was appointed to the High Court of Justice in 1946, and nine years later to the Court of Appeal, where he sat until his retirement in 1975. Among his most remembered trial court rulings came in the 1948 case *Noble and Wolf v Alley*, in which he upheld the right of a resort community to forbid the sale of houses to "any person of the Jewish, Hebrew, Semitic, Negro or coloured race or blood," a decision that was later overturned by the Supreme Court.

Known as one of the most erudite members of the legal community, Schroeder read philosophy in ancient Greek and Latin, and was renowned for his comprehensive and well-written judgments. Alongside John Aylesworth, he was also among the justices in the 1950s through 1970s who earned the court a reputation for belligerence and intimidation. "Some defence counsel thought the judges like Aylesworth and Schroeder were pro-crown," said Archie Campbell in his later years. "It was my view that they were equally rude to everybody. They would interrupt, they would demonstrate scorn, they would really challenge you ... They were brilliant men. They probably got it right in 95 cases out of 100. But they were rude."

* * *

Robert J. SHARPE, appointed to the court 1999

Robert Sharpe was born in Brantford, Ontario. He graduated from the University of Western Ontario with a BA in 1966, later earning an LLB from the University of Toronto and a doctorate of philosophy from Oxford.

Following his call to the bar in 1974, Sharpe became an associate at MacKinnon, McTaggart, where he practised in civil litigation. He was hired to teach in the University of Toronto's Faculty of Law only two years later, and remained there until 1988, when he took the position of executive legal officer at the Supreme Court of Canada. He became dean of law upon returning to U of T two years later, and in 1995 was appointed to the Ontario Court of Justice (General Division). He has sat on the Court of Appeal since 1999. Sharpe has written seven books on Canadian law and legal history, including *The Law of Habeas Corpus*, *The Charter of Rights and Freedoms*, and *The Persons Case: The Origins and Legacy of the Fight for Legal Personhood*, in addition to several articles.

* * *

Janet Marie SIMMONS, appointed to the court 2000

Janet Simmons graduated from the University of Toronto in 1974, and went on to earn an LLB from the University of Western Ontario. Called to the bar in 1979, Simmons practised in Brampton until her appointment to the Ontario Court (Provincial Division) in 1990. She moved to the Ontario Court (General Division) the following year, and in 2000 was named to the Court of Appeal.

* * *

Robert SMITH (1858–1942), member of the court 1923–7

Born and raised in Lanark County, Robert Smith began articling in 1880 and was called to the bar in 1885. He then moved to Cornwall, where he established his law practice and went on to become director of the Montreal and Cornwall Navigation Company.

A Liberal, he ran unsuccessfully for Parliament in 1904, but succeeded four years later. He declined to run for re-election in 1911, returning to private practice until his elevation to the High Court of Justice in 1922. Smith was appointed to the Court of Appeal the following year, and in 1927 was named to the Supreme Court of Canada, where he sat until his retirement in 1933.

* * *

John Godfrey SPRAGGE (1806–1884), member of Error and Appeal 1850–74 as justice of Chancery; chief justice of Ontario 1881–4

John Godfrey Spragge was born in the English town of New Cross, near London, and came to the town of York with his parents in 1820. He was home-schooled by his father Joseph, the master of the Upper Canada Central School, and in 1823 began articling under James Buchanan Macaulay, and later under Robert Baldwin. He was called to the bar in 1828, and throughout his years in private practice specialized in equity.

In 1837 he was made the first master of chancery and became responsible for establishing the rules and procedures of the new court. Like many other lawyers in Upper Canada, however, he became exasperated by the incoherence of the judicial system at the time, and in 1847 published an influential pamphlet lobbying the Attorney General for a strong court of appeal with judges from both Queen's Bench and the

Court of Chancery. These efforts helped build support for the court reform bill passed in 1849 by Solicitor General William Hume Blake. In 1850 Spragge was appointed to the chancery court, making him a member of Error and Appeal ex officio until 1874. In 1881 he succeeded Thomas Moss as the chief justice of Ontario, a position he held until his death three years later. "Though not a brilliant man," writes historian Brian Morrison, "he possessed qualities which made for a good jurist," being known for a meticulous assessment of the facts and patience and courtesy in court.

* * *

George STRATHY, appointed to the court 2013, chief justice of Ontario 2014

George Strathy earned a BA from McGill University in 1970, and the following year completed an MA in international relations at the University of Toronto. He graduated from the U of T Faculty of Law in 1974 with the gold medal, and went on to become a partner first at MacKinnon &McTaggart and later at the Faskens firm before establishing his own practice in 1991. Specializing in transport law, Strathy was closely involved in the Canadian Maritime Law Association and the Canadian Association of Maritime Arbitrations, and has published a book on marine insurance law.

Since his appointment to the Superior Court of Justice in 2008, he has presided over several class action lawsuits. He joined the Ontario Court of Appeal in April 2013. George Strathy was appointed chief justice of Ontario in June 2014.

* * *

Samuel Henry STRONG (1825–1909), member of the court 1869–75

Born in Dorset, England, Samuel Henry Strong came to Canada with his family in 1836, and grew up in Kingston, Ontario, and in Quebec City, where his father became an Anglican priest. He went on to study at Osgoode Hall, where he began to focus on equity law, and was called to the bar of Ontario in 1849.

He became a commissioner for the revision of the general statutes of Upper Canada and a lecturer at Osgoode Hall within a decade, but had also developed a reputation for impatience and arrogance in the courtroom. A friend and legal adviser to John A. Macdonald, Strong was chosen to draw up the first legislative proposal for the establishment of the Supreme Court of Canada in 1868, and was later appointed to Ontario's commission on the fusion of common and equity law. He joined the Court of Chancery in 1869, making him a member of Error and Appeal ex officio until its restructuring in 1874. In 1875 he was one of the four full-time judges appointed to the newly founded Supreme Court of Canada, where he sat for nearly thirty years and went on to become chief justice of Canada.

Though he had played an important role in the court's establishment and was by all accounts a highly gifted legal thinker, his belligerent attitude towards other judges and counsel eventually stoked conversation in Ottawa about his removal from office. Having appeared before Strong on several occasions, Robert Borden would later acknowledge his "preeminent intellectual qualities," but said that those talents were entirely offset by his "violent and bullying temperament."

* * *

Robert Baldwin SULLIVAN (1802–1853), member of Error and Appeal 1849–53 as justice of Common Pleas

Robert Baldwin Sullivan was born in Cork County, Ireland, and settled with his family in the Canadian town of York in 1819. Following the unexpected deaths of both his brother and his father, he was admitted as a student to the Law Society of Upper Canada with the support of his maternal uncle William Warren Baldwin, and called to the bar in 1828. His career as a litigator later thrived as he entered practice with his cousin Robert Baldwin.

He soon entered Upper Canada politics, joining the reform movement of his uncle and his cousin, though their early attempts to oppose the Family Compact Tories were met with frustrating setbacks. He was nonetheless elected as a Toronto alderman in 1835 and soon after appointed to the mayor's office, where he sat for one year during which he coordinated the construction of a sewer system – one of the city's first major public works.

Amidst the political crisis that emerged in the winter of 1836, Sullivan suddenly decided to join the conservative administration of Francis Bond Head – a move that seriously strained his relationship with his family, and provoked suspicion from Tories and Reformers alike. Though his legal practice with his cousin collapsed during this time period, he later worked as an adviser to Baldwin once he emerged as premier of Canada – presumably, writes Victor Russell, "more because of

Baldwin's stout family loyalty than because of [Sullivan's] chequered record as a political tactician."

But his career in the judiciary, beginning with his appointment to Queen's Bench in 1848, was marked by less controversy. He joined the court of Common Pleas when it was established the following year, and remained there until his death in 1853.

* * *

Walter Surma TARNOPOLSKY (1932–1993), member of the court 1983–93

Walter Tarnopolsky was born to Ukrainian parents in the town of Gronlid, Saskatchewan. He studied extensively throughout the 1950s and early 1960s, earning a BA and an LLB from the University of Saskatchewan, an MA from Columbia University, and a master of law from the London School of Economics. Specializing in human rights and civil liberties, he went on to teach at the University of Saskatchewan, the University of Ottawa, Osgoode Hall Law School, and the University of Windsor, where he was dean of law.

Throughout his academic career, Tarnopolsky served as chairman of several provincial inquiries in Ontario, and helped draft human rights legislations throughout Canada, including the Manitoba Bill of Rights, the Northwest Territories Human Rights Code, the federal Human Rights Act, and the Canadian Charter of Rights and Freedoms. He was also closely involved in a number of international judicial initiatives, sitting as president of the Canadian section of the International Court of Justice, Amnesty International, the International Commission of Jurists, and the UN Human Rights Committee.

In 1983 he was appointed to the Court of Appeal, and remained there until his death in September of 1993.

* * *

Donald Scarth THORSON (1925–1989), member of the court 1978–88

The son of Liberal MP Joseph Thorarinn Thorson, Donald Thorson was born and raised in Winnipeg. He studied law with Gowling, Osborne & Henderson in Ottawa, and went on to practise in the capital following his call to the bar in 1951.

He moved into the federal government in 1957, with his appointment as director of the legislative section of the department of justice, and four years later became assistant deputy minister of justice. Throughout his time in the Trudeau administration, Thorson was the chief legal counsel in the justice department, and played a central role in the drafting of the Canada Pension Plan, the *Divorce Act*, and the *Official Languages Act*. In 1973 he became deputy Attorney General, and in 1977 became a constitutional adviser to Trudeau. He was appointed to the Court of Appeal in 1978, and remained there until his retirement a decade later.

* * *

Michael H. TULLOCH, appointed to the court 2012

Michael Tulloch arrived in Canada from Jamaica at the age of nine, and grew up in the Brampton area. After graduating from Osgoode Hall Law School, he was called to the bar in 1991 and that same year was made an assistant Crown attorney.

He went on to establish a private practice, where he focused on criminal law and was known to take on a significant amount of pro bono work. He is a founding patron of the Second Chance Scholarship Foundation, which was established to assist young people with criminal records, and has served as president of the Canadian Association of Black Lawyers.

He was appointed to the Superior Court of Justice in 2003, and in 2012 became the first black person appointed to the Court of Appeal.

* * *

Philip Michael Matthew Scott VanKOUGHNET (1822–1869), member of Error and Appeal 1863–9 as justice of Chancery

Phillip VanKoughnet was born and raised in Cornwall and fought in the loyalist militia in 1837. He began studying law the subsequent year, and following his call to the bar in 1843 went into practice in Toronto with Robert Easton Burns and Oliver Mowat.

A Tory, he was elected to the legislative council in 1856 and at the suggestion of John A. Macdonald became president of the executive council and minister of agriculture. He went on to become commissioner of Crown lands and superintendent of Indian Affairs, where he prioritized the expansion of the colonial frontier through the settlement of land claims and construction of railroads.

In 1862 VanKoughnet was appointed chancellor of Upper Canada, where he became known for his clear and sympathetic judgments, and his practical revisions of the court's mandate. "A Conservative by birth, education, and party connections," wrote Mowat after his death, "in his court he was a Reformer."

* * *

Katherine M. van RENSBURG, appointed to the court 2013

After finishing a BA at the University of Toronto, Katherine van Rensburg earned an LLB from Queen's University and clerked under Justice William McIntyre at the Supreme Court of Canada. She was called to the bar of Ontario in 1983 and went on to earn an LLM from Cambridge in 1986. Upon returning to Toronto, she practised with Smith Lyons, where she specialized in civil litigation and commercial law. In 2006 she was appointed to the Brampton court of the Ontario Superior Court of Justice, and in 2013 to the Court of Appeal.

* * *

David WATT, appointed to the court 2007

David Watt received a BA in French and Criminology from the University of Waterloo in 1967 and graduated from Queen's Law School three years later. Following his call to the bar, he worked as counsel and then deputy director of the Criminal Appeals and Special Prosecutions Branch, and in 1977 became senior Crown counsel in criminal law in the office of the Attorney General of Ontario.

Watt has written several manuals on criminal procedure, has taught and lectured at Osgoode Hall Law School, Dalhousie, and the University of Toronto, and has been involved in continuing legal education programs across Canada. He was appointed to the Superior Court of Justice in 1985, to the Court of Appeal in 2007, and has sat on the Supreme Court of Yukon and the Court Martial Appeal Court of Canada.

* * *

Francis Stephen WEATHERSTON (1917–1984), member of the court 1977–84

Born and raised in Beverly Township, near Hamilton, Francis Weatherston graduated from Osgoode Hall Law School in 1940, and was called to the bar in the same year. He enlisted in the military with the beginning of the Second World War, and throughout the war served in the UK and Europe with the Royal Hamilton Light Infantry, earning the rank of captain by the time of his discharge.

Weatherston rapidly became a prominent personality within the Hamilton legal community, by 1952 sitting as president of the Hamilton Lawyers' Club and later as president of the Hamilton Law Association. In 1959 he became the acting solicitor for the city, and five years later began working as the general solicitor for the Toronto, Hamilton & Buffalo Railway Company. He also administrated the Legal Aid Plan in Hamilton from 1967 until his appointment to the High Court of Justice in 1974. He was appointed to the Court of Appeal in 1977, and remained there until his death.

* * *

Karen Merle Magnuson WEILER, appointed to the court 1992

Born in Spiritwood, Saskatchewan, Karen Weiler earned a BA from the University of Saskatchewan before attending at Osgoode Hall. She articled with Blake, Cassels & Graydon after her graduation in 1967, and was called to the bar two years later. She established a legal practice in Thunder Bay, and in 1972 returned to Toronto in order to complete a master of law at Osgoode Hall. She was hired as counsel to the Attorney General in 1975, later moving to the position of senior counsel in the Policy Development Division.

Weiler was appointed to the District Court of Ontario in 1980, to the High Court of Justice in 1989, and to the Court of Appeal in 1992. Fluently bilingual, she has presided over many of the court's French-language cases, and has additionally sat on the Ontario Status of Women Council and the Council on Children and Youth. She has been active in the judicial community throughout her time on the bench, having participated in the Canadian-American Legal Exchange and the Justice Minister's Advisory Committee for Judicial Appointments. She has sat as director of the American Judicature Society, the Canadian Judges Conference, and the Canadian Chapter of the International Association of Women Judges.

* * *

Dalton Courtwright WELLS (1900–1982), member of the court 1964–7

Born and raised in Toronto, Dalton Courtwright Wells graduated from the University of Toronto in 1922. He articled with McLaughlin, Johnson, Moorhead & McCaulay, and following his call to the bar in 1925 practised in Toronto. He went on to become the president of the Lawyers' Club in Toronto, and co-authored a book on Canadian taxation policy.

He was appointed to the High Court of Justice in 1946, and in 1964 joined the Court of Appeal. It was only three years, however, before he returned to the High Court, this time as chief justice. Though he was universally admired for his pleasant and relaxed disposition, several of his peers concurred that, in the words of John Arnup, "administration was definitely not his bag."

* * *

Adam WILSON (1814–1891), member of the court 1863–74

Born in Edinburgh, Adam Wilson came to Canada in 1830, first settling in Halton County, and four years later in Toronto where he articled under Robert Baldwin Sullivan and Robert Baldwin. Wilson established himself as a prominent barrister and an active bencher at the Law Society following his call to the bar in 1839. During his years in practice, he was appointed by John A. Macdonald to a panel responsible for consolidating the statutes of Canada, and later in his career played an instrumental role in the Ontario Law Reform Commission of 1871.

Sharing his mentors' reformist beliefs, in 1855 Wilson entered municipal politics as an alderman. Seeking to challenge the excessive sway held by railway developers in city hall, Wilson became mayor in 1859, in Toronto's first general election. Among his most important projects in office was to rationalize the city's by-laws, "then in indescribable confusion," according to the *Canadian Law Journal*. He remained mayor until 1861, by which time he had already become involved in national politics, holding the seat for York North in the legislative assembly.

His time in the assembly was brief, however, not least because of the turmoil within the government of John Sandfield Macdonald and Louis-Victor Sicotte with which he was aligned. He stepped down in 1863 and immediately joined the Court of Common Pleas, making him an ex officio judge of Error and Appeal until that court's restructuring in 1874. By the end of his career, he was the longest-serving judge in Ontario, and well respected at the bar for the "exhaustive research" that went into each of his judgments.

* * *

Bertha WILSON (1923–2007), member of the court 1975–82

Born to a working-class family in Kirkaldy, Scotland, Bertha Wilson went on to have a precedent-setting legal career in Canada.

She obtained an MA at the University of Aberdeen in 1944, and from there moved into teachers college. In 1949, Wilson arrived in Halifax and six years later enrolled in law at Dalhousie University. Following her call to the bar she moved to Toronto, where she joined Osler, Hoskin & Harcourt and became an innovative and distinguished legal researcher. In 1975, she became the first woman appointed to the Court of Appeal, and seven years later the first woman to sit on the Supreme Court of Canada.

Throughout her time on the bench, Wilson was known for adjudicating with a "distinctively principled and moral" approach, and, notes her biographer Ellen Anderson, was routinely "accused of judicial activism, but her record shows that she respects law's incremental development, frustratingly slow though it may be."

She ruled in several landmark cases in her time on the Supreme Court, during which the Charter of Rights and Freedoms came into effect and a cascade of cases on gender equality came before the courts. Her judgments covering the fields of family law, statutory rape, domestic abuse, and abortion all had a momentous effect on Canadian jurisprudence, and throughout her career she sought to broaden the scope of judicial understanding, to demonstrate that seemingly neutral laws could have disparate effects on women, minorities, and the poor. "It is so much easier," she stated in a 1990 speech, "to come up with a black and white answer if you are unencumbered by a broader context which might prompt you … to temper the cold light of reason with the warmer tints of imagination and sympathy."

* * *

John WILSON (1807–1869), member of Error and Appeal 1863–9 as justice of Common Pleas

John Wilson was born in Scotland, and at the age of sixteen settled in the Upper Canadian town of Perth, where he studied law under James Boulton. In the spring of 1830 he became embroiled in a petty altercation with a fellow law student named Robert Lyon after Lyon had made some disparaging remarks about his own fiancée. The spat culminated in a duel – reportedly the last in Upper Canada – in which Wilson killed Lyon.

Acquitted on charges of murder, Wilson was called to the bar five years later and established a law practice in London with his brother-in-law. He held a number of offices in the local civil service – including warden and district superintendent of education – and was elected to the legislative assembly in 1847. Though a Conservative, he was more moderate than the "ultra part of the Conservative Party," denouncing the loyalist riots that erupted in response to the 1849 Rebellion Losses Bill and on occasion allying himself with the Reformers. After leaving the legislature in 1857, he was appointed a judge of the Court of Common Pleas in 1863, where he remained until his death.

* * *

Warren Keith WINKLER (b. 1938), member of the court as chief justice of Ontario 2007–13

Born in Virden, Manitoba, Warren Winkler received a BA from the University of Manitoba and an LLB and LLM from Osgoode Hall Law School. Following his call to the bar in 1965, he established his practice in Toronto, specializing in civil litigation and specifically in labour law.

He was appointed to the Superior Court of Justice in 1993 and in 2007 became chief justice of Ontario. Throughout his time on the bench he has adjudicated several high-profile labour disputes and corporate restructurings, which have involved Ontario Hydro and Power, CanWest/Shaw, and Air Canada. He has additionally heard class action cases surrounding tobacco regulation, tainted water, mad cow disease, and residential schools. He has published extensively, received nine honorary degrees and multiple awards, and had several lectureships established in his honour. As chief justice, Winkler has taken an active interest in problems of access to justice, and has pushed for reforms that would diminish the costs and inefficiencies associated with litigation.

* * *

Thomas George ZUBER (b. 1927), member of the court 1975–90

Thomas Zuber was born in Kitchener and raised in Windsor. He graduated from the University of Western Ontario with a BA in 1948, and after studying at Osgoode Hall was called to the bar in 1951. He established his practice with Holden, McMahon, Zuber, Bondy & Cusinato in Windsor where he worked in both civil and criminal law, and in 1955 he began lecturing at the University of Windsor. He was appointed to the bench in 1968 as a junior judge in Essex County and, four years later, moved to the High Court of Justice. After publishing two widely-used introductory textbooks on Canadian law, he joined the Court of Appeal in 1975, and remained there until 1990 when he returned to the trial courts as a senior regional judge. Following his 2002 retirement, Zuber was awarded the Law Society Medal for his years of service on the bench and his contribution to the 1987 Ontario Courts Inquiry (also known as the Zuber Report), which sought to streamline judicial administration and influenced the subsequent restructuring of the Ontario court system.

Notes

Table of Abbreviations

AC	Law Reports, Appeal Cases
Alta L Rev	Alberta Law Review
Can Bar Rev	Canadian Bar Review
Can LJ (NS)	Canada Law Journal (New Series)
Can LT	Canadian Law Times
CCC	Canadian Criminal Cases
CRR	Canadian Rights Reporter
CS Prov C	Consolidated Statutes of the Provinces of Canada
DCB	Dictionaries of Canadian Biography
DLR	Dominion Law Reports
E & A	Grant's Upper Canada Error and Appeal Reports
L Soc'y Gaz	Law Society of Upper Canada Gazette
LAC	Library and Archives Canada
LSUC	Law Society of Upper Canada
OAC	Ontario Appeal Cases
OAR	Ontario Appeal Reports
OJ	Ontario Judgement (QuickLaw's Electronic Identifier, not a publication)
OLR	Ontario Law Reports
ONCA	Ontario Court of Appeal (A neutral identifier assigned by the courts, not a publication)

OR	Ontario Reports
Osgoode Hall LJ	Osgoode Hall Law Journal
OSOHI	Osgoode Society Oral History Interview Series
QL	QuickLaw (Electronic database, not a publication)
Rev Const Stud	Review of Constitutional Studies
RSC	Revised Statutes of Canada
RSO	Revised Statutes of Ontario
S Prov C	Statutes of the Provinces of Canada
SC	Statutes of Canada
SCR	Canada Supreme Court Reports
SO	Statutes of Ontario
UTLJ	University of Toronto Law Journal
Windsor YB Access Just	Windsor Yearbook of Access to Justice

General Notes on Case Reporter Citation Reading

Case reporter citations list the volume number, or the year in [ ] (depending on whether the reporter is organized by publication year or volume number), followed by the reporter's abbreviation, and end with the page in the reporter the case can be found at.

E.g: 1 E & A 251 = Volume 1 of Grant's *Upper Canada Error and Appeal Reports*, page 251.

1. Give Us the Court of Appeal, 1792–1874

1 Christopher Moore, *The Law Society of Upper Canada and Ontario's Lawyers, 1797–1997* (Toronto: University of Toronto Press, 1997) at 101–2. On the building and its modifications over time, see John Honsberger, *Osgoode Hall: An Illustrated History* (Toronto: Osgoode Society, 2004).

2 *An Act to repeal certain Parts of an Act, passed in the fourteenth Year of his Majesty's Reign, intituled, An Act for making more effectual Provision for the Government of the Province of Quebec, in North America; and to make further Provision for the Government of the said Province*, 1791 (UK), 31 Geo III, c 31 (The Constitutional Act).

3 *An Act to establish a superior court of civil and criminal jurisdiction and to regulate the court of appeal*, 1794 (UK), 34 Geo III, c 2 (The Judicature Act).

4 Ibid., s 36.

5 Peter Spiller, *The New Zealand Court of Appeal 1958–1996: A History* (Wellington: Brookers, 2002).

6 Francis Bergan, *History of the New York Court of Appeal 1847–1932* (New

York: Columbia University Press, 1985) at 9, 46, 49. For American judicial institutions in this period, see Lawrence Friedman, *A History of American Law*, 3d ed (New York: Touchstone Books, 2005) at 91–7.

7 David Bentley, *English Criminal Justice in the Nineteenth Century* (London: Hambleton Press, 1998) at xvi.

8 James Stephen, *History of the Criminal Law of England*, vol. 1 (London: Macmillan and Co., 1883) at 308.

9 *Upper Canada Assembly Journals* (13 January 1826) at 72. I am indebted to Professor Jim Phillips for this reference.

10 These developments are noted in standard histories; see, e.g., Gerald M. Craig, *Upper Canada: The Formative Years, 1784–1841* (Toronto: McClelland and Stewart, 1963) at 205–6. I have also relied on an as-yet-unpublished paper by Jim Phillips, "Judicial Independence in British North America, 1825–1867."

11 The panels in a group of cases from 1846–9 are listed in case reports; see Alexander Grant, *Reports of Cases Adjudged in the Court of Error and Appeal*, vol. 1 (Toronto: Carswell and Company, 1885) [Grant, *Error and Appeals Reports*]. Despite its title, the volume includes some cases heard "In the Executive Council," before the creation of Error and Appeal in 1849.

12 See ibid. Blake argued the first case in the volume, *Simpson v Smyth* (1846), and several others.

13 Moore, *The Law Society of Upper Canada and Ontario's Lawyers 1797–1997*.

14 The Act itself: *The Administration of Justice Act*, S Prov C 1849 (12 Vic), c 63. For Blake's major speech on the bill, see Elizabeth Abbott Gibbs, ed., *Debates of the Legislative Assembly of United Canada 1841–67*, vol. 8 (1849), part 3 (Montreal: Centre d'Études du Québec, 1974) at 2322–3.

15 Ibid. at 2322.

16 William Hume Blake, *A Letter to the Honorable Robert Baldwin upon the Administration of Justice in Western Canada* (Toronto: Printed by George Brown, 1845) at 4.

17 Blake to Robert Baldwin, 7 September 1848, quoted in John D. Blackwell, "William Hume Blake and the Judicature Acts of 1849," in David Flaherty, ed., *Essays in Canadian Legal History*, vol. 1 (Toronto: Osgoode Society, 1981) 132–74 at 153.

18 Toronto Reference Library, Special Collections, L5 Baldwin Papers A34 correspondence, #19, William Hume Blake to Robert Baldwin, 27 January 1845.

19 The Chancery reforms came in a separate act: *The Administration of Justice (Chancery) Act*, S Prov C 1849 (12 Vic), c64. It was passed on the same day.

20 Ibid.

21 The events are vividly described in John Ralston Saul, *Louis-Hippolyte La-Fontaine and Robert Baldwin* (Toronto: Penguin Books, 2010).

22 Elizabeth Nish, ed., *Debates of the Legislative Assembly of United Canada*, vol. 8 (Montreal: Centre d'Étude du Québec, 1976) at 2322–94, 2452, 2506, passim. Blake gave "a long speech" on the bill on 16 March, but it was not reported.

23 The Burns-led petition is appended to Blake's pamphlet, *Letter to the Hon. Robert Baldwin*, at 38–40.

24 Blake, *Letter to Baldwin*, at 11–12.

25 P.A. Howell, *The Judicial Committee of the Privy Council 1833–1876: Its Origins, Structure and Development* (Cambridge: Cambridge University Press, 1979).

26 Blake, *Letter to Baldwin*, at 12.

27 J.G. Spragge, *A Letter on the Subject of the Courts of Upper Canada* (Toronto: Scobie and Balfour, 1847), at 23.

28 "A Lawyer," *Globe* (Toronto), 16 March 1850, 2.

29 John D. Blackwell, "Jameson, Robert Sympson," *DCB*, vol. 8 (Toronto: University of Toronto Press, 1985) at 427–8.

30 Toronto Reference Library, Special Collections, L5 Baldwin Papers A34 correspondence, #19, William Hume Blake to Robert Baldwin, 27 January 1845.

31 A Member of the Kingston Bar, *A Proposal For Dividing the Jurisdiction of the Court of Queen's Bench and Establishing a Court of Appeal* (Kingston, 1845).

32 Blake, *Letter to Baldwin*, at 4.

33 "Courts, Lawyers, and Costs," *Globe* (Toronto), 5 February 1850, 2.

34 For analysis about the campaign for simplicity in law, see R.D. Gidney and W.P.J. Millar, *Professional Gentlemen: The Professions in Nineteenth-Century Ontario* (Toronto: University of Toronto Press, 1994) at 60–6.

35 Ibid. at 62.

36 Ibid. at 63.

37 Between October and December, the *Globe* (Toronto) reported most of the new appointments. Examples are 4 October and 18 December 1849.

38 George Metcalf, "Draper, William Henry," in *DCB*, vol. 10 (Toronto: University of Toronto Press, 1985) at 253–9.

39 Brian H. Morrison, "Burns, Robert Easton," in *DCB*, vol. 9 (Toronto: University of Toronto Press, 1976) at 104–8.

40 Hereward and Elinor Senior, "Boulton, Henry John," in *DCB*, vol. 9 (Toronto: University of Toronto Press, 1985) at 69–72. For more discussion of this issue, see Michael Cross, *A Biography of Robert Baldwin: The Morning Star of Memory* (Toronto: Oxford University Press, 2012).

41 Gordon Dodds, "Macaulay, James Buchanan," in *DCB*, vol. 8 (Toronto: University of Toronto Press, 1985) at 511–13.

42 Bruce W. Hodgins, "McLean, Archibald (1791–1865)," in *DCB*, vol. 9 (Toronto: University of Toronto Press, 1976) at 512–13.

43 Victor Loring Russell, Robert Lochiel Fraser, and Michael S. Cross, "Sullivan, Robert Baldwin," in *DCB*, vol. 8 (Toronto: University of Toronto Press, 1985) at 845–50.

44 Blackwell, "Jameson, Robert Sympson," at 246–7; "Vice-Chancellor Jameson's Pension," *Globe* (Toronto), 24 December 1850, 2.

45 Robert Hett, "Esten, James Christie Palmer," in *DCB*, vol. 9 (Toronto: University of Toronto Press, 1976) at 244–5.

46 Brian H. Morrison, "Spragge, John Godfrey," in *DCB*, vol. 11 (Toronto: University of Toronto Press, 1982) at 845–6.

47 Gibbs, ed., *Debates of the Legislative Assembly of United Canada 1841–67*, vol. 8 (1849), part 1 (at 717–32. For Blake's speech, see ibid. at 742–53.

48 Michael Cross, *The Morning Star of Memory: A Biography of Robert Baldwin* (Toronto: Oxford, 2012) at 352.

49 *Act to Confirm Judges' Rules*, S Prov C 1850 (13–14 Vic), c 51.

50 Mark D. Walters, "The Extension of Colonial Criminal Control over the Aboriginal Peoples of Upper Canada," (1996) 46 UT L J at 273 examines one case that did reach the Privy Council. I am indebted to Patrick Connor for advice on this point.

51 John Langbein, *Torture and the Law of Proof: Europe and England in the Ancien Régime* (Chicago: University of Chicago Press, 1976) at 8, 77–80; emphasis added.

52 This section draws on Bentley, *English Criminal Justice in the Nineteenth Century*, particularly chap. 25, "Appellate Remedies."

53 *An Act to Extend the Right of Appeal in Criminal Cases in Upper Canada*, S Prov C 1857 (20 Vic), c 61 (Assented to 10 June 1857).

54 *Act Respecting the Court of Error and Appeal*, S Prov C 1857 (20 Vic), c 5.

55 *R. v Gray* 1859, 1 E & A 501.

56 *Dickson v Ward*, 1863, 2 E & A 275.

57 *Procedure in Criminal Cases*, SC 1869 (32-33 Vic), c 29; Vincent M. Del Buono, "The Right to Appeal in Indictable Cases: A Legislative History," (1978) 16 Alta L Rev 446 at 449–50.

58 *Act Respecting the Court of Error and Appeal*, S Prov C 1857 (20 Vic), c 5.

59 Desmond H. Brown, *The Genesis of the Canadian Criminal Code of 1892* (Toronto: Osgoode Society, 1989).

60 Martin Friedland, *A Place Apart: Judicial Independence and Accountability in Canada* (Ottawa: Canadian Judicial Council, 1995) at 234.

61 *Act Respecting the Civil List*, SC 1868, c 33; *Tact Respecting the Civil List*, CS Prov C 1859 (22 Victoria) Title 2 c 10, s 4.

62 Data compiled from Walter Edwin Lear, ed., *Canadian Reports Appeal Cases: Appeals Allowed or Refused by the Judicial Committee of the Privy Council on Appeal from the Dominion of Canada*, vols. 2–7 (Toronto: A. Poole, 1910).

63 *Act Respecting the Court of Error and Appeal*, SO 1869, c 24, s 2.

64 R.C.B. Risk, "The Law and the Economy in Mid-Nineteenth Century Ontario: A Perspective," in David Flaherty, ed., *Essays in Canadian Legal History*, vol. 1 (Toronto: Osgoode Society, 1981) at 88–131, particularly at 116–18.

65 "Court of Appeal," (June 1874) 10 CLJ 154.

66 "A Disturbance on the Grand Trunk," *Globe* (Toronto), 25 October 1864, 1.

67 Ibid.

68 "Observer," (October 1864) 10 CLJ 334.

69 Ibid. Editorial, at 334.

70 *Act regarding Error and Appeal*, SCW 1862 (25 Vic), c 28, s 3.

71 *Act Respecting civil list and other functionaries*, SC 1868, c 33, s 3.

72 *Supplies and Expenditures*, SO 1869, c 1; *Act to remunerate certain members of the court of Error and Appeal Vic*, SO 1869, c 5, s 2.

73 See Grant, *Error and Appeal Reports*, passim.

74 Alexander Grant, *Reports of Cases adjudged in the Court of Error and Appeal* (Toronto: Carswell, 1885), vols. 2 and 3, passim.

75 *Coleman v McDermott* (1856), 1 E & A 445.

76 *Harvey v Smith* (1864), 2 E & A 480.

77 *Act Respecting the Court of Error and Appeal*, SO 1869, c 24; *Administration of Justice Act*, SO 1874, c 9.

78 *Brunskill v Harris* (1854), 1 E & A 322.

79 *Re Freeman, Craigie, Proudfoot* (1862), 2 E & A 109.

80 *Jamieson v Fisher* (1863), 2 E & A 242.

81 *Westcott v Powell* (1865), 2 E & A 525.

82 *Bettridge v Great Western* (1866), 3 E & A 49.

83 *Weir v Mathieson* (1866), 3 E & A 163. See Michiel Horn, *Academic Freedom in Canada: A History* (Toronto: University of Toronto Press, 1999) at 15–17, 283–5.

84 *Gamble v Great Western* (1866), 3 E & A 163.

85 *Shiriff v Holcomb* (1864), 3 E & A 156.

86 *Harvey v Smyth* (1864), 1 E & A 480; emphasis added.

87 *Henderson et al. v Graves* (1862), 2 E & A 9.

88 *Bank of Toronto v Wm Eccles* (1862), 2 E & A 53.

89 *Bettridge v Great Western* (1866), 3 E & A 49.

90 *Stanton v McKinley* (1858), 1 E & A 265.

91 *Desjardins Canal v Grand Trunk* (1864), 2 E & A 330.

92 Obituary Sir John Hawkins Hagarty, 20 *Law Times* (1900) at 170–8.

2. Oliver Mowat's Court, 1874–1912

1 Paul Romney, "Mowat, Oliver," in *DCB*, vol. 13 (Toronto: University of Toronto Press, 1994) at 724–41.

2 Ibid.

3 For useful information on the development of the province, see Peter Baskerville, *Sites of Power: A Concise History of Ontario* (Toronto: Oxford University Press, 2004).

4 Christopher Moore, *Law Society of Upper Canada and Ontario's Lawyers* (Toronto: University of Toronto Press, 1997).

5 "Legislative News, Administration of Justice," *Globe* (Toronto), 17 March 1874, 3.

6 Ibid.

7 Ibid.

8 *Amendments to Revised Statutes,* SO 1878, c 8, s 2.

9 *Judicature Act,* SO 1931, c 24, s 6(2). The enduring prevalence of four-judge panels is determined from our samplings of 100 cases per decade in the period.

10 *Act to make further provision for the due administration of Justice,* SO 1874, c 7 (Administration of Justice Act 1874); *Amendments to Revised Statutes,* SO 1878, c 8, s 2.

11 For a definition of the term, see Peter Russell, *The Judiciary in Canada: The Third Branch of Government* (Toronto: McGraw-Hill Ryerson, 1987) at 290–1.

12 "Legislative News, Administration of Justice," *Globe* (Toronto), 17 March 1874, 3.

13 "Legislation of Last Session" (1874) 10 Can LJ (NS) 124.

14 "The New Judges" (1874) 10 Can LJ (NS) 186.

15 Grant's appointments and other registry officials are noted in the annually published Law Lists, but they do not specify which courts various registrars served.

16 Ontario, Legislative Assembly, "Second Report of the Commissioners for Consolidating the Statutes," in *Sessional Papers,* vol. 8, no. 37 (1875) (Delivered to the Assembly Dec 23, 1875); *An Act to carry into effect certain suggestion made by the commissioners for Consolidating the Statutes and for other amendments of the law,* SO 1875–1876, c 7.

17 *An Act to Consolidate the Superior Courts,* SO 1881, c 5.

18 *Act to Amend the Judicature Act*, SO 1903, c 8.

19 Elizabeth Brown, "Equitable Jurisdiction and the Court of Chancery in Upper Canada" (1983) 21 Osgoode Hall LJ 275; John D. Blackwell, "William Hume Blake and the Judicature Acts of 1849: The Process of Legal Reform at Mid-Century in Upper Canada," in David H. Flaherty, ed., *Essays in the History of Canadian Law*, vol. 1 (Toronto: Osgoode Society, 1981) at 132–74.

20 Brown, "Equitable Jurisdiction and the Court of Chancery in Upper Canada" at 275, 313.

21 For this argument in the American context, see Morton J. Horwitz, *The Transformation of American Law 1780–1860* (Cambridge, MA: Harvard University Press, 1977) at 270–6.

22 David John Hughes and T.H. Purdom, *History of the Bar of the County of Middlesex* (London, ON: n.p., 1913) at 37. The opinion was given by Hughes in 1913, recalling the period when fusion was proceeding.

23 *High Court of Justice Act*, SC 1883, c 10.

24 SO 1883, c 6; SO 1885, c 13; SO 1897, c 13, ss 1–2, 4.

25 *The Judicature Act*, SO 1881, c 5, s 42.

26 For two examples of Court of Appeal panels made up entirely of trial court judges, see *Seyfang v Mann* (1898), 26 OAR 179, heard by W.J. Meredith, John Rose, and Hugh McMahon; *Badams v Toronto* (1896), 24 OAR 8, heard by John Boyd, Thomas Robertson, and W.J. Meredith.

27 *The Judicature Act*, SO 1881, c 5, s 29.

28 *Judicature Act 1895*, SO 1895, c 12; *Judicature Act*, RSO 1897, c 51, s 6.

29 *Amend Judicature Act*, SO 1904, c 11.

30 Ibid. ss 2, 76.

31 *To Amend the law regarding Crown Cases Reserved*, SC 1886, c 47.

32 *The Criminal Code*, SC 1892, c 29.

33 Ibid. ss 744, 746.

34 *R. v Brennan*, [1896] OR 659 (Div Ct).

35 Walter H.C. Boyd, *The Last Chancellor* (Hamilton, privately published, 1995), chap. 13, discusses the case.

36 *House of Commons Debates 1900* vol. 2 (14 & 18 May 1900) at 5291, 5703 (Britton).

37 *House of Commons Debates 1900* vol. 2 (18 May 1900) at 5703 (Powell). On Powell, see J.K. Johnson, *Canadian Directory of Parliament 1867–97* (Ottawa: Public Archives of Canada, 1968) at 472.

38 *Amend the Criminal Code Amendments*, SC 1900, c 46, s 744.

39 For coverage of some of these events, see Martin L. Friedland, *The Trials of Israel Lipski: A True Story of a Victorian Murder in the East End of London* (Toronto: University of Toronto Press, 1984).

40 *R. v Noel* (1903), 6 OLR 385.

41 *R. v Woods* (1903), 6 OLR 41; *R. v Burdell* (1906), 11 OLR 440; *R. v Ellis* (1909), 20 OLR 218.

42 *R. v Beboning* (1908), 17 OLR 23.

43 *R. v James* (1903), 6 OLR 109.

44 *Rex v Walsh and Lamont* (1904), 7 OLR 149.

45 *R. v Beboning* (1908) 17 OLR 23. Meredith had a similar complaint, see *R. v Henry* (1910), 20 OLR 494 at 494–7.

46 Walter Edwin Lear, ed., *Canadian Reports Appeal Cases: Appeals allowed or refused by the Judicial Committee of the Privy Council on appeal from the Dominion of Canada*, vols. 1–8 (Toronto: A Poole, 1910–16), passim.

47 "The Supreme Court Bill" (1875) 11 Can LJ (NS) 64.

48 On the origins of the Supreme Court, see James G. Snell and Frederick Vaughan, *The Supreme Court of Canada: History of the Institution* (Toronto: Osgoode Society, 1985) at 1–27.

49 "The Supreme Court Bill" (1875) 11 Can LJ (NS) 64.

50 Snell and Vaughan, *The Supreme Court of Canada* at 4; on personnel of court, ibid. at 12–15.

51 Ibid. at 11.

52 David B. Swinfen, *Imperial Appeal: The Debate on the Appeal to the Privy Council, 1833–1986* (Manchester: Manchester University Press, 1987) at 44.

53 To see the whole matter laid out, see Jacqueline D. Krikorian, "Canada, Criminal Appeals and the Judicial Committee of the Privy Council in the 1880s" (2001) 6:1 Rev Const Stud 44.

54 David B. Read, *Lives of the Chief Justices of Upper Canada* (Toronto: Rowsell & Hutchison, 1888) at 222–36; David John Hughes and T.H. Purdom, *History of the Bar of the County of Middlesex* (London, ON: n.p., 1913) at 16.

55 J.G. Snell, "Moss, Thomas," in *DCB*, vol. 11 (Toronto: University of Toronto/Université Laval, 1982) at 621–2.

56 *Act to Provide for Certain Amendments of the Law*, SO 1877, c 8, s 2.

57 Read, *Lives of the Chief Justices of Upper Canada* at 396, 400. Read has nothing but praise for all his subjects, but admiration on this very specialist point may be rooted in fact.

58 Brian H. Morrison, "Spragge, John Godfrey," in *DCB*, vol. 11 (Toronto: University of Toronto/Université Laval, 1982) at 845–6.

59 Graham Parker, "Hagarty, Sir John Hawkins," in *DCB*, vol. 12 (University of Toronto/Université Laval, 1990) at 399–400.

60 LAC, Macdonald Papers, vol. 321 at 47, M.C. Cameron to Adam Wilson, Chief Justice of Queen's Bench, Ontario, 8 February 1887.

61 Alexander Reford, "Moss, Sir Charles," in *DCB*, vol. 14 (Toronto: University of Toronto/Université Laval, 1998) at 771–3.

62 Wilfrid Laurier, a Catholic francophone, was prime minister in the latter part of this period, but Laurier was cautious about appointing Catholics and francophones outside Quebec. See Philip Girard, "Politics, Promotion, and Professionalism: Sir Wilfrid Laurier's Judicial Appointments," in Jim Phillips, Jack Saywell, and R. Roy McMurtry, eds., *Essays in the History of Canadian Law*, vol. 10 (Toronto: University of Toronto Press, 2008) at 169–99.

63 Curtis Cole, *Osler Hoskin and Harcourt: Portrait of a Partnership* (Toronto: McGraw-Hill Ryerson, 1995) at 35, 54.

64 Supreme Court of Canada, "Mr. Justice Christopher Salmon Patterson," http://www.scc-csc.gc.ca/court-cour/judges-juges/bio-eng.aspx?id=christopher-salmon-patterson, retrieved 5 March 2014.

65 *R. v Eli* (1886), 13 OAR 133.

66 *Furness v Mitchell* (1879), 3 OAR 510 at 535.

67 *Toronto General Trust Corporation v White* (1903), 5 OLR 21. Osler attributed the phrase to Chief Justice Adam Wilson.

68 Supreme Court of Canada, "Mr. Justice James Maclennan," http://www.scc-csc.gc.ca/court-cour/judges-juges/bio-eng.aspx?id=james-maclennan, retrieved 5 March 2014.

69 For his obituary, see "James Bethune, Q.C.," *Globe* (Toronto), 19 December 1884, 6.

70 *Kiely v Kiely et al.* (1878), 3 OAR 438.

71 *R. v Hodge* (1882), 7 OAR 246.

72 Fairty, Irving Stuart (c 1884–1974), "Reminiscences" (1978) 12:3 L Soc'y Gaz 245 at 252.

73 *In Re Toronto Railway Company Assessment* (1898), 25 OAR 135.

74 *Rooney v Rooney* (1879), 4 OAR 255.

75 *Driscoll v Green et al.* (1883), 8 OAR 366.

76 *Dillon v Twp of Raleigh* (1886), 13 OAR 53.

77 *Parsons v Standard Insurance* (1879), 4 OAR 326.

78 *Zumstein v Shrumm* (1895), 22 OAR 263.

79 *Wilson v Wilson* (1878), 3 OAR 400.

80 *Keewatin Power v Town of Kenora* (1908), 16 OAR 184.

81 Tyler Wentzell, "The Courts and the Cataract: The Creation of the Queen Victoria Niagara Falls Park and the Court of Appeal" (2014) 106:1 Ontario History 100.

82 Paul Romney, "Mowat, Oliver," in *DCB*, vol. 13 (Toronto: University of Toronto/Université Laval, 1994) at 724–41.

83 For the most recent and authoritative study, though more sympathetic to Macdonald than Mowat, see John Saywell, The *Lawmakers: Judicial Power and the Shaping of Canadian Federalism* (Toronto: University of Toronto Press, 2002), particularly chaps. 4 and 5.

84 *Leprohon v City of Ottawa* (1878), 2 OAR 522.

85 *R. v St Catharine's Milling*, [1886] OJ no 108 (QL). I am indebted to Carleigh Kityk, "Aboriginal Rights in the Court of Appeal" (paper presented to a legal history seminar on the court at the University of Toronto, fall of 2012), for its analysis of this question.

86 *Clarkson v Ontario Bank* (1888), 15 OAR 166 202.

87 A. Margaret Evans, *Sir Oliver Mowat* (Toronto: University of Toronto Press, 1992) at 154.

88 Saywell, *The Lawmakers* is the standard work on the subject. Saywell prefers the SCC decisions to those of the JCPC.

89 *Trumpour v Saylor* (1877), 1 OAR 100 at 107–8.

90 *Coll v Toronto Street Railway* (1898), 25 OAR 55.

91 *Erb et al. v Great Western Railway* (1879), 3 OAR 446.

3. The Meredith-Mulock-Rowell Courts, 1913–38: Experiments in Court Reform

1 Archives of Ontario, Whitney Fonds, F5-1 (Correspondence), items 7429, Whitney to Meredith, October 12, 1912; 7430, Whitney to Borden, 12 October 1912; 7442, Meredith to Whitney, 21 October 1912, and passim.

2 The standard biography is Charles W. Humphries, *Honest Enough to Be Bold: The Life and Times of Sir James Pliny Whitney* (Toronto: University of Toronto Press for the Ontario Historical Studies Series, 1985). The quotation is from Peter Oliver, *G. Howard Ferguson, Ontario Tory* (Toronto: University of Toronto Press, 1977) at 31.

3 Editorial, *Globe* (Toronto), 4 March 1909, 6.

4 Editorial, "Lawyers and Law Reform," *Globe* (Toronto), 5 February 1909, 4.

5 Ontario, *Journal of the Legislature of Ontario* (1908) at 351 (11 April 1908). Dissolution of the legislature for the provincial election meant the 1908 bill was not proceeded with.

6 Newspaper quotations from "Premier at Hamilton Rally Asks Electors for a Square Deal: Law Reform First on the Programme of the Party," *Globe* (Toronto), 6 May 1908, 1.

7 "Lawyers and Law Reform: Meeting of the Ontario Bar Association" (1909) 45 Can LJ 1.

8 "Decrease Cost and Lessen Delay of Litigation: Some Evils Must Be Remedied, Says Hon. Mr. Foy," *Globe* (Toronto), 4 February 1909, 1.

9 *Act for the Better Administration of Justice, to lessen the number of appeals and the cost of litigation, and for other purposes*, SO 1909, c 28 (proclaimed 1913).

10 R.C.B. Risk, "This Nuisance of Litigation: The Origins of Workers' Compensation in Ontario," in David H. Flaherty, ed., *Essays in the History of Canadian Law*, vol. 2 (Toronto: Osgoode Society, 1983) at 418–19.

11 "The Law Reform Act 190 in Ontario" (1913) 49 Can LJ 55.

12 *An Act Respecting the Supreme Court of Ontario and the Administration of Justice in Ontario*, SO 1913, c 19 (assented 6 May 1913), (The Judicature Act, 1913).

13 Ibid. ss. 12, 38–9.

14 Determined from our sample of cases 1911–20: 4 judges: 44 per cent; 5 judges: 34 per cent.

15 Election results determined from consulting the lists of First and Second Division judges provided annually in the Law Lists.

16 Archives of Ontario, Whitney Fonds, F5-1 (Correspondence) item 7442, W.R. Meredith to James P. Whitney 21 October 1912.

17 W.J. Loudon, *Sir William Mulock: A Short Biography* (Toronto: Macmillan, 1932) at 168–9. Loudon's is the only biography.

18 Charlotte Gray, *The Massey Murder: A Maid, Her Master, and the Trial that Shocked a Country* (Toronto: HarperCollins, 2013).

19 For a discussion of the case, see J.W. St.G Walker, *"Race," Rights and the Law in the Supreme Court of Canada* (Toronto: Osgoode Society, 1997) at 135–6.

20 Kerry Badgley, *Ringing in the Common Love of Good: The United Farmers of Ontario 1914–26* (Montreal: McGill-Queen's University Press, 2000).

21 Changes in registry personnel were tracked by reference to the annual Law Lists. On Hinds, see "Noted Registrar Darcy Hinds Is Dead," *Globe* (Toronto), 26 March 1948, 1.

22 Loudon, *Sir William Mulock*, at 168–9.

23 *Act to Amend the Judicature Act*, SO 1923, c 21; *The Judicature Act*, SO 1924, c 30.

24 *Re Judicature Act* (1924), 56 OLR 1. Mulock, Magee, Masten, and Smith, with Hodgins dissenting.

25 *Attorney General for Ontario v Attorney General for Canada*, [1925] AC 750.

26 *An Act to Amend the Criminal Code*, SC 1923, c 41, s 9.

27 *House of Commons Debates*, (1923) vol. 3 (1923) at 2283ff (Criminal Code Amendments).

28 *Senate Debates*, (1922) at 46ff (Criminal Code Appeals Bill – McMeans

urges appeal changes); *Senate Debates*, (1923) at 64ff, 1229ff (Criminal Code Amendments – McMeans's suggestions implemented); Martin L. Friedland, *The Trials of Israel Lipski* (Toronto: University of Toronto Press, 1984) covers the controversy in Britain.

29 For the evolution of English criminal appeals, see Rosemary Pattenden, *English Criminal Appeals 1844–1994: Appeals against Conviction and Sentence in England and Wales, 1844–1994* (Oxford: Clarendon Press, 1996).

30 *An Act to Amend the Criminal Code*, SC 1930, c 11, s 28.

31 For a detailed review of the right to appeal in Canadian criminal law, see Vincent M. Del Buono, "The Right to Appeal in Indictable Cases: A Legislative History" (1978) 16 Alta L Rev 446.

32 Jacqueline D. Krikorian, "British Imperial Politics and Judicial Independence: The Judicial Committee's Decision in the Canadian Case Nadan v. The King" (2000) 33:2 Can J Polit Scie 291 at 320, 328.

33. *Amend the Judicature Act*, SO 1931, c 24.

34 William Mulock, "Address of the Chief Justice of Ontario (to the bar dinner in honour of his 90th birthday, 1934)" (1934) 12 Can Bar Rev 32.

35 Osgoode Society Oral History Interview [hereafter OSOHI], "George Gale" (1981) at 21, retrieved from http://www.osgoodesociety.ca/Oral_History/Oral_History_Programme.html.

36 *House of Commons Debates 1935* vol. 5 (3 & 18 May 1933) at 4569–70, 4790–4808. (Amendment to *The Judges Act.*)

37 *The Judges Act*, RSC 1927, c 105, s 23; *Act Respecting Governor, Civil List, and Salaries of Certain Public Officials sets out judges pensions paid from the civil list*, CS Prov C 1859, Title 2, c 10.

38 *Senate Debates* (1933) at 505, 527. (On Bill c-84.)

39 William Mulock, "Independence of the Judges: Speech to the CBA Montreal" (1934) 12 Can Bar Rev 406.

40 *House of Commons Debates 1936* vol. 4 (1936) at 3359ff (Judges Act Amendment, Bennett's comment is at 3703-4, 16 June 1936).

41 OSOHI, "G. Arthur Martin" (1985) at 27.

42 LAC, MG 26-J13, Mackenzie King Dairies, 5 September 1936 (on Mulock resignation) and 27 April 1938 (on Ontario judges).

43 LAC, MG 26-J13, Mackenzie King Dairies, 5 September 1936 and 21 August 1938.

44 Margaret Prang, *N.W. Rowell, Ontario Nationalist* (Toronto: University of Toronto Press, 1975) at 489.

45 *In re Estate of Charles Millar, deceased*, [1937] OR 382. Prang reports Rowell's total written decisions. Mark Orkin, *The Great Stork Derby* (Toronto: General Publishing, 1981).

46 "Judges in Spat on Bench: 'Don't Care Tuppence' Is Cry," *Star* (Toronto), 13 October 1936, 1.

47 John D. Arnup, *Middleton: The Beloved Judge* (Toronto: Osgoode Society 1988).

48 OSOHI, "John Robinette" (1987), 245.

49 Arnup, *Middleton*, 49–52.

50 "Judge Would Flog all Bootleggers," *Globe* (Toronto), 13 March 1926, 1.

51 LAC, Mackenzie King Diaries, 5 September 1936.

52 J.W. McClung, *History of the Alberta Court of Appeal* (Edmonton: The Court of Appeal, n.d.) at 42–6.

53 Christopher Moore, *The British Columbia Court of Appeal: The First Hundred Years* (Vancouver: UBC Press, 2010) at 16–17, 26–7.

54 Henry F Pringle, *The Life and Times of William Howard Taft: A Biography* (New York: Farrack and Rinehart, 1939) at 971; Noah Feldman, *The Scorpions* (New York: Twelve Books, 2010) at 106–7.

55 James G. Snell and Frederick Vaughan, *The Supreme Court of Canada: History of the Institution* (Toronto: University of Toronto Press, 1985) at 60–1.

56 Ibid. at 125–6.

57 "Miscellany" (1975) 9:4 L Soc'y Gaz 314.

58 OSOHI, "Donald Morand" (1984) at 80; OSOHI, "Mayer Lerner" (1988) at 93.

59 "Obituary T.C. Robinette" (1920) 40 Can LT 335.

60 *R. v Mickey MacDonald*, [1939] OR 606; *Cf. R. v Dean*, [1942] OR 3. (An appeal on grounds of improperly introduced evidence.)

61 The following section draws on Constance Backhouse and Nancy L. Backhouse, *The Heiress Versus the Establishment* (Toronto: University of Toronto Press, 2004), which reproduces Elizabeth Campbell's entire memoir.

62 A.B. McKillop, *The Spinster and the Prophet: Florence Deeks, H.G. Wells, and the Mystery of the Purloined Past* (Toronto: McClelland and Stewart, 2000).

63 *An Act to provide in the province of Ontario for the dissolution and the annulment of Marriage*, SC 1930, c 14 [*The Divorce Act*]. I am indebted to Hayley Dilazzio, "Judicial Divorce in the Ontario Court of Appeal, 1930–68" (paper presented to the legal history class at the University of Toronto Law School, fall 2012).

64 *Godfrey v Good Rich Refining Co*, [1940] OLR 190.

65 *Shandloff v City Dairy Ltd. and Moscoe*, [1936] OR 579.

66 *Harrison v The Joy Oil Co Ltd et al.*, [1938] OR 679.

67 OSOHI, "Arthur Kelly" (1984) at 152.

68 R.C.B. Risk, "William R Meredith, CJO: The Search for Authority," in Risk,

ed., *A History of Canadian Legal Thought* (Toronto: University of Toronto Press, 2006) at 179–210.

69 *Toronto General Trusts Corporation v Canadian National Railway Co,* (1929) 64 OLR 622, OJ no 94 (QL).

4. The Robertson-Pickup-Porter Courts, 1938–67

1 Much of this description draws on C. Ian Kyer's history of the Fasken firm: Ian Kyer, *Lawyers, Families, and Businesses: The Shaping of a Bay Street Law Firm; Faskens 1863–1963* (Toronto: Irwin Law, 2013) particularly at 159–98.

2 Osgoode Society Oral History Interview [hereafter OSOHI], "John Robinette" (1987–8) at 203; OSOHI, "George Gale" (1981) at 21.

3 *Act To Amend the Judicature Act,* SO 1949, c 46.

4 The description of Pickup also draws on Kyer, *Lawyers, Families, and Businesses* at 199–220.

5 Bora Laskin, "Caesar Wright: A Personal Memoir" (1983) 33 UTLJ 148 at 161.

6 There is an insider's view of these rivalries in John Arnup, ed., "Swearing Out: An Inside Look at the Court of Appeal for Ontario and Some of its Judges" (unpublished MS, c1998, on file at LSUC Archives).

7 Ibid.

8 OSOHI, "Gregory Evans" (1997) at 180.

9 *House of Commons Debates* 1960, vol. 5 (1960) at 4885–914.

10 As yet there is no authoritative history of legal aid. For a brief note on its introduction, see Christopher Moore, *Law Society of Upper Canada and Ontario's Lawyers, 1797–1997* (Toronto: University of Toronto Press, 1997) at 274–7, 288–92.

11 "Justice Gillanders," *Globe and Mail* (Toronto), 6 May 1946, 6.

12 LAC, MG26-J13, Diaries of Prime Minister William Lyon Mackenzie King, entries of 2 February and 30 August 1943.

13 LAC, King Diaries, 30 August 1943, on McTague as labour minister, and 23 February 1944: "fed up." 23 April 1944 on King's reaction to McTague's new job.

14 McTague's labour-law activities are noted in Laurel Sefton MacDowell, *Renegade Lawyer: The Life of J.L. Cohen* (Toronto: University of Toronto Press, 2001) particularly at 122ff. On his later career in securities practice, see Christopher Armstrong, *Moose Pastures and Mergers: The Ontario Securities Commission and the Regulation of Share Markets in Canada, 1940–1980* (Toronto: University of Toronto Press, 2001) passim.

15 *Amendment to Judges Act (Annuities),* SC 1944–1945, c 45.

16 OSOHI, "Gregory Evans" (1997) at 176.

17 George D. Finlayson, *John J. Robinette Peerless Mentor* (Toronto: Osgoode Society, 2003).

18 W.J. Anderson, "1945–77: A View in Retrospect," in John Arnup, ed., "Swearing Out: An Inside Look at the Court of Appeal for Ontario and Some of its Judges" (unpublished manuscript, c1998, on file at LSUC Archives).

19 Anecdote told me by a current CA justice, who observed the court as a student in the early 1970s.

20 OSOHI, "Archie Campbell" (2008) at 41–2.

21 OSOHI, "John Brooke" (2000) at 219.

22 Anderson, "1945–77: A View in Retrospect."

23 Ibid.

24 Data on the 1960s is from our sampling; data for the whole period is from Philip Girard, *Bora Laskin: Bringing Law to Life* (Toronto: University of Toronto Press, 2005) at 350.

25 OSOHI, "Donald Morand" (1984–7) at 55–6.

26 *Beauregard v Canada*, [1986] 2 SCR 56.

27 William Kaplan, *Canadian Maverick: The Life and Times of Ivan C. Rand* (Toronto: University of Toronto Press, 2009), particularly chap. 4.

28 Girard, *Bora Laskin* at 249–52. Bora Laskin advised on the Drummond Wren case.

29 The case is covered in James W. St.G Walker, *"Race," Rights and the Law in the Supreme Court of Canada* (Toronto: Osgoode Society, 1997) at 182–245.

30 *Noble and Wolf v Alley*, [1949] O.R. 503.

31 *Noble et al. v Alley*, [1951] SCR 64.

32 St.G Walker, *"Race," Rights and the Law in the Supreme Court of Canada*, at 244.

33 This section draws on "The Ontario Court of Appeal and the *Canadian Bill of Rights*, 1960–1988: From Reaction to Cautious Progressivism" (an unpublished paper on the Court of Appeal's Bill of Rights jurisprudence by Jordan Birenbaum, presented to a legal history class at University of Toronto Law School, 2012). On the Bill of Rights generally, see Jordan Birenbaum, "Parliamentary Sovereignty Rests with the Courts: Constitutional Foundations of J.G. Diefenbaker's Canadian Bill of Rights" (PhD diss., University of Ottawa, 2012).

34 *R. v Sharpe* (1961), 131 CCC 75.

35 *R. v O'Connor*, [1965] 2 OR 773.

36 *R. v Prov Ct JJ, Ex parte Nevin*, [1971] 2 OR 25.

37 A point discussed in Walter S. Tarnopolsky, *The Canadian Bill of Rights* (Toronto: Carswell, 1966).

38 William Mulock, "Address of the Chief Justice of Ontario" (1934) 12 Can Bar Rev 35 at 38.

39 Risk finds many examples in the Annual Reports of the Canadian Bar Association in "Lawyers, Courts, and the Rise of the Regulatory State" (1984) 9 Dalhousie LJ 31.

40 R.C.B. Risk, "'This Nuisance of Litigation': The Origins of Workers' Compensation in Ontario," in David Flaherty, ed., *Essays in Canadian Legal History*, vol. 2 (Toronto: University of Toronto Press, 1983) 418–91.

41 *Re Ashby et al.*, [1934] OR 421.

42 The discussion here draws on Paul Davis, "Deference to the 'Despots': The Ontario Court of Appeal and the Ontario Securities Commission" (paper prepared for the UT legal history class on Court of Appeal history, 2012).

43 For the whole Robertson Trilogy, see *Re Manning*, [1946] OJ no 163 (QL); *Re the Securities Act and Morton*, [1946] OR 492; *Re the Securities Act and Gardiner*, [1948] OR 71, [1947] OJ no 561 (QL).

44 *Re the Securities Act and Morton*, [1946] OR 492.

45 *Regina v Prentice ex parte Smith*, [1959] OR 365; [1959] OJ No 673 (CA); *Re Williams and Williams*, [1961] OR 657; [1961] OJ No 578 (CA).

46 *Oil Chemical Atomic Workers and Polymer* (1961), 28 DLR (2d) 81. The case is discussed in Girard, *Bora Laskin* at 241–3. Laskin was the arbitrator whose authority was upheld.

47 For a case analysis, see Malcolm E. Davidson, "The Royal York Hotel Case: The Right to Strike – and Not be Fired for Striking," in Judy Fudge and Eric Tucker, eds., *Work on Trial: Canadian Labour Law Struggles* (Toronto: Irwin Law, 2010) 175–216.

48 Eric Tucker, "Hersees of Woodstock v Goldstein: How a Small Town Case made it Big," in Judy Fudge and Eric Tucker, eds., *Work on Trial: Canadian Labour Law Struggles* (Toronto: Irwin Law, 2010) 217–48.

49 OSOHI, "W.B. 'Bill' Common" (1979) at 21–2.

50 OSOHI, "G. Arthur Martin" (1985) at 96.

5. Renewal: The Gale-Estey-Howland Courts, 1967–90

1 John Arnup, ed., "Swearing Out: An Inside Look at the Court of Appeal for Ontario and Some of its Judges" (unpublished MS, c1998, on file at LSUC Archives).

2 Ellen Anderson, *Judging Bertha Wilson: Law as Large as Life* (Toronto: University of Toronto Press, 2001) at 125; see also Osgoode Society Oral History Interview [hereafeter OSOHI], "Willard Estey" (1983) at 445.

3 Philip Girard, *Bora Laskin: Bringing Law to Life* (Toronto; University of Toronto Press, 2005) at 319.

4 Arnup, ed., "Swearing Out."

5 OSOHI, "John Arnup" (1983) at 357.

6 OSOHI, "John Brooke," interview with Christopher Moore, 31 October 2012.

7 OSOHI, "Willard Estey" (1979–80) at 154.

8 Gale described this event in G.A. Gale, "The Problem of Television in the Courtroom" (1974) 8:1 L Soc'y Gaz 4 at 4–7.

9 OSOHI, "William Howland" (1992) at 459.

10 Ibid.

11 Sydney Robins, personal communication with the author, 28 October 2013.

12 OSOHI, "George Gale" (1981) at 98.

13 Martin L. Friedland, *A Place Apart: Judicial Independence in Canada* (Ottawa: Canadian Judicial Council, 1995) at 241–3.

14 Anderson, *Judging Bertha Wilson* at 83–6.

15 John Honsberger, *Osgoode Hall: An Illustrated History* (Toronto: Osgoode Society, 2004) at 250–9.

16 OSOHI, "Willard Estey." Estey led an inquiry into Air Canada's financial operations in 1975.

17 OSOHI, "William Howland."

18 Perry S. Millar and Carl Baar, *Judicial Administration in Canada* (Montreal: McGill-Queen's University Press, 1971). Millar was a British Columbia judge and court administrator; Baar was an Ontario academic. Both participated in the changes they documented in this work.

19 Patrick Boyer, *A Passion for Justice: The Legacy of James Chalmers McRuer* (Toronto: Osgoode Society, 1994).

20 McRuer's quotation is from Martin L. Friedland, *My Life in Crime and Other Academic Adventures* (Toronto: University of Toronto Press, 2007) at 125, drawing on material in Friedland's 1968 study prepared for the Ouimet Committee, *Toward Unity: Criminal Justice and Corrections: The Report of the Canadian Committee on Corrections* (Roger Ouimet, chair).

21 Royal Commission into Civil Rights, J.C. McRuer, Commissioner, Report No 1 (Toronto: Queen's Printer, 1968).

22 Ouimet, *Towards Unity*, particularly chap. 9 at 165–74.

23 Among McRuer's first critics was the administrative law scholar John Willis. See John Willis, "The McRuer Report: Lawyers' Values and Civil Servants' Values" (1968) 18 UTLJ 351. On Boyer's biography of McRuer, see also Jim Phillips, "Recent Publications in Canadian Legal History" (1997) 78:2 Canadian Historical Review 236.

24 *Act to Amend the Judicature Act,* SO 1970, c 97 (establishes Divisional Court); *Act to Amend the Judicature Act,* SO 1971, c 57 (judicial review powers defined).
25 Ian Bushnell, *The Federal Court of Canada: A History 1875–1992* (Toronto: University of Toronto Press, 1996) at 162.
26 Ibid. at 163.
27 Ibid. at 159ff; Richard Pound, *Chief Justice W.R. Jackett: By the Law of the Land* (Toronto: Osgoode Society, 1999) at 216ff, 239ff. Jackett, a former deputy minister of justice, did much of the planning for the new federal court and became its first chief justice.
28 Archives of Ontario RG 4-18, Kelly Commission Papers, Box 7, includes the Aylesworth report, "Presentation to Law Reform Commission from Judges of Supreme Court of Ontario" (31 May 1971), and other related studies. For summaries of the various studies and proposals, see John McCamus and Donald F. Bur, *Appellate Court Reform in Ontario: A Consultation Paper* (Toronto: Ministry of Attorney General of Ontario, 1994) at 16ff.
29 McCamus and Bur, *Appellate Court Reform in Ontario.*
30 Archives of Ontario, RG 4-49: Minutes of Monthly Meeting of the Court of Appeal for April 7, 1977, Letter to the court from the Criminal Lawyers Association.
31 McCamus and Bur, *Appellate Court Reform in Ontario;* Roy McMurtry, *Memoirs and Reflections* (Toronto: University of Toronto Press, 2013); OSOHI, "Roy McMurtry."
32 OSOHI, "Roy McMurtry" (1999) at 509.
33 Jules Deschênes, *Masters in Their Own House: Independent Judicial Administration of the Courts* (Ottawa: Canadian Judicial Council, Canadian Judges Conference and Canadian Institute for the Administration of Justice, 1981).
34 OSOHI, "William Howland"; OSOHI, "Roy McMurtry"; McMurtry, *Memoirs and Reflections.*
35 *Courts of Justice Act,* SO 1984, c 11.
36 Names and titles are drawn from *The Canadian Law List* (Toronto, 1967–90). For discussion of roles, see OSOHI, "William Howland."
37 OSOHI, "William Howland."
38 Staff statistics are drawn from *The Canadian Law List* (Toronto, 1967–90).
39 OSOHI, "William Howland."
40 Friedland, *A Place Apart,* particularly "Chief Justices and Their Courts" at 225–31. See also T. David Marshall, *Judicial Conduct and Accountability* (Toronto: Carswell, 1995).

41 *Order in Council regarding prerogatives of the Prime Minister,* PC 1935-3374. See Ed Ratushny, "Judicial Appointments: The Lang Legacy," in Allen Linden, ed., *The Canadian Judiciary* (Toronto: Canadian Institute for the Administration of Justice, 1976) at 31–46.

42 *Act to Amend the Judges Act,* RSC 1985, c J-1, s 32.

43 The decision in the unsuccessful 1998 appeal of Kuldip Singh Samra against his murder conviction covers the facts of the case: http://www.ontariocourts.on.ca/decisions/1998/september/samra.htm.

44 OSOHI, "Arthur Kelly" (1984) at 135.

45 OSOHI, "John Arnup."

46 For a survey of the foundation of the CJC, see Pound, *Chief Justice W.R. Jackett* at 197–213.

47 D.C. McDonald, "The Role of the Canadian Institute for the Administration of Justice in the Development of Judicial Education in Canada," in W. Kaplan and D. McRae, eds., *Law, Policy and International Justice, Essays in Honour of Maxwell Cohen* (Montreal: McGill-Queen's University Press, 1992) at 455–480.

48 W.A. Stevenson, "Towards the Creation of a National Judicial Education Service for Canada" (Ottawa: Canadian Judicial Council, 1986). See also *The 25th Annual Report of the Canadian Judicial Council 1996–97* (Ottawa: Canadian Judicial Council, 1997) at 5–12.

49 OSOHI, "William Howland."

50 For McMurtry's views on bilingual services in the courts, see McMurtry, *Memoirs and Reflections,* 193–8.

51 For Howland's perspective on bilingual courts, see OSOHI, "William Howland" at 624ff.

52 Deschênes, *Masters in Their Own House* at 21, quoting Garry D. Watson in Allen Linden, ed., *The Canadian Judiciary* (Toronto: Osgoode Hall Law School, 1976) at 182.

53 Friedland, *A Place Apart,* at 186.

54 Archives of Ontario, RG 4-49: Minutes of Monthly Meeting of the Court of Appeal, 22 November 1975.

55 For Nemetz's views on intermediate appeal, see Christopher Moore, *The British Columbia Court of Appeal: The First Hundred Years* (Vancouver: UBC Press, 2010).

56 Archives of Ontario, RG 4-18, Records of the Appellate Jurisdiction Committee (The Kelly Committee).

57 Archives of Ontario, RG 4-18, The Appellate Jurisdiction Committee (The Kelly Committee), Box 1, Final Report, 13ff.

58 Archives of Ontario, RG 4-49: Minutes of Monthly Meetings of the

Court of Appeal, 1972–80, particularly 19 October 1976 and subsequent meetings.

59 Ontario, *Report of the Future of the Court Committee* ("the MacKinnon Report"); Ontario, *Report of the Ontario Courts Inquiry* ("the Zuber Report"); and Joint Committee on Court Reform, "Report of the Sub-Committee on Appeal Court Reform." MacKinnon chaired a committee of Court of Appeal judges, Zuber was commissioned by the Attorney General, and the Joint Committee was formed by several Ontario legal organizations, including the Law Society of Upper Canada.

60 OSOHI, "Roy McMurtry" (1999) at 722.

61 Ian Scott with Neil McCormick, *To Make a Difference: A Memoir* (Toronto: Stoddart, 2001) at 31.

62 Robert Sharpe and Patricia McMahon, *The Persons Case: The Origins and Legacy of the Fight for Legal Personhood* (Toronto: University of Toronto Press, 2007).

63 OSOHI, "William Howland" (1992) at 461.

64 Ibid., at 471.

65 Ibid., at 459.

66 *Courts of Justice Act*, RSO 1990, c 43, s 8.

67 *Reference re an Act to Amend the Education Act*, 1986 CanLII 2863.

68 *Reference re Bill 30 An Act to Amend the Education Act*, [1987] 1 SCR 1148.

69 *Regina and Beason* (1983) 42 OR (2d) 65.

70 *R. v Askov*, [1990] 2 SCR 1199.

71 *R. v Shand* (1977), 13 OR (2d) 65.

72 OSOHI, "Stephen Borins" (2006) at 148–9.

73 *Seneca College v Bhaudaria*, 27 OR (2d) 142.

74 *Seneca College v Bhadauria*, [1981] 2 SCR 181.

75 *Re Blainey and Ontario Hockey Association*, 1986 CanLII 145.

76 OSOHI, "William Howland" at 462.

77 Ibid.

78 Ibid. at 885.

6. The Dubin-McMurtry Courts, 1990–2007

1 Some of the detail comes from a eulogy to Dubin by his colleague Robert Armstrong, retrieved from http://www.ontariocourts.ca/coa/en/ps/speeches/CharlesLeonardDubin.htm, 1 March 2014.

2 Sydney Robins, personal communication to author, November 2013.

3 Ian Scott with Neil McCormick, *To Make a Difference: A Memoir* (Toronto: Stoddart, 2001) at 176.

4 OSOHI, "William Howland" (1992) at 925.

5 Scott, *To Make a Difference* at 179.

6 Thomas G. Zuber, *Report of the Ontario Courts Inquiry* (Toronto: Ministry of the Attorney General of Ontario, 1987).

7 Carl Baar, "The Zuber Report: Decline and Fall of Court Reform in Ontario" (1988) 8 Windsor YB Access Just, 105–49.

8 *Courts of Justice Act*, RSO 1990 c 43.

9 Ibid.

10 Ian Scott, "The Concept of a Single Court" (paper presented at a Civil Litigation Seminar, Mont-Ste-Marie, Quebec, 17 November 1989).

11 *R. v Shand* (1977), 13 OR (2d) 65.

12 *R. v Rowbotham* (1984), 11 CRR 302.

13 OSOHI, "Stephen Borins" (2006) at 176.

14 Roy McMurtry, *Memoirs and Reflections* (Toronto: University of Toronto Press, 2013).

15 Zuber, *Report of the Ontario Courts Inquiry*, particularly chap. 6.

16 *Courts of Justice Act*, s 2.

17 McMurtry, *Memoirs and Reflections* (Toronto: University of Toronto Press, 2013) at 698.

18 Ibid.

19 Ibid.

20 Pro Bono Law, retrieved from http://www.pblo.org/our-impact/, 12 January 2014.

21 *Judges Act*, RSC 1985, C-J1, s 32.

22 Ontario, Ministry of the Attorney General, *Ontario Court of Appeal Review, Final Report* (Toronto: Ministry of the Attorney General of Ontario, July 1998), and *Final Report Recommendations* (Toronto: Ministry of the Attorney General of Ontario, July 1999).

23 Christopher Moore, interview with Dennis O'Connor, Court of Appeal, Osgoode Hall, Toronto, ON, 26 September 2012.

24 Ibid.

25 *Ontario Court of Appeal Review, Final Recommendations* at i.

26 Moore, interview with Dennis O'Connor, 26 September 2012.

27 McMurtry, *Memoirs and Reflections*.

28 Information about registry personnel drawn from Law Lists and from Law Society of Upper Canada files on lawyers who served as registrars.

29 OSOHI, "William Howland" (1992) at 459.

30 Christopher Moore, interview with Registrar Huguette Thomson, Toronto, 29 January 2014, and interview with senior legal officer John Kromkamp, Toronto, 19 January 2012.

31 Ibid.

32 Ontario, Ministry of the Attorney General, *Court of Appeal Review, Final Report*, and *Final Report Recommendations*.

33 Ontario, Ministry of the Attorney General, *Court of Appeal Review, Final Report* at 86.

34 Kromkamp, personal communication, 29 January 2014.

35 Christopher Moore, interview with Warren Winkler, Osgoode Hall, Toronto, ON, 23 April 2013.

36 Thomson, personal communication, 29 January 2014.

37 OSOHI, "Stephen Borins" (2006) at 190–3.

38 For example, 167 unanimous to 14 split in the 1970s; 173 to 21 in the 1980s; 166 to 9 in the 1990s; 187 to just 5 in the 2000s. A few single-judge or five-judge rulings completed the sample each decade.

39 I draw here on personal communications from several members of the court and my own observations of courts in progress.

40 Robert Sharpe and Kent Roach, *Brian Dickson: A Judge's Journey* (Toronto: University of Toronto Press, 2003), particularly part 5, 285–442 on Charter jurisprudence.

41 OSOHI, "John Brooke" (2000) at 283.

42 *Ontario English Catholic Teachers' Assn v Ontario (AG)* (1999), 172 DLR (4th) 193 (Ont CA).

43 Mr Justice Stephen T. Goudge, "The Five Most Important Decisions of the Past Year" (speech made to the CBA Continuing Education program, Toronto, 1999), retrieved from http://www.ontariocourts.ca/coa/en/ps/speeches/five.htm , 15 March 2014.

44 *Halpern v Canada (AG)* (2003), 169 OAC 172.

45 See Christopher Moore, *The British Columbia Court of Appeal: The First Hundred Years* (Vancouver: UBC Press, 2010) at 231–40.

46 *Re Truscott* (2007), 226 OAC 200.

47 Ibid. at para 3.

7. Into the Twenty-First Century: The Winkler Court, 2007–13

1 Some of this material is based on author's interview with Chief Justice Warren Winkler, Osgoode Hall, Toronto, ON, 23 April 2013.

2 Roy McMurtry, *Memoirs and Reflections* (Toronto: University of Toronto Press, 2013).

3 Winkler interview.

4 The Annual Reports since 2009 are available at http://www.ontariocourts.ca/coa/en/ps/, accessed 1 March 2014.

5 Winkler interview.

6 *Courts of Justice Act*, RSO 1985, c C43, s 77.

7 Memorandum of understanding, Chief Justice Warren Winkler and Attorney General John Gerritson, 24 May 2012.

8 Cristin Schmitz, "Harper Appoints Large Number of Crowns, Few Women to Bench," *Lawyers Weekly*, 18 March 2011, 1.

9 *R. v Khawaja*, 2010 ONCA 862, 103 OR (3d) 321.

10 *Canada (AG) v Bedford*, 2012 ONCA 186, 109 OR (3d) 1.

11 *R. v Smickle*, 2013 ONCA 678, 311 OAC 288.

12 *Keewatin v Ontario (Natural Resources)*, 2013 ONCA 158, 114 OR (3d) 401.

13 *Yaiguaje v Chevron Corporation*, 2013 ONCA 758, 118 OR (3d) 1.

14 *Rasouli v Sunnybrook Health Sciences Centre*, 2011 ONCA 482, 107 OR (3d) 9.

15 *Jones v Tsige*, 2012 ONCA 32, 108 OR (3d) 241.

16 The court began producing annual reports in 2009, with statistics on its caseload back to 2004. See Court of Appeal for Ontario, http://www.ontariocourts.ca/coa/en/ps/.

17 Michael H. Lubetsky and Joshua Krane, "Appealing Outcomes: A Study of the Overturn Rate of Canada's Appellate Courts" (2009) 47:1 Osgoode Hall LJ 131.

18 Court of Appeal Annual Reports, 2009–2013, retrieved from http://www.ontariocourts.ca/coa/en/ps/, January 2014.

19 Lubetsky and Krane, "Appealing Outcomes."

20 Ibid. at 147.

21 Donald R. Songer, *The Transformation of the Supreme Court of Canada* (Toronto: University of Toronto Press, 2008) at 158.

22 Peter McCormick, "Evolution of Coordinate Precedential Authority in Canada: Interprovincial Citations of Judicial Authority, 1922–92" (1994) 32 Osgoode Hall LJ 271 at 279.

23 Ibid. at 287.

24 Ibid. at 294.

Illustration Credits

Archives of Ontario: William Henry Draper (RG 22-522 40, AO4297); John Hawkins Hagarty (RG 22-522 18, AO4294); George William Burton (RG 22-522 74, AO4300).

Canadian Heritage Gallery (canadianheritage.ca): Oliver Mowat (ID #20110).

City of Toronto Archives: Chief Justice Dana Porter (Fonds 1257 it 4028).

Court of Appeal: Chief Justice Warren Winkler (Postel Video Gabriel Koncz photo); The Law Clerks group, 2010 (David Batten photo); The Winkler Court, 2013 (David Batten photo).

Glenbow Museum: William Hume Blake (NA-1375-5).

Law Society of Upper Canada Archives: Osgoode Hall (P171); Featherston Osler (P2734); The Supreme Court, 1891 (P414); Chief Justice William Ralph Meredith (P962); The Meredith Court, 1923 (P688); Justice William R.R. Riddell (P15); Justice Francis Latchford (P799); Judges at Cards, 1931 (P797); The Mulock Court, 1934 (P420); The Robertson Court, 1951 (P2769); Chief Justice John W. Pickup (2009006-23P); The Pickup Court, 1956 (P810); Chief Justice George Gale (P530); The Gale Court, 1976 (P1433); Chief Justice Roy McMurtry (1600-22).

Index

Abella, Rosalie, 174, 175, 179; biography, 211
Administration of Justice Act (1874), 41–4, 67
Administration of Justice (Canada West) Act (1849), 9–12, 17–18
Alberta, judges of, 91
alternate dispute resolution (ADR), 194–5
American Bar Association, on judgment writing, 139
Anderson, J.T., 33
Anderson, W.J., 109–10
appeal court panels, 8, 11, 33, 48, 64, 143, 188; size of, 37, 42, 48, 64, 143, 188
appellate bar: at Error and Appeal, 32–3; and criminal appeals, 54; late nineteenth century, 62–3; early twentieth century, 92–3; post-war and 1960s, 119–22; and procedural rules, 169; "vanishing," 194
Appellate Division of the Supreme

Court of Ontario, 76–85; First Division, 77–81; Second Division, 77–80
Arar, Maher, 185n
Arbour, Louise, 174, 176; biography, 212
Armour, Eric, 54
Armour, John Douglas, 52, 60; biography, 212–13
Armstrong, Robert, 174–6; biography, 213
Arnup, John, quoted, 90, 104, 122–3, 126, 128; as lawyer, 119, 124; as judge, 126, 130, 139, 151–2, 155–8; biography, 213–14
associate chief justice of Ontario, 125–6, 136–9, 160, 165–9, 172, 185
attorney, defined, 47
Austin, Allan McNiece, biography, 214
Aylesworth, Allen, 63
Aylesworth, John, 104, 109–11, 124–6, 149; report of, 135; biography, 214

2014   Christopher Moore, *The Court of Appeal for Ontario: Defining the Right of Appeal, 1792–2013*
        Paul Craven, *Petty Justice: Low Law and the Sessions System in Charlotte County, New Brunswick, 1785–1867*
        Thomas GW Telfer, *Ruin and Redemption: The Struggle for a Canadian Bankruptcy Law, 1867–1919*
        Dominique Clément, *Equality Deferred: Sex Discrimination and British Columbia's Human Rights State, 1953–1984*

2013   Roy McMurtry, *Memoirs and Reflections*
        Charlotte Gray, *The Massey Murder: A Maid, Her Master, and the Trial that Shocked a Nation*
        C. Ian Kyer, *Lawyers, Families, and Businesses: The Shaping of a Bay Street Law Firm, Faskens 1863–1963*
        G. Blaine Baker and Donald Fyson, eds., *Essays in the History of Canadian Law, Volume XI: Quebec and the Canadas*

2012   R. Blake Brown, *Arming and Disarming: A History of Gun Control in Canada*
        Eric Tucker, James Muir, and Bruce Ziff, eds., *Property on Trial: Canadian Cases in Context*
        Shelley Gavigan, *Hunger, Horses, and Government Men: Criminal Law on the Aboriginal Plains, 1870–1905*
        Barrington Walker, ed., *The African Canadian Legal Odyssey: Historical Essays*

2011   Robert J. Sharpe, *The Lazier Murder: Prince Edward County, 1884*
        Philip Girard, *Lawyers and Legal Culture in British North America: Beamish Murdoch of Halifax*
        John McLaren, *Dewigged, Bothered, and Bewildered: British Colonial Judges on Trial, 1800–1900*
        Lesley Erickson, *Westward Bound: Sex, Violence, the Law, and the Making of a Settler Society*

2010   Judy Fudge and Eric Tucker, eds., *Work on Trial: Canadian Labour Law Struggles*
        Christopher Moore, *The British Columbia Court of Appeal: The First Hundred Years*
        Frederick Vaughan, *Viscount Haldane: 'The Wicked Step-father of the Canadian Constitution'*
        Barrington Walker, *Race on Trial: Black Defendants in Ontario's Criminal Courts, 1858–1958*

2009   William Kaplan, *Canadian Maverick: The Life and Times of Ivan C. Rand*
        R. Blake Brown, *A Trying Question: The Jury in Nineteenth-Century Canada*
        Barry Wright and Susan Binnie, eds., *Canadian State Trials, Volume III: Political Trials and Security Measures, 1840–1914*
        Robert J. Sharpe, *The Last Day, the Last Hour: The Currie Libel Trial* (paperback edition with a new preface)
2008   Constance Backhouse, *Carnal Crimes: Sexual Assault Law in Canada, 1900–1975*
        Jim Phillips, R. Roy McMurtry, and John T. Saywell, eds., *Essays in the History of Canadian Law, Volume X: A Tribute to Peter N. Oliver*
        Greg Taylor, *The Law of the Land: The Advent of the Torrens System in Canada*
        Hamar Foster, Benjamin Berger, and A.R. Buck, eds., *The Grand Experiment: Law and Legal Culture in British Settler Societies*
2007   Robert Sharpe and Patricia McMahon, *The Persons Case: The Origins and Legacy of the Fight for Legal Personhood*
        Lori Chambers, *Misconceptions: Unmarried Motherhood and the Ontario Children of Unmarried Parents Act, 1921–1969*
        Jonathan Swainger, ed., *A History of the Supreme Court of Alberta*
        Martin Friedland, *My Life in Crime and Other Academic Adventures*
2006   Donald Fyson, *Magistrates, Police, and People: Everyday Criminal Justice in Quebec and Lower Canada, 1764–1837*
        Dale Brawn, *The Court of Queen's Bench of Manitoba, 1870–1950: A Biographical History*
        R.C.B. Risk, *A History of Canadian Legal Thought: Collected Essays*, edited and introduced by G. Blaine Baker and Jim Phillips
2005   Philip Girard, *Bora Laskin: Bringing Law to Life*
        Christopher English, ed., *Essays in the History of Canadian Law: Volume IX – Two Islands: Newfoundland and Prince Edward Island*
        Fred Kaufman, *Searching for Justice: An Autobiography*
2004   Philip Girard, Jim Phillips, and Barry Cahill, eds., *The Supreme Court of Nova Scotia, 1754–2004: From Imperial Bastion to Provincial Oracle*
        Frederick Vaughan, *Aggressive in Pursuit: The Life of Justice Emmett Hall*
        John D. Honsberger, *Osgoode Hall: An Illustrated History*
        Constance Backhouse and Nancy Backhouse, *The Heiress versus the Establishment: Mrs Campbell's Campaign for Legal Justice*
2003   Robert Sharpe and Kent Roach, *Brian Dickson: A Judge's Journey*
        Jerry Bannister, *The Rule of the Admirals: Law, Custom, and Naval Government in Newfoundland, 1699–1832*

George Finlayson, *John J. Robinette, Peerless Mentor: An Appreciation*

Peter Oliver, *The Conventional Man: The Diaries of Ontario Chief Justice Robert A. Harrison, 1856–1878*

2002 John T. Saywell, *The Lawmakers: Judicial Power and the Shaping of Canadian Federalism*

Patrick Brode, *Courted and Abandoned: Seduction in Canadian Law*

David Murray, *Colonial Justice: Justice, Morality, and Crime in the Niagara District, 1791–1849*

F. Murray Greenwood and Barry Wright, eds., *Canadian State Trials, Volume II: Rebellion and Invasion in the Canadas, 1837–1839*

2001 Ellen Anderson, *Judging Bertha Wilson: Law as Large as Life*

Judy Fudge and Eric Tucker, *Labour before the Law: The Regulation of Workers' Collective Action in Canada, 1900–1948*

Laurel Sefton MacDowell, *Renegade Lawyer: The Life of J.L. Cohen*

2000 Barry Cahill, *'The Thousandth Man': A Biography of James McGregor Stewart*

A.B. McKillop, *The Spinster and the Prophet: Florence Deeks, H.G. Wells, and the Mystery of the Purloined Past*

Beverley Boissery and F. Murray Greenwood, *Uncertain Justice: Canadian Women and Capital Punishment*

Bruce Ziff, *Unforeseen Legacies: Reuben Wells Leonard and the Leonard Foundation Trust*

1999 Constance Backhouse, *Colour-Coded: A Legal History of Racism in Canada, 1900–1950*

G. Blaine Baker and Jim Phillips, eds., *Essays in the History of Canadian Law: Volume VIII – In Honour of R.C.B. Risk*

Richard W. Pound, *Chief Justice W.R. Jackett: By the Law of the Land*

David Vanek, *Fulfilment: Memoirs of a Criminal Court Judge*

1998 Sidney Harring, *White Man's Law: Native People in Nineteenth-Century Canadian Jurisprudence*

Peter Oliver, *'Terror to Evil-Doers': Prisons and Punishments in Nineteenth-Century Ontario*

1997 James W.St.G. Walker, *'Race,' Rights and the Law in the Supreme Court of Canada: Historical Case Studies*

Lori Chambers, *Married Women and Property Law in Victorian Ontario*

Patrick Brode, *Casual Slaughters and Accidental Judgments: Canadian War Crimes and Prosecutions, 1944–1948*

Ian Bushnell, *The Federal Court of Canada: A History, 1875–1992*

1996 Carol Wilton, ed., *Essays in the History of Canadian Law: Volume VII – Inside the Law: Canadian Law Firms in Historical Perspective*

William Kaplan, *Bad Judgment: The Case of Mr Justice Leo A. Landreville*

Murray Greenwood and Barry Wright, eds., *Canadian State Trials: Volume I – Law, Politics, and Security Measures, 1608–1837*

1995 David Williams, *Just Lawyers: Seven Portraits*

Hamar Foster and John McLaren, eds., *Essays in the History of Canadian Law: Volume VI – British Columbia and the Yukon*

W.H. Morrow, ed., *Northern Justice: The Memoirs of Mr Justice William G. Morrow*

Beverley Boissery, *A Deep Sense of Wrong: The Treason, Trials, and Transportation to New South Wales of Lower Canadian Rebels after the 1838 Rebellion*

1994 Patrick Boyer, *A Passion for Justice: The Legacy of James Chalmers McRuer*

Charles Pullen, *The Life and Times of Arthur Maloney: The Last of the Tribunes*

Jim Phillips, Tina Loo, and Susan Lewthwaite, eds., *Essays in the History of Canadian Law: Volume V – Crime and Criminal Justice*

Brian Young, *The Politics of Codification: The Lower Canadian Civil Code of 1866*

1993 Greg Marquis, *Policing Canada's Century: A History of the Canadian Association of Chiefs of Police*

Murray Greenwood, *Legacies of Fear: Law and Politics in Quebec in the Era of the French Revolution*

1992 Brendan O'Brien, *Speedy Justice: The Tragic Last Voyage of His Majesty's Vessel Speedy*

Robert Fraser, ed., *Provincial Justice: Upper Canadian Legal Portraits from the Dictionary of Canadian Biography*

1991 Constance Backhouse, *Petticoats and Prejudice: Women and Law in Nineteenth-Century Canada*

1990 Philip Girard and Jim Phillips, eds., *Essays in the History of Canadian Law: Volume III – Nova Scotia*

Carol Wilton, ed., *Essays in the History of Canadian Law: Volume IV – Beyond the Law: Lawyers and Business in Canada, 1830–1930*

1989 Desmond Brown, *The Genesis of the Canadian Criminal Code of 1892*

Patrick Brode, *The Odyssey of John Anderson*

1988 Robert Sharpe, *The Last Day, the Last Hour: The Currie Libel Trial*

John D. Arnup, *Middleton: The Beloved Judge*

1987 C. Ian Kyer and Jerome Bickenbach, *The Fiercest Debate: Cecil A. Wright, the Benchers, and Legal Education in Ontario, 1923–1957*

1986 Paul Romney, *Mr Attorney: The Attorney General for Ontario in Court, Cabinet, and Legislature, 1791–1899*

Martin Friedland, *The Case of Valentine Shortis: A True Story of Crime and Politics in Canada*

1985   James Snell and Frederick Vaughan, *The Supreme Court of Canada: History of the Institution*

1984   Patrick Brode, *Sir John Beverley Robinson: Bone and Sinew of the Compact*
       David Williams, *Duff: A Life in the Law*

1983   David H. Flaherty, ed., *Essays in the History of Canadian Law: Volume II*

1982   Marion MacRae and Anthony Adamson, *Cornerstones of Order: Courthouses and Town Halls of Ontario, 1784–1914*

1981   David H. Flaherty, ed., *Essays in the History of Canadian Law: Volume I*